Encyclopedia of
the Persian Gulf War

# ENCYCLOPEDIA OF
# THE PERSIAN GULF WAR

Richard A. Schwartz

McFarland & Company, Inc., Publishers
*Jefferson, North Carolina, and London*

*On the cover:* Launching of a Tomahawk cruise missile
(photograph courtesy of the U.S. Department of Defense).

British Library Cataloguing-in-Publication data are available

Library of Congress Cataloguing-in-Publication Data

Schwartz, Richard Alan, 1951–
    Encyclopedia of the Persian Gulf War / Richard A. Schwartz
      p.  cm.
    Includes bibliographical references (p.    ).
    ISBN 0-7864-0451-5 (case binding : 50# alkaline paper) ∞
    1. Persian Gulf War, 1991—Encyclopedias.   I. Title.
DS79.72.S39   1998
956.7044'2'03—dc21                  97-51886
                                            CIP

Manufactured in the United States of America

*McFarland & Company, Inc., Publishers
  Box 611, Jefferson, North Carolina 28640*

To Ana-Maria,
who teaches the
peaceful uses of technology

# Contents

# Introduction

Between January 17 and February 28, 1991*, an international military coalition sanctioned by the United Nations and led by the United States defeated a large, well-equipped Iraqi army and forced it to withdraw from occupied Kuwait. The Persian Gulf War was the first U.S. military action after the Cold War, which, after enduring in a protracted stalemate for almost 45 years, had come to an unexpectedly rapid conclusion only months earlier, when Communist governments fell throughout Eastern Europe in 1989 and 1990. The allied offensive, whose military code name was Operation Desert Storm, involved ground troops from 19 countries (*see* **Operation Desert Storm**). Coalition participants joined together from virtually every region on the globe: North America, South America, Western Europe, Eastern Europe, the Middle East, Africa, Asia, and Australia (*see* **Coalition**).

The immediate cause of the Persian Gulf War was Iraq's conquest of Kuwait on August 2, 1990. Iraq's rapid success in overpowering Kuwait left Iraqi armored divisions suddenly poised on the Saudi Arabian border. Though the Iraqi Army stopped at the border and began erecting defensive fortifications, it was also positioned to occupy the oil-rich Saudi provinces adjoining Kuwait and Iraq.

Or it could even try to conquer all of Saudi Arabia. Iraq's armed forces were not only the largest and most formidable in the region, apart from Israel's, they were also mobilized and in position. By contrast, the sudden conquest of Kuwait had taken the Saudis and their allies by surprise, and the comparatively small Saudi armed forces were not at a high state of readiness. Consequently, Saudi Arabia was highly vulnerable to attack, and much of the world feared an invasion might be imminent† (*see* **Causes of the War**, **Invasion and Occupation of Kuwait**).

An Iraqi conquest of Saudi Arabia would have left approximately 40 percent of the world's proven oil reserves under the control of Saddam Hussein, the dictator whose Baath Party had created a Stalin-like police state in Iraq and who was known for his brutal suppression of domestic enemies, his desire to destroy Israel, and his ambition to create and lead a new, Pan-Arabic empire in the Middle East that would achieve a status comparable to the Cold War superpowers. Ultimately, the Persian Gulf War was fought because the United States and its Western allies would not allow control of almost half of the world's oil reserves—and the immense political and economic power that would accompany it—to

*All dates are for local time in the Middle East unless otherwise noted. The war began on the afternoon of January 16 and concluded on midnight of February 27, Eastern Standard Time (EST). The Middle East is in a time zone eight hours ahead of Washington, D.C., and three hours ahead of Greenwich mean time, which in the military is known as Zulu. When events occurred between midnight and 8 A.M. in Saudi Arabia, Kuwait, or Iraq, it was the afternoon or evening of the previous day in the United States.

†Some commentators argue that had Hussein indeed continued the invasion and at least seized the ports and oil fields in eastern Saudi Arabia, he might have fared better in the Persian Gulf War. Not only would he have had most of the Middle East's oil reserves under his direct control, he could also have denied the allies any Saudi port of entry on the Persian Gulf, thereby considerably impeding their ability to land troops and supplies in the contested regions.

One possible explanation for Hussein's failure to take this course of action is that he may not have expected a military response to his seizure of Kuwait and did not want to provoke one by invading Saudi Arabia.

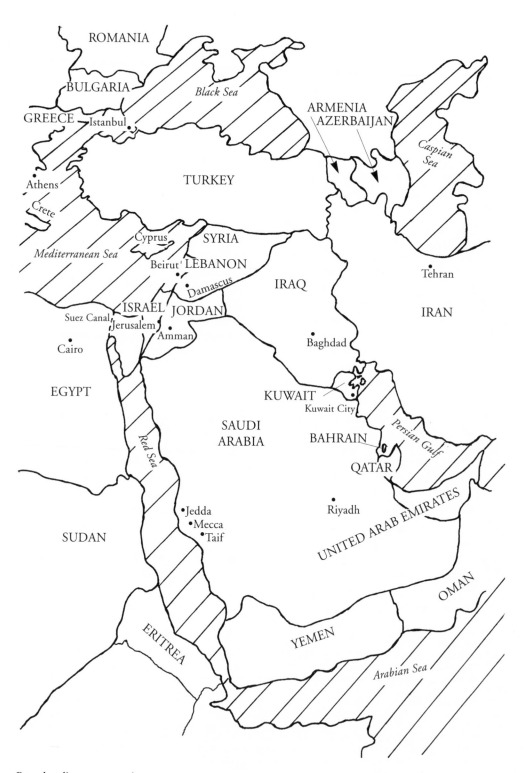

**Boundary lines are approximate.**

•Baghdad

*Euphrates River*

*Tigris River*

As Samawah

An Nasiriyah

Shattal Arab

IRAN

Basra

•As-Salmān Airfield

Umm Qasr

Safwan

•Rafha

IRAQ

KUWAIT

Warbah Island

Bubiyan Island

Al Jahra

Wadi al Batin

Kuwait City

Nisab

SAUDI ARABIA

Khafji

*Persian Gulf*

BAHRAIN

Dhahran

• Riyadh

**Boundary lines are approximate.**

fall to Hussein (*see* **Saddam Hussein, Ba'ath Party**).

The invasion of Kuwait came just as the Cold War was ending, and a "new world order" was beginning to emerge. This dramatic change in political environment made it possible for Iraq to be universally condemned for conquering Kuwait and for a worldwide coalition to be organized against it. During the Cold War most of the world had been polarized into two opposing camps, one led by the United States and the other by the Soviet Union. Iraq had been a client state of the Soviet Union. During the Cold War the Soviets would almost certainly have defended its ally against U.S.-led retaliation. But in the new world order they were more interested in cultivating closer ties with the United States than in supporting a renegade ally. Consequently, even the Soviet Union and its other allies joined in condemning Iraq, and though it did not fight in the Persian Gulf War, the Soviet Union did not oppose the U.S.-led military offensive to eject Iraqi troops from occupied Kuwait (*see* **Soviet Union**).

On the evening of Iraq's invasion of Kuwait, the United Nations Security Council condemned the action and called for an immediate Iraqi withdrawal. (Only Yemen, an Iraqi ally in the Middle East, did not support the resolution; Yemen abstained). Prior to the commencement of the war the Security Council passed 12 resolutions condemning Iraqi behavior (*see* **United Nations**). On August 6, the Security Council voted to impose a full trade embargo against Iraq to force Hussein to comply. On the same day, the United States received permission from Saudi Arabia's King Fahd to send some 200,000 troops to Saudi Arabia to defend it from an anticipated Iraqi invasion. In return, Saudi Arabia agreed to increase its oil production by 2 million barrels a day to help compensate for the 4.1 million barrels lost to the world market when Iraq stopped exporting its own oil and Kuwait's. The Saudis later agreed to provide substantial funding and military support as well.

The deployment of enough troops to guarantee the defense of Saudi Arabia lasted about two months. The first of the American troops arrived on August 9. They were later joined by forces from other nations, notably France, Great Britain, Egypt, Syria, and the countries in the Persian Gulf Cooperation Council. Saudi ground and air forces also contributed to the defense of their homeland. Turkey sent no troops to Saudi Arabia, but it agreed to allow U.S. planes to use its airbases and permitted the United States to expand its military presence in Turkey. It also positioned some 150,000 troops on its border with Iraq to create a potential second front and divert Iraqi forces from Kuwait (*see* **Operation Desert Shield, France, Great Britain, Egypt, Saudi Arabia, Syria, Gulf Cooperation Council, Turkey**).

As defensive troops continued to arrive in Saudi Arabia, U.S. President George Bush assembled commitments from other nations throughout the world (*see* **George Bush**). These countries contributed ground troops, ships, and medical units. Germany and Japan, which were prohibited by their post–Word War II constitutions from sending armies, contributed considerable sums of money. Bush's ability to assemble such a broad international coalition was a major diplomatic achievement, and forces from other nations made substantial achievements during the war. Nonetheless, U.S. troops constituted well over half of the coalition force, most of which fell under the command of General Norman Schwarzkopf, the commander-in-chief of the U.S. Central Command. The ground troops from Arab and Islamic countries were under the command of the Saudi-led Joint Forces Command, which coordinated with the Central Command. The Coalition Coordination, Communications, and Control Integration Center coordinated the two commands. Moreover, U.S. Special Forces teams served as liaisons with the Joint Forces (*see* **Norman Schwarzkopf, U.S. Central Command, Joint Forces Command**).

As the anti–Iraqi coalition grew in the late summer and fall of 1990, Hussein was not passive. On August 8, Iraq formally annexed Kuwait as the nineteenth Iraqi province, thereby in a single stroke eliminating its huge debt to Kuwait, gaining all of Kuwait's assets, and acquiring long-sought ports on the Persian Gulf. On August 15, Hussein offered to grant Iran all of the concessions it was demanding in order to formally end the Gulf War that the two nations had waged between 1980 and 1988. Iran accepted and Hussein immediately redeployed 24 divisions—some 300,000 troops—from the Iran border to Kuwait and the Saudi border areas. By reopening the border with Iran, Hussein also created a long frontier where outside goods could be smuggled into Iraq, in violation of the U.N. embargo (*see* **Iran**). In addition, Hussein refused to permit the thousands of foreign nationals in Kuwait and Iraq to leave. Instead, he tried to employ them as bargaining chips to enhance his diplomatic leverage, and he threatened to make them into "human shields" by placing them around sensitive target areas to prevent the coalition countries from bombing those targets (*see* **Hostages**). Hussein also called for all Islamic nations to support him in a *jihad*—a holy war—against the United States and its allies, and he sought to undermine the governments of those Arab countries that opposed him—notably Egypt and Syria—by appealing directly to their citizens for support. He also threatened to launch missiles with chemical weapons against Israel if the coalition countries attacked Iraq, even though Israel was not part of the coalition (*see* **Israel**). And Hussein tried unsuccessfully to link an Iraqi withdrawal from occupied Kuwait to Israeli withdrawal from the West Bank and Syrian withdrawal from Lebanon (*see* **Diplomacy**). Since the United States was Israel's chief ally in the region, Hussein managed to win considerable popular support throughout the Arab world. However, he did not succeed in destabilizing the Arab governments that opposed him or in lessening their commitment to the coalition.

On August 25, the Security Council voted to permit military enforcement of the embargo against Iraq (*see* **Naval Action**). The plan was to pressure Hussein to withdraw from Iraq by using the trade sanctions to de-

bilitate the Iraqi economy until he did. Estimates were that the sanctions would require six months to two years to succeed, if they would succeed at all (*see* **Embargo**). However, by late September Bush concluded that the situation needed to be resolved more quickly, since the Iraqis were pillaging Kuwait, terrorizing Kuwaiti citizens, and abducting Kuwaiti boys and military-age men to Iraq. And though Hussein was releasing small numbers of foreign hostages as prominent leaders from throughout the world came to Baghdad to ask for their freedom, thousands of British and American hostages remained in Kuwait and Iraq against their will. Moreover, holding the disparate coalition together for two years while sanctions took effect would have been problematic, especially since Hussein tried to splinter the coalition by making political concessions to some countries but not others. Sustaining popular support in the United States for maintaining a force in excess of 200,000 troops in the desert for two years would also have been difficult, especially since Bush had called up reservists who left their families and civilian jobs to serve. Therefore, in October, Bush asked for Schwarzkopf and Colin Powell, the chairman of the Joint Chiefs of Staff, to present plans for a military offensive to remove the Iraqis from Kuwait (*see* **Colin Powell, Offensive War Preparations for Liberating Kuwait**).

Schwarzkopf and Powell concluded that an offensive would require almost twice as many troops as were on hand for the defense of Saudi Arabia. Consequently, on November 8, two days after the midterm Congressional elections, Defense Secretary Richard Cheney began calling up additional reserve units, and by January over 400,000 U.S. troops were deployed in the Middle East. On November 29, the Security Council voted to authorize war if Iraq did not withdraw by January 15, 1991.

The deployment of U.S. troops to defend Saudi Arabia enjoyed broad support within the United States, but there was considerable opposition to an offensive war to liberate Kuwait. Experts were estimating that a war would result in 10,000 to 20,000 U.S.

casualties, and many Americans believed that Bush was too eager to fight; they wanted to give diplomacy and economic sanctions more time to compel Hussein to withdraw. Others believed American soldiers were being sent to risk their lives primarily for the economic interests of the oil industry, with which Bush had close political and personal connections. Others had qualms about sending U.S. troops to restore a nondemocratic monarchy that deprived its citizens of many of the basic freedoms that Americans traditionally cherish. Still other citizens objected to Americans being used essentially as hired guns to fight for Saudis and Kuwaitis, who had done precious little to protect themselves. Some Jewish Americans, and other Americans as well, feared that Hussein would carry out his threat to attack Israel with chemical weapons if the allies started a war, and they did not think Kuwait was worth that risk. Moreover, Congressional hearings featured testimony against fighting a war from, among others, Admiral William Crowe, a former chairman of the Joint Chiefs, and former Secretary of Defense Robert McNamara, the architect of the Vietnam War, the memory of which was never far from mind in the Persian Gulf War debate. Sam Nunn, the influential chairman of the Senate Armed Services Committee, also opposed the war. Consequently, Congress was divided in its support for the war, and antiwar demonstrations took place throughout the country (*see* **Popular Support for the War**). However, on January 12, following the failure of a last-ditch effort to obtain an Iraqi withdrawal by diplomatic means, the majority of Congress voted to authorize a war.

On January 17, Operation Desert Storm began as coalition planes and missiles struck against Iraq. Between January 17 and February 24, the coalition waged an air campaign whose objectives were to destroy the Iraqi Air Force and air defenses in order to obtain complete air supremacy, to disrupt Iraqi command and control, to destroy Iraqi chemical, biological and nuclear weapons stockpiles and or production facilities, and to weaken Iraqi ground forces and defensive fortifications

through repeated bombings (*see* **Air Campaign**). On January 18, Iraq responded to the air attacks by launching the first of 40 Scud missiles against Israel. Hussein's rationale was to provoke Israel into retaliating and thereby create a rift within the coalition, since the Arab countries would presumably refuse to fight alongside Israel. To prevent Israel from joining the war, the United States agreed to send batteries of Patriot antimissile missiles to Israel and to make attacking Iraqi Scud launchers a major military priority in the air campaign. In addition, Special Forces units were inserted into western Iraq to hunt for mobile Scud launchers (*see* **Scud Missiles, Patriot Missiles, Special Operations Forces**). Though Hussein had threatened to use chemical warheads against Israel and the coalition troops, he did not because he feared nuclear retaliation. He did, however, launch a "scorched earth" policy against Kuwait by ordering over 500 oil wells set on fire and the pumping of millions of barrels of oil into the Persian Gulf (*see* **Environmental Warfare**).

During the air war, General Schwarzkopf ordered the secret redeployment of most of his armored divisions several hundred miles to the west, so he could launch a surprise attack against the Iraqi flank. The westward shift, known as Operation Hail Mary, was a major logistical achievement, as over 117,000 troops, 5,000 tanks, and enough food, water, and ammunition to sustain them in the desert for 60 days were secretly moved as far as 530 miles across the desert to positions as far as 250 miles inland along the Saudi-Iraqi border. The redeployment lasted about three weeks (*see* **Operation Hail Mary**). At the same time, the 1st Marine Expeditionary Force and the Joint Forces Command also redeployed from their positions by the coast to new attack positions further inland and closer to the Kuwaiti border.

On February 24, Schwarzkopf initiated a two-pronged ground attack. The first prong was an assault by U.S. Marines and pan-Arab forces against the Iraqi fortifications in Kuwait. After breaching the Iraqi defenses, they proceeded north to Kuwait City, which was liberated on February 27 (*see* **Battle for Kuwait**). The second prong constituted the main coalition attack, as U.S. and British armored divisions west of the Iraqi lines crossed into Iraq and then swung around to strike at the exposed flank of the elite Republican Guard armored divisions. Farther to the west a French armored division and U.S. airborne troops protected the allied flank against a counterattack. During 100 hours of fighting the allies trapped most of the Republican Guard in a pocket in northern Kuwait, inflicting heavy casualties and destroying most of Iraq's tanks and armored vehicles (*see* **Battle Against the Republican Guard**).

According to the U.S. Air Force, the Iraqi Army lost about 76 percent of its tanks, 55 percent of its armored personnel carriers, and 90 percent of its artillery. About 1,430 Iraqi personnel carriers and 700 tanks managed to escape. On the other hand, the allies destroyed about 3,700 tanks, took over 70,000 prisoners, and rendered 33 Iraqi divisions ineffective. Approximately 20 to 30,000 Iraqi soldiers were killed from bombings and ground combat, and many others died from diseases and other desert-related illnesses. Moreover, an estimated 100,000 Iraqi soldiers deserted during the air campaign. In addition, approximately 2,300 Iraqi civilians died in the bombings and another 6,000 were wounded. Additional civilian casualties followed from the poor sanitary conditions and breakdown in support services caused by the air attacks.

By contrast, the coalition forces suffered fewer than 300 combat fatalities. Forty-two coalition troops were captured. However, after the war, tens of thousands of veterans—as many as one-third of those who served in the Middle East—began experiencing such symptoms as fatigue, nausea, depression, severe headaches, memory loss, disturbed sleep, dizziness, sexual impotence, muscle pain and muscle fatigue, rashes, confusion, and the inability to concentrate. To date, efforts to treat and account for the cause of these ailments remain unsuccessful (*see* **Gulf War Syndrome**).

Bush ordered the cessation of offensive actions at 8 A.M. on February 28 (midnight, February 27, EST). At that point all of the coalition's stated objectives had been achieved: Iraqi troops had been forced from Kuwait and Iraq's ability to wage offensive war within the region had been eliminated (*see* **Objectives, Cease-fire**). However, several hundred Iraqi tanks were able to escape back into Iraq, and these were soon used to suppress rebellions within Iraq by disaffected Kurds and Shīa Muslims (*see* **Aftermath, Kurdish Rebellion, Shīʿite Rebellion**). Thus, Bush's decision to end the war before the Republican Guard was completely destroyed remains one of the most controversial aspects of the war.

The Persian Gulf War was notable in several respects. It was the first American war waged by all-volunteer military forces. The technologically advanced coalition forces successfully employed many highly sophisticated, computerized weapons (*see* **Weapons Systems and Advanced Technology**). Satellite communications systems and cable television allowed for instantaneous and nearly continuous media coverage; at the same time the military subjected battlefront journalists to more stringent restrictions than ever before (*see* **Media Coverage**). Finally, female soldiers played a much more active role in combat than in any other U.S. military action (*see* **Women in the Military**).

# The Encyclopedia

**Air Campaign**—The air campaign was the initial phase of Operation Desert Storm, and it lasted from January 17, 1991, until the cessation of hostilities on February 28, 1991 (*see* **Operation Desert Storm**).

Colonel John A. Warden III submitted the first plans for an air campaign to General Schwarzkopf in early August 1990 under the code name Instant Thunder. Though subsequently revised, Warden's basic strategy was retained throughout the war (*see* **Instant Thunder**).

Primarily a strategic campaign to destroy Iraqi leadership and command and control capabilities and eliminate Iraq's ability to reinforce its ground forces in Kuwait, the final plan also called for establishing air supremacy over Kuwait, inflicting heavy casualties on the Iraqi Army prior to the ground offensive, destroying Republican Guard tanks and artillery, and providing air support during the ground campaign.

Altogether, 12 kinds of targets were identified to achieve these goals. These included leadership command facilities, 45 of which were in Baghdad; electricity production facilities; telecommunications and command, control, and communications nodes; the Iraqi strategic integrated air defense system; Iraqi air forces and air fields; nuclear, biological, and chemical weapons facilities; Scud missiles, Scud launchers, and Scud production and storage facilities; naval forces and port facilities; oil refining and distribution facilities; railroads and bridges; and Iraqi army units and the Republican Guard forces within the Kuwaiti theater of operations. Historical, archaeological, economic, religious, and politically sensitive sights were removed from target lists, and care was taken to avoid schools, hospitals, and mosques close to targets.

U.S. Air Force Lieutenant General Charles A. Horner commanded all coalition air forces and assumed ultimate responsibility for prosecuting the air war (*see* **Charles A. Horner**). Brigadier General Buster C. Glosson was the chief targeter and commander of all U.S. Air Force wings in the Persian Gulf. Lieutenant Colonel David A. Deptula, who had been one of Warden's assistants, was in charge of maintaining the master plan.

The air war began at 1 A.M. on January 17, 1991 (U.S. time, 5 P.M., January 16, EST), one day after the U.N. deadline for an Iraqi withdrawal from Kuwait. It took place under the worst weather conditions in the 14 years that the Air Force had maintained records for the region. Consequently, numerous sorties were canceled or redirected. Though the U.S. Air Force flew most of the missions (59 percent), U.S. Navy and Marine Corps jets accounted for about 25 percent of the sorties. Warplanes from Great Britain, France, Canada, Italy, Saudi Arabia, Qatar, and Kuwait flew a combined total of about 16 percent of the 112,000 sorties launched during the war. U.S. Army and Marine helicopters and gunships also flew missions and were especially useful for providing ground support and destroying Iraqi tanks and vehicles during the ground offensive.

Throughout the air campaign the allies made extensive use of advanced technology, employing state-of-the-art aircraft, cruise missiles, remote-piloted drones, sophisticated electronic equipment, satellite data, and laser-guided "smart bombs" and Hellfire missiles, as well as more conventional weapons (*see* **Weapons Systems and Advanced Technology**).

The first order of business was to gain air dominance over the Kuwaiti theater of operations, and that was achieved on the first day. By January 27, the allies had achieved air supremacy, which meant that coalition planes essentially had unchallenged control of the skies. This was accomplished against heavily fortified air defenses armed with Soviet-made surface-to-air missiles (SAMs), sophisticated radar systems, numerous antiaircraft installations, and advanced Soviet-made MiGs and French-made Mirage jets armed with Exocet missiles.

The initial allied strikes were conducted by helicopters against Iraq's early-warning radar sites in order to establish an attack corridor over which allied planes could fly undetected deep inside Iraq. The helicopter attacks were followed by Tomahawk cruise missiles launched from U.S. warships in the Persian Gulf and Red Sea. These were directed at heavily defended targets within Baghdad. Stealth F-117A fighter bombers were also chosen to attack well-defended sites because the Stealth bombers could approach the targets without being detected. By 2:30 A.M. Iraqi command and control centers in Baghdad were under heavy attack.

Not only did their quick mastery of the air allow the allies to bomb subsequent targets safely, it also deprived Iraq of reconnaissance capabilities. As such the Iraqis frequently had no idea where the allied ground forces were. This proved crucial to the success of the ground war. Meanwhile, the allies often enjoyed very good intelligence about Iraqi locations, provided by aerial reconnaissance and sophisticated satellite photographs.

Heat-detecting infrared sensors enabled some reconnaissance cameras to detect enemy troops, tanks, and vehicles that were camouflaged and otherwise invisible. Eliminating Iraqi reconnaissance enabled Schwarzkopf to secretly set up the surprise flanking attack that ultimately trapped and destroyed most of the Republican Guard.

Schwarzkopf initiated the westward redeployment, which he called Operation Hail Mary, on January 17, the day he launched the air campaign (*see* **Operation Hail Mary**).

The air campaign passed through several phases as it accomplished successive objectives. From January 17–21, Iraqi air defense radars and air defense control centers constituted the primary targets. The Iraqi air defense was controlled by a network of over 50 fixed and mobile radars near the Saudi border and 12 larger surveillance radars deeper inside Iraq. These were all eliminated during the first week of fighting. In addition, some antiaircraft guns had their own radars, but these were typically destroyed as soon as they were detected, and they could be detected within 20 seconds of being turned on. Without their radar, most of the Iraqi SAMs and antiaircraft artillery were rendered ineffective, and subsequent allied air attacks became only two to three times more dangerous than peacetime training missions.

Thus most of the allied air losses occurred during the first weeks of the war. The antiradar missions were flown primarily by F-117A Stealth bombers armed with laser-guided "smart bombs" and F-15E, F-4G, E-6, and F-111 fighter bombers. The last, affectionately dubbed Wild Weasels, carried sophisticated electronic equipment for detecting the enemy radars, which they destroyed with high-velocity antiradiation missiles (HARMs). Sometimes, unmanned drones were launched to trick the Iraqis into turning on their radars, thereby revealing the radar locations and making them vulnerable to subsequent air strikes. Unmanned Tomahawk cruise missiles were also employed for taking out heavily defended radar and control centers.

Iraqi air bases, airfields, and flying aircraft were also targeted at the beginning of the air campaign in order to secure air supremacy. Though these remained targets throughout the war, the most intensive efforts against them occurred between January 17 and February 2. Wild Weasels and low-flying British Tornados were used most extensively against these targets, though all types of fighters and bombers attacked them. With their ground-based radar and control facilities destroyed, airborne Iraqi fighters became more vulnerable and less effective because they depended on those radar systems for direction. Iraqi planes rarely challenged allied jets in the air. Coalition air planners speculated that the Iraqis were trying to save their planes for use in surprise attacks later in the war, perhaps during the ground offensive. However, most of the Iraqi Air Force was destroyed before that could happen. Some air encounters did take place, and allied planes downed 40 Iraqi fighters in air-to-air combat. Only one coalition plane was shot down by an Iraqi jet. That took place on the first night of the war when an Iraqi MiG-25 shot down a U.S. carrier-based jet.

By destroying runways and refueling equipments, the allies were able to keep many Iraqi jets on the ground, inside hardened bunkers that later became targets. Approximately 140 Iraqi combat aircraft were destroyed inside their bunkers; another 80 or more escaped destruction by flying to Iran, where they were impounded for the duration of the war. Hundreds of Iraqi helicopters were also destroyed on the ground.

With the Iraqi Air Force effectively eliminated from the fighting, the allies were able to concentrate on other bombing priorities. Between January 19 and February 15, Iraqi strategic command and communication centers emerged as primary targets for Stealth bombers and F-15E fighter bombers using laser-guided smart bombs. Wild Weasels and other planes also bombed these targets. Without their command and communication centers, the Iraqi high command could not effectively direct and deploy their forces, arrange for supplies, or communicate important information.

On January 18, the day after the air war began, Iraq launched its first Scud missile against Israel. The Israelis were prepared to retaliate, but the allied leaders feared that Israeli participation in the war would cause the coalition to splinter, as the participating Arab countries might refuse to fight alongside Israel against another Arab nation.

Consequently, President Bush took several steps to keep Israel out of the war. He immediately sent Patriot missile systems to defend against subsequent Scud attacks, and despite Schwarzkopf's objections that Scuds were not a major military target, Bush insisted that destroying Scud launchers be made a top priority. (He also threatened the Israelis by refusing to give them the codes to identify their planes as friendly aircraft. Israeli jets would thus have been exposed to friendly fire from the allies).

To Schwarzkopf's frustration, "Scud hunting" accounted for as much as 40 percent of all air sorties in late January. The allies quickly destroyed the Iraqis' fixed-position Scud launchers, but destroying mobile Scud launchers was far more difficult, and Scud hunting remained a top priority throughout the war, as allied jets were assigned to crisscross over some 28,000 square miles of desert searching for mobile launchers. J-STAR jets were used for detecting the movements of Scud launch vehicles. (*See* **Scud Missiles, Patriot Missiles**.)

The allies also feared Iraq would use chemical weapons as it had during its Gulf War against Iran and in its attacks on Kurdish civilians in northern Iraq during that war (*see* **Iran-Iraq Gulf War**). The Iraqis had also been developing biological weapons and had long been trying to build nuclear weapons as well.

No one knew for sure if they had succeeded in making a nuclear device or if they had warheads capable of delivering one. But to be safe, the allies targeted Iraqi chemical, biological, and nuclear facilities throughout the entire war. Stealth bombers, and A-6, F-15E, and A-10 bombers were employed against these targets (*see* **Biological Warfare, Chemical Warfare, Nuclear Warfare**).

By January 26, the Iraqi Army and its logistical and support facilities emerged as new priorities for the allies, who employed Army and Marine attack helicopters and every type of bomber against them. General Colin Powell, the chairman of the Joint Chiefs of Staff, had stated that the allies would cut off the Iraqi Army and kill it.

Destroying the army's source of supplies enabled the allies to cut it off, and bombing Iraqi troops on the ground played a major role in killing it. Thus, prior to the beginning of the ground war, allied planes and helicopters attacked Iraqi fortified positions, fieldworks, bunkers, tanks, and artillery pieces. B-52s specialized in carpet bombings to cover large areas of the Iraqi defensive positions. Flying around the clock, they attacked frontline forces, breaching sites, and Iraqi staging areas near the Euphrates river. B-52 raids accounted for about 30 percent of the bomb tonnage dropped during the war. They inflicted substantial damage and had the additional effect of terrorizing Iraqi troops on the ground. B-52s and other aircraft also dropped millions of leaflets in English and Arabic encouraging the Iraqi soldiers to surrender (*see* **Psychological Operations**).

Coalition planes also targeted the trucks and railroads necessary for delivering food, water, fuel, ammunition, medical supplies, replacement parts, clothing, and other materials essential to the Iraqi Army. They struck at Iraq's electric power generators to further cripple the army's ability to sustain itself. Moreover, Tomahawk cruise missiles scattered thousands of carbon filaments through the air over Baghdad. These were intended to fall onto electrical power lines and short them out.

Some disputes arose between the U.S. Army and the Air Force over target selection during the middle of the air campaign, as the Army complained that the Air Force was assigning too many of its sorties to strategic targets in Iraq and not enough to bombing the Iraqi ground troops on the battlefield in Kuwait. Schwarzkopf, who wanted to reduce Iraqi ground strength by 50 percent before initiating his ground offensive, concurred. Therefore, in early February he assigned his deputy, Lieutenant General Calvin Waller, to approve the daily bombing targets to ensure that adequate effort went into "shaping" the battlefield. By the time the ground war began on February 24, the Iraqi ground troops suffered from a severe lack of food and water, and

many were ill. Consequently, both their stamina and morale were low. Once the ground war began, Iraqi troops and armored vehicles became targets for allied bombers and helicopters as the Iraqi forces deployed from their concealed positions into the open desert.

The allies tried to refrain from bombing civilians for both humanitarian and political reasons. Politically, they feared that if Arab civilians were routinely shown as victims of allied bombings, public outrage in the Arab countries within the coalition might force those governments to withdraw from the war. Indeed, after CNN showed the remnants of a bomb shelter in which 204 noncombatants were killed on February 13, the allies severely restricted their targets in Baghdad and decided to move ahead with the ground war (*see* **Al-Firdos Bunker**). The United States claimed that the shelter had been used as a military command and control center and supplied evidence to support that claim. But the disaster remained a public relations victory for Iraq. Altogether, Iraq reported some 2,300 civilians were killed and 6,000 wounded by allied air attacks. The Iraqi military lost 40 planes in the air (confirmed) and several hundred on the ground.

The allies suffered 42 combat losses and 33 noncombat losses during the air campaign at a rate of 31 losses per 100,000 sorties. (The peacetime rate is about 14 per 100,000). The estimated replacement cost of lost aircraft was $82 billion. The estimated additional maintenance costs for fixed-wing aircraft was $400,000, and the estimated cost of munitions expended in the air war was $500 million.

**Aftermath**—Not wanting to become bogged down in a long-term military occupation, the allies moved quickly to restore stability to the region after the success of Operation Desert Storm. On March 1, the U.S., British, French, and Canadian embassies opened in Kuwait City, and the international airport became operational. On March 2, 1991, the Security Council passed Resolution 686, setting down the conditions for a cease-fire. It demanded that Iraq cease all hostile military action and renounce any aggressive intentions toward Kuwait, disclose the locations of mines, return all POWs and other detainees (including the Kuwaiti citizens taken hostage after August 2, 1990), rescind its annexation of Kuwait, return Kuwaiti property, and accept responsibility for damages it inflicted. The vote was 11–1, with Cuba opposing and India, Yemen, and China abstaining. Iraq accepted the cease-fire on the next day and demonstrated its good faith on March 4 by releasing some allied POWs. (The first of the released POWs returned to Washington, D.C. on March 10. *See* **Cease-fire**.) On March 8, the harbor of Kuwait City reopened, following two weeks of minesweeping. On March 14, the Emir of Kuwait, Sheik Jaber Al-Sabah, returned to Kuwait City from his exile in Saudi Arabia.

On the diplomatic scene, Iraq officially accepted the U.N. terms for a formal cease-fire on April 6. Three days later the Security Council passed Resolution 689 establishing an observer mission to monitor the permanent cease-fire, and on April 11, the Security Council announced that Operation Desert Storm had officially concluded (*see* **United Nations**).

The cease-fire agreement forbade Iraqi troop movements within the Kuwaiti theater and any flights by Iraqi military planes. Violations of these provisions provoked several U.S. strikes after the cease-fire concluded. On March 1, U.S. armored vehicles destroyed a convoy of 1,000 Iraqi vehicles moving north of the Rumalia oil field. On the following day, the U.S. 24th Mechanized Infantry Division destroyed two battalions of Republican Guards traveling west on Highway 8. A number of Iraqi civilians were also killed. In both instances the Iraqis attacked the U.S. troops, though critics maintain the U.S. response was disproportionate. On March 20 and 22, U.S. jets shot down Iraqi warplanes flying over northern Iraq.

On March 3, Schwarzkopf met with rank-ing Iraqi officers to establish the procedural details for enforcing the cease-fire. They prepared to exchange POWs (the Iraqis held 41; the allies had taken over 70,000) and information about missing soldiers, and the Iraqis provided details about the positions of their land mines. Prior to this meeting Schwarzkopf had retained his standing order to shoot down any Iraqi warplane flying over Iraqi airspace. But at the meeting he acceded to a request to permit helicopter flights, after the Iraqis pointed out how the allies had destroyed most of their strategic bridges and roads. They claimed helicopters were necessary to transport government officials who were trying to implement the terms of the cease-fire. However, soon afterward the Iraqi Army employed its helicopters to suppress the Shī'ite uprising in southern Iraq near Basra and the Kurdish rebellion in northern Iraq that had sprung up during Desert Storm. On March 13 and 14, Bush criticized Hussein's use of the helicopters against his own people, but took no steps to curtail it.

Bush tolerated Hussein's suppression of the Kurds and Shī'ites because he did not want to enmesh the U.S. military in a bloody and prolonged occupation or peacekeeping operation. Moreover, the Sunni-led Saudis may have preferred having a weakened Hussein in power in Iraq to seeing an independent Shī'ite nation established on its border, right beside the portion of Saudi Arabia that contains the greatest oil reserves and has a large Shī'ite population.

Likewise, Turkey, which had its own difficulties with Kurdish separatists on its southern border, was not anxious to see an independent Kurdish state formed in northern Iraq. Whatever the reasons, the coalition forces treated Hussein's war against the Kurds and Shī'ites as an internal Iraqi matter for which they had no U.N. mandate to intervene. They denounced Hussein's brutal actions that drove more than 500,000 Kurds into refugee camps in Iran and Turkey, but apart from enforcing

*Bush received considerable public criticism for his decision not to oppose Hussein's violent suppression of the insurrections, especially because the president had helped provoke the uprisings by publicly calling on the Iraqi people to overthrow*

the terms of the cease-fire, they took no military action to stop Hussein. Consequently, with the use of the helicopters Schwarzkopf had permitted them and some of the troops and tanks that had escaped almost certain destruction when Bush terminated the attack, Hussein's forces succeeded in suppressing the uprisings by early April. Some observers maintain that Hussein had retained sufficient forces within Iraq to suppress the rebellions, regardless of whether or not he could also use those that survived Desert Storm. In any event, the threat to Hussein's grip on power inside Iraq largely disappeared* (see **Kurdish Rebellion**, **Shī'ite Rebellion**).

On April 7, the United States and Great Britain inaugurated Operation Provide Comfort to assist Kurdish refugees, and on April 16 they established safety zones for the Kurds. U.N. forces assumed responsibility for the safety zones in June, but subsequently the United States placed a rapid deployment force in Turkey to protect the Kurds. To date, in accordance with the terms of the peace agreement that ended the war, coalition planes continue to enforce zones over northern Iraq where Iraqi military aircraft are forbidden to fly, and periodically Iraqi jets have been shot down. More recently, the situation has been further complicated by fighting between the two major Kurdish independence movements.

While Hussein was prosecuting his war against the Kurds and Shī'ites, coalition leaders were anxious to bring their troops back home. On March 8, Operation Desert Farewell began, as the first 5,000 American troops departed from Dhahran. By April 1, 165,000 troops had returned to the United States.

In the years since the Persian Gulf War the Iraqis have failed to give U.N. inspection teams complete access to their nuclear, chemical, and biological warfare facilities. Consequently, the

United Nations has refused to lift its economic and military embargo against Iraq. However, in August 1991, the Security Council's Resolution 706 permitted Iraq to sell a limited amount of oil for six months to generate funds to provide for humanitarian needs of its citizens, compensate war victims, and pay for U.N. monitoring teams. In December 1996, the United Nations also permitted Iraq to sell a limited amount of oil under similar conditions. In late 1997 tensions flared again as Hussein denied U.N. monitors access to biological weapons facilities.

**AirLand Battle Doctrine**—Conceived after the Vietnam War, the AirLand battle doctrine called for full coordination between the U.S. ground and air forces, something that had been lacking since World War II, after which the Army Air Corps separated from the Army and became the Air Force. Though used against Iraq in the Persian Gulf War, the Cold War military doctrine was originally designed for fighting a war against Soviet and Warsaw Pact armored divisions in Europe.

The plan calls for fully integrated, comprehensive warfare in which ground forces coordinate their operations with air forces. During World War II such coordination existed. But when the Air Force became a separate branch of the military, its officers typically concentrated on strategic bombing raids and other elements of air campaigning and relegated air support for ground troops to relatively low priority. Indeed, even as late as 1990 some Air Force officers suggested turning over their A-10 ground support aircraft to the Army, so the Air Force could concentrate on its own missions. However, that proposal was rejected, and during the Persian Gulf War the branches of the military service worked closely together.

Instead of focusing primarily on the main battle fronts where the opposing armies face

---

(continued) *Hussein. Indeed, the televised attacks on the Kurds and Shī'ites subjected Bush to even more criticism for his decision to end the war early, before Hussein's military capability was entirely destroyed. In response the president's popularity, which during Desert Storm was at the highest level of any president since World War II, began to falter. The fact that Hussein remained firmly entrenched in power in the fall of 1992, and the Kurds and Shī'ites had clearly been suppressed, led some critics to contend that the United States had, after all, failed to win the war. Though inaccurate on many counts, this perception no doubt contributed to Bush's failure to win reelection that November.*

each other, AirLand doctrine views the battle arena something like a chessboard where various pieces may operate behind the main enemy lines to disrupt the enemy's ability to coordinate its movements and actions. According to the Army manual:

> AirLand Battle doctrine is based on securing or retaining the initiative and exercising it aggressively to defeat the enemy. Destruction of the opposing force is achieved by throwing the enemy off balance with powerful initial blows from unexpected directions and then following up rapidly to prevent his recovery. Army units will attack the enemy in depth with fire and maneuver and synchronize all efforts to attain the objective. They will maintain the agility necessary to shift forces and fire to the points of enemy weakness. Our operations must be rapid, unpredictable, violent and disorienting to the enemy.

During Operation Desert Storm the doctrine called for the Air Force to use missiles, planes, and helicopters to strike deep within enemy territory to disrupt movement of troops and supplies and to attack enemy troops on the ground. At the same time, ground-based artillery was directed against Iraqi air defenses, thereby enabling Air Force jets to fly safely over the battlefields to take out enemy artillery and tanks. Airborne soldiers also landed behind enemy positions to further disrupt their defenses. Meanwhile, reconnaissance aircraft monitored enemy troop movements and kept the ground forces appraised. Moreover, the main thrust of the ground offensive, the surprise "left hook" in which armored divisions unexpectedly attacked the Republican Guard's western flank, was a strategy consistent with AirLand doctrine's penchant for the unexpected.

The doctrine emphasizes matching the strike force to the mission, calling for the use of specific kinds of weapons, equipment, and troops for specific tasks. In this way it seeks to optimize resources. The Persian Gulf War was the first major test of the AirLand doctrine, and it worked exceedingly well.

**Al-Firdos Bunker**—On February 13, 1991, two F-117 fighters dropped two 2,000-pound, laser-guided bombs on the Al-Firdos bunker in Baghdad, also known as Public Shelter Number 25. The target was a hardened bunker containing what U.S. intelligence officers believed was the Iraqi Internal Security Directorate. Whether the facility was actually being used by Iraqi intelligence remains a matter of controversy. That Iraqi civilians were using it as an air raid shelter at the time of the bombing is undisputed. Two hundred four civilians were killed in an intense firestorm; many others were wounded.

During Operation Desert Shield, American intelligence officers had identified the bunker as one of ten that had been extensively hardened with reinforced concrete ceilings and protected against electromagnetic pulses emitted by nuclear explosions. They assumed these precautions were taken to protect an important Iraqi command and control facility in the event of a nuclear attack. However, although the bunkers were placed on a tentative target list in early January, Lieutenant Colonel Dave Deptula, who was in charge of maintaining the master plan for the strategic bombing campaign, removed them because he could find no satellite evidence that they were being used for command and control activities.

In early February, though, the CIA detected radio emanations from the vicinity of the Al-Firdos bunker and, believing it had been a command bunker during the Iran-Iraq Gulf War, concluded that it had now been taken over by the General Intelligence Department, whose headquarters had been bombed early in the war. Satellite photos showing military vehicles near the facility reinforced their suspicions. A specific query to the Defense Intelligence Agency from Schwarzkopf's intelligence chief, Brigadier General Jack Leide, yielded the answer that there was no evidence that the bunker was being used as a civilian shelter. Nonetheless, Brigadier General Buster Glosson, who was responsible for selecting allied bombing targets, rejected the evidence that the bunker was an Iraqi command site as too circumstantial.

However, in the second week of February a top official in the Iraqi government who was spying for the United States claimed that Iraqi intelligence officials were using Shelter Number 25. The spy's information had been accurate in the past, and on the strength of his claim Glosson reversed his decision and authorized bombing the facility. On February 11, the Al-Firdos bunker was added to the master plan of targets, and on February 13 it was hit.

CNN broadcast images of the ruined bunker and the casualties, and its on-the-spot reporter, Peter Arnett, reported to the entire world that the Iraqi government claimed the facility had been used solely as a civilian bomb shelter and that he could see no evidence that it had been employed for any military use. Despite the fact that CNN soon after presented military experts who reviewed the videotape and pointed out considerable evidence to suggest that the bunker was, indeed, a command and control facility, Iraq won a big public relations victory. During the war it consistently used the media to try to intensify the considerable opposition to the war in the Arab countries that were coalition members, especially Egypt and Syria. The pictures of American bombs killing Arab civilians in what was ostensibly a deliberate attack thus became a potent weapon in Iraq's media campaign.

On the other hand, the incident apparently did little to undermine support for the war in the United States. A poll taken soon afterwards showed that about 80 percent of Americans blamed the Iraqi government for the tragedy, and only 13 percent advocated greater precautions to avoid additional civilian deaths. Nonetheless, as a result of the bombing, the allied military planners restricted their targets in Baghdad and took greater efforts to avoid civilian casualties. Stating that "The amount of additional damage we might inflict compared to the consequences of that damage takes on more policy and political overtones.... We don't want to take a chance on something like this happening again," General Colin Powell, the chairman of the Joint Chiefs of Staff, thereafter assumed personal responsibility for approving targets within Baghdad. The incident also increased the pressure to begin the ground war more quickly.

Reports after the war support the contention that an Iraqi military intelligence unit, in fact, had been using the shelter, at least during the daytime (see **The Air Campaign**).

**Amphibious Landing**—Preparations for an amphibious assault on the Kuwaiti shore began as early as October 1, 1990, when most of the U.S. naval ships in the Persian Gulf rehearsed a landing off of Oman during Operation Camel Sand. The original plan for Operation Desert Storm called for some 17,000 Marines on ships offshore to land at Ash-Shu'aybah, a port on the Persian Gulf about 20 miles south of Kuwait City. The landing, code-named Desert Saber, would provide a supply base for the land-based 1st Marine Expeditionary Force pushing north into Kuwait from the Saudi border, 50 miles inland from the coast. The amphibious assault would also provide a force to cut off an Iraqi counterattack against the land attack. In fact, however, Schwarzkopf concluded in early February that an amphibious landing through heavily mined waters and against heavily defended shores would cost too many Marine lives and incur too much damage to Kuwaiti property. The allies would have had to destroy all of the high-rise buildings along the shoreline to eliminate potential Iraqi gun emplacements. Schwarzkopf was afraid that the Iraqis could detonate a liquid gas plant next to the port, turning it into what Marine planners called "the nuke on the beach." In addition to desperately wanting to save American lives, Schwarzkopf repeatedly told Colin Powell, "I can't destroy Kuwait in the process of saving Kuwait," alluding to the Vietnam War practice of destroying villages in order to save them. Moreover, extensive minesweeping and battlefield preparation necessary for an amphibious assault would have postponed the ground offensive planned for the third week of February.

Thus Schwarzkopf ordered several practice assaults code-named Sea Soldier I-IV to keep the sea-based Marines ready if their land-based comrades needed them. But their primary mission now was to serve as a ruse to divert Iraqi defenses to the coast, where they would be useless against the main attack (see **Deceptions, Feints, and Ruses**).

On the evening before the ground offensive began, Navy SEALs simulated an attack at Mīnā Saʿūd, Kuwait, to convince Iraqi defenders that an amphibious attack against the Kuwaiti coastline had begun. They detonated high explosives and shot at the beach with .50-caliber machine guns and grenade launchers, which they fired from four special warfare speedboats. SEALs continued to simulate attacks throughout the ground war. From February 20 to February 22, helicopter raids were conducted against Faylaka Island to lend credence to the possibility of an amphibious assault, and on February 24, the first day of the ground war, a raid was feigned at Ash-Shuʿaybah. Later feints were made at Al-Fāw, Faylakah, and Būbiyān islands.

The ruses succeeded, as the Iraqis ultimately tied up at least three divisions and hundreds of artillery pieces in anticipation of an amphibious assault against the Kuwaiti coast.

**As-Salmān Airfield**—During the coalition's redeployment prior to the ground war, the positions farthest to the west were occupied by the French 6th Light Armored Division (the Daguet Division) and the 2nd Brigade of the U.S. 82nd Airborne Division, which was under French operational control (*see* **Operation Hail Mary**). On February 23, the day before the main ground attack began, advanced units crossed the border into Iraq and seized control of a position overlooking a major highway. On the following day, the main force pushed north. Its objective was to capture the As-Salmān airfield, about 90 miles deep into Iraq and 120 miles east of Kuwait. The allied force passed unopposed across the border but later encountered the 45th Iraqi Mechanized Infantry Division. After a brief battle in which French helicopters attacked dug-in Iraqi tanks and bunkers, the French forces prevailed, taking some 2,500 prisoners. They then proceeded without opposition to Objective Rochambeau, a position about 45 miles inside Iraq, and assumed defensive positions for the night. Their success and that of the U.S. 101st Airborne Division at Forward Operating Base (FOB) Cobra enabled the 24th Mechanized Infantry Divi-

sion to move up its attack by five hours (*see* **Forward Operating Base Cobra**).

On February 25, the Daguet Division and the 2nd Brigade of the 82nd Airborne Division reached the southern outskirts of As-Salmān, while the rest of the 82nd Airborne Division entered FOB Cobra. On the following day, February 26, the Daguet Division completed its capture of the airfield and then advanced north to the Euphrates River Valley to join up with the 101st Airborne Division on Highway 8 near As-Samāwah. On February 27, their combat operations concluded when they fought at Ash-Shabakah and at an observation post to the west. At the end of the fighting elements of the Daguet Division were less than 90 miles east of Baghdad, with fewer than two Iraqi brigades intervening between them and the Iraqi capital. The 3rd Helicopter Regiment penetrated farther north than any other coalition force when it advanced 25 miles south of As-Samāwah.

Capturing the As-Salmān airfield was important because it eliminated Iraqi air support in the tank battles against the Republican Guard that took place to the east. Moreover, the French forces and the U.S. 82nd and 101st Airborne divisions formed a protective barrier on the western flank, and they were subsequently able to cut off the strategic Highway 8 to prevent supplies and reinforcements from reaching the beleaguered Republican Guard. Two French soldiers and seven American engineers were killed while clearing the As-Salmān area of mines, booby traps, and cluster bombs (*see* **Battle Against the Republican Guard, U.S. Army 18th Airborne Corps**). For additional reading, see James Cooke, *100 Miles from Baghdad*.

**Baʿath (Baʿth) Party**—In addition to being Iraq's head of state and commander-in-chief of its military, Hussein is the leader of the Baʿath political party which has ruled the country since 1968 (*see* **Saddam Hussein**). Michel ʿAflaq founded the Baʿath Socialist Party in Syria in 1943 to promote the principle of Pan-Arabism. Pan-Arabism maintains that all Arabs are essentially countrymen. It rejects the British and French division of the

Arab lands after World War I and calls for the unification of those arbitrarily created Arab states into a single, Arab nation. Despite its ties to Islam, the Ba'athist philosophy is essentially secular. 'Aflaq emphasized the importance of nurturing ties to the historical past and envisioned recreating the Arab nation that, prior to the Ottoman conquests in the 16th century, had expanded from North Africa along the Mediterranean Coast through Egypt, Israel, Lebanon, Syria, and Turkey, and west through Arabia to eastern Iran.

Fuad al-Rikabi founded the Iraqi branch of the Ba'ath Party in 1952. Hussein joined the party in 1957. In 1958, General Abdul Karim Kassem's Communist-backed Free Officers Movement overthrew the ruling monarchy and established the Republic of Iraq. The Ba'ath Party initially supported Kassem and cooperated with the new regime in hopes that it would join the United Arab Republic (UAR) with Egypt and Syria. But neither the Communists nor Kassem wanted to join a Pan-Arabic state at the cost of subordinating Iraqi interests, and their own, to those of Egypt, which was the dominant partner in the UAR.* As the Communists gained influence within the government, the Ba'athists felt they were being squeezed out of power, and they came to oppose Kassem's regime. Consequently, in July 1959, after Kassem sat idly while Communist street fighters massacred Ba'athists in the northern town of Kirkūk, Rikabi decided to go ahead with a plan to assassinate Kassem. Hussein was one of the would-be assassins, but the plot failed and he fled first to Damascus and then to Egypt, where he became a full member of the Ba'ath inner party. Several of the other members of the hit squad were captured, and a public trial condemned 78 Ba'athists. But their open defiance of the court, despite having been tortured, won admiration for the Ba'ath Party among the masses, and Kassem delayed implementing some of the death sentences in fear that a pan–Arab uprising might ensue.

Meanwhile, the Iraqi Ba'athists split among themselves over the propriety of the assassination attempt, and Rikabi lost the party leadership. 'Ali Saleh Saadi, a prominent critic of the attempted assassination, emerged as the new general secretary after the Ba'ath Party reorganized in 1962. Hussein's antagonism for the left-leaning Saadi dates from the failed assassination.

In Syria the Ba'athists drew support from conservative Muslims, but in Iraq they appealed most strongly to the impoverished and alienated lower class. The Ba'athists competed for the allegiance of Iraqi workers with the Iraqi Communist Party, the largest Communist party in the Middle East. Both parties called for secular internationalism, but whereas Communist theory appealed to the common interests of all workers, regardless of nationality, race, religion, or ethnicity, the Ba'athists emphasized the shared background, religion, history, and concerns of all Arabs. The similarities in their philosophical outlook led to some cooperation between the Communists and Ba'athists. For instance, in the formative days of the Iraqi Ba'ath Party, the Communist Party gave the Ba'athists their first printing press. In 1972, their cooperation culminated with a 15-year friendship agreement between Ba'athist-ruled Iraq and the Soviet Union, which was the bastion of world Communism.

However, despite their affinities and moments of goodwill, the Ba'athists and Arab Communists were natural rivals who were each trying to assert themselves as the dominant power in the Middle East. Because of this inherent antagonism, as part of its Cold War strategy the United States turned to the Ba'athists to curb the spread of Communism in the Middle East during the 1960s. Hussein himself was suspected of having CIA connections while he was in exile in Egypt. When a 1963 Ba'athist military coup toppled Kassem in 1963, the CIA was widely believed to have been involved.

*On the other hand, under 'Aflaq's leadership the Syrian Ba'athist Party agreed to voluntarily dissolve as a gesture of support for the formation of the UAR, which was a first step toward Pan-Arabism. Egypt's President Nasser distrusted all political parties, including Ba'athists and Communists. The decision to dissolve caused a split among the Syrian Ba'athists that ultimately led to 'Aflaq's exile and a growing antagonism between the Iraqi and Syrian branches of the party.

The coup was engineered by Ba'athist officers in the military, led by Aḥmad Ḥassan al-Bakr and by Saadi. Bakr was Hussein's cousin and patron, and Hussein served as his personal bodyguard after returning to Iraq from Egypt following the coup. Abdel Salem 'Aref served as president of the new regime. Like Bakr, he had been one of the revolutionary military officers who overthrew the monarchy and brought Kassem to power in 1958, but Kassem later purged 'Aref and sentenced him to death. (As per his customary practice, however, Kassem did not carry out the execution. 'Aref declined to return the favor, and he ordered Kassem killed the day after the 1963 coup). Saadi became deputy premier, and Bakr served as vice-president, though Bakr later emerged as leader of the centrist faction that eventually dominated the government.

In addition to temporarily bringing the Ba'athists to power, the coup also served U.S. interests by eliminating Kassem's threat to the oil holdings of Western multinational corporations. It also suppressed Communist influence in Iraq, a Cold War objective of the United States. On the other hand, Communists opposed the coup. They organized street demonstrations and fought against Ba'athist gangs on the streets of Baghdad. But Communist resistance ended after the Ba'athists executed Kassem and displayed his disfigured corpse on television.

The Ba'athist-led *junta* ruled from February through November 1963. They consolidated power by attacking their rivals. The Ba'ath-controlled Iraqi National Guard, with which Hussein was affiliated, used information furnished by the CIA to track down and arrest hundreds of Communists, other leftists, and other political opponents. Despite assurances to the Americans that the prisoners would receive trials, the prisoners were routinely tortured and executed.

However, even while the party consolidated its power, internal power struggles within the party quickly surfaced. Saadi wanted to introduce socialist reforms and limit the power of 'Aref, Bakr, and other military officers who had participated in the coup. Hussein was elected to the general council of the Ba'ath Party's command after he publicly criticized Saadi and privately offered to assassinate him. When the internal party conflicts threatened to grow out of control, Michel 'Aflaq, the party founder, came to Baghdad from Damascus to resolve them. 'Aflaq ordered the expulsion and exile of Saadi and his leftist followers, and 'Aflaq subsequently became Hussein's chief mentor and promoter. In response to their expulsion, Saadi's supporters organized the massive public demonstrations in the streets.

But the National Guard's brutal excesses and the widespread civil disturbances convinced the Iraqi military officers that the Ba'athists could not govern effectively. Consequently, in November another military coup removed the Ba'athists from power. 'Aref remained head of state, but the Ba'athists were eliminated from all positions of power within the government. 'Aref ordered 'Aflaq arrested and then deported back to Syria, and he dissolved the National Guard, which had been used almost exclusively to subjugate and intimidate Ba'athist foes. To protect himself against subsequent coups, 'Aref formed the Republican Guard as a military unit personally loyal to the president (*see* **Republican Guard**). Bakr remained vice-president before being removed the following year.

For the next five years the Ba'athists regrouped in secret, while 'Aref and his brother led a series of civilian-military governments that promoted a version of pan–Arabism advocated by Egypt's President Gamal Abdel Nasser. During this time Hussein took command of the underground Jihaz Hunain, an intelligence/assassination unit that became his power base within the party and eventually enabled him to dominate it. He also joined a conspiracy to assassinate 'Aref, but it was foiled when a sympathetic military officer was transferred before he could give the would-be assassins access to 'Aref's conference room.

In 1964, Hussein traveled to Syria to convince 'Aflaq to dissolve the Iraqi branch of the party. 'Aflaq obliged and named Hussein head of a caretaker leadership. Hussein held the position alone for three months until 'Abdel-

Karim al-Shaikhli was appointed to share the post. Hussein also became the full-time organizer of the civilian portion of the party. In 1966, he made himself deputy secretary by threatening the leadership with weapons. To consolidate his power Hussein created an inner circle of people he could trust—mostly relatives and party members from Tikrīt, his hometown in northern Iraq.

On July 17, 1968, Bakr, Hussein, other Ba'ath leaders, and senior military officers removed 'Aref in a bloodless coup. The coup took place the day after Great Britain announced that by December 1971 it would withdraw all of its military forces currently stationed east of the Suez Canal, an act that created a vast power vacuum and greatly influenced subsequent developments in the Middle East. Among the military leaders who participated in the coup were Abd al-Razaq al-Nayyef, the deputy head of Iraqi intelligence, and Ibrahim al-Daoud, the commander of the Presidential Guard. Nayyef took an anti–Western position and announced his intention of renegotiating contracts between Iraq and the major oil companies. This prompted British agents to contact Ba'athist leaders and indicate their support for a coup that would topple Nayyef and leave the Ba'ath Party in control. Two weeks after the first coup, a second one purged the non–Ba'athists, giving the Ba'ath Party complete power within the Iraqi government. Bakr emerged as president and Hussein as deputy chairman in charge of internal security.

The successful coup led to a new round of bloody battles between the Ba'athists and the Communists, but as Iraq's relations with the Soviet Union improved a truce was arranged and the Communist Party was invited to join Bakr's ruling National Front in 1972. Although the Communists never received significant power within the government, Iraq and the Soviet Union signed their friendship treaty that year and the Soviets became a major supplier of weapons for Ba'athist-led Iraq. The alignment with the Soviet Union coincided with the strengthening of Iran's military alliance with the United States that same year, and

Iraq's relationship with the United States remained cold and often hostile.

In 1979, the shah of Iran was deposed and an anti–American regime of Islamic fundamentalists seized power. The emergence of Iran as the most virulent enemy of the United States within the region eventually led the United States to look to Iraq as a buffer against expansion of Iran's Shī'ite-led Islamic revolution. By the end of the Iran-Iraq Gulf War the United States was actively supporting Hussein against the Iranian fundamentalists.

The Ba'athist regime sent troops to fight against Israel in the 1973 Yom Kippur War. After the Arab defeat, members of the Organization of Petroleum Exporting Countries (OPEC) almost quadrupled the price of oil within one year and temporarily stopped shipping oil to the United States in order to punish the country for supporting Israel and pressure it to change its pro–Israeli Middle Eastern policies. Iraq took even stronger steps by nationalizing the holdings of U.S.-owned corporations, Exxon and Mobil. Its income due to higher prices amounted to over $80 billion between 1973 and 1980, doubling the nation's gross national product (GNP) and greatly enriching the Ba'ath Party and its members. This new wealth enabled the Ba'athists to retain their grip on power more firmly and to purchase advanced weapons systems from the Soviet Union, France, and other countries. Hussein subsequently used his upgraded military against both external and domestic foes. For example, among the additions to his arsenal were the French Mirage jets and Exocet missiles the Iraqi Air Force later employed against the coalition in the Persian Gulf War.

Hussein used his control of the police and other internal security apparati to consolidate his position. In 1973 he charged the head of the secret police with plotting against the government and had him and 36 of his followers executed. This left the Ba'ath Party in complete control of the internal security forces within Iraq. By the mid 1970s, Hussein was commonly recognized to be the most powerful figure within the government. However, he was not officially made chairman of the Revolutionary Command Council and president of Iraq until 1979, when Bakr was forced aside on the dubious grounds of ill health.

After Hussein officially came to power, the Iraqi Ba'ath Party became primarily an instrument for Hussein's personal power and aggrandizement. Under his rule the Ba'athist rhetoric changed from Pan-Arabism to a vision of a dominant new Babylon that would embrace and nurture the Arab world under the leadership of Iraq and himself. In a 1979 interview Hussein stated, "The Arab nation is the source of all prophets and the cradle of civilization. And there is no doubt that the oldest civilization in the world is that of Mesopotamia. It is not an Iraqi civilization in isolation from the Arab nation. It is a civilization which developed thanks to the strength and ability of the Iraqi people, coupled with the efforts and heritage of the nation."

Moreover, in spite of Ba'athist secularism and Hussein's suppression of Islamic fundamentalism (he expelled the Ayatollah Khomeini from Iraq in 1978, a year before Khomeini came to power in Iran), Hussein also drew on Islam as a source of popular support. To gain legitimacy as an Islamic leader he made a highly publicized pilgrimage to Mecca and had his family tree forged to show that he was a descendant of Muhammad, the founder of Islam.

By establishing links to Islamic heritage and ancient Babylonian glory, Hussein created a Stalin-like personality cult around himself. He presented himself as the new Nebuchadnezzar, the Biblical conqueror of Israel, as well as a descendant of the Prophet of Islam, and he drew personal power from the allegiance the Iraqi people gave him. Like Stalin, Hussein also used secret police and terror to acquire and retain power, and he was quick to purge real and imagined rivals within government and the party. The Republican Guard, the best-trained and best-equipped military unit in the Iraqi Army, was loyal to him personally.

In the 1980s Hussein further consolidated his power during the war with Iran. Even his crushing defeat in the Persian Gulf War did little to loosen his grip on the Ba'ath Party or the Iraqi government. Indeed, in the long run it offered him another excuse to purge his internal rivals and further consolidate his control.

**Bahrain**—A member of the Persian Gulf Cooperation Council, Bahrain provided port facilities and airfields for coalition ships and air forces. Before the war the United States deployed fuel, ammunition, and supplies in Bahrain, which is an island in the Gulf of Bahrain between Qatar and Saudi Arabia. Its air and naval forces participated in Operation Desert Storm, and the Bahraini Infantry Company was part of the Arab Joint Forces Command–East that fought along the Kuwaiti coast and helped liberate Kuwait City. Two Bahraini soldiers were wounded in action (*see* **Gulf Cooperation Council, Joint Forces Command**).

**Battle Against the Republican Guard**—The ground war phase of Operation Desert storm had two components. The first, conducted by the U.S. 1st Marine Expeditionary Force and the Arab Joint Forces Command, involved a straightforward assault across the Saudi border into Kuwait. Its primary objective was to convince the Iraqis that the allies' main attack was coming up through southern Kuwait, thereby diverting Iraqi reserve units away from the allied thrust to the west. Secondarily, if all went well, the Marine and Arab forces would also liberate Kuwait City (*see* **Battle for Kuwait**). The allies' main attack was the Battle against the Republican Guard, and it took place in the desert in Iraq and western Kuwait. Its mission was to destroy Iraq's elite Republican Guard armored divisions and to decimate Iraq's war-making capability (*see* **Republican Guard**). Conducted by the U.S. Army's 7th Corps and the U.S. 18th Airborne Corps (which together comprised the U.S. 3rd Army), the French 6th Light Armored Division (the "Daguet Division"), and the British 1st Armoured Division, the Battle Against the Republican Guard incorporated the AirLand battle doctrine developed in the 1980s to combat a potential Soviet invasion of Europe. That doctrine called

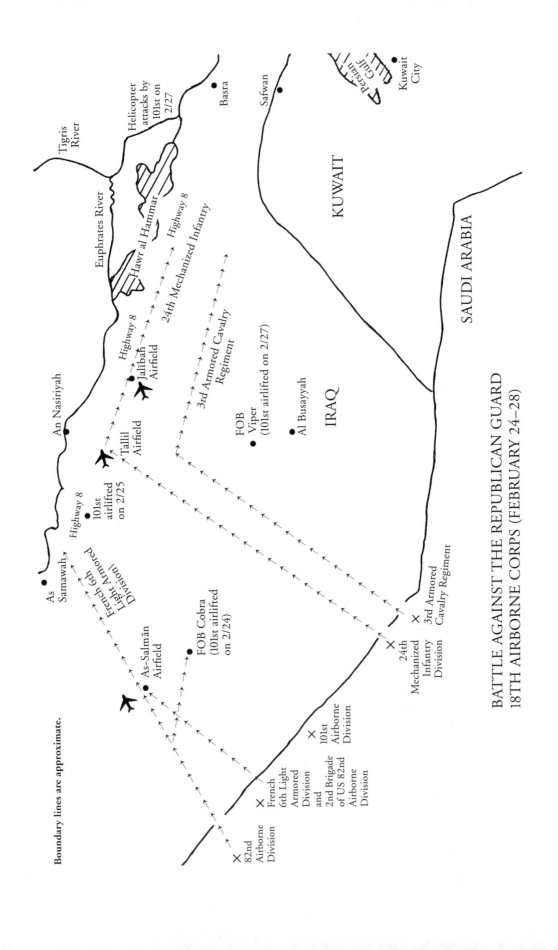

BATTLE AGAINST THE REPUBLICAN GUARD
18TH AIRBORNE CORPS (FEBRUARY 24–28)

for surprise, rapid thrusts deep within enemy territory, and coordination among the different military services. Ultimately, the campaign involved deception, rapid deployment of airborne units to points deep inside Iraq, and massive tank battles (*see* **AirLand Battle Doctrine**).

The battle against the Republican Guard took place in poor weather often characterized by driving rain, heavy winds, and sandstorms. Though the weather reduced air support, it gave an advantage to the coalition forces, because, unlike their Iraqi counterparts, U.S. and British tanks were equipped with thermal gun sights that allowed them to identify distant enemy tanks even when visibility was poor. Moreover, Firefinder radar systems could locate enemy artillery units as soon as they fired. The British and American tank cannons were also effective at longer range, and the U.S. M-1A1 and British Challenger tanks were more heavily armored than Iraq's Soviet-made T-72s (*see* **Weapons Systems and Advanced Technology**). Moreover, allied air supremacy over the Kuwaiti theater of operations severely restricted Iraqi reconnaissance capabilities and enabled the coalition forces to advance undetected over vast amounts of territory and strike with surprise. Coalition helicopters were also able to attack and destroy Iraqi tanks without fear of interference from Iraqi air forces (*see* **Air Campaign**).

During the air campaign between January 17 and February 20, 1991, the allied airborne and armored divisions secretly shifted hundreds of miles to the west before the ground war began (*see* **Operation Hail Mary**). On February 24, the forces that had deployed to the west pushed northward from Saudi Arabia into Iraq. After some initial delay, 7th Corps proceeded 70 to 100 miles into Iraq, approximately halfway to the Euphrates River Valley, before making a right turn on February 26 and attacking the Republican Guard's flank just west of the northwestern border between Kuwait and Iraq. Meanwhile, the British 1st Armoured Division crossed into Iraq on February 25 and pushed eastward into Kuwait. Starting about 75 miles west of the

7th Corps' center on February 24, the 24th Mechanized Infantry Division raced north to the Euphrates Valley and late on February 25 turned east to approach the Republican Guard positions from the northwest. Meanwhile, on February 24, in the desert about west of this action, the 1st Brigade of the 101st Airborne Division established a forward operating base (FOB) about 90 miles inside Iraq for landing supplies. The next day, the division's 3rd Brigade airlifted some 150 miles north to capture Highway 8, a key Iraqi supply route (*see* **Forward Operating Base Cobra**). And west of them, the French 6th Light Armored Division, accompanied by a brigade from the U.S. 82nd Airborne Division, captured the Iraqi airfield at As-Salmān to protect the allies' western flank (*see* **As-Salmān Airfield**). Thus, within three days, 7th Corps, the British 1st Armoured Division, and the 24th Mechanized Infantry Division had trapped the Republican Guard within a pocket between northern Kuwait and the Iraqi city of Basra, and the 101st Airborne Division had cut it off from reinforcements and supplies. The allied troops inflicted enormous casualties on the Republican Guard and were on the verge of entirely destroying it when President Bush called an end to the offensive action on the morning of February 28 (midnight, February 27, EST).

The first actions in the desert battle came in the weeks before the main assault. In the month preceding the ground war, the U.S. Army 1st Cavalry Division, which served as a reserve force during the initial assault and remained under the operational command of the U.S. Central Command (CENTCOM) for most of the battle, initiated a series of feints designed to convince the Iraqis that the main assault would come up through the Wadi al-Bāṭin at the Saudi-Kuwaiti border. (A *wadi* is a river or stream bed that is usually dry, except during the rainy season. It makes a natural invasion route in desert terrain. *See* **Wadi al-Bāṭin, Ruqi Pocket**.)

Moreover, General Norman Schwarzkopf, the coalition commander-in-chief in the Kuwaiti theater of operations, issued public statements reminding the world, including the

Iraqis, of a planned amphibious assault on the Kuwaiti shore. Though Schwarzkopf had decided in early February not to go ahead with the landing, code-named Desert Saber, because it would incur too many casualties, do too much damage to Kuwaiti property, and delay the commencement of the ground war, he ordered several practice assaults in order to convince the Iraqis that an amphibious attack was coming, and for the shipboard Marines to be on call in case the land-based Marine assault ran into trouble and an amphibious assault proved necessary to render assistance (*see* **Amphibious Landing**). The allies employed a number of other deceptions to convince the Iraqis to deploy their troops, tanks, and artillery in places where the coalition did not plan to attack (*see* **Deceptions, Feints, and Ruses**).

As the ground war approached, the Air Force turned more of its attention to bombing Iraqi troops, tanks, and fortifications on the battlefield. Schwarzkopf's intention was to reduce Iraqi ground strength by 50 percent before launching his ground assault. Two days before the main attack, army engineers began cutting holes in the Iraqi berms, tall dirt embankments, to allow the coalition troops to penetrate (*see* **Berms**), and on the night before the ground offensive, Special Forces landed reconnaissance units inside Iraq to report on Iraqi positions and movements (*see* **Special Operations Forces**). In the desert to the west, the French Daguet Division and troops from the U.S. 82nd Airborne Division conducted reconnaissance missions deep inside Iraq and seized control of a position overlooking a major highway.

The Marines initiated the ground war by attacking Iraqi positions in Kuwait early on the morning of February 24. At the same time, in the west, the French Daguet Division and the 2nd Brigade of the 82nd Airborne Division began moving toward their first objective, the As-Salmān airfield about 90 miles inside Iraq. They passed unopposed across the border but later encountered the 45th Iraqi Mechanized Infantry Division. After a brief battle in which French helicopters attacked dug-in Iraqi tanks and bunkers, the French forces prevailed, taking

some 2,500 prisoners. They then proceeded without opposition to Objective Rochambeau, a position about 45 miles inside Iraq, and assumed defensive positions for the night. Thus, seven hours into the offensive, the French Daguet Division and the 2nd Brigade of the 82nd Airborne Division had achieved their first-day objectives and secured the coalition's west flank. Subsequently, the remaining two brigades of the 82nd Airborne Division cleared and secured a two-lane highway in southern Iraq designated as Main Supply Route (MSR) Texas, which was used to move troops, supplies, and equipment north in support of the corps' advance.

Later in the morning, the U.S. 101st Airborne Division's 1st Brigade began airlifting troops and supplies to establish FOB Cobra about 93 miles inside Iraq and halfway to the Euphrates River. Thus, the allies prepared to secure their western flank before beginning the main assault by the heavily armored 7th Corps. The initial plan called for the 7th Corps to launch its main attack on the following day, but the Marines' rapid success on the eastern front prompted Schwarzkopf to move up the main western assault to that afternoon.

At noon, five hours ahead of schedule, the 3rd Armored Cavalry Regiment led the assault of the 24th Mechanized Infantry Division, which was positioned between the 101st Airborne Division and 7th Corps. Using a "regimental wedge," the regiment pierced the Iraqi berms and, encountering only light enemy resistance, raced northward. Using long-range electronic navigation, image enhancements scopes and goggles, infrared and thermal imagining systems, and Global Positioning Satellite receivers, the 24th Mechanized Infantry Division was able to continue moving at full speed throughout the night. By midnight first day the 3rd Armored Cavalry Regiment had penetrated some 75 miles into Iraq, spearheading the 24th Mechanized Infantry Division's unprecedented fast drive into the Euphrates River Valley, in which the mechanized unit covered almost 220 miles in four days. Along the way it overran two airfields, collected numerous prisoners, and blocked the path of Iraqi forces retreating back toward Baghdad.

The most potent American force was by far 7th Corps. Backed by the British 1st Armoured Division, which was under its operational control, 7th Corps was a highly mechanized unit that had come to the Middle East from Germany, where its mission had been to fight off Soviet tanks in the event of a Warsaw Pact invasion of Western Europe.

At 3 P.M. on February 24, 15 hours ahead of schedule, 7th Corp launched its attack, as the U.S. Army 1st Mechanized Infantry Division successfully breached the Iraqi minefields and berms in two hours and captured an Iraqi security zone on the Corps' eastern flank, thereby depriving the enemy of the ability to direct artillery fire or gather intelligence about the allied forces (*see* **Iraqi Fortifications**). The 1st Infantry Division left a battalion in the breach to guard against a counterattack while the British 1st Armoured Division prepared to follow through the lanes that the 1st Infantry had opened. The British 1st Armoured Division thus protected the Corps' eastern flank from an Iraqi armored counterattack.

As the 1st Infantry Division breached minefields at the Corps' center, the U.S. 2nd Army Cavalry Regiment swung wide to the west and bypassed the Iraqi lines. The U.S. 1st and 3rd armored divisions followed on either side behind it, likewise sidestepping the Iraqi defenses.

By nightfall, the 1st Infantry Division had successfully breached about half of the Iraqi obstacle belt and forward defenses and captured hundreds of prisoners. (Many prisoners taken in the campaign indicated that their decision to give up was influenced by leaflets and radio and loudspeaker broadcasts assuring them of safe and humane treatment if they surrendered (*see* **Psychological Operations**). In the evening the 1st Infantry consolidated, repositioned its artillery, and coordinated for the 1st British Armoured Division's passage through its lines the next day. Rather than attempt breaching the remaining defenses at night, when friendly fire casualties would be more likely, Corps commander Lieutenant General Frederick Franks, Jr., halted the Corps' progress for the night. The 1st and 3rd armored divisions

and the 2nd Army Cavalry Regiment had not been hampered by obstacles or serious opposition and had already proceeded almost 50 miles into Iraq. Not wanting them to outpace the Corps' center and eastern flank, Franks ordered them to halt for the night as well.

Schwarzkopf was anxious to cut off and destroy the retreating Republican Guard, and when he saw the next morning that the 7th Corps had stopped, he became extremely upset. He repeatedly urged Franks to quicken the pace of the attack and engage the enemy before it could escape. Franks was proceeding more slowly because he wanted to concentrate his force for a knockout blow.

On the morning of the second day, February 25, the U.S. 1st Armored Division engaged the Iraqi 26th Infantry Division on the Corps' western flank shortly after daybreak, destroying 40 to 50 tanks and armored personnel carriers in ten minutes. It then continued on toward Al Buşayyah, about 70 miles into Iraq, and in the early afternoon attacked a dug-in Iraqi brigade, destroying artillery pieces and several vehicles and taking almost 300 prisoners. Just to the east, the 2nd Cavalry Regiment and 3rd Armored Division continued north before turning eastward around nightfall. They encountered isolated pockets of resistance as high winds and heavy rains began. That evening the 2nd Cavalry Regiment encountered elements of the Republican Guard's Tawakalna Division and the 50th Brigade of the Iraqi 12th Armored Division. It destroyed the 50th Brigade and then assumed defensive positions while awaiting to resume the attack at dawn the next day.

Meanwhile, the British 1st Armoured Division passed through the breach lanes opened by the 1st Infantry Division around noon on February 25. While the 1st Infantry Division enlarged the breach by attacking and overwhelming the enemy defenses directly ahead of them, the British 1st Armoured Division turned east to attack the Iraqi 52nd Armored Division, which it destroyed. The British troops then engaged in nearly continuous combat for the next two days as they continued moving east into Kuwait.

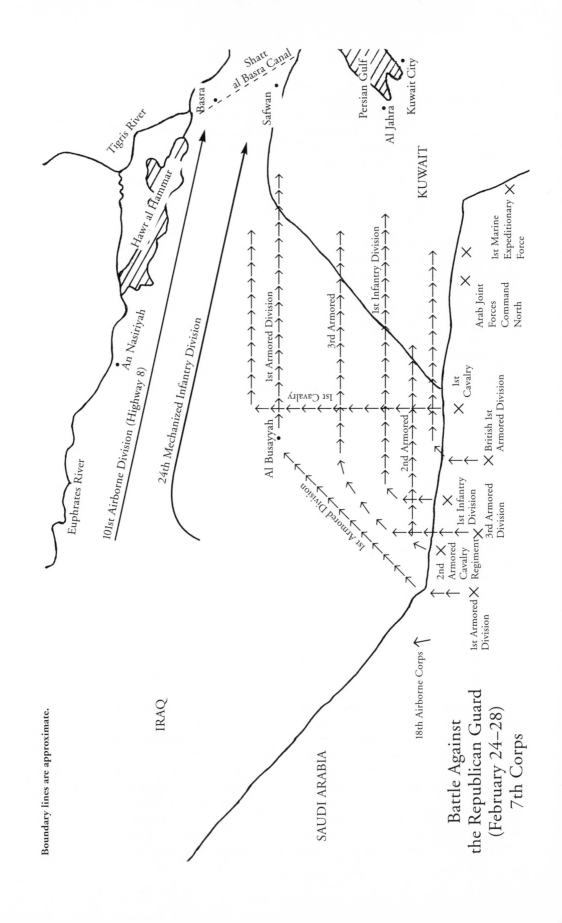

Boundary lines are approximate.

Euphrates River

Tigris River

Hawr al Hammar

An Nasiriyah

101st Airborne Division (Highway 8)

24th Mechanized Infantry Division

Basra

Shatt al Basra Canal

Safwan

Persian Gulf

Al Jahra

Kuwait City

KUWAIT

1st Armored Division

3rd Armored

1st Infantry Division

1st Cavalry

2nd Armored

Arab Joint Forces Command North

1st Marine Expeditionary Force

British 1st Armored Division

1st Cavalry

Al Busayyah

1st Armored Division

1st Infantry Division

3rd Armored Division

2nd Armored Cavalry Regiment

1st Armored Division

18th Airborne Corps

IRAQ

SAUDI ARABIA

Battle Against
the Republican Guard
(February 24–28)
7th Corps

Farther to the west on the second day of battle, the 24th Mechanized Infantry Division concluded its unprecedented drive northward into the Euphrates River Valley near An-Nāṣirīyah, an Iraqi town about 100 miles northwest of Basra. On February 24 and 25, the division covered almost 150 miles in 24 hours, faster than any mechanized ground force had ever traveled during warfare. During the first four days of battle, it averaged about 55 miles a day. After establishing a forward operating base, placing brigades in blocking positions in the Euphrates Valley, and taking thousands of prisoners, the 24th Mechanized Infantry Division turned eastward toward Basra to cut off Republican Guard forces that were retreating from 7th Corps. Meanwhile, the 101st Airborne Division's 3rd Brigade airlifted some 150 miles from its base in Saudi Arabia to a point in the Euphrates Valley between An-Nāṣirīyah and As-Samāwah, a town farther west. After completing the deepest air assault in military history, the paratroopers from the 101st Airborne Division marched some 20 miles on foot through heavy rain and thick mud to capture a portion of Highway 8, a key Iraqi supply route. They then established defensive positions and awaited an Iraqi counterattack that never materialized.

Even farther west, the French Daguet Division and the 2nd Brigade of the 82nd Airborne Division reached the southern outskirts of As-Salmān, while the rest of the 82nd Airborne Division entered FOB Cobra. On the following day, February 26, the 82nd Airborne Division and Daguet Division completed their capture of the airfield and then advanced north to the Euphrates River Valley to join up with the 101st Airborne Division on Highway 8. By the day's end they had achieved all of their objectives, having blocked reinforcements to the Iraqi forces in the Kuwaiti theater of operations and protected the coalition's western flank. They were within 100 miles of Baghdad when the fighting ended.

With the airborne forces protecting its western and northern flanks, on the afternoon of February 26 the 24th Mechanized Infantry Division moved into the Euphrates Valley. As it approached the Iraqi airfields at Jalībah and Tallil in the midst of an intense dust storm, the division encountered its heaviest resistance of the war. The Iraqi 47th and 49th infantry divisions and the Republican Guard Nebuchadnezzar Infantry Division and 26th Commando Brigade defended their positions with artillery and automatic weapons dug into rocky escarpments. But after four hours of intense fighting, the 24th Mechanized Infantry Division prevailed, using its Firefinder radars to locate and destroy enemy artillery and tanks in the dust storm and employing attack helicopters and armored personnel carriers to spot and attack Iraqi tanks at distances of over 3500 meters—well before the Iraqis could locate them. By nightfall, the division had destroyed six Iraqi artillery batteries and captured hundreds of prisoners. It was in position to attack the airfields on the following day, but needed to refuel. The division had moved so quickly that fuel tankers had difficulty keeping up, and lead elements were not certain where to rendezvous with them in the desert. But several junior officers used their initiative to solve the problem, and the division was refueled by midnight.

Also on February 26, 7th Corps and the British 1st Armoured Division began their "left hook" against the Republican Guard's armored divisions and fought what became the largest tank battle since World War II. As the 7th Corps rotated clockwise to attack eastward into the Republican Guard's western flank, its forces were positioned with the 1st Armored Division assuming the northernmost line of attack. The 3rd Armored Division was in the center, the 2nd Armored Cavalry Regiment below that, and the 1st Infantry Division to the south. Below them, the British 1st Armoured Division formed the southernmost line of attack.

Just after daybreak the 3rd Armored Division captured map designation Collins, east of Al-Buṣayyah. It then continued its eastward advance directly into Republican Guard strongholds. Then, in the early afternoon, the 2nd Armored Cavalry Regiment moved east through a sandstorm to the southern sector of Objective Collins. It was screening in front of the 1st Infantry Division, which had just arrived after clearing the mine belt by the Saudi border. The Iraqis, who had expected the attack to come from the south and east, were desperately repositioning hundreds of tanks, armored personnel carriers, and artillery pieces to meet the assault from the west.

At around 2 P.M., the 2nd Cavalry Regiment received fire from a building on the 69 Easting, a north-south line designation on the map. It answered the fire and continued east, receiving more enemy fire over the next two hours. At 4 P.M. the regiment encountered dug-in Iraqi tanks and soldiers along a ridge near the map designation 73 Easting. The six-hour Battle of 73 Easting produced some of the fiercest fighting of the war, as the desperate Republican Guard sent waves of tanks and motorized infantry against the 2nd Armored Cavalry's 2nd Squadron, which had closed an escape route between the 7th Corps to the east and the 24th Mechanized Infantry Division to the west. The unsuccessful Iraqi tank attack was one of the few Iraqi offensive operations of the war, but it was stopped cold by the American tanks' more effective firepower, which could hit the Iraqi tanks while still out of range from Iraqi fire. The Americans' thermal gunsights also proved valuable in the sandstorm that raged during the battle. The 2nd Armored Cavalry Regiment destroyed at least 29 Iraqi tanks and 24 armored personnel carriers and took 1,300 prisoners in the Battle of 73 Easting.

That evening, the 1st Infantry Division passed through the regiment and continued the attack eastward. At the same time, to the north the 3rd Armored Division attacked through heavy wind, rain, and sandstorms into the Republican Guard's Tawakalna Division, which was entrenched in westward-facing defensive positions. The poor weather reduced visibility to 100 meters and eliminated air support. Nonetheless, the 1st and 2nd brigades of the 3rd Armored Division launched a combined tank and artillery attack that destroyed many Iraqi tanks and armored vehicles in intense fighting that effectively destroyed the Tawakalna Division as a coherent fighting unit. Later, as the weather cleared, an Apache helicopter attack battalion, guided by intelligence from a JSTARS airplane, spotted an Iraqi mechanized infantry task force apparently attempting to reinforce other elements of the Tawakalna Division. The Apaches destroyed 8 tanks and 19 armored vehicles.

At Wadi Al-Bāṭin to the south, the British 1st Armoured Division cut behind two dug-in Iraqi infantry divisions that had been opposing the U.S. 1st Calvary Division. The British forces overran the infantry's rear positions and attacked Iraqi mechanized troops, who began to surrender in mass. The British 1st Armoured Division destroyed 40 tanks and captured an Iraqi division commander.

Those actions left the remaining Republican Guard armored units trapped in a pocket between Basra and northern Kuwait, and Schwarzkopf released the 1st Cavalry Division, which he had been holding in reserve, to assist in the final attack against the Republican Guard. The 1st Cavalry immediately proceeded north to a position behind the 1st and 3rd armored divisions at the northern border of Kuwait.

On the next morning, February 27, the 24th Mechanized Infantry Division completed its mission of securing the Euphrates Valley by capturing the Tallil airfield about 20 miles south of An-Nāṣirīyah and the Jalībah airfield east of it, near the western edge of the large shallow lake Hawr Al-Ḥammār. Some controversy exists over whether taking the Tallil air base unnecessarily slowed the division's progress. Colonel Frank Akers, the operations officer for the 18th Airborne Corps, has maintained that the attack diverted attention from the main assault against the Republican Guard and enabled some Republican Guard units to escape. On the other hand, General Barry McCaffrey, the division commander, claimed that the enemy air base threatened his plan to erect a fuel depot nearby. McCaffrey maintained that any delays were caused by the need to wait for food and fuel, not by taking the airfield. McCaffrey received authorization for the attack from his commander, Lieutenant General Gary Luck, who commanded the 18th Airborne Corps (see Gary **Luck**).

Meanwhile, south of the 24th Mechanized Infantry Division, the 2nd Brigade of the 101st Airborne Division and the 12th Combat Aviation Brigade left FOB Cobra to attack 95 miles east and establish a new forward operations base, FOB Viper, southwest of Jalībah. Throughout the afternoon four battalions of Apache helicopters based at FOB Viper attacked the causeway leading over the Hawr Al-Ḥammar lake and the marshlands north of Basra. They destroyed all traffic on the Basra causeway and blocked further movement. This effectively cut off most of the Republican Guard's northern escape route, trapping it between the 24th Mechanized Infantry Division moving east on Highway 8, the 7th Corps coming up from the southwest, and the Euphrates River to the north. However, a 30-mile seam between the 24th Mechanized Division and the 7th Corps ultimately allowed most of the Republican Guard infantry divisions, the Adnan, Nebuchadnezzar, and Al Faw, to escape across the Euphrates or into Basra. Attempts to destroy the bridges and causeways leading into Basra or across the river were only partially successful, as bad weather hampered the ability of coalition planes and helicopters to attack them.

The 24th Mechanized Infantry Division and the 3rd Armored Cavalry accompanying it linked up with the 1st Cavalry Division on February 27, and that afternoon and evening they destroyed hundreds of Iraqi vehicles that were trying either to redeploy to meet the American attack or escape across the river. By the evening, the coalition forces were moving eastward from positions extending south to north from about 50 miles above of the Saudi border, where the British 1st Armoured Division was conducting its offensive, to the northwest corner of Kuwait, where the 7th Corps was concentrated, to the Euphrates Valley, where the 24th Mechanized Infantry Division was pushing towards Basra. The 101st Airborne Division had plans to airlift a brigade along Highway 6 on the following morning to cut

off Basra from the north, but this was forestalled by the cease-fire.

The 7th Corps also began a coordinated assault against the Republican Guard's mechanized Tawakalna, Medina, and Hammurabi divisions. The 1st Infantry Division, which had passed through the 2nd Armored Cavalry Regiment the night before, attacked from the south, while the 1st and 3rd armored divisions came from the west, and the 1st Cavalry Division struck on the northern flank to cut off that escape route. Later that night it joined up with the 24th Mechanized Infantry Division. These forces continued to close in on the Republican Guard divisions trapped in northern Kuwait and southern Iraq, and Apache helicopter attacks that night in the rear of the Iraqi 10th Armored Division broke the continuity of their defense and forced them to abandon their positions and much of their equipment. Meanwhile, a frontal attack by the 3rd Armored Division completed the rout of Iraq's 10th Armored Division when it forced the Iraqi forward lines to retreat into their own disorganized rear elements.

The Republican Guard made its last significant defensive stand when its Medina Division pivoted to the west and dug in behind a desert ridge in northwest Kuwait. Forming a battle line six to seven miles long, the Iraqis hoped to ambush the approaching U.S. 1st Armored Division. However, the thermal gun sights on the American tanks were able to detect the enemy tanks two miles away. As in the Battle of 73 Easting, the Americans began firing while still out of range of the Iraqi T-72 tanks. Artillery units and Apache helicopters soon joined the battle, and within about 40 minutes the 1st Armored Division destroyed approximately 300 Iraqi tanks and armored vehicles while suffering only one combat death. According to Major General Wafic al-Sammarai, Hussein's chief of military intelligence who was with him, Hussein fell into a state of despair after learning of the destruction.

Following the Battle of Medina Ridge, the allies were positioned to eliminate most of the remaining Republican Guard. To the south, the British 1st Armoured Division destroyed

**U.S. Army 18th Airborne Corps: Soldiers from the 101st Airborne Division in training exercises during Operation Desert Storm (photograph courtesy of the Department of Defense).**

the Iraqi 52nd Armored Division and overran three infantry divisions, and the 1st Infantry Division overran the Iraqi 12th Armored Division. Although running low on fuel, the 7th Corps was in the process of completing a double encirclement of the Republican Guard that night. It subjected the remaining Iraqi units to an intense artillery barrage in preparation for a final attack. However, President Bush ordered all offensive combat operations to cease at 8 A.M. on February 28, local time, because Kuwait had been liberated and Iraq defeated. Bush, his civilian cabinet advisers, Chairman of the Joint Chiefs of Staff Colin Powell, and General Schwarzkopf all concurred that their mission had been accomplished and that further slaughter of Iraqi troops would be pointless and inhumane (*see* **George Bush**, **Objectives**, **Cease-fire**).

In a press conference describing the military situation at the time the cease-fire was announced, Schwarzkopf declared that the Iraqi armored divisions were totally trapped within the Basra Pocket: "The gates are closed. There is no way out of here." In fact, however, the roads leading to Basra were not entirely cut off: a 30-mile gap existed between the 7th Corps and the 18th Airborne Corps. Nor were all the bridges leading across a key canal outside of Basra destroyed, despite allied bombings. It was initially believed that only infantry carrying small arms were able to escape into Basra. But later the Defense Intelligence Agency estimated that as many as one-third of the Republican Guard's tanks made their way into the city, along with 70,000–80,000 soldiers. Approximately 800 tanks and 1,400 armored personnel carriers survived.

Bush's order allowed the allies to take defensive action and halt the movement of Iraqi forces back to Iraq. On March 1, an Iraqi brigade attacked the 3rd Armored Cavalry Regiment, which destroyed the Iraqi unit in an hour-long battle near the Rumalia oil field. On March 2, a tank battalion from the U.S. 24th Mechanized Infantry Division was fired upon by infantry from the Republican Guard's Hammurabi Division, which was traveling west deeper into Iraq on Highway 8. The American tanks fired back in force, and a battle ensued which lasted for several hours. After calling in artillery and helicopter support, the Americans destroyed 177 Iraqi tanks and armored personnel carriers, 11 battlefield missile systems, and 23 trucks in the fighting. Several hundred Iraqi soldiers were killed. So were a number of civilians, including a group of Iraqi school children riding in a bus that was struck during an air attack. Critics have maintained that the American response in this action was disproportionate to the initial provocation, which consisted of small-arms fire and threatening behavior by Iraqi tanks that directed their gun turrets against American tanks.

Following the cease-fire, the U.S. forces implemented several humanitarian operations, treating 30,000 Iraqi civilians in military health care facilities, supplying over 1 million meals, and reopening the health clinic and school in Safwān, an Iraqi city just north of Kuwait. In addition, 7th Corps protected 12,000 refugees in Safwān and a camp in Iraq near Rafḥā, a Saudi town in the west, where the 18th Airborne Corps had deployed before the battle began. The U.S. Army built another refugee camp north of Rafḥā capable of holding an additional 30,000 refugees. It also provided transportation for refugees who chose to leave Iraq.

**Battle for Kuwait**—The ground war consisted of two major allied thrusts. The main attack took place in the desert to the west, as U.S., British, and French armored divisions moved north from Saudi Arabia into Iraq and then turned east in a surprise attack against the western flank of the Iraqi Republican Guard that was positioned in northwest Kuwait (*see* **Battle Against the Republican Guard**). The Battle for Kuwait was fought at the Kuwaiti border to the south, by the U.S. 1st Marine Expeditionary Force (the 1st and 2nd Marine divisions and the U.S. Army's Tiger Brigade—1st Brigade of the 2nd Armored Division—which was under the Marines' operational control) and by the Arab and Islamic Joint Forces Command (JFC). The main objective of

the battle was to convince the Iraqis that the allies' main attack was coming up through southern Kuwait and thereby divert Iraqi reserve units away from the allied thrust to the west. Secondarily, if all went well, the Marine and Arab forces would also liberate Kuwait City.

Prior to the battle, the Marines redeployed about 50 to 70 miles inland from the coast along the Saudi-Kuwaiti border. The JFC-East flanked the Marines on their right and was responsible for coastal operations. The mobile, highly mechanized force was comprised primarily of Saudi troops, but also included units from the other Persian Gulf States: the United Arab Emirates, Qatar, Oman, Bahrain and Kuwait. The more armor-intensive JFC-North flanked the Marines on their left. It included troops from Egypt, Saudi Arabia, Syria and other Arab countries (*see* **Joint Forces Command**). The Marines and the JFC-North had to overcome dug-in Iraqi defensive positions that were fortified with minefields, fire trenches, and protective berms—ridges of dirt and sand approximately 2 kilometers long (1¼ miles) and 3–4 meters high (9 to 13 feet) (*see* **Iraqi Fortifications**, **Berms**).

Originally, plans also called for a Marine amphibious landing at Ash-Shu'aybah, a port on the coast about 20 miles south of Kuwait City. The landing, code-named Desert Saber, was to provide a supply base for the land-based Marines pushing north into Kuwait from the Saudi border. The amphibious assault would also provide a force to cut off an Iraqi counterattack against the land attack. However, General Schwarzkopf, the allied commander-in-chief in the Kuwaiti theater of operations, concluded in early February that an amphibious landing through heavily mined waters and against heavily defended shores would cost too many Marine lives, incur too much damage to Kuwaiti property, and delay the commencement of the ground offensive. Nonetheless, he ordered several practice assaults in order to convince the Iraqis that an amphibious attack was coming so that they would deploy troops along the coast, away from the main attack sites. Some three Iraqi divisions and hundreds of artillery pieces were di-

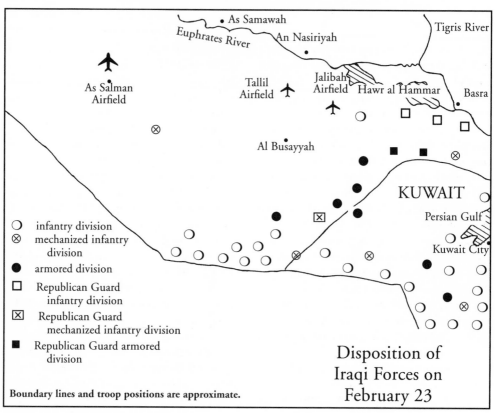

· As Samawah

Euphrates River    An Nasiriyah

Tigris River

As Salman
Airfield

Tallil
Airfield

Jalibah
Airfield    Hawr al Hammar

Basra

Al Busayyah

KUWAIT

Persian Gulf

○  infantry division
⊗  mechanized infantry
   division
●  armored division
□  Republican Guard
   infantry division
⊠  Republican Guard
   mechanized infantry division
■  Republican Guard armored
   division

Kuwait City

Boundary lines and troop positions are approximate.

## Disposition of
## Iraqi Forces on
## February 23

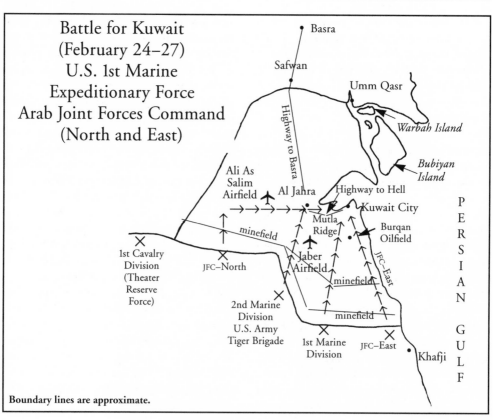

## Battle for Kuwait
## (February 24–27)
## U.S. 1st Marine
## Expeditionary Force
## Arab Joint Forces Command
## (North and East)

· Basra

Safwan

Umm Qasr

Warbah Island

Bubiyan
Island

Highway to Basra

Ali As
Salim
Airfield    Al Jahra

Highway to Hell

Kuwait City

minefield

Mutla
Ridge

Burqan
Oilfield

1st Cavalry
Division
(Theater
Reserve
Force)

✕
JFC–North

Jaber
Airfield

JFC–East

minefield

2nd Marine
Division
U.S. Army
Tiger Brigade

1st Marine
Division    JFC–East

minefield

Khafji

P
E
R
S
I
A
N

G
U
L
F

Boundary lines are approximate.

verted in this way. The practice amphibious attacks also allowed the ship-based Marines to be on call in case the land-based Marine assault ran into trouble and an amphibious landing proved necessary to render assistance (*see* **Amphibious Landing**; **Deceptions, Feints, and Ruses**).

Though the major offensive began on February 24, on February 20 engineers from the 2nd Marine Division began preparing attack routes by cutting holes through the berm. The next day, the 2nd Light Armored Infantry Battalion began screening actions to divert the Iraqis from the actual breaching sites. In the process they engaged Iraqi troops, artillery and tanks, and took 120 prisoners and destroyed 12 tanks. On February 22, U.S. and British artillery bombarded Iraqi artillery units, U.S. aircraft dropped napalm and fuel-air explosives on oil-filled trenches to burn off the oil, and that night Marine ground patrols passed through the berm and reconnoitered the Iraqi minefields. Four U.S. battalions moved into Kuwait to provide spotters and advanced fire support for the ground attack and to clear and mark lanes through the minefields. They were assisted on February 23 by a group of Iraqi defectors who helped them identify passageways through the mine fields. That night a team of Navy SEALs simulated an attack on the Kuwaiti coast to convince the Iraqis that an amphibious assault was being launched and fool them into redeploying defensive troops to the coast, away from the actual assault positions.

At 4 A.M. on February 24, the main assault began. Advancing on foot, Marines from the 1st Division followed paths that had been cleared for them by artillery fire and mine plows–attached tanks. The Marine 2nd Division began its attack 90 minutes later. (The Israeli-manufactured mine plows were also used to smash Iraqi bunkers and firing pits, sometimes burying the defenders alive and often provoking massive surrenders). The Marines wore special suits to protect them from the chemical attacks which Hussein had threatened but apparently did not use (*see* **Chemical Warfare**).

The 1st Division quickly breached the first of two minefields cluttered with barbed wire and other obstacles. But it was subjected to intense Iraqi artillery fire as it proceeded against the second minefield. The Iraqi defensive plan had been to trap the attacking forces between the minefields and subject them to devastating artillery fire. However, allied artillery units employed their Firefinder radars to quickly locate the Iraqi artillery positions and return the fire, taking out many of the Iraqi guns. AH-1 Cobra helicopter gunships and A-6 attack planes also supported the Marines (*see* **Weapons Systems and Advanced Technology**).

On the Marines' western flank, the 2nd Division took nine hours to pass through the defenses, but by mid-afternoon they penetrated them and assumed defensive positions. They also opened 20 attack lanes for forces behind them. To the east, the 1st Marine Division breached the Iraqi lines somewhat more easily. It then captured the Burqan oil field, bypassing the nearby Al-Jaber air base for the time being, with the intention of subduing it with infantry the next day. Suffering fewer than 50 casualties in the breaching operation, the Marines achieved all of their objectives for the day within the first 12 hours. Subsequently, their progress was slowed by the large number of prisoners they took. The 2nd Marine Division alone captured between 700 and 800 soldiers in the morning attack and destroyed an attacking armored unit. As the first day of battle progressed, thousands more Iraqi soldiers surrendered, and by the end of the day, the two divisions had taken some 8,000 prisoners and advanced about 20 miles into Kuwait. The Marine assault was so successful that Schwarzkopf decided to move up the main attack in the west by 15 hours, from the morning of February 25 to the afternoon of February 24.

At noon on February 24, the Tiger Brigade passed through the breaches opened by the 2nd Division and proceeded northeast toward Kuwait City. The thermal gun sights on the Tiger Brigade's M-1A1 tanks enabled its gunners to identify targets through the thick, black smoke from burning oil wells that covered the

**U.S. 1st Marine Expeditionary Force: A Marine checks his weapon during Operation Desert Storm (photograph courtesy of the Department of Defense).**

battlefield, and the M-1A1 cannon's superior range enabled them to fire at Iraqi tanks from a relatively safe distance. (The Marines used older M-1 and M-60A1 tanks that were not as modern or as well equipped).

On the eastern flank, the JFC-East began its attack at 8 A.M. and moved from Khafji, Saudi Arabia, into Kuwait. Supported by gunfire from U.S. battleships offshore, it proceeded north along the coast.

Saudi and Egyptian forces from the JFC-North crossed into southwest Kuwait at 4 P.M., breached the defenses, and then turned eastward to assault Iraqi positions from the flank before stopping for the night. It too captured thousands of prisoners. Many of the prisoners were reservists who reported how their Regular Army officers had abandoned their units prior to the ground offensive. Many also indicated that their decision to give up was influenced by leaflets and radio and loud-

speaker broadcasts assuring them of safe and humane treatment if they surrendered (*see* **Psychological Operations**).

On the second day of battle, February 25, the 1st Marine Division turned back a stiff Iraqi counterattack near the Burqan oil field south of Kuwait City. The fighting was the fiercest the Marines encountered during the ground war, and much of it took place at close distance in near darkness caused by bad weather and heavy smoke from burning oil wells the Iraqis had ignited before the ground offensive began (*see* **Environmental Warfare**). After the tank battle infantry from the 1st Division completed clearing the Al-Jaber airfield. The division then proceeded north to within ten miles of Kuwait City. Meanwhile, elements of the 2nd Marine Division and the Tiger Brigade fighting west of the oil field repulsed an armored counterattack with artillery, tanks, TOW missiles, and air support that devastated the attacking Iraqis before they could approach the Marine units. Altogether, the Marines destroyed 34 or 35 enemy tanks in what proved to be the largest tank battle in Marine Corps history.

Late that night Marine aircraft detected Iraqi convoys fleeing from Kuwait City, and throughout the night and next day U.S. Air Force, Navy, and Marine planes attacked thousands of trucks, private cars, and other vehicles proceeding along the 6th Ring Road, damaging and destroying 3,000–4,000 of them along the so-called "Highway to Hell" or "Highway of Death." (See **Highway to Hell**.)

By the afternoon of February 25, the JFC-East had also overcome its opposition and proceeded up the coastal highway toward Kuwait City, and the JFC-North seized most of its objectives and consolidated their positions, though Egyptian forces were slowed in their breaching operations and unable to secure all of their objectives by midnight.

On February 26, Hussein announced on Baghdad Radio that Iraq was withdrawing its troops from Kuwait. In response, President Bush called the announcement "an outrage. He is not withdrawing. His defeated forces are retreating. The coalition forces will continue to prosecute the war with undiminished intensity." Aircraft continued to bomb the Highway to Hell, and the Tiger Brigade destroyed 33 armored vehicles and captured the police station at the main highway south of Kuwait City in the Battle of Mutla Ridge. In so doing, the Tiger Brigade occupied the highest ground in the region and trapped the remaining Iraqi troops in the Kuwait City area. It then added its destructive firepower to that of the bombers attacking the Iraqi vehicles stranded on the Highway to Hell.

Meanwhile, the 2nd Marine Division encountered stiff resistance at Al-Jahra, a suburb of Kuwait City that it captured on February 26. The 1st Marine Division also encountered heavy resistance at Kuwait International Airport, where it engaged a large number of tanks on February 26. It finally captured the airport in the early morning of February 27, destroying more than 250 tanks and 70 armored vehicles. Elsewhere, Marine aircraft attacked Iraqi troops at Faylakah and Būbiyān islands in the Persian Gulf north of Kuwait City. Following an afternoon tank battle, 12 Marines from the 2nd Force Reconnaissance unit became the first Americans to enter Kuwait City, where they retook the U.S. Embassy at around 10 P.M. However, Iraqi resistance continued until the next day.

Egyptian forces from the JFC-North proceeded toward the 'Ali as-Salīm airfield west of Kuwait City, and the JFC-East approached Kuwait City and prepared to enter it the following day.

With the Iraqi defenses around the Kuwaiti International Airport destroyed on the morning of February 27, Schwarzkopf held up the Marine advance and let the Arab forces proceed through American lines to give them the privilege of liberating the nation's capital. The Egyptians captured the 'Alī as-Salīm airfield early in the morning and around 9 A.M. the JFC-North passed through the 2nd Marine Division into the western portion of Kuwait City. Saudi and Kuwaiti troops from the JFC-East joined up with them and entered Kuwait City in force from the east. Meanwhile, the Marines and Tiger Brigade held their positions outside the city and cleaned up remaining pockets of resistance.

The fighting ceased at 8 A.M. on February 28, after President Bush ordered the cessation of offensive actions. During Desert Storm the 1st and 2nd Marine divisions ultimately damaged or destroyed 1,060 tanks, 432 artillery pieces, 608 armored personnel carriers, and 2 Scud launchers. They also discovered an Iraqi bunker containing chemical artillery shells. Twenty-four Marines were killed and ninety-two were wounded. Two soldiers from the Tiger Brigade and seventy-one soldiers from the Joint Forces Command also died in the fighting, and 344 were wounded.

**Battle of Būbiyān**—Būbiyān is an island off northern Kuwait, near the Iraqi border. On January 29 and 30, 1991, it was the scene of a major naval engagement in which much of the Iraqi Navy was destroyed. The battle began on the night of January 29, when an A-6E Intruder attack jet on reconnaissance spotted four suspicious vessels south of the Al-Fāw Peninsula traveling with their lights out toward Iranian coastal waters. After some delay while an E-2C airborne early warning aircraft positively identified the vessels as Iraqi gunboats, the Intruder was authorized to attack. It dropped a 500-pound laser-guided bomb on the leading boat, scoring a direct hit and causing the other ships to scatter. Another bomb hit a second boat, destroying its superstructure and causing it to go dead in the water. Meanwhile, the E-2C called in an F/A-18 Hornet Strike Fighter to assist. The Intruder directed a laser signal onto a third ship, and the Hornet dropped a laser-guided bomb that followed the signal, scoring another direct hit. After that attack, however, both planes were out of ordnance. Therefore, the E-2C directed two Canadian jets against the remaining vessel. The Canadian jets were armed for a combat patrol mission and did not have any bombs, so they strafed the gunboat with 20mm guns. The first three ships were later found capsized; the fourth was located in an Iranian port with substantial strafing damage to its superstructure.

On the next day several more Iraqi ships based at the Iraqi ports of Az-Zubayr and Umm Qaṣr were detected trying to flee to Iran. Coalition aircraft engaged the vessels 21 times near Būbiyān Island, over a 13-hour period. Four Iraqi missile boats, three amphibious ships, and one minesweeper were damaged, many of them heavily. Only two of the damaged ships managed to escape to Iranian ports.

Subsequent air strikes over the next few days did more damage to Iraqi ships, and by February 2, all 13 Iraqi surface craft capable of delivering missiles against coalition ships were either destroyed or disabled. The Iraqi Navy was then considered combat ineffective, and on February 8, the coalition claimed sea control of the northern Persian Gulf.

**Berms**—As part of their defensive fortifications, Iraqi engineers built company and battalion-sized triangular strongpoints along the Saudi border with Kuwait and portions of southeastern Iraq. Positioned behind fortified mine fields and antitank ditches, these strongpoints consisted of a triangle of berms, or ridges, of dirt and sand approximately 2 kilometers long (1¼ miles) and 3–4 meters high (9 to 13 feet). Additional berms were constructed within the mine fields and along the Saudi-Kuwaiti border and the eastern part of the Saudi-Iraqi border to impede the allied advance (*see* **Iraqi Fortifications**).

Unlike some of the U.S. and French troops farther to the west, the Marines and the Joint Arab Forces attacked northward, directly into Kuwait and heavily fortified Iraqi defenses. Therefore, prior to the commencement of the ground assault Marine engineers cut openings through the berms to create paths for the attacking ground troops to follow. The 2nd Marine Division's 2nd Combat Engineer Division began cutting through the berms on February 20 and concluded on February 22, allowing the 3rd Battalion of the 2nd Marine Division to advance into Kuwait to provide security for artillery survey units. The 1st and 2nd Marine divisions passed through these holes in the berms on the first day of Operation Desert Storm. To the west, engineers

from the U.S. Army 7th Corps also cut holes through the berms, so the 1st Infantry Division and the British 1st Armoured Division could pass through (*see* **Battle Against the Republican Guard, Battle for Kuwait**).

**Biological Warfare**—One of the allies' greatest concerns was that Iraq would employ chemical and or biological weapons during the ground war. In fact, though they had such weapons stockpiled, the Iraqis apparently did not use them because they feared nuclear retaliation. They are believed to have begun large-scale production of anthrax bacteria and botulism toxin in 1989 at four facilities near Baghdad. Botulism was a particular concern, because it is three million times more potent than the nerve agent Sarin, and a single Scud warhead filled with botulism toxins could contaminate 3,700 square kilometers.

To deal with these threats, troops were issued protective clothing. However, only a limited number were also immunized because there were insufficient supplies of the vaccine. One hundred and fifty thousand troops were inoculated against anthrax, and eight thousand against botulism. At the start of the crisis, the sole supply of the antibotulism vaccine came from two Army horses, Abe and First Flight, that had developed immunity to the disease.

The United States also deployed a special force of over 6,000 soldiers to detect and decontaminate biological weapons. Iraqi research, development and production plants for chemical and biological weapons were a top priority throughout the air campaign, and all of its known production facilities were incapacitated and its refrigerated storage capacities destroyed.

**Boomer, Walter**—The commander of the 1st Marine Expeditionary Force, Lieutenant General Boomer was responsible for leading the assault against the dug-in Iraqi fortifications in Kuwait (*see* **U.S. 1st Marine Expeditionary Force, Battle for Kuwait**). He was born in 1938 and commissioned as a second lieutenant in the Marine Corps upon his graduation from

**Walter Boomer (photograph courtesy of United States Marine Corps).**

Duke University in 1960. Boomer served two tours of duty in Vietnam. He received a master of science in the technology of management from American University in 1973 and subsequently served as chairman of the Department of Management at the U.S. Naval Academy. After assuming a series of commands within the Marine Corps, Boomer was promoted to lieutenant general on August 15, 1990—less than two weeks after Iraq invaded Kuwait. He was then named commander of the 1st Marine Expeditionary Force. During the Persian Gulf War that force included the 1st and 2nd Marine divisions, the 3rd Marine Aircraft Wing, and the U.S. Army's Tiger Brigade from the 2nd Armored Division.

Boomer had favored going ahead with a planned amphibious landing at the Kuwaiti port of Ash-Shu'aybah, about 20 miles south of Kuwait City. The landing, code-named Desert Saber, would provide a supply base for the land-based 1st Marine Expeditionary Force pushing north into Kuwait from the Saudi border, 50 miles inland from the coast. It would also provide a force to cut off an Iraqi counterattack against the land attack. But on February 2, Boomer acquiesced to Schwarz-

kopf's decision to cancel the landing because it threatened to be too costly, to do too much damage to the Kuwaiti coast, and to delay the ground offensive (*see* **Amphibious Landing**). Later, at Boomer's request, the ground offensive was delayed from February 22, 1991, to February 24, so the Marines would have more time to prepare after they redeployed to new attack positions about 50 miles inland.

After the war Boomer served as commander of the Marine Corps Combat Development Command until September 1992, when he was promoted to four-star general and named assistant commandant of the Marine Corps.

**British 1st Armoured Division**—The main British ground force during Operation Desert Storm was the 1st Armoured Division. Commanded by Major General Rupert Smith, it served under the operational control of the U.S. Army's 7th Corps, which Lieutenant General Frederick Franks commanded. The 1st Armoured Division was comprised of the 4th Brigade and the 7th Armoured Brigade. The latter was called the Desert Rats after its service in World War II against the great German tank commander Erwin Rommel, who was known as the "Desert Fox." The division was equipped with British-made Challenger tanks, a high-performance tank comparable to the U.S. M-1A1 but with an even greater firing range.

On the second day of the ground war, the British 1st Armoured Division passed through the breach in the Iraqi defensive lines opened by U.S. 1st Infantry Division. It immediately turned east to protect the 7th Corps from a counterattack and, after encountering and destroying an Iraqi armored division, fought almost continuously for two days while executing the southernmost line of the corps' eastward attack against the Republican Guard. On February 27, the British 1st Armoured Division destroyed the Iraqi 52nd Armored Division and overran three infantry divisions as it cut behind forces battling the U.S. 1st Infantry Division (*see* **Battle Against the Republican Guard**).

**Bush, George Herbert**—Elected president of the United States in 1988, Bush was Saddam Hussein's adversary in the Persian Gulf War. Although Iraq was a client state of the Soviet Union, the United States' Cold War enemy, Bush implemented conciliatory policies toward Iraq prior to its invasion of Kuwait on August 2, 1990. Moreover, he had been vice president during the Gulf War when, under the leadership of President Reagan, the United States had actively supported Iraq against Iran (*see* **Iran-Iraq Gulf War**). However, Bush immediately took an unwavering position against the Iraqi occupation and subsequent annexation of Kuwait, and he was responsible for assembling the international coalition that opposed and defeated Iraq.

Bush acquired considerable political experience during the Cold War. He began his career as a Republican congressman from Texas in 1967. After he lost a 1970 Senate election, President Nixon appointed him ambassador to the United Nations, where he supported the Middle East peace proposals initiated by Secretary of State William Rogers. Bush also defended the administration's support of Pakistan during its December 1971 war with India, but in May he offered U.S. relief aid to Bangladesh. He also defended the U.S. blockade of North Vietnam before the United Nations.

After the 1972 election Nixon named Bush chairman of the Republican National Committee. Bush set out to broaden the party by appealing more to workers and ethnic groups but quickly became distracted by the ongoing Watergate scandal that dominated much of Nixon's second term. Bush did not directly involve the party in defending the president; nonetheless his effectiveness in promoting party goals suffered from the scandal. Following Nixon's resignation, Bush accepted an appointment by President Ford to lead the U.S. Liaison Office in the People's Republic of China (PRC). He impressed the Chinese with his friendliness and informality, touring Beijing on a bicycle and hosting hot dog and hamburger parties in the American compound. He also helped host Ford's state visit to China in 1975.

In November 1975, Ford appointed Bush director of the CIA, and he held the post through the remainder of Ford's presidency. Bush implemented policies to improve the agency's professionalism, and he promoted younger personnel. He also supported claims by a group of advisers outside the agency that the Soviet Union was preparing to win a nuclear war with the United States, in violation of the premise of mutually assured destruction that underlay the 1970s détente. Bush's position later became the basis for the massive arms buildup during the 1980s under President Reagan. Bush contended for the Republican vice-presidential nomination in 1976, but Ford chose Senator Robert Dole instead. After Ford's defeat in the general election, Bush returned to private life, serving as chairman of the First National Bank of Houston. In 1980 he challenged frontrunner Ronald Reagan for the presidential nomination but lost in a surprisingly close contest. Reagan named Bush as his running mate, and Bush served as vice president from 1981 to 1989. During that time he supported the president and cultivated ties to right-wing Republicans who were suspicious of his commitment to the conservative cause. Though he maintained that he had been "out of the loop" in the Iran-Contra scandal, a 1992 special prosecutor's report concluded that Bush had been involved in the scheme which sold U.S. arms to Iran for use against Iraq in the Gulf War. In return the Iranians promised to arrange for the release of American hostages in Lebanon. The scheme, which ultimately managed to win the release of only three of the seven hostages, illegally diverted profits from the arms sales to support the anti–Communist Contras in Nicaragua and conduct other covert activities. Bush's role in Iran-Contra had not been established in 1988, when he defeated Democrat Michael Dukakis for the presidency. However, the long-awaited special prosecutor's report, issued just prior to the 1992 election, contributed to Bush's loss to Bill Clinton.

Bush campaigned in 1988 by taking a hard line against Soviet Premier Mikhail Gorbachev. However, the quickly spreading collapse of Communism in Eastern Europe and the

**President Bush greets the troops during Operation Desert Shield (photograph courtesy of George Bush Presidential Library and Museum).**

Soviet Union forced Bush to re-evaluate and offer Gorbachev greater support. Bush presided over the "official" end of the Cold War in November 1990, when leaders of all the European states, the United States, Canada, and the Soviet Union met in Paris to sign the Conventional Forces in Europe Treaty. He proclaimed, "We have closed a chapter of history. The Cold War is over."

By 1990 Bush and Gorbachev had come to some basic agreements. Both wanted to preserve political stability during these times of immense change. In the aftermath of the Cold War they worked together to promote "a new world order." Though a vague projection of the world's future power structure, the new world order presumably called upon the United States, the sole remaining superpower, to use its influence to stabilize world affairs and curtail unacceptable behavior among nations.

In his first year as president, Bush ordered an invasion of Panama which led to the ouster and arrest of President Manuel Noriega, whom Bush accused of promoting drug smuggling. The invasion established Bush's willingness to employ military force to achieve U.S. goals. The Bush administration continued its Cold War policies of supporting the right-wing military dictatorship in El Salvador in its civil war against pro–Communist populists and of maintaining a hard line against Castro in Cuba and against the ruling Marxist Sandinistas in Nicaragua.

During the first year and a half of Bush's presidency, the State Department tolerated Hussein because, even if his methods were fascistic and inhumane, he provided a check against Iran and its virulently anti–American Islamic fundamentalist revolution. It was for this reason that the United States actively supported Iraq during the Gulf War while Bush was vice president, providing naval escorts for Kuwaiti tankers carrying Iraqi oil and offering other kinds of aid. While he was president, virtually up to the moment of the invasion, Bush continued to cultivate Hussein as a stabilizing influence in the Gulf whose interests coincided, up to a certain point, with those of the United States.

On July 25, one week before the invasion,

Hussein conferred with Ambassador April Glaspie to learn how the United States would respond to an Iraqi military action and to threaten against U.S. interference. According to a transcript of the meeting that Iraq later leaked to the press, Glaspie replied, "We have no opinion on Arab-Arab conflicts, like your border disagreement with Kuwait." Glaspie added that "President Bush is an intelligent man. He is not going to declare an economic war against Iraq." She complimented Hussein's "extraordinary efforts" to rebuild Iraq and expressed Bush's desire for improved relations with Iraq.

On July 27, as Iraq was massing its armies on the Kuwaiti border, the State Department acknowledged that Iraq's threatening behavior toward Kuwait had "caused us concern," but it criticized the Senate for banning agricultural loans to Iraq, arguing that such bans "would not help achieve our goals." Two days before the invasion, Assistant Secretary of State John Kelly's statement before the House Foreign Affairs Committee similarly signalled the Bush administration's tolerance for Iraq's aggressive posture against Kuwait: "We have no defense treaty relationship with any Gulf country. That is clear.... We have traditionally avoided taking a position on border disputes or on internal OPEC deliberations, but we have certainly ... resoundingly called for the peaceful settlement of disputes and differences in the area" (*see* **Causes of the War**).

After the invasion, Iraqis argued that when Glaspie assured Hussein that the United States took no position on the border dispute, she was implying that the United States tacitly approved an Iraqi military action. The State Department maintained that Glaspie's statements were never intended as assertions of U.S. policy and that they did not in any case imply approval of Iraqi aggression. More likely, her statements and Kelly's probably were intended to signal that the Bush administration would tolerate a limited incursion into northern Kuwait and a readjustment of the border at the Rumalia oil field and the offshore islands of Bubiyān and Warbah. But their comments were probably never meant to imply that the United States would approve the conquest and annexation of the entire country, although some cynical commentators have speculated that they may have been intended to hoodwink Hussein into invading Kuwait in order to give the United States justification for waging a war to destroy him.

Despite past support for Hussein, Bush immediately took a firm stand against Iraq. Great Britain's Prime Minister Margaret Thatcher, a close Cold War ally of President Reagan, met with him in Colorado on August 2 and encouraged him to take a hard line against Hussein. Three days later, Bush publicly described the Iraqis as "international outlaws and renegades" and declared, "I view very seriously our determination to reverse this aggression.... This will not stand." And although Gorbachev tried to reach a negotiated settlement with Iraq, which had been a Soviet client state, both superpower leaders agreed that the new world order could not tolerate Hussein's annexation of Kuwait.

On the day of the invasion the Bush administration called for the immediate withdrawal of Iraqi troops, the freezing of all Iraqi and Kuwaiti assets, and a halt to arms shipments to Iraq. It also supported U.N. Security Council Resolution 660 condemning the conquest and demanding an immediate withdrawal. The next day, August 3, Soviet Foreign Minister Eduard Shevardnadze and Secretary of State James Baker jointly called for the unconditional withdrawal of Iraqi troops, the restoration of Kuwait's sovereignty, and an end to arms deliveries to Iraq. Bush himself indicated that he would provide military assistance to Saudi Arabia if Iraq invaded it. On August 4, Bush learned that land- and carrier-based aircraft could arrive in the region within days, but that it would require several weeks to establish a ground defense and 17 weeks to launch a ground attack. The next day he publicly declared that nothing short of a total withdrawal from Kuwait would be acceptable.

On August 6, Bush sent Defense Secretary Richard Cheney to negotiate an agreement with King Fahd, allowing the United States to station military forces in Saudi Arabia in order to protect the kingdom from an Iraqi attack.

On August 8, the day Iraq annexed Kuwait, Bush initiated Operation Desert Shield when he ordered a rapid deployment force to Saudi Arabia. Anticipating an imminent Iraqi invasion of Saudi Arabia, the soldiers were prepared to fight immediately upon debarking in Dhahran. As he ordered the troops into possible combat, Bush defined the U.S. objectives in a televised address to the American people. The first goal was Iraq's withdrawal from Kuwait. Bush also called for the restoration of the legitimate Kuwaiti government, security and stability in the Persian Gulf, and the safety of Americans abroad. Elements from the U.S. Army 82nd and 101 airborne divisions arrived unopposed in Dhahran the following day (*see* **Operation Desert Shield**).

Bush's most impressive achievement during the Persian Gulf War was his ability to assemble and lead a broad, international coalition against Iraq. Altogether, a total of 36 countries joined Bush's coalition from virtually every region on the globe: North America, South America, Western Europe, Eastern Europe, the Middle East, Africa, Asia, and Australia. Japan and Germany were forbidden by restraints in their post–World War II constitutions to send ground troops, but they and Saudi Arabia contributed significantly in helping the United States underwrite the cost of the war. Germany also contributed minesweeping ships that participated in Operation Desert Storm. The Soviet Union refused to participate in an army led by the United States instead of the United Nations, but it supported the effort in other ways (*see* **Coalition**).

Though Desert Shield was purely a defensive operation, Bush never wavered from his initial position that the Iraqi invasion was unacceptable and would not be allowed to stand. The United Nations had imposed a strict economic and military embargo against Iraq, and the diplomatic strategy was to allow the embargo to devastate the Iraqi economy and thereby pressure Hussein to evacuate from Kuwait. Most officials estimated the embargo

would require one to two years to achieve results (*see* **Embargo**).

But Bush did not believe the embargo would succeed, and he quickly began to explore military options. If there was to be a war, General Schwarzkopf was anxious to start it in January or February, since his troops would by then be ready to attack and the desert conditions would be optimal. If they waited until late February or March to begin the war, seasonal rain and dust storms could impede maneuvers and threaten to jam the sophisticated machines and technology that gave the allies their advantage. After March, the fierce summer heat would be too intense for fighting. So, if Operation Desert Storm did not commence in January or early February, the coalition would have to wait until the following autumn, and that would entail many political risks, domestically and within the coalition.

The argument against the January-February timetable was that it did not give ample time for a diplomatic solution to be worked out. Indeed, one of the main criticisms of Bush's handling of the crisis was that he did not try hard enough—or not hard at all—to resolve the conflict by diplomatic means, or give the economic embargo sufficient time to change the political climate inside of Iraq and force Hussein to relent. During the early stages of Operation Desert Shield, Secretary of State James Baker and Chairman of the Joint Chiefs of Staff Colin Powell advocated giving the sanctions more time to force Hussein to accede to the U.N. demands. But Bush overruled them.

Bush's defenders maintain that prospects for a negotiated settlement appeared slim right from the beginning, especially as the allies were unwilling to compromise on their basic demands: release of all hostages, complete Iraqi withdrawal from Kuwait, renunciation of the annexation of Kuwait and of aggressive intentions against it, and reparations to Kuwait. Hussein had given no indication that he would simply walk away from his victory in Kuwait. Indeed, his rhetoric became more bellicose over time, not less. Given the absolute nature of Hussein's dictatorship, it was doubtful that economic devastation could topple him. For instance, years of economic ruin due mainly to the U.S. embargo against Cuba had not driven Castro, another dictator, from power. Furthermore, waiting for sanctions to work would require Bush to take the unpopular step of maintaining hundreds of thousands of troops in Saudi Arabia, many of whom were reservists who had been called away from families and jobs. Moreover, a prolonged U.S. military presence in Saudi Arabia would have been politically unpalatable to the Saudis, who had heretofore resisted having foreign bases on their soil. And the coalition troops would have to passively stand by in their defensive positions while Hussein remained free to plunder Kuwait, abuse the human rights of its citizens, and threaten new actions against Israel and elsewhere. Plus, the American diplomats and citizens held in Iraq and Kuwait would have remained hostages to Hussein, who released them only in December 1990, after the United Nations voted to permit an offensive war against Iraq.

Consequently, both as a means of putting more pressure on Hussein to leave Kuwait immediately and as a prelude to waging war if he did not, throughout the end of 1990 Bush continued to strengthen the U.S. forces in Saudi Arabia (*see* **Offensive War Preparations for Liberating Kuwait**). On November 8, two days after the mid-term Congressional elections, he ordered an additional 150,000 air, sea, and ground troops to the Persian Gulf. He had approved the buildup earlier but delayed announcing it so it would not become an election issue (*see* **Popular Support for the War**). This buildup introduced a second phase in Desert Shield and enabled Schwarzkopf and his staff to prepare for Desert Storm. Bush celebrated Thanksgiving in Saudi Arabia with the American armed forces there, and he continued to increase allied troop strength until the commencement of the war in mid–January, by which time the United States alone had deployed some 450,000 troops, and the total coalition forces numbered over 700,000. On the other side of the border, Iraq had amassed over 540,000 troops in the Kuwaiti theater of operations.

Bush's insistence that any diplomatic solution require Iraq to immediately withdraw from Kuwait, free its hostages, and annul its annexation of Kuwait did not leave much room for negotiation. Moreover, he refused to link Iraq's withdrawal from Kuwait to Israel's withdrawal from the West Bank and Syria's evacuation from Lebanon, as Hussein had proposed on August 12. Bush claimed Hussein's plan imposed preconditions and did not comply with the U.N. demands. In addition to these stated reasons, Bush no doubt opposed the plan for precisely the same reason Hussein offered it. He was unwilling to concede a major political victory to Hussein or to undermine Israel's position within the region. Hussein probably knew Bush would reject his peace proposal. But merely by making the offer he recast Israel and Syria, instead of Iraq, as the oppressors (*see* **Diplomacy**).

After rejecting Hussein's attempt to link the Kuwaiti occupation to other military occupations in the region, Bush made no counteroffer to Hussein, other than to reiterate his basic demands. Although he told the U.N. General Assembly on October 1 that the United States was still seeking diplomatic solutions, it was not until November 30—the day after the United Nations voted to permit a war to remove the Iraqis—that Bush suggested direct talks with Iraq. But on December 19, the meeting between Iraq's Foreign Minister Tariq Aziz and U.S. Secretary of State James Baker was postponed indefinitely because the two sides could not agree on a reciprocal visit by Baker to Iraq. Baker and Aziz finally met in Geneva on January 9, but the meeting yielded no results, nor had anyone seriously expected it to. But the conference enabled Bush to claim his administration had taken every extra step possible to negotiate an acceptable resolution, only to receive "a total stiff-arm" for its efforts. And on January 12, Congress voted that if Iraq did not withdraw from Kuwait by the U.N.'s January 15 deadline, Bush was authorized to use military force to remove Iraq from Kuwait. On January 15,

France submitted a last-minute proposal that the U.N. Security Council hold an international conference on the Palestinian situation if Iraq would agree to withdraw from Kuwait. However, Bush and British Prime Minister John Major strongly opposed the proposal, and it failed.

The Persian Gulf War reflected many lessons learned from the failure of the Vietnam War. Bush and Powell agreed that it was essential to have a clearly defined mission and to give the military the full resources and freedom of action to complete the job quickly and effectively, with as few casualties as possible. "This will not be another Vietnam. This will not be a protracted, drawn-out war," Bush declared. "If there must be a war, we will not permit our troops to have their hands tied behind their backs. If one American soldier has to go into battle, that soldier will have enough force behind him to win and then get out as soon as possible." It was for this reason that Bush agreed to an immediate massive buildup of troops and a callup of reservists, despite the political risks such a move entailed.

During the war, Bush applied another lesson learned from Vietnam: he stayed out of the day-to-day military decision making. Whereas President Johnson, in particular, had micro-managed the war in Vietnam, even calling for bombing missions against specific targets, Bush stayed abreast of events but allowed his generals to run the war.

Bush did his role to sustain popular support for the war, making speeches and public appearances. For instance, on February 15, he toured the Raytheon plant in Massachusetts that produced the Patriot missiles. Declaring, "We are going to prevail, and our soldiers are going to come home with their heads high" and "Thank God for the Patriot missile," he received a standing ovation and loud applause.

Bush's greatest involvement in the war came on February 27, when he decided to terminate hostilities on the morning of February 28 (local time), as the allied armies were poised to finish demolishing the Republic Guard's armored divisions. Despite criticisms from

Thatcher, among others, he has never publicly questioned that decision, and in January 1996 he defended it to British interviewer David Frost on BBC television:

> The mission was to end the aggression, it wasn't to decimate, further decimate, the Republican Guard. It wasn't to increase the body count by stacking up another 50,000 Iraqi dead. It was not to go in to find Saddam Hussein.... I don't think war is immoral, but I don't think you measure the totality of its success by whether you can shoot down, kill another 50,000 fleeing soldiers, murderous though they had been in Kuwait.

Bush added that it would have been unrealistic to demand Hussein to "hand over his sword," though he acknowledged that the allies should have insisted that the surrender be conducted by a higher ranking Iraqi official, perhaps a top Iraqi politician or soldier, "just one step below Hussein." But he pointed out the difficult situation the allies would have been in if they had demanded Hussein to personally surrender and he refused. "There we would be, in downtown Baghdad, America occupying a foreign land, searching for this brutal dictator who had the best security in the world, involved in an urban guerrilla war. That is not a formula I wanted to contemplate, and I think history will say we did the right thing." He also pointed out that pursuing the war further could have split the coalition, with some Arab countries and even some European states objecting.

Bush also added that the United States never considered using its nuclear weapons. "I suppose you could conjure up some horrible scenario that would call for the use of battlefield tactical nuclear weapons or something but it was not something that we really contemplated at all."

He discussed how the United States pressured Israel not to retaliate after being struck by Iraqi Scud missiles. "We said, 'We're not going to give you the codes and thus your aircraft are going to be flying and exposed to the threat of friendly fire.'" He added that the decision to keep Israel out of the war, which was necessary to keep the coalition together, was in the best interests of Israel's security. In return for Israel's agreement to remain out of the war, Bush consented to making the destruction of the Scud missiles a top priority, despite the objections of Schwarzkopf, who did not believe Scuds posed a major military threat.

Prior to and during the war, Bush kept up a steady stream of rhetoric denouncing Hussein, whom he likened to Hitler, and there was a sense that his antagonism for Hussein became personal as well as political. On February 15, Bush called for "the Iraqi military and the people of Iraq to take matters into their own hands to force Saddam Hussein the dictator to step aside." This statement and later ones after the conclusion of Desert Storm suggested to Iraqi Kurds and Shī'ites that the United States would support their postwar insurrections against Hussein, though that support was never given.

Bush may have tolerated Hussein's suppression of the Kurds and Shī'ites because he did not want to enmesh the U.S. military in a bloody and prolonged occupation or peacekeeping operation. Moreover, like the Iraqi military, the Sunni-led Saudis may have preferred having a weakened Hussein in power to seeing an independent Shī'ite nation established on its border, right beside the portion of Saudi Arabia that contains the greatest oil reserves and has a large Shī'ite population. Likewise, Turkey, which had its own difficulties with Kurdish separatists on its southern border, was not anxious to see an independent Kurdish nation formed in northern Iraq. Whatever the underlying reasons, Bush officially took the position that Hussein's war against the Kurds and Shī'ites was an internal Iraqi matter for which there was no U.N. mandate to intervene (*see* **Kurdish Rebellion**, **Shī'ite Rebellion**).

Regardless of the relative merits of his decisions not to eradicate the Republican Guard, remove Hussein from power, or intervene on behalf of the Kurds and Shī'ites, Bush was not rewarded politically for his temperate policies. Immediately following the overwhelming success of Desert Storm he enjoyed the highest approval rating of any U.S. president since World War II, but his popularity plummeted in subsequent months as Hussein consolidated his power, massacred Kurdish civilians at will, and violated the terms of the U.N. cease-fire. Hussein's postwar flaunting of the international community contributed to Bush's failure to win reelection in 1992, along with a weak economy and the revelation of his role in the Iran-Contra scandal.

From April 14–16, 1993, Bush visited Kuwait, where he was welcomed as a hero. According to FBI and CIA investigations, while there he was apparently the target of an Iraqi assassination plot that did not materialize. In response to the alleged plot, President Clinton authorized a reprisal. Twenty-three missiles were launched against Iraqi intelligence headquarters in Baghdad from U.S. Navy vessels in the Persian Gulf and Red Sea. The headquarters was destroyed, but some missiles missed their target and caused civilian casualties.

**Carter Doctrine**—On December 25, 1979, the Soviet Union invaded Afghanistan in order to prop up the regime they had installed there. In response, President Carter issued the Carter Doctrine, declaring, "Any attempt by any outside force to gain control of the Persian Gulf will be regarded as an assault on the vital interests of the United States of America and such an assault will be repelled by any means necessary, including military force." The Carter Doctrine later became a justification for the Persian Gulf War.

**Causes of the War**—The roots of the Persian Gulf War extend back at least to Iraq's eight-year Gulf War with Iran that concluded in 1988, and possibly as far back as Hussein's Ba'ath Party's assumption of power in Iraq in 1968, or the establishment of the Republic of Iraq in 1958, or British High Commissioner Percy Cox's arbitrary redrawing of boundaries to resolve border disputes among Saudi Arabia, Iraq, and Kuwait in 1922, or the 1916 Sykes-Picot agreement that first parceled the former Ottoman Empire into regions of British and French influence following World

War I. However, the immediate cause was Iraq's conquest of Kuwait on August 2, 1990.

Iraq's conquest of Kuwait was the first challenge to the post–Cold War "new world order" in which the United States was the sole superpower, and President Bush did not want to establish the precedent of tolerating such bold-faced aggression against sovereign states in his new world order. More importantly, he could not permit Iraq to acquire the economic and political stranglehold over the West that control of Kuwaiti oil would give it.

Hussein justified the invasion, occupation, and annexation of Kuwait on several grounds. He revived historical claims that Kuwait, in fact, had always belonged to Iraq. This argument dated back to 1922, when Cox redrew the borders, giving some Kuwaiti territory to Saudi Arabia and Iraq, but not as much as Iraq demanded. In 1961, Kuwait was established as an independent and sovereign nation over Iraqi objections. At that time Iraq massed soldiers along the border but backed off after British troops landed to defend Kuwait, and Kuwait won recognition from the Arab League. Iraq did not formally withdraw its claim to Kuwait until October 1963. In 1965, it demanded the two Persian Gulf islands of Warbah and Būbiyān, along with other Kuwaiti territory close to the Iraqi border, in order to create space to construct a port at Umm Qaṣr and a railway line attached to it. This would have given Iraq a major port on the Persian Gulf, but Kuwait refused, offering instead to lease Warbah to Iraq for 99 years. The issue was never resolved. In 1973, Iraq again demanded Būbiyān and briefly occupied a portion of Kuwait, but withdrew after Saudi Arabian forces moved into the country, world opinion turned against it, and Iran threatened to take military action. In 1978, Iraq offered to rent half of Būbiyān, declaring "Iraq is committed to the principle that the border should be defined in such a way that it guarantees a naval position for Iraq." Iraq's desire for a secure port on the Persian Gulf was the primary cause of its war with Iran in 1980.

Hussein also claimed that he was liberating the Kuwaiti people from an unpopular ruling family. In fact, invading Iraqi soldiers frequently informed Kuwaitis that they had come to liberate them. The emir had closed down the Kuwaiti National Assembly in 1986 in response to tensions caused by the Iran-Iraq Gulf War, and indeed there had been some popular pressure to reinstate the assembly and otherwise open the government to wider representation of the citizenry. However, Hussein's claim that the invasion was at the behest of the Kuwaiti people was belied by his inability to find a single Kuwaiti citizen to head the new government of occupied Kuwait. Moreover, Iraq's annexation of Kuwait less than a week after the invasion and its officially sanctioned plundering of Kuwaiti industry and other assets were hardly the acts of a liberator.

Two weeks before the invasion, Hussein also accused Kuwait of stealing $2.4 billion worth of Iraqi oil by drilling into the Rumaila oil field, which he claimed belonged solely to Iraq even though the final five kilometers reside on Kuwait's side of the border. Moreover, Hussein also accused Kuwait of aggressive military action because it had repositioned its border and customs posts closer to the Iraqi border. Kuwait, whose 17,000 member armed services were dwarfed by Hussein's million-man army, rejected the charge of aggression, pointing out that the changes were made solely for administrative purposes and to expedite the flow of traffic, and that the posts remained within Kuwait's territory.

Finally, Hussein charged that by exceeding the oil production quotas agreed upon by the Organization of Petroleum Exporting Countries (OPEC), Kuwait was driving down the price of oil and thereby weakening Iraq by depressing the value of its primary resource. He insisted that Kuwait, Saudi Arabia, and the other Persian Gulf states should forgive the billions of dollars they loaned to Iraq during its war with Iran since Iraq had fought the war to protect them from Iranian-sponsored, revolutionary Islamic fundamentalism that threatened to depose them.

These last arguments had greater credibility, though the second is only partially accurate. Hussein wanted to increase the price of oil in order to finance postwar reconstruction and improve the economy. But in 1990, Kuwait and the United Arab Emirates were exceeding the quotas allowed by OPEC and were thereby keeping prices down. Kuwait not only owned vast reserves of oil in the ground, it also had invested heavily in refineries, filling stations, and such petroleum-dependent products as petro-chemicals. Consequently, high oil production benefitted Kuwait, even though the practice deflated prices for crude oil, since Kuwaiti filling stations and petroleum-based industries would be able to purchase oil and gasoline at lower costs. Therefore, Kuwait was producing as much as one million barrels of oil per day more than OPEC permitted. On the other hand, Iraq's main source of revenue came from its crude oil reserves, not from production and spin-off industries. Consequently, the lower prices reduced the value of its main asset and weakened its economy. Thus Hussein complained to U.S. Ambassador April Glaspie on July 25, 1990, that by depressing the price of oil Kuwait was threatening the jobs of Iraqi workers, and "harming even the milk our children drink and the pension of the widow who lost a husband during the war and the pensions of the orphans who lost their parents."

Hussein's last claim was that he had fought the Gulf War against Iran to protect the interests of the Gulf states, as well as his own, and that they should therefore forgive the approximately $40 million in loans Iraq owed them. In fact, he waged the war primarily to advance Iraqi interests, but the war did coincidentally help the Sunni-led Persian Gulf states by suppressing Iran's Shī'ite-led Islamic revolution.

In 1980, Hussein initiated Iraq's eight-year Gulf War with Iran primarily to gain control of the Shaṭṭ al-'Arab waterway and Iran's oil-rich, predominantly Arabic border province of Khūzestān (called *Arabistan* in Iraq). These would have given Iraq direct shipping access to the Persian Gulf, something it had desired since 1969 when the shah of Iran unilaterally revoked a 1937 treaty that had given Iraq control over most of the Shaṭṭ al-'Arab, a deep-channel estuary at the border between the two nations. The war lasted eight years, cost between 500,000 and one million lives, and ended essentially in a stalemate. Although Iraq failed to realize its own objectives, it did succeed in impeding the spread of revolutionary Islamic fundamentalism, as the war depleted Iran's resources and left its economy and government in a state of disarray. Consequently, Iran could not effectively extend its fundamentalist revolution beyond its borders to overthrow the secular, Sunni regimes that controlled the Persian Gulf region. Thus the war did, in fact, achieve the goals of Saudi Arabia, Kuwait, and the other Persian Gulf states. But it also left Iraq with a well-equipped standing army of some one million soldiers. And with Iran at least temporarily eliminated as a major force in the Gulf, there was no other military power in the region that could challenge Hussein (*see* **Iran-Iraq Gulf War**).

Apart from the reasons he gave for the invasion, Hussein conquered Kuwait for economic and political reasons as well. The United States and its allies opposed him for economic and political reasons that transcended their most frequently stated reason for fighting: to defend the principle of national sovereignty which Iraq trampled when it conquered Kuwait. By annexing Kuwait, Hussein could simultaneously gain vast oil reserves, acquire a major port on the Persian Gulf, and eliminate the $13 billion debt Iraq owed Kuwait.

In addition to these economic benefits, Hussein could acquire tremendous political leverage over the industrial world and Iraq could establish itself as a major player in world politics. Iraq exported about one billion barrels of oil annually. If it annexed Kuwait, it could control another billion barrels a year. And if it went on to conquer Saudi Arabia, it would add another 1.3 billion barrels. The combined oil resources in Iraq, Kuwait, and Saudi Arabia accounted for about one-third of the world's annual oil production and 55–60 percent of the world's proven oil reserves. In 1990, the United States was importing about 45 percent of its oil needs. The Western allies were even more dependent, importing over 90 percent of their oil. Combined, they imported about two billion barrels annually from the Persian Gulf region, about one-quarter of their total oil imports.

In a high-tech world increasingly dependent on ample and affordable energy, Hussein's control over such a large portion of the worldwide oil supply would have given him considerable leverage over the industrial nations. This in turn would have enabled him to pursue his goal of making Iraq a power comparable to or greater than the United States and the Western European countries. For this reason Hussein had also been developing chemical and biological weapons and was trying to build nuclear weapons. Such military and economic power might have enabled him to curtail U.S. support for Israel and create the new Babylon he often spoke of: an anti-Western, anti–Israeli, Iraqi-led, Pan-Arabic superpower. The United States and the coalition allies fought the war against Hussein because they found it unacceptable to permit him to acquire such an economic and political stranglehold over them. (*See* **Diplomacy**.)

**Cease-fire**—President Bush decided unilaterally to end offensive action in Operation Desert Storm at 8 A.M. February 28, 1991 (local time, midnight on February 27, EST). The cease-fire came after the coalition had achieved all of its proclaimed objectives and fulfilled the mandate called for by the U.N. Security Council's Resolution 678, which authorized the war. The Iraqi forces had been forced from Kuwait and most of the elite Republican Guard armored divisions were either destroyed or trapped in a pocket between northern Kuwait and the Iraqi city of Basra (*see* **Objectives**). By the time of the cease-fire, the Iraqi Army had lost about 76 percent of its tanks, 55 percent of its armored personnel carriers, and 90 percent of its artillery. Moreover, Iraq had lost its ability to wage an offensive war against other nations in the region, though, as subsequent events proved, Hussein could still suppress rebellions within Iraq (*see* **Kurdish Rebellion**, **Shī'ite Rebellion**).

Bush's decision to terminate the fighting before the Republican Guard was entirely destroyed and while Hussein retained power inside Iraq remains one of the most controversial aspects of the Persian Gulf War. No members of the National Security Council, including Defense Secretary Richard Cheney and Chairman of the Joint Chiefs of Staff Colin Powell, opposed the decision. And although General Schwarzkopf believed that, given more time, his armies could achieve more, he raised no objections to ending the hostilities when he was consulted. Schwarzkopf was aware that in addition to ending what was turning into a massacre of Iraqi troops, the cease-fire undoubtedly also saved American lives and those of soldiers from other coalition countries. As Powell later pointed out, the United States had no mandate to overthrow Hussein or pursue the war into Iraq once the Iraqi troops had been ejected from Kuwait, and it was likely that the Arab nations within the coalition would have strongly objected to such an action. Moreover, Bush's advisers believed that media coverage of the carnage inflicted upon the Iraqis retreating from Kuwait City might lead to a public outcry to stop the fighting (*see* **Highway to Hell**).

Nonetheless, Hussein's ability to remain in power and suppress all internal opposition after his devastating defeat led to considerable criticism of Bush's decision to end the war before the Republican Guard was entirely destroyed. The Republican Guard was loyal to Hussein, personally, and was a crucial component of his power base (*see* **Republican Guard**). Indeed, Hussein's survival and his use of Republican Guard units that survived Desert Storm to brutally squelch the Kurdish and Shī'ite uprisings no doubt contributed to Bush's failure to be reelected in 1992.

When the order to implement the cease-fire was passed through the chain of command, there was some confusion as to whether it was for 5 A.M. Zulu time (8 A.M. local time) or 5 A.M. local time. (Zulu is the military designation for Greenwich mean time, which is three hours behind local time in Kuwait and five hours ahead of Eastern Standard Time.)

Consequently, for some four hours elements of the U.S. Army erroneously prepared to stop fighting at 5 A.M. local time. As a result, the army did not proceed as close to Basra as intended. Erroneous reports that the army had captured the Safwān airfield in southern Iraq prompted General Schwarzkopf to suggest Safwān as the site for his meeting with Iraqi generals on March 3, where they would work out the details of the cease-fire. When Schwarzkopf discovered that Safwān was in enemy hands, he became enraged and ordered its capture, despite the fact that the cease-fire had already begun. When the Iraqis refused to retreat from Safwān, Schwarzkopf issued an ultimatum, and they evacuated the area on the afternoon of March 1.

Bush's order to cease offensive action permitted coalition forces to defend themselves, and on March 1, U.S. armored vehicles destroyed a convoy of 1,000 Iraqi vehicles near the Rumaila oil field after the Iraqi troops attacked them. Likewise, on the following day the U.S. 24th Mechanized Infantry Division was fired upon by infantry from the Republican Guard's Hammurabi Division traveling west on Highway 8, back into Iraq. In a battle that lasted for several hours, the Americans destroyed 177 Iraqi tanks and armored personnel carriers. Several hundred Iraqi soldiers were killed. So were a number of Iraqi civilians, including a group of school children riding in a bus that was struck during an air attack. Critics have maintained that the American response in this action was disproportionate to the initial provocation, which consisted of small arms fire and threatening behavior by Iraqi tanks that directed their gun turrets against American tanks.

On March 2, the U.N. Security Council passed Resolution 686, establishing the conditions for a permanent cease-fire. Resolution 686 demanded that Iraq accept the 12 previous U.N. resolutions, specifically insisting that Iraq rescind its annexation of Kuwait, accept liability for losses incurred by its invasion and occupation of Kuwait, release all Kuwaiti and foreign nationals it had detained, and return all Kuwaiti property it had seized. The resolution also required Iraq to cease all military actions, including missile attacks and flights of combat aircraft, meet with military commanders from the coalition to arrange for the military aspects of the cessation of hostilities, release all prisoners of war, return the remains of those killed in action, and provide information and assistance in identifying mines and chemical and biological weapons in the war zone. The Security Council later passed additional resolutions calling for inspection of Iraq's chemical, biological, and nuclear weapons facilities, making arrangements for Iraq to pay war reparations, and condemning its treatment of Kurdish civilians (*see* **United Nations**).

As per Resolution 686, Iraqi generals met with Schwarzkopf and other coalition military leaders in a tent at Safwān on March 3. The Iraqis agreed to show their good faith by immediately releasing some POWs, which they began to do the following day. On March 8, Operation Desert Farewell began as the first 5,000 American troops left for home (*see* **Aftermath**).

**Chemical Warfare**—One of the greatest fears of coalition leaders was that Iraq would employ chemical weapons as it had in its Gulf War with Iraq and against Kurdish rebels in the late 1980s (*see* **Iran-Iraq Gulf War**). Consequently, Iraqi chemical weapons production facilities were heavily targeted during the air campaign, and coalition ground troops were issued protective garments that they wore during breaching operations and afterward, and some received anti–nerve gas vaccinations. Fears of chemical warheads on Scud missiles prompted the Israeli government to issue gas masks to its citizens and have them seal their apartments during Scud attacks. However, according to the Pentagon, the Iraqis did not employ chemical weapons during the war. Foreign Minister Tariq Aziz stated in a 1996 *Frontline* documentary that Iraq feared nuclear retaliation if it launched chemical attacks.

Nonetheless, some veterans and analysts maintain that Iraq did in fact employ chemical agents in sporadic and uncoordinated instances. Many people present at Khafji, Saudi Arabia, on January 20, 1991, believe that an overhead explosion that produced a mysterious mist was a chemical attack, although the Pentagon maintains the mist was rocket propellant from an Iraqi Scud missile that detonated in the air. The mist burned the skin and triggered chemical alarms, and personnel present at the time appear to be at higher risk for Gulf War Syndrome, according to a 1997 study conducted at the University of Texas (*see* **Khafji**, **Gulf War Syndrome**).

According to Jonathan Tucker, director of a chemical weapons nonproliferation project at the Monterey Institute of International Studies, logs, command chronologies, and statements by intelligence officers and forward-deployed troops indicate the Iraqis sporadically employed chemical weapons. Tucker, a former staff member of the Presidential Advisory Committee on Gulf War Veterans' Illnesses, claims he was fired because he became skeptical of government explanations and sought information outside of official channels. In April 1997, Tucker maintained that military records showed that numerous sensors on the battlefield detected chemical use. Moreover, intercepted Iraqi military communiques indicate that Hussein authorized frontline commanders to use chemical weapons once the ground war began. Iraqi documents show that chemical munitions were probably stored more widely in frontline areas than the Pentagon has acknowledged. And one captured military document suggests that the Iraqis may have contaminated some burning oil wells with chemical agents. The document orders Iraqi saboteurs to send a representative "to receive the chemical preparations distributed to your units."

Iraq had a large stockpile of chemical agents, including thousands of tons of lethal nerve gas and blister-producing mustard gas. Its delivery systems included missile warheads, artillery shells, aerial bombs, rockets, and spray tanks mounted on aircraft. During the war at least 75 percent of Iraq's chemical warfare production capacity was destroyed. None-

theless, sizeable stockpiles remained after the war, and Iraq's refusal to cooperate completely with U.N. inspection teams sent in to destroy them led to the continuation of the embargo against Iraq following the war (*see* **Embargo**, **United Nations**).

In June 1996, the Pentagon acknowledged that as many as 20,000 soldiers might have been exposed to low levels of toxic chemicals shortly after the war, when army engineers demolished an Iraqi ammunition bunker containing cyclosarin, a deadly nerve gas, near the village of Khamisiyah. The engineers had been told that the depot contained no chemical weapons. In April 1997, the CIA acknowledged that it mishandled the information about Khamisiyah, stating that it had found evidence of chemical weapons activity there as early as 1984 but failed to communicate it.

**Cheney, Richard B.**—As secretary of defense during the Persian Gulf War, Cheney was responsible for the U.S. conduct of the war. In the chain of command, Chairman of the Joint Chiefs of Staff Colin Powell reported to Cheney, who reported directly to President Bush. Cheney was also in direct contact with Gen-

**Richard B. Cheney (photograph courtesy of the Department of Defense).**

eral Norman Schwarzkopf, the commander-in-chief of the allied forces in the Kuwaiti theater of operations, but Schwarzkopf typically communicated through Powell.

Born in Lincoln, Nebraska, in 1941, Cheney grew up in Wyoming and received his bachelor's degree from the University of Wyoming in 1965 and his master's degree in 1966. He served in the Nixon administration and then as President Ford's chief of staff. From 1979 to 1989, Cheney represented Wyoming in the House of Representatives, and in 1989 Bush appointed him secretary of defense after the Senate refused to confirm John Tower.

During Operation Desert Shield, Cheney fired Air Force Chief of Staff Michael Dugan for making public statements about U.S. plans in the event of a war with Iraq. He appointed General Merrill "Tony" McPeak to succeed Dugan. Cheney also criticized Schwarzkopf's initial plan for a ground war because it called for a direct attack into Iraqi fortified positions and promised to incur heavy losses. He subsequently approved Schwarzkopf and Powell's request to double U.S. troop strength, an act that made possible the new, highly successful strategy for the ground offensive.

In early October, Cheney ordered Powell to assess nuclear strike options against the Iraqi Army. Cheney told Powell, who opposed even assessing the possibility of employing nuclear weapons, that he was not seriously considering using them, but that he wanted to be thorough and was curious about what a tactical nuclear strike would entail. Presumably, one would be employed only upon extreme provocation, such as an Iraqi nuclear attack or a devastating chemical or biological attack against allied ground forces. The team Powell assembled concluded that a large number of small tactical weapons would be necessary just to damage a single division. Powell showed the results to Cheney and then destroyed them; the use of nuclear forces was not contemplated any further.

On February 8, 1991, Cheney, Powell, and Paul Wolfowitz, the undersecretary of defense, flew to Saudi Arabia to meet with Schwarzkopf and set the date for commencing the ground offensive. The next day Schwarzkopf briefed them thoroughly on his plans and indicated that he would be ready to begin on February 21, with perhaps three or four days latitude to deal with unexpected contingencies. Cheney found Schwarzkopf's plan acceptable, and they adopted his time frame. Cheney was later among the president's advisers who concurred with Bush's decision to end the fighting at 8 A.M. on February 28, after the Iraqi ground forces had been routed.

**Coalition**—Among the 36 members of the coalition against Iraq were most of the members of the U.S.-led North American Treaty Organization (NATO) that was formed in 1949 in Cold War opposition to the Soviet Union and its Communist allies in Europe. But during the Persian Gulf War, the Soviet Union and some of its former client states, for the first time since World War II, united with NATO countries against a common enemy. So too were several Arab countries whose relationships with the United States had often been strained over the past three decades, primarily due to American support of Israel and the affiliation of some of the Arab states with the Soviet Union during the Cold War. The NATO members included the United States, Great Britain, France, Canada, Turkey, Italy, Denmark, Greece, Norway, Belgium, Portugal, Spain, the Netherlands, and Germany, which had been reunified into a single nation only months earlier. The former Warsaw Pact countries were Czechoslovakia, Poland, and Hungary, which contributed 100 medics. Though the Soviet Union supported the U.N. resolution authorizing the war, it did not join the coalition because it would not allow its troops to serve directly under U.S. command. It did, however, contribute four ships to the effort to enforce the embargo against Iraq. The Arab states allied against Iraq, also an Arab state, were the Persian Gulf nations of Saudi Arabia, Kuwait, the United Arab Emirates, Bahrain, Qatar, and Oman (collectively these comprised the Gulf Cooperation Council), and Egypt, Syria, and Morocco. Muslim Bangladesh and Afghanistan contributed offensive troops against Muslim Iraq. Pakistan, another Muslim country, sent a brigade of soldiers specifically to defend Saudi Arabia, but these did not participate in the offensive actions against Iraq. Unlike the NATO troops, the Arab forces did not serve under the United States Central Command (CENTCOM); instead they served under a Saudi-led Joint Forces Command that coordinated with CENTCOM (*see* **Joint Forces Command**). Nigeria, Senegal, Argentina, Honduras, South Korea, New Zealand, and Australia also committed ground, air, and/or naval forces. Japan was forbidden by its post–World War II constitution to send armed forces, but it contributed money, supplies, and logistical support. Germany had similar constitutional constraints but supplied five minesweepers and money and assumed greater responsibility for defending Western Europe after U.S. forces stationed there were redeployed to the Middle East. Israel also offered to assist in Saudi Arabia's defense, but the offer was declined because it was feared that Israel's participation would cause the Arab countries to withdraw from the coalition. In fact, during the war Hussein launched missile attacks against Israeli cities, presumably with the intention of drawing Israel into the war and thereby causing the coalition to disintegrate. However, at the behest of the United States, Israel did not retaliate and the coalition remained intact.

**Coast Guard**—During Operations Desert Shield and Desert Storm the U.S. Coast Guard provided security at all 14 major ports where U.S. troops shipped out to the Middle East. Furthermore, ten law enforcement detachments, each consisting of one officer and three enlisted men, served in the Persian Gulf, where they employed their expertise in interdicting and boarding ships in the navy's effort to enforce the embargo against Iraq. A coast guard team was also ordered to Saudi Arabia to advise on cleaning up the massive oil spill in the Persian Gulf that was part of Iraq's environmental warfare (*see* **Environmental Warfare**). During the war 877 coast guard reservists were called up to active duty.

**Conscientious Objectors**—Since the Persian Gulf War was the first war in which the U.S. armed services were comprised entirely of volunteers, the number of conscientious objectors was quite low in comparison to other wars. According to the Pentagon, during the Persian Gulf War it received 400 applications for conscientious objector status and approved 217 of those requests.

**Daguet Division** *see* **French 6th Light Armored Division.**

**Deceptions, Feints, and Ruses**—General Schwarzkopf, the coalition's commander-in-chief in the Kuwaiti theater of operations, was a student of military history, and among the works that influenced him was *The Art of War*, written by the Chinese military philosopher Sun Tsu over 2,000 years earlier. One of Sun Tsu's admonitions was that "a military operation involves deception. Without deception you cannot carry out strategy, without strategy you cannot control the opponent. When you are going to attack far away, make it look as if you are going just a short distance." Schwarzkopf employed this principle as a cornerstone of Operation Desert Storm.

The main thrust of the ground war was based on deception. Schwarzkopf believed that the Iraqis expected the coalition to attack directly into Kuwait, moving up the Wadi al-Bātin, where the Saudi, Kuwaiti, and Iraqi borders converge (*see* **Wadi al-Bātin**). The assault by the 1st Marine Expeditionary Force and the Arab Joint Forces Command against entrenched Iraqi fortifications along the Kuwait border was primarily a massive diversion (*see* **Battle for Kuwait**). Though it ultimately proved overwhelmingly successful and led to the liberation of Kuwait City, the Marines' primary objective was to divert the Iraqi high command's attention from the main allied assault, in which armored and airborne divisions crossed into Iraq hundreds of miles to the west and then swung right, executing a powerful, unexpected "left hook" into the western flank of the Republican Guard in northern Kuwait (*see* **Battle Against the Republican Guard**).

The surprise flanking attack was made possible when the U.S. 18th Airborne Corps, the French 6th Light Armored Division, the heavily armored U.S. 7th Corps, and the British 1st Armoured Division secretly shifted hundreds of miles to the west during the first weeks of the air campaign (see **Operation Hail Mary**). Air strikes that grounded the Iraqi Air Force kept the Iraqis from detecting the massive movement of troops, tanks, and equipment.

Schwarzkopf took additional steps to maintain the secret. He restricted bombing operations against Iraqi ground forces in the west, because he feared such bombings might signal to the Iraqi command that the coalition planned to strike there. For the same reason, he limited special forces operations in the area. Furthermore, to convince the Iraqis that the coalition forces were still positioned south of Kuwait, he ordered the creation of a network of phony camps at the Saudi-Kuwaiti border. For instance, Forward Operation Base (FOB) Weasel was established to give the impression that the headquarters of the 18th Airborne Corps was about 30 miles west of the Kuwaiti bootheel—the point about 50 miles inland where the border line suddenly turns from horizontal to diagonal. In fact, the 18th Airborne Corps had relocated about 200 miles farther west.

Manned by a few dozen soldiers, FOB Weasel employed simulated radio traffic that was designed to emulate normal communications within the corps. A computer controlled the transmissions, most of which were scrambled as in normal wartime operating conditions. A deception platoon moved throughout the sector at night broadcasting tape recordings of tanks and trucks repositioning. The platoon would also spew smoke from generators to indicate the presence of vehicular activity. Moreover, the Americans created depots filled with dummy tanks, helicopters, Humvees, and fuel drums, so Iraqi reconnaissance teams would report the presence of a large armored force. Heat strips powered by generators emitted the same infrared frequencies as M-1A1 tanks.

In addition to these elaborate deceptions, the allies executed several feints to convince the Iraqis that the main attack would come up the Wadi al-Bātin. In the month preceding the ground war, the U.S. Army 1st Cavalry Division launched several limited operations near Wadi al-Bātin to simulate the kind of probes that would normally precede a full-scale attack (see **Ruqi Pocket**). Among those deceptive feints was Operation Berm Buster. On the night of February 15, army engineers blew a hole in the Smugglers' Berm separating Saudi Arabia and Iraq to convince the Iraqis that the allies were opening up an invasion route. A psychological unit provided taped recordings of tracked vehicles to enhance the deception, while an army unit passed through the breech made by the engineers and established security on the Iraqi side of the berm. They later withdrew back to their defensive positions in Saudi Arabia. Artillery barrages to soften the Iraqi defensive fortifications also contributed to the illusion of an imminent invasion.

Moreover, Schwarzkopf issued public statements reminding the world, including the Iraqis, of a planned amphibious assault on the Kuwaiti shore. Though Schwarzkopf had decided in early February not to go ahead with the landing, code-named Desert Saber, because it would incur too many casualties, do too much damage to Kuwaiti property, and delay the commencement of the ground war, he ordered several practice assaults in order to convince the Iraqis that an amphibious attack was coming. On the evening before the ground offensive began, Navy SEALs in fast patrol boats simulated an attack at Mīnā Saʿūd to convince Iraqi defenders that an amphibious attack against the Kuwaiti coastline had begun. The SEALs swam in close to shore, stringing a line of buoys used to mark amphibious landing zones and planting plastic explosives which detonated after they returned to their boats, simulating a naval bombardment. The SEALs then raced along the shoreline in their boats, firing at defensive positions with machine guns. Additional feints continued during the first days of the ground war.

The diversions succeeded, as the Iraqis assigned at least three divisions and hundreds of artillery pieces to the Kuwaiti coast in expectation of an assault that never came (*see* **Amphibious Assault**).

**Desert Shield** *see* **Operation Desert Shield.**

**Desert Storm** *see* **Operation Desert Storm.**

**Diplomacy**—Several diplomatic efforts to resolve the Iraq-Kuwait dispute took place at different times during the crisis: prior to Iraq's invasion of Kuwait, immediately after the invasion, during Operation Desert Shield, during Operation Desert Storm, and after the cease-fire that ended the fighting. However, before the invasion Iraq remained inflexible in its demands upon Kuwait, and afterward the U.S.-led coalition refused to settle for anything less than what the United Nations had demanded: an Iraqi withdrawal from Kuwait, an annulment of its annexation of Kuwait, a return of all foreign hostages, and reparations to Kuwait for damages. The United Nations imposed a complete economic and military embargo against Iraq on August 6, 1990, in hopes of forcing Iraq to withdraw from Kuwait and negotiate an acceptable settlement, but that did not happen (*see* **Embargo**).

### Diplomacy Prior to Iraq's Invasion of Kuwait

Hussein first denounced Kuwait in late May 1990, and added to his list of charges throughout the summer. However, apart from issuing threats, he never took serious steps toward negotiating a peaceful settlement with Kuwait.

Hussein made his first charges against Kuwait in the emergency summit meeting of the Arab League he hosted in Baghdad beginning May 28, 1990. Ostensibly the meeting was convened to discuss the threat posed by the new influx of Jewish emigres from the Soviet Union to Israel. But in addition to condemning the United States and Israel, Hussein used the occasion to justify his military buildup and assert himself as leader and protector of the Arab community. He also chastised Kuwait for driving down the price of oil and stealing oil from Iraq's Rumaila field at the Kuwaiti border, and he implicitly accused Kuwait of waging economic warfare against Iraq: "War takes place sometimes through soldiers…. At other times, war is launched through economic means. To those who do not mean to wage war against Iraq, I say that this is a kind of war against Iraq."

On July 16, Hussein formalized his accusations against Kuwait when he published an open letter to the Arab League charging Kuwait with stealing $2.4 billion of oil from the Rumaila field and acting aggressively against Iraq by advancing its border and customs posts northward. Around this time Hussein also ordered Lieutenant General Ayad Futayih al-Rawi, commander of the elite Republican Guard, to prepare his troops to invade Kuwait. (*See* **Causes of the War**.)

Kuwait responded by placing its military on high alert. It accused Iraq of trying to intimidate it and other countries into canceling Iraq's $40 billion in war debts, something Kuwait refused to do. Kuwait, whose 17,000-member armed services were dwarfed by Hussein's million-man army, further rejected the charge of aggression, pointing out that the changes in its border posts were made solely for administrative purposes and to expedite the flow of traffic, and that the posts remained within Kuwait's territory. It also rejected the accusation that it had been stealing from the Rumaila oil field, though this presumably could have been a matter for negotiation had serious talks taken place.

Two days after Hussein published his open letter to the Arab League, Iraq accused Kuwait of preparing grounds for justifying foreign intervention into a dispute among Arabs, and the Iraqi spokesman chastised Kuwait for abandoning the option of having the Arab community resolve their dispute. Diplomats throughout the Arab League understood this statement to signal that Hussein was seeking an Arab-negotiated settlement, and leaders from Saudi Arabia, Egypt, and other Arab nations began exploring a diplomatic solution. In particular, Egypt's President Hosni Mubarak conferred in Cairo with the foreign ministers of various Arab nations and then flew to the capitals of Iraq, Kuwait, and Saudi Arabia to speak with the leaders of those countries. According to Mubarak, Hussein said he had no intention of attacking Kuwait while talks were ongoing. Mubarak and the U.S. State Department understood Hussein's statement to mean that he would seek a negotiated settlement, but his promise proved instead to mean that he would refrain from attacking until he abruptly canceled negotiations.

On July 19, the improved prospects for a diplomatic resolution led Kuwait to cancel its military alert. But by July 22, Iraq had massed some 30,000 troops at the Kuwaiti border, and Kuwait reinstated the alert.

Prior to the invasion Hussein revived historical claims that Kuwait, in fact, had always belonged to Iraq. He also maintained that he was liberating the Kuwaiti people from an unpopular ruling family. However, these claims were apparently made more to pressure Kuwait into concessions and or justify war than to place substantive issues on the bargaining table. Certainly Hussein's assertion that the invasion was at the behest of the Kuwaiti people was belied by his inability to find a single Kuwaiti citizen to head the new government imposed in occupied Kuwait, by his annexation of Kuwait less than a week after the invasion, and by the officially sanctioned plundering of Kuwaiti industry and other assets.

Hussein's charge that Kuwait was waging economic warfare against Iraq had greater credibility and was the focus of the limited diplomatic efforts that did take place. Hussein needed to increase the price of oil in order to finance reconstruction following his eight-year war with Iran, to underwrite his military buildup, and to improve Iraq's economy. But in 1990, Kuwait and the United Arab Emirates were greatly exceeding the quotas allowed by the Organization of Petroleum Exporting Countries (OPEC) and were thereby keeping oil prices down. The deflated prices were wrecking havoc on Iraq's economy and thereby threatening Hussein's hold on power, and they were one of the primary reasons for the state of belligerence between the two countries.

Hussein later complained to the U.S. ambassador that Kuwait was threatening the jobs of Iraqi workers, and "harming even the milk our children drink and the pension of the widow who lost a husband during the war and the pensions of the orphans who lost their parents."

Moreover, Hussein insisted that Kuwait, Saudi Arabia, and the other Persian Gulf states should forgive the billions of dollars worth of loans they made to Iraq during its war with Iran, since Iraq had fought the war to protect them from Iranian-sponsored, revolutionary Islamic fundamentalism that threatened to depose them.

Saudi Arabia agreed to cancel Iraq's approximately $22 billion debt, but Kuwait refused to write off the $13 billion Iraq owed it. Hussein's claim that he had fought the Gulf War on their behalf was only partly true. In 1980, Hussein initiated the eight-year Gulf War with Iran primarily to gain control of the Shaṭṭ al-'Arab waterway and Iran's oil-rich, predominantly Arabic border province of Khūzestān (called *Arabistan* in Iraq). These were Iraqi objectives, not those of the Persian Gulf states. At the same time, however, the war also impeded the spread of Ayatollah Khomeini's Islamic fundamentalist revolution and did, thereby, advance the interests of the Persian Gulf states. The leaders of Saudi Arabia, Kuwait, and the other Gulf states feared Iran's fundamentalist Shī'ite revolution because, like Hussein, they were Sunni Muslims governing either majority or large minority Shī'ite populations (*see* **Iran-Iraq Gulf War**).

On July 25, Hussein conferred with the U.S. ambassador, April Glaspie, both to learn how the United States would respond to an Iraqi military action and to threaten against U.S. interference. According to a transcript of the meeting that Iraq later leaked to the press, Hussein warned that the United States should not become involved in his dispute with Kuwait, and Glaspie replied, "We have no opinion on Arab-Arab conflicts, like your border disagreement with Kuwait." Hussein also threatened that if the United States were to intervene, "Yours is a society which cannot accept 10,000 dead in one battle … we know that you can harm us although we do not threaten you. But we can harm you. Everyone can cause harm according to their ability and their size." Hussein also suggested the possibility of terrorist attacks within the United States: "We cannot come all the way to you in the United States but individual Arabs may reach you."

Hussein later softened his tone, declaring that he did not count the United States among Iraq's enemies, but he reiterated that the United States must "not push us to consider war as the only solution to live proudly and to provide our people with a good living. We know that the United States has nuclear weapons but we are determined either to live as proud men or we will die."

Hussein also complained about a recent Voice of America (V.O.A.) editorial that applauded the populist overthrow of Communist tyrannies in Poland, Romania, and Czechoslovakia and implicitly advocated the removal of other governments where secret police forces still prevailed: China, North Korea, Iran, Iraq, Syria, Libya, Cuba, and Albania. The Iraqi foreign minister, Tariq Aziz, had already objected to the editorial from what Iraq considered an official news forum for the U.S. government, since the V.O.A. is government sponsored. In particular, Aziz protested that the broadcast was a "flagrant interference in the internal affairs of Iraq." Glaspie apologized to Aziz, assuring him "It is absolutely not United States policy to question the legitimacy of the government of Iraq."

Glaspie added that "President Bush is an intelligent man. He is not going to declare an economic war against Iraq." She complimented Hussein's "extraordinary efforts" to rebuild Iraq and expressed Bush's desire for improved relations with Iraq. She reiterated that "I was in the American embassy in Kuwait during the late sixties. The instruction we had during this period was that we should express no opinion on this issue and that the issue is not associated with America. [Secretary of State] James Baker has directed our official spokesman to emphasize this instruction."

The conversation concluded with Hussein announcing that he had agreed to meet in Saudi Arabia for a meeting with high-level representatives from Kuwait. Glaspie congratulated Hussein on that development.

After the August 2 invasion, Iraqis leaked the transcript of this meeting to the press. They argued that when Ambassador Glaspie assured Hussein that the United States took no position on the border dispute, she was implying that the United States tacitly approved an Iraqi military action. The State Department maintained that Glaspie's statements were never intended as assertions of U.S. policy and that they did not, in any case, imply approval of Iraqi aggression. More likely, they probably were intended to signal that the United States would tolerate a limited incursion into northern Kuwait and readjustment of the border at the Rumaila oil field and the offshore islands of Būbiyān and Warbah. But Glaspie's comments were probably never meant to imply that the United States would approve the conquest and annexation of the entire country, although some commentators have speculated that they may have been intended to hoodwink Hussein into invading Kuwait in order to give the United States justification for waging a war to destroy him.

Four days before the invasion, diplomats seemingly resolved one of the most important issues—the matter of oil prices and production levels. On July 27 and 28, OPEC ministers met in Geneva, Switzerland, and in deference to Iraqi demands for a 38.8 percent price increase, agreed to raise prices by 16.5 percent and impose more stringent quotas on oil production. They also agreed to strictly enforce the production quotas that Kuwait had been flaunting. The resolution of the oil issues by OPEC, in which Saudi Arabia and Kuwait made major concessions to Iraq, generated new optimism that the dispute between Iraq and Kuwait would be resolved peacefully.

But Iraq continued to mass troops along the border and postponed until August 1 the high-level talks with Kuwaiti officials that Saudi Arabia's King Fahd hosted at his summer palace in Jiddah near the Red Sea. The purpose of those talks was to peacefully resolve the outstanding differences between the two countries, but the Iraqis apparently did not come to bargain in good faith. Kuwait agreed to negotiate Iraq's war debt but refused to concede any territory or admit that it should pay for oil it had taken from the Rumaila field. After making intractable demands that the Kuwaitis would not accept, the Iraqi representatives walked out of the meeting in protest. The invasion commenced in the early hours of the next day.

It does not appear that Hussein ever seriously sought a diplomatic solution to the Kuwaiti dispute. After all, by the time of the invasion he had achieved substantial gains on the two most important issues: he won major concessions at the OPEC meeting in Geneva, and Kuwait had indicated willingness to negotiate the war debts. Certainly, he showed no patience in resolving the outstanding differences. The time frame between Hussein's first formal charges against Kuwait and the invasion was little more than two weeks. Significantly, Hussein ordered preparations for the invasion at the same time he first accused Kuwait in his open letter to the Arab League, and he began massing troops at the border shortly thereafter. At the very least, by massing over 100,000 troops at the border he was forcing the Kuwaitis literally to negotiate under the gun.

But Hussein had much to gain by defeating Kuwait on the battlefield instead of the bargaining table. Annexing Kuwait could solve his economic woes in a single stroke and take him one step closer toward his ultimate goal of creating a Pan-Arab state under his leadership. Iraq would simultaneously gain vast oil reserves, acquire a major port on the Persian Gulf, and eliminate the $13 billion debt it owed Kuwait. In addition, Hussein would acquire tremendous political leverage over the industrial world, and the Iraqis could establish themselves as major players in world politics.

Iraq exported about one billion barrels of oil annually. If it annexed Kuwait, it could control another billion barrels a year. And if it went on to conquer Saudi Arabia, it would add another 1.3 billion barrels. The combined oil resources in Iraq, Kuwait, and Saudi Arabia accounted for about one-third of the world's annual oil production and 55–60 percent of the world's proven oil reserves.

In a high-tech world increasingly dependent on ample and affordable energy, Hussein's control over such a large portion of the worldwide oil supply would have given him considerable leverage over the industrial nations. This, in turn, would have enabled him to pursue his goal of making Iraq a power comparable to or greater than the United States and the Western European countries. For this reason Hussein had also been developing chemical and biological weapons and trying to build a nuclear bomb. Such military and economic power might have enabled him to curtail U.S. support for Israel and create the new Babylon he often spoke of: an anti-Western, anti–Israeli, Iraqi-led, Pan-Arabic superpower.

### Diplomacy Immediately After the Invasion

The conquest of Kuwait met immediate worldwide condemnation. On August 2, the same day as the invasion, the U.N. Security Council passed Resolution 660, calling for Iraq's complete withdrawal. The following day Hussein announced that he was merely teaching Kuwait a lesson and would withdraw his troops within two days, so long as it did not appear that he was being coerced. They would then resolve their differences in negotiations at a summit meeting with Arab heads of state. Of course, even if Saddam Hussein had been sincere, Kuwait would have been negotiating under the gun, with the Republican Guard still massed at its border and its own armed forces destroyed.

But Kuwait rejected the Arab summit proposal and turned to the United Nations instead. Also on August 3, the Arab League also voted to condemn Iraq, and Hussein retracted his promise to withdraw his troops and negotiate a settlement. After his efforts to install a puppet government in Kuwait failed, he annexed the country as Iraq's nineteenth province on August 8.

On August 6, the Security Council reiterated its call for an Iraqi withdrawal and imposed a total military and economic embargo upon Iraq. On August 9, it rejected the annexation of Kuwait; on August 25, it authorized member states to enforce the embargo by stopping ships in the Persian Gulf and inspecting their cargos. The embargo became the basis for the U.N. diplomatic strategy against Hussein.

Unlike many Cold War–era embargoes, which were only partially enforced, this one enjoyed the support of most of the world's governments, and it threatened to wreak havoc on the Iraqi economy and eventually to provoke popular discontent that might lead to a weakening of Hussein's rule. Thus, the basic U.N. diplomatic strategy was to enforce the embargo until the deteriorating situation in Iraq compelled Hussein to withdraw from Kuwait. Most officials estimated that the economic sanctions would require one to two years to succeed (see **Embargo, United Nations**).

Despite support for that strategy from Secretary of State James Baker, Chairman of the Joint Chiefs of Staff Colin Powell, and others within the administration, President Bush believed the time frame was too long to be politically viable. Thus he tried the embargo for only five months before resorting to force. During that period he also brought the coalition force to the full strength necessary to fight an offensive war, both as a means of putting more pressure on Hussein to leave Kuwait immediately and as a prelude to waging war if he did not (see **Offensive War Preparations for Liberating Kuwait**).

### Diplomacy During Operation Desert Shield (August 6, 1990–January 16, 1991)

As allied troops amassed in Saudi Arabia to defend that country from a possible Iraqi invasion, three major avenues of diplomacy developed. First, Iraq improved its relations with Iran and retained the support of Jordan. Second, Hussein alternatively threatened and made proposals to the international community. Meanwhile, the Bush administration assembled the international alliance against Iraq (see **Coalition**).

Although the Gulf War cease-fire took effect in 1988, Iran and Iraq did not reach a peace agreement until August 15, 1990—two weeks after the invasion of Kuwait. Anxious to eliminate an enemy on his eastern flank while preparing to defend against the international forces to the south, Hussein conceded everything Iran had been asking for since the cease-fire began. He agreed to withdraw from all occupied Iranian territory, exchange prisoners immediately, and establish the middle of the Shatt al-'Arab as the border between the countries.

Iran accepted the offer, and Iraq began dismantling its field fortifications there on August 18, and on August 19, Iraqi ground troops began withdrawing from Iranian territory they had occupied since the conclusion of the Gulf War. Iran and Iraq resumed diplomatic relations on September 10 (see **Iran-Iraq Gulf War**).

By removing his troops and opening the border with Iran, Hussein both reinforced his armies in the south and created a long frontier where outside goods could be smuggled into Iraq, despite the U.N. embargo. Within two days of resolving the war with Iran, the Iraqis began moving 24 divisions—some 300,000 troops—from the Iran border to Kuwait and the Saudi border areas. (Later, during Desert Storm, Iraqi planes fled to Iran to avoid destruction by coalition air forces.)

Hussein's first proposal to the international community came on August 12, 1990, when he offered to link an Iraqi withdrawal from Kuwaiti-occupied territory to the withdrawal of all foreign forces from all occupied territory in the Middle East. The plan was probably more a gesture to win support among Arabs than a serious attempt at settling the Kuwait crisis through diplomacy. It would have required Israeli troops to leave the West Bank of the Jordan River and other lands seized after the 1967 Six-Day War, and it would have compelled Syria, Hussein's other enemy in the region, to withdraw from Lebanon. Moreover, the plan would have insisted that the Israelis and Syrians remove their troops before the Iraqis had to withdraw theirs.

If accepted, the plan would have been an enormous diplomatic victory for Hussein. For one thing, he would weaken and humiliate his Syrian rival, General Hafez al-Assad. But much more importantly, as the liberator of the Israeli occupied territories, Hussein would enormously enhance his prestige among Arabs and take a large step towards his ultimate goal of establishing himself as the leader of a Pan-Arab nation. Some members of the international community whose relations with Israel were either cool or outright hostile—such as France and the Soviet Union—appeared willing to link the resolution of the Kuwaiti situation to the larger regional issues in the Middle East.

But Bush predictably rejected Hussein's proposal. The reasons he gave were that it imposed preconditions and did not comply with the U.N. resolutions calling for Iraq's immediate evacuation from Kuwait, the release of foreign hostages, and annulment of Iraq's annexation of Kuwait. In addition to these stated reasons, the United States and Britain no doubt opposed the plan for precisely the same reason Hussein offered it. They were unwilling to concede such a major political victory to Hussein or to undermine Israel's position within the region. Hussein probably knew Bush would reject his peace proposal. But merely by making the offer he recast Israel and Syria, instead of Iraq, as the oppressors. Though not successful in the United States or Britain, this strategy of vilifying Israel won Hussein further support among Arabs—especially Palestinians and Jordanians. Later, even after he lost the war, Hussein retained much of his popularity among Arabs from the lower economic classes because he had attacked Israel, demanded Palestinian rights, and stood up to the Western powers and survived.

At a conference on Palestine in Geneva on August 29, PLO Chairman Yasser Arafat proposed a peace plan for the Gulf calling for a U.N. peacekeeping force to replace U.S. and coalition troops and for the lifting of all sanctions against Iraq. The plan was to be part of a broader solution to all outstanding problems in the Middle East, but it found no support in the West.

Hussein also tried to enhance his negotiating position against the allies by taking hostage thousands of Westerners who had been caught in Kuwait during the invasion. Some 4,000 British and 2,500 U.S. citizens were in Kuwait alone, as well as Soviet advisers and Europeans from other countries trapped in both Kuwait and Iraq. On August 18, the Security Council demanded the release of the foreign captives. In return, Hussein tried to use them for political gain. He declared that he would free them only if the United States promised to remove its forces from the Persian Gulf region. Subsequently, Hussein announced that the male hostages would be used as human shields to be placed at sensitive targets in Iraq, so any allied air attack against those targets would also kill the hostages (*see* **Hostages**).

At the same time, Hussein selectively freed the hostages from individual countries to try to create rifts within the coalition. For example, he rewarded Austria, Sweden, Finland, and Portugal for not participating in Operation Desert Shield by releasing some of their hostages. Periodically, he released additional hostages following personal appeals from high-profile world leaders. And following a secret meeting between Iraq's Foreign Minister Tariq Aziz and France's former foreign minister, Claude Cheysson, Iraq agreed to unconditionally release the approximately 300 French hostages it held. Even so, he retained thousands of Westerners as potential human shields, especially British and American citizens.

On August 24, Hussein ordered the U.S. embassy in Kuwait closed, and approximately 100 U.S. officials, Marine guards, and civilians were taken to Baghdad. The hostage-taking of personnel from the American embassy pointedly evoked memories from November 1979, when Islamic fundamentalists humiliated the United States and politically incapacitated President Carter by taking hostage 66 members of the U.S. embassy in Iran. Hussein no doubt hoped that President Bush would prove as ineffectual in dealing with this new hostage situation as Carter was during the Iranian crisis and as President Reagan had been in his efforts to free American hostages in Lebanon in the 1980s. (Reagan's failed efforts, in which then–Vice President Bush played a significant role, culminated in the Iran-Contra fiasco that politically debilitated Reagan during his second term.)

Perhaps in response to world opinion, Hussein released all female and child hostages on August 29. However, he retained the male hostages and continued to use them as human shields around sensitive target areas until he finally released them on December 6, a week after the United Nations voted to authorize war if Iraq did not withdraw from Kuwait by January 15.

Though the captives afforded Hussein some leverage over the allies, by taking diplomats and private citizens hostage he flouted international law and further turned world opinion against Iraq. He also greatly intensified his confrontation with the allies. And although the hostages may have given him an additional card to play in negotiations, the hostage-taking also increased the likelihood that negotiations would fail and that the issues would be resolved by war. Taking hostages also made Hussein vulnerable to the rhetorical attacks the West had initiated against him, in which he was being depicted as a ruthless, barbaric, dictator—another Hitler who could not and must not be appeased.

Hussein offered few diplomatic initiatives to peacefully resolve the situation. Aziz met on August 31 with U.N. Secretary General Perez de Cuellar, but they failed to make any progress towards an acceptable resolution. Meanwhile Bush steadfastly maintained his uncompromising position that any peace agreement would have to satisfy the conditions of all of the Security Council's resolutions. Consequently, the Americans and the British consistently insisted as preconditions

for negotiations that any agreement would require Iraq to withdraw from Kuwait, annul its annexation of Kuwait, return all foreign hostages, and repay Kuwait for damages. They also refused to link the Kuwait situation to other issues in the Middle East.

During the autumn, France submitted a few unsuccessful proposals. President François Mitterrand offered a four-step plan before the United Nations on September 24, calling for free elections in Kuwait, the restoration of Kuwait's sovereignty, and an international conference on all major issues in the Middle East. In general, French diplomats were more willing than their British and American counterparts to appease Hussein's demand that an Iraqi withdrawal from Kuwait be linked to the Israeli occupation of the West Bank and the Syrian occupation of Lebanon. In early October, France proposed a peace initiative linking the Palestinian issue to the occupation of Kuwait, but the Saudis rejected it. And on January 10, Defense Minister Jean-Pierre Chevenement called for the United States to agree to an international peace conference on the Middle East as a face-saving mechanism to enable Hussein to withdraw from Kuwait before the January 15 deadline. However, the United States rejected that proposal as well.

On November 30, the day after the Security Council authorized war against Iraq, Bush made his first offer to conduct direct negotiations. But on December 19, the meeting between Aziz and Secretary of State Baker was postponed indefinitely because the two sides could not agree on a reciprocal visit by Baker to Iraq. Baker and Aziz finally met in Geneva on January 9, but the meeting yielded no results, nor had anyone seriously expected it to. The conference did, however, enable Bush to claim his administration had taken every extra step possible to negotiate an acceptable resolution, only to receive "a total stiff-arm" for its efforts.

On January 12, Congress voted that if Iraq did not withdraw from Kuwait by the United Nation's January 15 deadline, President Bush was authorized to use military force to remove Iraq from Kuwait. On January 15, France submitted a last-minute proposal that the U.N. Security Council hold an international conference on the Palestinian situation, if Iraq would agreed to withdraw from Kuwait. However, the United States and Great Britain strongly opposed the proposal, and it failed.

### Diplomacy During Operation Desert Storm
### (January 17—February 28)

No direct talks took place between the adversaries during Operation Desert Storm. However, during the initial air campaign the Soviets increased their efforts to find a diplomatic solution. Soviet envoy Yevgeni Primakov met with Hussein and Aziz in Baghdad on February 12 and submitted a plan in which the Iraqis would unconditionally withdraw from Kuwait.

On February 18, Aziz came to Moscow, where Gorbachev told him that if Iraq began to withdraw immediately, the survival of Hussein's regime would be guaranteed, no reparations would be required, and other regional disputes—including those with Israel—would eventually be addressed. After insisting that Iraq act without delay, Gorbachev cabled a summary of his plan to Bush, who had not been previously consulted. The next day Iraq announced it would comply with the plan, but Bush rejected the proposal and insisted that any new plan require Iraq to evacuate Kuwait within four days (instead of the six weeks Gorbachev had offered), release all POWs immediately, and disclose the location of all land and water mines.

Aziz returned to Moscow on February 21 and informed Gorbachev that Iraq was willing to announce an unconditional withdrawal from Kuwait and immediately return the POWs, but it would not accept the four-day timetable for withdrawal. Moreover, Aziz insisted that all U.N. resolutions be nullified once the withdrawal was two-thirds complete. On the early morning of February 22 (local time), Gorbachev and Aziz announced an eight-point peace agreement.

Gorbachev phoned Bush, who received the call shortly before 7 P.M. EST, on Thursday,

February 21. Gorbachev described the plan to Bush, Baker, and Deputy National Security Adviser Robert Gates. Bush told Gorbachev that the proposal still did not comply with all of the allies' conditions, and it failed to satisfy all of the requirements of the U.N. resolutions.

The proposal would have annulled the U.N. condemnation of Iraq's annexation of Kuwait and eliminated the demand that Iraq repay Kuwait for the damage done by its occupation, by the oil it spilled into the Persian Gulf, and by the fires it set in the Kuwaiti oil fields. The Soviet proposal also failed to secure freedom for the thousands of Kuwaiti citizens being held captive in Iraq or to fulfill another major U.N. objective—to create conditions for peace and security within the region. Gorbachev promised to continue negotiations.

Later that night Colin Powell, the chairman of the Joint Chiefs of Staff, brought up the possibility of setting a deadline for an Iraqi withdrawal. He suggested that Bush tell Gorbachev, "If you get them out by noon Saturday [February 23], Mr. Gorbachev, you get the Nobel Prize. If you don't, we kick Hussein's ass." If Hussein did agree to the deadline, Iraq would have four days to complete the withdrawal. (This was later expanded to a week at the behest of France and Great Britain. In either case, the short timetable would require Hussein to abandon most of his heavy combat equipment and stocks of ammunition.) Once Hussein agreed to withdraw, bombing attacks would be suspended for two hours to give the Iraqis time to begin their retreat. Then, as long as the withdrawal continued, the bombing raids would remain suspended. In addition, Iraq would be required to abandon Kuwait City immediately, release all POWs within two days, withdraw from all of its defensive positions along the Iraqi-Saudi border and the islands in the Persian Gulf, and reveal the locations of all minefields.

France's President Mitterrand requested that Hussein be given at least 72 hours to announce a withdrawal, but as he and Bush were speaking on the phone, Bush received satellite photos showing that the Iraqis had ignited hundreds more oil wells in Kuwait, and Bush used this information to defend his short deadline. And on Friday morning, February 22, he replied publicly to Gorbachev's proposal by demanding that Hussein announce a withdrawal by noon Saturday. Hussein did not comply, and the Soviet effort to mediate a settlement failed.

### The Diplomacy of the Cease-fire (March 3, 1991)

The only fruitful negotiations during the crisis came three days after Bush terminated the hostilities. The allies had devastated the Iraqi regular army and the elite Republican Guard that was loyal to Hussein personally and was a major foundation of his power base. According to his head of intelligence, Major General Wafic al-Sammarai, Hussein was depressed by his massive defeat and afraid that the allies would continue into Baghdad to depose him. He thus was anxious to quickly set terms for a formal cease-fire in order to halt the allies' advance and avoid giving them a pretext to destroy his remaining forces.

On March 2, the Security Council passed Resolution 686, setting down the conditions for a cease-fire. It demanded that Iraq cease all hostile military action and renounce any aggressive intentions toward Kuwait, disclose the locations of mines, return all POWs and other detainees (including the Kuwaiti citizens taken hostage after August 2), rescind its annexation of Kuwait, return Kuwaiti property, and accept responsibility for damages it inflicted. The Security Council later required Iraq to allow the United Nations to monitor its nuclear, biological, and chemical weapons facilities (see Cease-fire).

On March 3, the top Iraqi generals met with General Schwarzkopf and other top allied officers in a tent at Safwān airfield in southern Iraq, where the Iraqis accepted the U.N. terms for a permanent cease-fire and the generals worked out the details of its implementation.

On April 6, the Iraqi government formally accepted the U.N. cease-fire that officially concluded the war.

In a 1995 interview on *Frontline*, Schwarzkopf maintained that prior to the meeting in Safwān he received no instructions at all from the State Department. Consequently, he and his staff formulated the details of the cease-fire and submitted them for approval. Following the cessation of hostilities on February 28, Schwarzkopf had issued a standing order to shoot down any Iraqi warplanes flying over Iraq. But at the meeting he acceded to a request to permit helicopter flights, after the Iraqis pointed out how the allies had destroyed most of their strategic bridges and roads. They claimed helicopters were necessary to transport government officials who were trying to implement the terms of the cease-fire. However, soon afterward the Iraqi Army employed its helicopters to suppress the Shī'ite uprising in southern Iraq near Basra and the Kurdish rebellion in northern Iraq that had sprung up during Desert Storm. The United States, Great Britain, and the other coalition allies declined to intervene because they had no U.N. mandate to do so, and the rebellions were internal Iraqi affairs (see **Kurdish Rebellion, Shī'ite Rebellion**).

Former British Prime Minister Margaret Thatcher, one of the architects of the war, has maintained that the allies could have brought down Hussein by humiliating him before the Iraqi people and the Arab world. Thatcher stepped down in November 1990, and thus was not in power when the war concluded. She stated on *Frontline* that the Iraqis should have been made to surrender all of their military equipment to further weaken Hussein and demonstrate to the Iraqi people that he was responsible for the defeat. Likewise, Bush's national security adviser, Brent Scowcroft, believes that the coalition should have required Hussein to personally negotiate the cease-fire so he would be publicly viewed as a loser. Instead, the Iraqi population identified the defeat with the generals who signed the armistice.

**Egypt**—Egypt played an important role in the Persian Gulf War, both militarily and politically. During the summer of 1990, prior to Iraq's invasion of Kuwait, Egyptian President Hosni Mubarak tried to negotiate a peaceful settlement between the two countries. Days before the invasion he met with Hussein, who assured him that Iraq would not attack while negotiations were ongoing. Mubarak reported this to the United States, and he was taken by surprise when Iraq abruptly called off negotiations on August 1 and then invaded the following day. Subsequently, Mubarak led the elements within the Arab League that condemned the invasion on August 4, and he played a central role in winning the league's support of the U.N. sanctions against Iraq. Prior to the outbreak of war, he tried to convince Hussein to withdraw, declaring that the Iraqi leader was living in a fantasy world if he believed he could defeat the United States and its allies. But Mubarak was condemned and ridiculed for his efforts.

Egypt was the first Arab country to support the United States in its defense of Saudi Arabia in Operation Desert Shield. Mubarak met with Defense Secretary Cheney on August 7, the day after Cheney gained permission to base U.S. troops in Saudi Arabia. Mubarak agreed to allow U.S. warships to pass through Egypt's Suez Canal, and later that day a carrier battle group headed by the USS *Dwight D. Eisenhower* passed from the Mediterranean Sea through the Suez Canal into the Red Sea. Access to the Suez Canal played an important role throughout the crisis. The first Egyptian troops arrived in Saudi Arabia on August 11. In return for Egypt's support during the crisis, the United States forgave approximately $6.7 billion of Egypt's debt.

Mubarak took an early position that Egyptian troops would not invade Iraq, and he reiterated it at the beginning of Operation Desert Storm. But he committed an armored army corps of some 40,000 troops to the defense of Saudi Arabia, and ultimately these were used in the liberation of Kuwait, where they served as part of the Arab Joint Forces Command—North that flanked the U.S. 1st and 2nd Marine Divisions on their west (*see* **Joint Forces Command**). On the first day of

battle the Egyptian troops advanced through Iraqi fire trenches and mine fields towards Kuwait City. Three days later, on February 27, they achieved their main objective by taking the 'Alī as-Salīm airfield outside of Kuwait City. Egyptian forces captured some 1,500 Iraqi troops during Operation Desert Storm. Twelve Egyptian soldiers were killed in action and ninety-five were wounded.

Though the Egyptian government firmly backed the coalition, much of the general population supported Hussein, and massive demonstrations against the war took place during the ground offensive, especially among students at Cairo University. Hussein encouraged the protests in hopes that popular discontent with Egypt's participation in the coalition would either force the government to pull out or lead to a revolution that would depose the government. But neither scenario materialized.

**82nd Airborne Division** *see* **Battle Against the Republican Guard, U.S. Army 18th Airborne Corps.**

**Embargo**—On August 6, 1990, the U.N. Security Council passed Resolution 661 to pressure Iraq to withdraw from Kuwait, which it had conquered four days earlier. The resolution imposed a complete military and economic embargo against Iraq and occupied Kuwait, except for food, medical supplies, and other goods intended for humanitarian purposes. It froze all Kuwaiti and Iraqi assets, except for payments made exclusively for medical or humanitarian purposes. The resolution also established a committee of the Security Council, composed of all the members of the council, to oversee the implementation of the embargo. The intention of the embargo was to cause sufficient hardship within Iraq to force Hussein to withdraw his troops from Kuwait. Most experts agreed that the economic sanctions would require one to two years to achieve that goal, if they could achieve it at all (*see* **Diplomacy**).

On August 25, Resolution 665 authorized member states to enforce the embargo against

**Sailor testing his weapon while on patrol enforcing the embargo (photograph courtesy of the Department of Defense).**

Iraq by stopping ships in the Persian Gulf and inspecting and verifying their cargos. On September 25, Resolution 670 extended the embargo to air shipments and flights into and out of occupied Kuwait and Iraq. Resolution 666 (September 13) called for close monitoring of the human deprivation in Iraq and Kuwait caused by the embargo, especially in terms of the availability of food, and it called upon the Secretary General to use his good offices to facilitate the delivery and distribution of food to Kuwait and Iraq through the Red Cross and or other appropriate humanitarian agencies (*see* **United Nations**).

Ships from several coalition countries were very successful in enforcing the embargo by stopping vessels in the Persian Gulf to ensure they were not carrying cargo from or bound for Iraq. Great Britain and the United States were especially active in this area, though ships from several other countries also participated. On September 14, British, Dutch, French, and Italian officials designated areas in the Persian Gulf and Strait of Hormuz that their navies would patrol. The nations of the Gulf Coop-

eration Council likewise played a significant role in enforcing the embargo (*see* **Gulf Cooperation Council**). Though not part of the coalition, the Soviet Union also contributed four vessels. Beginning on August 16, 1990, coalition ships intercepted some 7,673 merchant ships in the Persian Gulf, north Arabian Sea, the Red Sea, and the Gulf of Aden and boarded 964 of them. Fifty-one ships were turned back for trying to violate the embargo, and 11 warning shots were fired. There was no disabling fire (*see* **Naval Action**). In compliance with the U.N. resolutions, Jordan closed its Red Sea port of Aqaba to Iraqi shipping, and at considerable cost to itself, Turkey shut off the flow of Iraqi oil through the pipelines that ran through the country to the port of Ceyhan.

The allies were not as successful in stopping the flow of goods overland, into and out of Iraq. Jordan supported Iraq during the crisis and did not strictly enforce the embargo on goods proceeding across its border (*see* **Jordan**). Iran was the other weak link in enforcing the embargo. On August 15, Hussein proposed to make peace with Iran by granting everything it demanded at the close of their Gulf War in 1988. Iran accepted Hussein's proposal, and the two countries resumed diplomatic relations on September 10. By removing his troops and opening the border with Iran, Hussein both reinforced his armies in the south and created a long frontier where outside goods could be smuggled into Iraq, despite the U.N. embargo (*see* **Iran**). Hussein also offered free oil to any nation that would ship goods to Iraq, but he had no good way to deliver it, and the offer never achieved anything.

Despite the porous borders in Jordan and Iran, the embargo was highly effective in limiting Iraq's access to consumer goods and military equipment and in decimating Iraq's economy by taking away its ability to export oil. Nonetheless, President Bush quickly decided that waiting one to two years for sanctions to force Hussein from Kuwait would be too long; it would be politically difficult to sustain the coalition for that period or to maintain popular support within the United States for deploying over 200,000 troops in the Middle East. He also feared that the cost of waiting up to two years would be prohibitive, that Hussein would gain too much prestige in the Middle East if he succeeded in engaging the United States in a prolonged standoff, and that Kuwait would suffer too much damage at Iraq's hand while waiting for sanctions to work. Therefore, although such key advisers as Secretary of State James Baker and Chairman of the Joint Chiefs of Staff Colin Powell and such powerful members of Congress as Sam Nunn (D–Georgia), the chair of the Senate Armed Services Committee, favored giving sanctions more time to have an effect, Bush opted to give Hussein an ultimatum to withdraw by January 15 or face a war (*see* **Offensive War Preparations for Liberating Kuwait**).

After the war, experts estimated that, at the time of its invasion of Kuwait, Iraq was within one year of being able to assemble a crude nuclear device. Thus, had the coalition waited one to two years for sanctions to succeed, there is a strong possibility Iraq would have been able to produce a nuclear device during that period.

After the success of Operation Desert Storm, Resolution 687 retained the arms embargo against Iraq and tied the lifting of the economic embargo to Iraq's compliance with the resolution, which set the terms for the formal cessation of hostilities. Among those terms was a stipulation that Iraq agree to on-site inspections of its nuclear, chemical, and biological warfare facilities and permit future ongoing monitoring and verification of its compliance. Because Iraq failed to comply fully with this provision, the embargo has remained in place since August 6, 1990 (*see* **United Nations**). However, in August 1991, Resolution 706 permitted Iraq to sell $1.6 billion of oil over a six month period, with the provision that the revenue be used to compensate war victims, pay for U.N. weapons monitoring in Iraq, and provide food and supplies for the Iraqi populace. In December 1996, the Security Council voted to allow Iraq to sell $2 billion in oil over a 180-day period. The next day, in a public ceremony, Hussein opened the valve on the pipeline to resume the flow of oil to Turkey's Yumurtalik terminal on the Mediterranean.

**Environmental Warfare**—During the Persian Gulf War, Hussein ordered over 500 Kuwaiti oil wells set on fire and millions of barrels of oil from offshore tankers and Kuwait's Sea Island oil tanker terminal spilled into the Persian Gulf. The threat of igniting the wells and destroying a large portion of the world's oil reserves was one of the ways Hussein had tried to intimidate the allies before the war began. Likewise, he raised the spectre of polluting the Persian Gulf presumably to turn Western environmentalists against the war. Spite and vindictiveness appear to have been his primary motivations after the war began.

The first fires were set on January 22, 1991, five days after the commencement of the air campaign against Iraq. Hundreds more fires were ignited in the days just prior to the start of the ground offensive on February 24. In fact, U.S. President Bush was on the telephone with French President Mitterrand on February 22, when he received satellite photos showing the new rash of oil fires. Bush insisted that they proved the urgency of beginning the ground offensive immediately, despite Mitterrand's objections that the allies should give Hussein more time to withdraw from Kuwait. Later that morning Bush announced that Hussein "has now launched a scorched-earth policy against Kuwait, anticipating perhaps that he now will be forced to leave. He is wantonly setting fires to and destroying the oil wells, the oil tanks, the export terminals, and other installations of that small country. Indeed, they are destroying the entire oil-production system of Kuwait." Bush then issued an ultimatum for Hussein to begin withdrawing from Kuwait by noon the next day or face a ground war.

The main purpose of the fires was to ruin the future economy of Kuwait and turn the emirate into an environmental wasteland. The heavy smoke from the fires offered the additional advantage of screening Iraqi troops from allied air reconnaissance and allowed greater freedom of movement for supply convoys and redeploying troops who were targets of allied bombing raids. On the other hand, during the ground war the limited visibility near the burning oil fields proved a greater liability to Iraqi tanks, which relied on visual gunsights. U.S. tanks, by contrast, were equipped with thermal gunsights that enabled them to spot and identify Iraqi armored vehicles not visible through the smoke.

After the war, despite fears that it might require two to three years to put out all of the fires, expert firefighters extinguished the blazes in about eight months. The emir of Kuwait doused the last one in a special ceremony on November 6, 1991. The Kuwait Oil Company estimated that nearly three billion barrels of oil had been lost—approximately three percent of Kuwait's total reserves. Five million barrels of oil (260 million gallons) burned each day from 508 wells, producing one-half million tons of thick black smoke. The Gulf Emergency Response Team estimated that the fires

emitted 100,000 tons of particulate, 50,000 tons of sulfur, and 850,000 tons of carbon dioxide daily. Though predictions of a "nuclear winter" caused by the soot or "greenhouse warming" did not prove accurate, a veil of oil smoke covered an area twice the size of Alaska, and black snow was reported as far away as the Himalaya Mountains in India.

The oil spill was intended to damage and pollute Saudi Arabia's desalinization plants that furnished fresh water for much of the kingdom. If Iraq could pollute the allies' supply of fresh water, it would severely limit their capacity to wage war. However, the desalinization plants were not damaged. Another possible motive may have been to impede an amphibious landing on the Kuwaiti beaches.

The oil was first released into the Persian Gulf on January 25, eight days after the beginning of the air campaign. Within two days the oil slick was 35 miles long and 10 miles wide. Military analysts consulted with petroleum experts in the United States and engineers who had escaped from Kuwait. They developed a plan to bomb the two pumphouses containing the valves that controlled the spill. However, the plan was delayed after the Kuwaiti government-in-exile expressed its fears that a bombing raid would destroy the oil field in the process of stemming the spill. After a day's delay to ensure that the oil field would not be destroyed, General Schwarzkopf personally approved the attack, and on January 27, four U.S. Air Force jets passed through heavy antiaircraft defenses and employed laser-guided bombs to destroy the manifolds. By then the spill was estimated to contain seven to nine million barrels of oil (460 million gallons). After the air raid, several workers from the Kuwait Oil Company reportedly took advantage of the confusion from the raids to sneak into the tank farms and close the valves manually. Though some controversy remains over whether the bombing raid or the Kuwaiti oil workers were most responsible, the result was that the flow of petroleum was stopped at its source, although the oil remaining in the 13-mile pipeline leading to the sea terminal continued to drain into the Gulf.

Further pollution occurred as oil continued to spill onto the ground in the oil fields. The pollution of the Gulf and its shores was considerable: at least 30,000 sea birds died, and the damage to fish and the seabed was extensive.

**1st Armored Division** *see* **Battle Against the Republican Guard, U.S. Army 7th Corps.**

**1st Brigade of the Army 2nd Armored Division (Tiger Brigade)** *see* **Battle for Kuwait, U.S. 1st Marine Expeditionary Force.**

**1st Cavalry Division** *see* **Battle Against the Republican Guard, U.S. Army 7th Corps.**

**1st Infantry Division (Mechanized)** *see* **Battle Against the Republican Guard, U.S. Army 7th Corps.**

**1st Marine Division** *see* **Battle for Kuwait, U.S. 1st Marine Expeditionary Force.**

**1st Marine Expeditionary Force** *see* **Battle for Kuwait, U.S. 1st Marine Expeditionary Force.**

**Forward Operating Base Cobra**—During Operation Hail Mary the U.S. Army's 101st Airborne Division secretly deployed in the desert some 250 miles inland along the Saudi border opposite Iraq (*see* **Operation Hail Mary**). On February 23, the day prior to the start of the ground offensive, the 101st initiated deep reconnaissance into Iraq, and on the day of the attack its helicopters moved supplies and troops 93 miles north into Iraq, where the 101st's 1st Brigade established Forward Operating Base (FOB) Cobra, a refueling and rearming base for helicopters and air-assault troops advancing deeper into Iraq, toward the Euphrates River.

The initial attack had been scheduled for 5 A.M. but was delayed for two hours by bad weather. Caught by surprise, the Iraqi forces in the area were scattered and disorganized, and most quickly surrendered. Over 300 helicopter sorties then ferried troops, ammuni-

tion, supplies, refueling equipment, and building materials in the largest heliborne operation in military history.

On the next day, the 82nd Airborne Division arrived at FOB Cobra. Meanwhile, the 3rd Brigade of the 101st Airborne Division departed from its base in Saudi Arabia to conduct the deepest air assault in military history. One thousand paratroopers airlifted to a point some 150 miles north in the Euphrates Valley, between the towns of As-Samāwah and An-Nāṣirīyah. The gunships that ferried them immediately turned around and headed for necessary refueling at FOB Cobra. After proceeding an additional 20 miles on foot through heavy rain and mud, the 3rd Brigade captured Highway 8, a key Iraqi supply route, and established defensive positions. An anticipated Iraqi counterattack never materialized. The 101st Airborne Division thus cut off the Republican Guard from reinforcements and supplies while protecting the flank of the 24th Mechanized Infantry Division and the 7th Corps, which were beginning to engage Republican Guard armored units. On February 27, the 101st's 2nd Brigade and the 12th Combat Aviation Brigade airlifted over 90 miles east from FOB Cobra to establish a new forward operating base, FOB Viper. Apache helicopter battalions then proceeded to attack the causeways leading from Basra from the north. Meanwhile, the French 6th Light Armored Division, having completed its capture of As-Salmān airfield, moved to a position just west of the 101st's base on Highway 8 (*see* **As-Salmān Airfield**).

By the end of the third day of battle the 101st Airborne Division had deployed 380,000 gallons of fuel at FOB Cobra, allowing the 18th Airborne Corps to move infantry and helicopters north to quickly reinforce their positions along Highway 8 (*see* **Battle Against the Republican Guard**).

**France**—An important member of the coalition against Iraq, France made substantial political and military contributions to the effort to remove Iraqi troops from Kuwait. As a permanent member of the Security Council,

France's support of U.N. resolutions condemning Iraq was crucial. Immediately after the Iraqi invasion of Kuwait, France, who had been a major arms supplier of Iraq in the 1980s, called for an immediate Iraqi withdrawal, the freezing of Iraqi and Kuwaiti assets, and a moratorium on weapons deliveries to Iraq. On August 9, 1990, France announced it would send combat planes to the region to assist in the defense of Saudi Arabia, and on September 15, it agreed to send 4,000 troops to Saudi Arabia. French light armor and helicopters were by then already deployed. Eventually France committed some 14,000 troops, 40 fighter planes, and 14 ships.

During the Iran-Iraq Gulf War in the 1980s, France cultivated relations with Iraq, and the French government transferred weapons valued at $15–$17 billion, including advanced Etendard jets armed with Exocet missiles, and French civilian corporations sold Hussein an additional $5 billion in munitions (*see* **Iran-Iraq Gulf War**). Iraq employed some of these weapons against French and other coalition forces during the Persian Gulf War. Moreover, French Mirage jets were used sparingly during the air campaign because they could not be easily distinguished from the Mirage jets in the Iraqi Air Force.

Prior to the outbreak of war, French diplomats actively sought a diplomatic solution to the crisis. President François Mitterrand pursued unsuccessful proposals in the United Nations, including one made on September 24 in which he presented a four-stage plan calling for free elections in Kuwait, the restoration of Kuwait's sovereignty, and an international conference on all major issues in the Middle East. In general, French diplomats were more willing than their British and American counterparts to appease Hussein's demand that an Iraqi withdrawal from Kuwait be linked to the resolution of all military occupations within the Middle East (i.e., the Israeli occupation of the West Bank and the Syrian occupation of Lebanon). In early October, France proposed a peace initiative linking the Palestinian issue to the occupation of Kuwait, but the Saudis rejected it. On January 10, Defense Minister Jean-Pierre Chevenement called for the United States to agree to an international peace conference on the Middle East as a face-saving mechanism to enable Hussein to withdraw from Kuwait before the January 15, 1991, deadline. However, the United States rejected that proposal as well. A last-minute proposal before the U.N. Security Council on January 15 also failed (*see* **Diplomacy**).

Chevenement, a founding member of the French-Iraqi Friendship Society, resisted going to war against Iraq, but Mitterrand ultimately overruled him, and Chevenement resigned shortly after the air campaign began. On February 21, Mitterrand urged President Bush to give Hussein more time to withdraw before initiating the ground war, but while they were speaking on the phone Bush received satellite photos showing that the Iraqis had set fire to hundreds more oil wells, and he insisted on giving Hussein no more than 24 hours to begin withdrawing.

French planes participated in the air campaign, and the 6th Light Armored Division (the Daguet Division) anchored the allies' western flank during the ground war, in which they captured the strategic As-Salmān airfield. Elements of the U.S. 82nd Airborne Division fell under French operational command, which in turn was under the operational command of the U.S. Army 18th Airborne Corps. Two French soldiers were killed in Operation Desert Storm and 38 were wounded (*see* **As-Salmān Airfield, French 6th Light Armored Division, Battle Against the Republican Guard**).

**Franks, Frederick M., Jr.**—Lieutenant General Franks commanded the U.S. Army 7th Corps during the Persian Gulf War (*see* **U.S. Army 7th Corps**). Born in 1936, he graduated from West Point in 1959, after which he received his commission as a second lieutenant of armor. He received his Master of Arts degree in 1966 and a Master of Philosophy degree in 1975, both from Columbia University. From 1969 to 1970 Franks served with the 11th Armored Cavalry Regiment in Vietnam, where he lost a leg in a land mine explosion. In 1989,

**Frederick Franks (photograph courtesy of the Department of Defense).**

he assumed command of the 7th Corps, a heavily armored unit based in Germany. Its primary assignment was to protect against a Soviet invasion of Western Europe.

The 7th Corps provided the main muscle of the allied attack during the ground war. Along with the attached British 1st Armoured Division, the 7th Corps secretly moved some 300 miles to the northwest during Operation Hail Mary to positions 150 miles inland at the Saudi-Iraqi border. There, they set up the surprise flanking attack that ultimately trapped and destroyed most of the Republican Guard (*see* **Operation Hail Mary**). General Schwarzkopf criticized Franks during the first days of the ground attack for not engaging the enemy quickly enough. Fearing that the Republican Guard might escape, Schwarzkopf at one point threatened to replace Franks with someone who would move more swiftly. Franks, on the other hand, wanted to proceed more slowly so he could concentrate his troops and strike with full force, instead of with sparring jabs. Franks was also concerned that his troops might accidentally shoot each other in the rain and sandstorms, and he wanted to maintain resupply lines for fuel.

Ultimately, the 7th Corps did engage the Republican Guard with its full force and inflicted extremely heavy casualties. According to the Defense Department report to Congress, "VII Corps achieved devastating results against the best units of the Iraqi Army. VII Corps reported destroying more than a dozen Iraqi divisions; an estimated 1,300 tanks, 1,200 fighting vehicles and APCs [armored personnel carriers], 285 artillery pieces, and 100 air defense systems; and captured nearly 22,000 enemy soldiers." After the war Franks was promoted to four-star general and chosen to command the army's Training and Doctrine Command at Fort Monroe, Virginia (*see* **Battle Against the Republican Guard**).

**French 6th Light Armored Division**—The French 6th Light Armored Division, nicknamed the Daguet Division, occupied the allies' western flank during Operation Desert Storm. *Daguet* is French for "young deer." Originally assigned to serve with the Saudi-led Joint Forces Command, the Daguet Division was reassigned to anchor down the westernmost flank on January 20, 1991, after its commander, Brigadier General Jean-Charles Mouscardes, privately expressed his suspicions of Saudi military incompetence to General Schwarzkopf, the commander-in-chief of most of the allied forces in the Kuwaiti theater of operations. Mouscardes fell ill in early February and was replaced on February 9 by Brigadier General Bernard Janvier, who commanded the division during the ground offensive.

The Daguet Division included two regiments of the French Foreign Legion, the 1st Hussars Airborne Regiment, the 4th Dragoon Regiment, a commando unit, and engineer and artillery units. During Operation Desert Storm the Daguet Division also had under its operational control the 2nd Brigade of the U.S. 82nd Airborne Division. In turn, the Daguet Division itself served under the operational control of the U.S. 18th Airborne Corps commanded by General Gary Luck. Two French soldiers were killed while clearing mines in As-Salmān after the airfield was captured. Thirty-eight soldiers were wounded in action (*see* **As-Salmān Airfield, Battle Against the Republican Guard**).

**Friendly Fire**—One of the great concerns of coalition military leaders was to avoid deaths by friendly fire—accidental fire from one's own troops. Of the 146 U.S. soldiers killed in action, 35 were killed by friendly fire, and 78 of the 467 wounded were victims of friendly fire. In addition, U.S. friendly fire inadvertently killed 9 British soldiers and wounded 11. One of the worst friendly fire incidents occurred at the battle of Khafji, in January 1991, when 11 Marines were killed by their own troops: seven by a U.S. Maverick missile that struck a Marine Light Attack Vehicle and four more when an American TOW missile struck a vehicle. Four Saudis were also killed during the battle when a mixed flight of U.S. and Qatari planes accidentally bombed their position (*see* **Khafji**).

In another friendly fire incident, on February 17, U.S. Army Apache helicopters mistakenly fired on two American armored personnel carriers from the 1st Infantry Division located in a forward position three miles inside Iraq. Two soldiers were killed and six more were wounded. Nine British soldiers died when U.S. warplanes mistook their armored vehicles for Iraqi vehicles on February 26; eleven more were wounded. The British liaison officer claimed that he had radioed instructions designating a target that was far from the point of attack, but the pilots maintained that they did not receive any instructions from him, other than assurances that there were "no friendlies within ten kilometers."

To avoid friendly fire incidents, coalition vehicles were painted with an inverted "V" for easy identification, but this was not as successful as hoped for. The planes that destroyed the British armored vehicles, for instance, had searched for the sign but were unable to see it. It was later discovered that the "V" was not visible above 5,000 feet, and efforts were increased after the war to devise new ways for avoiding friendly fire casualties.

**Great Britain**—Great Britain was among the earliest members of the coalition and one of the strongest supporters of the efforts against Iraq. Britain had a long history of involvement in the Middle East, especially with the Persian Gulf States. Following World War I, the region was divided into British and French mandates, and in 1922 British High Commissioner Percy Cox redrew the boundaries of Saudi Arabia, Iraq, and Kuwait to resolve their border disputes. The arbitrariness of his action later contributed to the continued disputes among those countries. In 1961, Britain landed troops to defend Kuwait against Iraq after Kuwait was established as an independent and sovereign nation over Iraqi objections. When Britain evacuated its bases east of the Suez Canal in 1971, it created a power vacuum that greatly influenced subsequent developments in the Middle East (*see* **Causes of the War**).

As a permanent member of the U.N. Security Council, Britain supported all of the resolutions against Iraq following the invasion of Kuwait. These included the August 2, 1990, resolution that condemned the Iraqi invasion of Kuwait earlier that same day, the August 6 decision to impose economic sanctions against Iraq, and the November 29 authorization to wage war if Iraq did not remove its troops by January 15, 1991 (*see* **United Nations**). Prime Minister Margaret Thatcher took an especially hard line against Hussein from the very beginning, and her meeting with President Bush on August 2 played a significant role in Bush's decision to take a firm stand. On August 9, three days after the commencement of Operation Desert Shield, Thatcher agreed to deploy the Royal Air Force in the Persian Gulf. Parliament affirmed its support on September 6, when it met in emergency session and strongly endorsed the Desert Shield operations. On October 1, Thatcher insisted on American television that Iraq must pay compensation for the damages inflicted on Kuwait. That same day British Defense Secretary Tom King announced that Sir Peter de la Billiere would be the British forces commander for Operation Granby—the British name for operations Desert Shield and Desert Storm. (Billiere later described his experiences in *Storm Command: A Personal Account of the Gulf War*.) Air Chief Marshall Sir Patrick Hine was the overall commander of British forces in the Gulf War. Though ultimately under British control, British forces served under the tactical command of the U.S. Central Command led by General Schwarzkopf (*see* **U.S. Central Command**).

Many of the foreign nationals held hostage in Kuwait and Iraq after the invasion were British. During the invasion on August 2, 1990, Iraqi forces took control of the airport and captured the passengers and crew of a British Airways plane that had just landed in Kuwait City for a stopover en route to India. The men from that flight were subsequently taken to Baghdad to be among the first "human shields" whom Hussein deployed around sensitive targets inside Iraq. Some 4,000 British citizens were held hostage in Kuwait alone. On October 22, former British Prime Minister Edward Heath created a controversy when he met with Hussein in Baghdad and returned with 33 of the hostages. Hussein finally announced that he would release all of the hostages on December 6, and the last left Baghdad about one week later (*see* **Hostages**).

After the United States and Saudi Arabia, Great Britain made the most substantial contribution to the coalition effort: some 5,500 military personnel were deployed in the region. Britain furnished 26 ships, and the Royal Navy played a major role in enforcing the embargo during Operation Desert Shield and destroying the Iraqi fleet during Operation Desert Storm. The Royal Navy was also very active in clearing mines (*see* **Naval Action**). The first British planes arrived in Saudi Arabia on August 12. During the war the Royal Air Force deployed 158 aircraft and helicopters and flew numerous sorties. Seven aircraft were lost: six to ground fire while on low-level bombing raids, and one to a noncombat flying accident.

The British 1st Armoured Division made a significant contribution to the ground war. On February 25, it breached the Iraqi defensive lines and attacked the Iraqi 52nd Armored Division, destroying 40 tanks and capturing approximately 4,000 prisoners. On February 27, it overran three Iraqi infantry divisions (*see* **Battle Against the Republican Guard**).

Twenty-five British troops died during the war, including nine who were killed by friendly fire when an American plane mistook a British vehicle for an Iraqi vehicle (*see* **Friendly Fire**). Forty-five troops were wounded, and eleven were taken prisoner.

**Gulf Cooperation Council** (GCC) — The GCC is comprised of the six oil producing states along the Persian Gulf: Saudi Arabia, Kuwait, the United Arab Emirates, Oman, Qatar, and Bahrain. These supported Iraq during its Gulf War with Iran, and Iraq owed war debts to several member states, notably Saudi Arabia and Kuwait. Iraq's demand for forgiveness of these debts was a major reason behind its invasion of Kuwait. Also, before the invasion Kuwait and the United Arab Emirates were exceeding their OPEC oil production quotas, thereby driving down the price of oil and hurting Iraq's economy.

The GCC countries helped enforce the embargo against Iraq (*see* **Embargo**). They also contributed to Operation Desert Shield and Operation Desert Storm by sending troops and making their airfields and port facilities available to the United States and other coalition members (*see* **Naval Action**). The troops were part of the Arab Joint Forces Command–East which drove up the coast to Kuwait City during the ground war (*see* **Joint Forces Command**, **Saudi Arabia**, **United Arab Emirates**, **Oman**, **Qatar**, and **Bahrain**).

**Gulf War Syndrome** — After the war, tens of thousands of veterans — as many as one-third of those who served in the Middle East — began experiencing such symptoms as fatigue, nausea, depression, severe headaches, memory loss, disturbed sleep, dizziness, sexual impotence, muscle pain and muscle fatigue, rashes, confusion, and inability to concentrate. Since Iraq had known chemical warfare capabilities that Hussein had threatened to employ against the allies, many veterans believed they were exposed to nerve gas or some other toxic gas and that their symptoms stemmed from this exposure. However, finding no evidence that Iraq used its chemical arsenal during the war, the Pentagon denied for several years that any U.S. personnel had been exposed. But in June 1996, the Pentagon acknowledged that as many as 20,000 soldiers might have been exposed to low levels of toxic chemicals shortly after the war, when army engineers demolished an Iraqi ammunition bunker containing cyclosarin, a deadly nerve gas, near the village of Khamisiyah. The engineers had been told that the depot contained no chemical weapons. However, in April 1997, the CIA acknowledged that it mishandled the information about Khamisiyah, stating that it had found evidence of chemical weapons activity there as early as 1984 but failed to communicate it (see **Chemical Warfare**).

Though critical of the Pentagon's desultory initial efforts to study Gulf War Syndrome or its possible connection to chemical exposure, the Presidential Advisory Committee on Gulf War Veterans' Illness reported on January 7, 1997, that it could find no evidence to suggest that exposure to toxic chemicals was responsible for the symptoms afflicting the veterans, since the symptoms typically related to nerve gas differ significantly from those the veterans reported. But the committee called for further research into the effects of exposure to low levels of nerve gas, because most of what is known about the effects of nerve gas comes from incidents where people have been exposed to large doses of the chemicals.

The committee was unable to identify any other specific cause of Gulf War Syndrome. However, it did suggest that the extreme stress caused by wartime conditions might be a major factor. Other government studies, including a study of 4,000 Iowa veterans funded by the Centers for Disease Control and Prevention, have also pointed to stress as a probable cause. Both the director of the Centers for Disease Control and the presidential committee, as well as other independent researchers, noted that veterans of other wars have experienced similar symptoms. Soldiers re-

turning from World War II, and even veterans of the Civil War, complained of the same ailments. Two studies published in the *New England Journal of Medicine* in November 1996 concluded that the death rates from disease and the rates of hospitalization for Persian Gulf War veterans did not vary significantly from those experienced by veterans of other wars. In a 1996 article published in the *Annals of Internal Medicine*, Navy doctors Kenneth Hyams and Stephen Wignall and Dr. Robert Roswell from the Department of Veterans Affairs suggested, "If an analogous illness affected veterans of other wars, its cause may be related to common wartime experience rather than to a unique event during the Persian Gulf War." Elaine Larson, dean of Georgetown University's School of Nursing and a member of the presidential committee, acknowledged that Gulf War syndrome is "a serious problem, and it is something related to the biologic aspects of stress."

However, the day after the committee released its report, researchers at the University of Texas suggested another possible cause: organophosphate-induced delayed polyneuropathy. This rare disorder is caused by exposure to chemicals that block an enzyme necessary for the proper functioning of the human nervous system. The scientists have hypothesized that this neuropathy may have been caused by flea collars and insecticides used to ward off pervasive desert sand fleas, or by the anti–nerve gas pills taken to protect against chemical attacks. Although the pet collars usually carry warnings that they are harmful to humans, many soldiers resorted to wearing them because the flea problem in the desert was so severe. Some soldiers who were otherwise exposed to insecticides also showed symptoms.

In the Texas study of 249 veterans, those with the most severe ailments had taken PB, an anti–nerve gas tablet, and they may have been exposed to an Iraqi chemical attack. Especially at risk were personnel who had taken PB and been exposed to the stinging mist from a mysterious explosion above Khafji, Saudi Arabia, on January 20, 1991. The Pentagon claims the mist was rocket propellant from an Iraqi Scud missile that detonated in the air. But some veterans who were present believe the mist, which burned the skin and triggered chemical alarms, was an Iraqi gas attack. Moreover, veterans who took PB and also used a concentrated insect repellent appeared to be at higher risk for Gulf War Syndrome. Prior to the study, other veterans had already complained of ailments they believed were side effects from PB.

Though suggestive, the Texas study was inconclusive, and the possibility that Gulf War Syndrome may be organophosphate-induced polyneuropathy remains a hypothesis. Moreover, even if the hypothesis proves correct, the study does not provide doctors with a way to diagnose or cure the disorder.

The Pentagon's initial reluctance to take the veterans' complaints seriously or to answer honestly all their queries contributed to the growing cynicism about the U.S. government, which had been increasing since the Vietnam War. Many veterans believed they were being lied to and/or their complaints were not being taken seriously. The revelation, five years after the fact, that the government suppressed the incident at Khamisiyah underscored their suspicions. Moreover, the presidential committee, which applauded other aspects of the government's response, supported the veterans' contention, complaining that the Pentagon's early investigations of exposure to toxic chemicals have "lacked vigor, fallen short on investigative grounds, and stretched credibility." The committee held these shortcomings responsible for the "mistrust that now surrounds every aspect of Gulf War veterans' illness."

The outrage over the mistreatment of suffering war veterans has both political and social ramifications. President Clinton's appointment of the committee in 1996 was both a sincere effort to discover the real facts surrounding the Gulf War Syndrome and a way to demonstrate his concern for the veterans' plight during an election year. But even the suggestion that stress might be the underlying cause has prompted political responses, since some veterans feel the "catch-all" term trivializes and dismisses their symptoms. Consequently, both Democratic and Republican politicians were quick to criticize the suggestion that stress is the main culprit. On the other hand, some veterans groups welcomed the conclusion that severe stress can result in real disabilities. According to Matt Puglisi of the American Legion, stress is "not something that only weaklings or those who can't handle difficult situations fall victim to."

Though politically divisive, the Gulf War Syndrome has also brought many veterans together, creating a sense of community among the afflicted. The Internet has provided a vehicle for veterans to share descriptions of their symptoms and to come together for mutual support and communal action. The *Gulf War Veteran Resource Pages* at http://www.gulfweb.org on the World Wide Web is an especially useful starting point.

**Highway to Hell (Highway of Death)** — Iraqi troops fleeing Kuwait City on the night of February 25 and on February 26 and 27 were trapped in a seven-mile stretch where they were subject to repeated air attacks. Officially known as the 6th Ring Road, or the Jahrah Road, it was dubbed the "Highway to Hell" by soldiers who witnessed the carnage. Others called it the "Highway of Death."

Late on the night of February 25, Marine planes supporting the 1st Marine Expedition's advance in Kuwait spotted an Iraqi convoy of about 1,500 vehicles fleeing north towards Basra. The convoy consisted of some 200 tanks, other military vehicles, and cars and trucks stolen from Kuwaiti civilians. In addition to carrying military equipment, the Iraqi vehicles were filled with loot stolen from the stores and homes of Kuwaitis. The bombers immobilized the column by destroying the vehicles at its head and rear, leaving everything in between stationary targets for later bomb runs. The next day the U.S. Army's Tiger Brigade attached to the 2nd Marine Division closed off the road at the Mutlah Ridge police station, just west of Kuwait City. Commanding the high ground overlooking all of the roads leading from the city, the Tiger Brigade added its firepower to the destructive power of the bombers. Many Iraqis abandoned their vehicles and fled into the desert, but many others were trapped and killed. Graphic pictures of the slaughter helped induce President Bush to cease offensive operations at midnight on February 27, EST, as he feared public reaction against the massacre might undermine support for the war (*see* **Battle for Kuwait, U.S. 1st Marine Expeditionary Force**).

**Horner, Charles A.**—Lieutenant General Charles A. Horner was the commander of 9th U.S. Air Force and the Air Force Component of the Central Command (CENTAF) during the Persian Gulf War. He was responsible for approving and implementing the plan used in the air campaign. Born in 1936, Horner graduated from the University of Iowa in 1958, after which he joined the Air Force as a second lieutenant. He served two tours of duty in Vietnam, flying a total of 111 combat missions. Horner assumed command of the 9th Air Force and CENTAF in 1987. During the war he oversaw a coalition fleet of some 2,700 aircraft from 14 separate nations or service components. Prior to the beginning of the ground war they flew nearly 100,000 sorties, of which approximately 60 percent were combat missions.

The air campaign was extremely effective and is credited for much of the success the coalition enjoyed during the war. Though Horner did not get along well with Colonel John A. Warden III, who devised Instant Thunder, the initial plan for the air campaign, Horner retained the basic structure of Instant Thunder as the basis of his strategy, and he placed Warden's deputy, Lieutenant Colonel David A. Deptula, in charge of maintaining the master plan for the strategic campaign. Horner appointed Air Force Brigadier General Buster Glosson in charge of selecting targets (*see* **Air Campaign**).

In 1992, Horner was promoted to four-star general and appointed commander-in-chief of NORAD, commander-in-chief of the U.S. Space Command, and commander of the Air Force Space Command.

**Hostages**—During the invasion of Kuwait on August 2, 1990, Iraqi forces took control of the airport and captured the passengers and crew of a British Airways plane that had just landed in Kuwait City for a stopover en route to India. The men from that flight were subsequently taken to Baghdad to be among the first "human shields" that Hussein deployed around sensitive targets inside Iraq.

Despite initial assurances that foreigners would be well treated, Hussein refused to provide exit visas to several thousand Westerners who happened to be in Kuwait or Iraq when the invasion took place. Some 4,000 British and 3,000 U.S. citizens were in Kuwait alone. An additional 500 Americans were in Iraq at the time of the invasion. Thousands of Soviets and Europeans from other countries were also trapped in both Kuwait and Iraq.

Ignoring the U.N. Security Council's Resolution 664 calling for the hostages' release, Hussein initially called them "guests" and "heroes of peace." But on August 15, he ordered all Westerners to report to three specified hotels. Most reported, but many found secret shelter in the homes of Kuwaitis who risked severe punishment if Iraqi soldiers discovered the fugitives. On August 19, Hussein announced that he would not release the Westerners unless the United States promised to remove its forces from the Persian Gulf region. He insisted that the Security Council fix a timetable and guarantee that the troop withdrawal would not take longer than the troop deployment required in the first place. Moreover, the Iraqi ambassador in Paris and the head of Iraq's National Assembly further warned that the treatment of foreigners would be dictated by how their countries behaved toward Iraq and how scrupulously they enforced the U.N.-approved sanctions against Iraq. Using a carrot-and-stick approach to create rifts within the coalition, Hussein freed some hostages from Austria, Sweden, Finland, and Portugal to reward those countries for not participating in Operation Desert Shield. Plus he periodically released small numbers of additional hostages after meetings with such high-profile world leaders as Austrian Presi-

**Charles Horner (photograph courtesy of the U.S. Air Force).**

dent Kurt Waldheim; former British Prime Minister Edward Heath; former West German Chancellor Willy Brandt; former Danish Prime Minister Anker Jorgensen; former New Zealand Prime Minister David Lange; Jean-Marie Le Pen, the leader of the French National Front; and Edgar Oehler, who headed a Swiss parliamentary delegation. Moreover, following a secret meeting between Iraqi Foreign Minister Tariq Aziz and former French

Foreign Minister Claude Cheysson, Iraq agreed to unconditionally release the approximately 300 French hostages it held. Even so, Iraq retained thousands of Westerners as potential human shields, especially British and Americans.

On August 20, Hussein applied the stick when he ordered many of the foreigners transferred to potential military targets throughout Iraq, where they were used as human shields to preclude allied attacks. The idea was that the United States and its allies would refrain from bombing those targets in order to avoid killing their own citizens.

Three days later Hussein told 15 British hostages during an internationally televised meeting that he sympathized with their situation, but he was detaining them to avoid "the scourge of war" and that would all be "heroes for maintaining peace." He then singled out a 7-year-old boy, Stuart Lockwood, and, patting him on the head, asked the child about his well-being and whether he was receiving his milk. Though Hussein was ostensibly exhibiting his concern for Lockwood and another boy who was present, most viewers throughout the world regarded the broadcast as a thinly veiled threat that Hussein would use these children and the other men and women in the group as human shields if the then-forming coalition were to attack Iraq. However, his attempt to intimidate the Western powers backfired, as world opinion denounced his implied threat against the innocent children.

On August 24, Hussein ordered the U.S. embassy in Kuwait closed, and approximately 100 U.S. officials, Marine guards, and civilians were removed to Baghdad, bringing the total number of American hostages in Iraq to 1,000. The hostage-taking of personnel from the American embassy pointedly evoked memories from November 1979, when Islamic fundamentalists humiliated the United States and politically incapacitated President Carter by taking hostage 66 members of the U.S. embassy in Iran. Hussein no doubt hoped that President Bush would prove as ineffectual in dealing with this new hostage situation as

Carter was during the Iranian crisis and as President Reagan had been in his efforts to free American hostages in Lebanon in the 1980s. Those failed efforts, in which then–Vice President Bush played a significant role, culminated in the Iran-Contra fiasco that politically debilitated Reagan during his second term.

Perhaps in response to world opinion, Hussein released all female and child hostages on August 29. However, he retained the male hostages and continued to use them as human shields around sensitive target areas. The United Nations continued to pressure Iraq to release all of the hostages, and on September 13, Security Council Resolution 666 reiterated Iraq's responsibility for ensuring the well-being of all foreign hostages. Three days later Resolution 667 condemned Iraqi actions against diplomats and again demanded the immediate release of hostages.

Finally, on November 18, perhaps in response to negative world opinion or to the additional 150,000 troops Bush ordered to the Persian Gulf, Hussein announced that Iraq would release the remaining 2,000 Western hostages between Christmas and March 25, "unless something would take place that mars the atmosphere of peace." However, Hussein's offer was not sufficient to preclude the Security Council on November 29 from authorizing war if Iraq did not free the hostages and withdraw from Kuwait by January 15. To back up the threat, the United States called up an additional 115,000 reservists on December 1. A week later, on December 6, Hussein agreed to free the hostages, who departed Baghdad between December 10 and 14.

**Hussein, Saddam**—Chairman of Iraq's Revolutionary Command Council, commander-in-chief of its military, head of the ruling Ba'ath Party, and president of Iraq since 1979, Saddam Hussein initiated the Persian Gulf War when he ordered the Iraqi conquest of Kuwait on August 2, 1990.

Hussein, whose given name means "fighter who stands steadfast," has been likened to both Hitler and Stalin for his willingness to employ violence, terror, secret police, and a personality cult to obtain, sustain, and expand power. He was born to a peasant woman, Subha Tulfah, on April 28, 1937, in the village of al-Ouja. The village is located in northern Iraq near Tikrīt, a farming town 100 miles north of Baghdad on the Tigris river, and most of Hussein's inner circle comes from this region. Though Hussein later had his family tree altered to show that he was a direct descendant of Muhammad, the founder of Islām, the future president of Iraq grew up in poverty. He lived in a shack built of mud bricks in a community of Sunni Muslims that was governed primarily by tribal and family customs. Though Sunnis constitute the majority of Muslims in the Arab world, in Iraq they are heavily outnumbered by members of the Shī'ah sect, the sect that came to power in neighboring Iran in 1979 and that revolted unsuccessfully against Hussein after his defeat in Operation Desert Storm. Hussein's father probably died before he was born. After his mother remarried, his stepfather frequently beat him, and Hussein was shunned and abused by others in the community. Hussein's only friend was his cousin, Adnan Khairallah, whose father, Khairallah Tulfah, essentially adopted and raised him and gave him his first gun at the age of 10. After Hussein came to power, Adnan became Iraq's defense minister and his father was appointed governor of Baghdad. Hussein married Adnan's sister, Sajida, in 1963, and Adnan later died in a suspicious helicopter accident that occurred after he vehemently objected on his sister's behalf to Hussein's intimate relationship with a mistress.

Hussein's community was poor, violent, and corrupt, and his family had a reputation for violence. It voiced commonly held prejudices against Iranians and Jews, prejudices that Hussein soon acquired and later acted upon when he waged the Gulf War that killed hundreds of thousands of Iranians, and when he ordered Scud missiles launched against Israeli cities during the Persian Gulf War.* Hussein grew to be a rugged and tough young man with a reputation as a murderer and thug. He killed his first man, one of Khairallah's rivals, when he was a teenager.

In his late teens Hussein moved to Baghdad and enrolled in law school. He also became attracted to the Ba'ath Socialist Party, which he joined in 1957, the year before a military coup deposed Iraq's king and brought the Communist-backed General Kassem to power. When Kassem's Free Officers Movement overthrew the monarchy and established the Republic of Iraq in July 1958, the Ba'ath Party initially supported it (see **Ba'ath Party**). But as the Communists gained influence within the new regime, the Ba'athists felt they were being squeezed out of power, and they came to oppose Kassem. In 1959, Fuad al-Rikabi, the founder of the Iraqi branch of the Ba'ath Party, organized an assassination plot against Kassem, and Hussein was selected and trained to be one of the assassins. The plan did not enjoy the approval of the entire party leadership, but after Kassem sat idly on July 14, while Communist street fighters massacred Ba'athists in the northern town of Kirkūk, Rikabi decided to implement it.

The plan involved blocking the path of Kassem's car as it drove through a narrow street in Baghdad. Then armed assassins were to open fire on the stationary automobile. However, according to one version of the story, the driver of the car that was to block the street mislaid his keys. When Kassem's car arrived unimpeded, the gunmen opened fire on the moving vehicle, but their gunfire did more damage to themselves than to Kassem. They succeeded only in wounding the president and killing his driver. (According to one account, Hussein was responsible for those casualties.) On the other hand, one of the gunmen was killed by a bullet fired by another assassin across the street. A second assassin was shot in the chest, and Hussein suffered a superficial leg wound. After fleeing to a safe

*In 1981, during Iraq's Gulf War with Iran (formerly known as Persia), Hussein republished a Ba'athist treatise by Khairallah entitled "Three Whom God Should Not Have Created: Persians, Jews, and Flies."

house where a Ba'athist medical student, Tahsin Moallah, treated his wound, Hussein and two others involved in the plot escaped first to Damascus and then to Egypt.

Several of the other members of the hit squad were captured, and a public trial condemned 78 Ba'athists, including Selim Zibaq, the man who allegedly misplaced his car keys. But their open defiance of the court, despite having been tortured, won admiration for the Ba'ath Party among the masses, and Kassem delayed implementing some of the death sentences in fear that a Pan-Arab uprising might ensue. Other Ba'athist participants in the plot survived government reprisals but later came to unfortunate ends under Hussein's rule. Hussein jailed one of the gunmen, Ahmad al-Azzuz. Another would-be assassin, Abdel-Karim al-Shaikhli, was briefly made foreign minister and then ambassador to the United Nations. However, he was assassinated soon after the start of the Gulf War. Dr. Moallah, whom the Kassem regime imprisoned for six months for treating Hussein and the others, had been one of the founders of Iraq's Ba'ath Party, and he remained one of the more prominent members after the party regained power in 1968. But he fled the country in 1976, a day before an order was issued forbidding his exit, and in 1977 Moallah avoided assassination when he discovered a bomb planted in his car.

The Iraqi Ba'athists split among themselves over the propriety of the assassination attempt, and Rikabi lost the party leadership. Ali Saleh Saadi, a prominent critic of the botched assassination, emerged as the new general secretary after the Ba'ath Party reorganized in 1962. Hussein's antagonism for the left-leaning Saadi presumably dates from the failed assassination.

After coming to power, Hussein embellished his role in the assassination attempt to underscore his dedication, courage, and resourcefulness. He maintained that he removed the bullet himself from his leg, that he traveled to Syria alone, disguised as a bedouin and armed only with a knife, that he lived on a sparse diet of bread and dates, and so on. The mythologizing of the botched assassination was one of the ways Hussein projected himself to the people as a folk hero, and it contributed to his effort to create a personality cult and to establish himself as a new Nebuchadnezzar ready to build a new Babylon.

Hussein stayed in Damascus for a few months before moving to Egypt in February 1960. In 1958 Egypt and Syria had joined to form the United Arab Republic (UAR), which Egypt soon dominated. The UAR, which only lasted until 1961, was ruled by Egypt's Gamal Abdel Nasser, a Pan-Arabist who tolerated the presence in Cairo of a large community of exiled Ba'athists, since they also promoted the Pan-Arab cause. In fact, the Syrian Ba'ath Party had played a large role in creating the UAR. But Nasser's secret police maintained surveillance on the exiled Ba'athists, whom they suspected of having dealings with the CIA. Hussein may have been among those dealing with the agency, as he reportedly visited the U.S. embassy in Cairo on a regular basis. Though ostensibly a student, he spent most of his time and energy establishing himself within the Ba'ath Party and gaining full membership into the ruling inner party. Little else is known about Hussein's exile in Egypt, except that he regarded his time in exile as a prison sentence.

Hussein returned to Baghdad in 1963, shortly after a Ba'athist-led coup overthrew Kassem and seized power in Iraq. The coup, which was widely believed to have CIA backing, was engineered by Ba'athist officers in the military led by Ahmad Hassan al-Bakr and by Saadi, the leftist head of Iraq's reorganized Ba'ath Party who had vehemently criticized the failed attempt to kill Kassem in 1959. Bakr was Hussein's cousin and patron, and Hussein served for a while as his personal bodyguard. Abdel Salem 'Aref was named president of the new regime. Like Bakr, he had been one of the revolutionary military officers who overthrew the monarchy and brought Kassem to power in 1958, but Kassem later purged 'Aref. Saadi became deputy premier, and Bakr served as vice president, though he later emerged as leader of the centrist faction that eventually dominated the government.

The Ba'athist-led *junta* ruled from February through November, 1963. They consolidated power by attacking their rivals. The Ba'ath-controlled Iraqi National Guard, with which Hussein was affiliated, used information furnished by the CIA to track down and arrest hundreds of Communists, other leftists, and other political opponents. Despite assurances to the Americans that the prisoners would receive trials, the captives were routinely tortured and executed. According to eyewitnesses, Hussein actively participated in the torture.

Power struggles also broke out within the party leadership, pitting Saadi and the party's left wing against Bakr and the military. Hussein was elected to the general council of the party's command after he publicly criticized and privately offered to assassinate Saadi. When the internal party conflicts threatened to grow out of control, Michel 'Aflaq, the party founder, came to Baghdad from Damascus to resolve them. 'Aflaq ordered the expulsion and exile of Saadi and his leftist followers, and 'Aflaq subsequently became Hussein's chief mentor and promoter. In response to their expulsion, Saadi's supporters organized massive public demonstrations in the streets.

But the National Guard's brutal excesses and the widespread civil disturbances convinced the Iraqi military officers that the Ba'athists could not govern effectively. Consequently, in November another military coup removed the Ba'athists from power. 'Aref remained head of state, but the Ba'athists were eliminated from all positions of power within the government.

For the next five years the Ba'athists regrouped in secret. During this time Hussein took command of the underground Jihaz Hunain, an intelligence and assassination unit that became his power base within the party and eventually enabled him to dominate it. He also joined a conspiracy to assassinate 'Aref, but it was foiled when a sympathetic military officer was transferred before he could give the would-be assassins access to 'Aref's conference room.

In 1964, Hussein traveled to Syria to convince 'Aflaq to dissolve the Iraqi branch of the party. 'Aflaq obliged and named Hussein head of a caretaker leadership. Hussein held the position alone for three months until Abdel-Karim al-Shaikhli was appointed to share the post.

Iraqi police discovered a second assassination plot against 'Aref in September 1964, and many Ba'athists were arrested, including Hussein. Unlike the others, however, Hussein was released without suffering torture, a fact that led some opponents to charge that he had given up secret information about the party in order to escape punishment.

In 1964, Hussein became the full-time organizer of the civilian portion of the party. In 1966, he made himself deputy secretary by threatening the leadership with weapons. To consolidate his power Hussein created an inner circle of people he could trust and rely on—mostly relatives and party members from Tikrīt, his hometown in northern Iraq.

On July 17, 1968, Bakr, Hussein, other Ba'ath leaders, and senior military officers removed 'Aref in a bloodless coup. Among the military leaders were Abd al-Nayyef, the deputy head of Iraqi intelligence, and Ibrahim al-Daoud, the commander of the Presidential Guard. Nayyef took an anti–Western position and announced his intention of renegotiating contracts between Iraq and the major oil companies. This prompted British agents to contact Ba'athist leaders and indicate their support for a coup that would topple Nayyef and leave the Ba'ath Party in control. Two weeks after the first coup, a second reorganization purged the non–Ba'athists, giving the Ba'ath Party complete power in Iraq. Bakr emerged as president and Hussein as deputy chairman in charge of internal security. According to Herdan al-Tikriti, one of the leaders of the original coup, Hussein personally threatened Nayyef with a pistol and then, after Nayyef begged on his knees for mercy, ordered him into exile. Ten years later Nayyef was assassinated in London on Hussein's orders.

Hussein used his control of the police and other internal security apparati to consolidate his position. In 1973 he charged the head of the secret police with plotting against the government and had him and 36 of his followers executed. This left the Ba'ath Party in complete control of the internal security forces within Iraq. By the middle 1970s, Hussein was commonly recognized to be the most powerful figure within the government. However, he was not officially made chairman of the Revolutionary Command Council and president of Iraq until 1979, when Bakr stepped aside on the dubious grounds of ill health. Bakr was subsequently placed under house arrest.

During the period when Hussein was deputy chairman, Iraq began to develop close relationships with France and the Soviet Union, both of which sold weapons to Iraq. France cultivated business and cultural ties with the Ba'athist regime, and in 1975 Hussein made an official visit to Paris in his only trip ever to a Western country. Three years earlier, Iraq and the Soviet Union signed a 15-year friendship treaty.

In 1974, Hussein took charge of a program to develop chemical and nuclear weapons in order to give Iraq parity with Israel, which was commonly believed to possess nuclear weapons. Hussein also believed that a chemical, biological, and nuclear arsenal would give Iraq greater leverage in its dealings with the West and enable Iraq to assert itself as a major world power. In 1975, in a deal Hussein personally supervised, France agreed to provide Iraq with a nuclear power plant. Although the French maintained that the plant would be used solely for peaceful purposes, Israeli intelligence concluded that the Iraqis planned to use it to build nuclear weapons. Consequently, Israeli planes bombed and destroyed the nuclear plant at Osirak on June 7, 1981. Despite that setback, during the next decade Hussein continued to try to build a chemical, biological, and nuclear arsenal. He employed Dr. Gerald Bull to build a supergun, an artillery piece capable of delivering a nuclear warhead to Israel, and in 1989 and 1990, British and American customs officials caught Iraqi agents trying to smuggle out triggers for nuclear bombs. Iraq's chemical, biological, and nuclear weapons development and production plants later became top-priority targets during the coalition's air campaign. In December 1989, Iraq announced that it had successfully tested a three-stage rocket capable of launching a satellite into space. It also claimed that it had tested two missiles with ranges of 1,200 miles—sufficient to strike Israel.

With Hussein's backing, Iraq sent troops to fight against Israel in the 1973 Yom Kippur War. After the Arab defeat, members of the Organization of Petroleum Exporting Countries (OPEC) almost quadrupled the price of oil and temporarily stopped shipping oil to the United States in order to punish America for supporting Israel and pressure it to change its pro–Israeli Middle Eastern policies. Iraq took even stronger steps by nationalizing the holdings of U.S.-owned corporations, Exxon and Mobil. Its increased income due to higher prices amounted to over $80 billion between 1973 and 1980, doubling the nation's gross national product (GNP) and greatly enriching Hussein and Ba'ath Party members, as well as the government of Iraq. This new wealth enabled Hussein to retain his grip on power more firmly and to purchase advanced weapons systems from the Soviet Union, France, and other sources. Hussein subsequently used his upgraded military against both external and domestic foes. For instance, among the additions to his arsenal were the French Mirage jets and Exocet missiles the Iraqi Air Force used against the coalition in the Persian Gulf War.

During the early 1970s Hussein tried unsuccessfully to suppress an Iranian-backed Kurdish uprising in northern Iraq. Finally, in 1975 he was compelled to negotiate an agreement with the shah of Iran in order to end Iranian support for the rebels. In return, Hussein agreed to accept the middle of the Shaṭṭ al-'Arab as their border, conceding half control of the waterway to Iran. (In 1969, the shah had unilaterally revoked a 1937 treaty giving Iraq control over most of the deep-channel estuary at the border between the two nations.) Hussein desired control of the Shaṭṭ al-'Arab in order to gain shipping access to the

Persian Gulf, and five years later, after the shah was driven from Iran, Hussein revoked the 1975 Algiers Accord and launched the Gulf War. However, the formal peace agreement he signed with Iran in 1990 restored the terms of the accord.

After Hussein officially became head of state, he worked to enhance his personal power and aggrandizement. To protect himself against a military coup, he built up the Republican Guard, made it the best trained and best equipped military unit in the Iraqi Army, and ensured that it would remain loyal to him personally (*see* **Republican Guard**). He also began promoting himself as a leader of all Arabs. He projected himself as the would-be liberator of Palestine (Israel), and after Iran counterattacked and invaded Iraq in the Gulf War, he represented himself as the protector of the Arabs against the Persians. He also articulated a vision of a revived Babylon that would embrace and nurture the Arab world under his leadership. Indeed, he even built reproductions of Babylonian buildings on the archeological site of the ancient city and appeared in posters showing him and Nebuchadnezzar superimposed against Babylon. In a 1979 interview Hussein stated, "The Arab nation is the source of all prophets and the cradle of civilization. And there is no doubt that the oldest civilization in the world is that of Mesopotamia. It is not an Iraqi civilization in isolation from the Arab nation. It is a civilization which developed thanks to the strength and ability of the Iraqi people, coupled with the efforts and heritage of the nation."

Moreover, in spite of Ba'athist secularism and Hussein's suppression of Islamic fundamentalism (he expelled the Ayatollah Khomeini from Iraq in 1978, a year before Khomeini

came to power in Iran), he also drew on Islām as a source of popular support. To gain legitimacy as an Islāmic leader, Hussein made a highly publicized pilgrimage to Mecca and had his family tree forged to show that he was a direct descendant of Muhammad, the founder of Islām.

By establishing links to Islamic heritage and ancient Babylonian glory, Hussein created a Stalin-like personality cult around himself. He drew personal power from the allegiance the Iraqi people gave him. He presented himself as a folk hero: a descendant of Hammurabi, the great law-giver from ancient times; a new Nebuchadnezzar, the Biblical conqueror of Israel;* and a descendant of the Prophet of Islam. Despite his complete lack of military training, Hussein was the commander-in-chief of the Iraqi armed forces, and like Stalin, portraits of him in military uniform lined the streets of cities and towns everywhere. Later, when the war was not going well, he disassociated himself from his military image, and posters and other forms of mass media identified him instead with Hammurabi; Nebuchadnezzar; Sargon the Great, another ancient ruler from Mesopotamia; and Saladin, the Kurdish hero who vanquished Richard the Lionhearted and his Christian Crusaders. Other posters showed Hussein wearing Western business suits and casual wear and the traditional garb of Kurds from the north and of Arabs from southern Iraq.

Like Stalin, Hussein also used terror to acquire and retain power and to gain revenge against his enemies. He maintained a secret police force and an extensive network of informers to instill widespread fear among the people, and he maintained a torture chamber in Baghdad called Qasr al-Nihayyah, the "Palace of the End," where political prisoners

---

*In a 1979 interview Saddam stated:

Nebuchadnezzar stirs in me everything relating to pre–Islamic ancient history. I am reminded that any human ... can act wisely but practically, attain his goals, and become a great man who makes his country into a great state. And what is most important to me about Nebuchadnezzar is the link between the Arabs' abilities and the liberation of Palestine. Nebuchadnezzar was, after all, an Arab from Iraq ... [who] brought the bound Jewish slaves from Palestine. This is why I like to remind the Arabs, Iraqis in particular, of their historical responsibilities. It is a burden that should not stop them from action, but rather spur them into action because of their history.

Source: John Bullock and Harvey Morris, Saddam's War.

were subjected to horrific treatment. A March 1989 report from the human rights group Amnesty International described approximately 30 forms of torture employed in Iraqi prisons, ranging from beatings to gouging out eyes and amputating limbs, noses, ears, breasts, and penises. The report also included accounts from witnesses who described how children were tortured in order to extract confessions from their parents. Among the incidents reported to Amnesty was a description of how, in 1985, "some of the 300 children and youths ... were beaten, whipped, sexually abused and given electric shocks." According to another report by a political prisoner who had been jailed in the Palace of the End, on one occasion Hussein personally lifted a Shī'ite prisoner who had confessed under torture, dropped him into a vat of acid, and watched the body dissolve.*

In addition to terrorizing the civilian population and his political opponents outside the Ba'ath Party, Hussein employed terror within his government, too. Shortly after being named president in 1979, he accused several inner party members of participating in an alleged Syrian-backed plot to overthrow him. Among the accused traitors were some of the party's top figures, including five of the twenty members of the ruling Revolutionary Command Council. Hussein commanded the remaining Ba'ath leaders to accompany him to where the prisoners were detained. Then they were given guns, and he ordered them to join him as he executed the accused traitors. In this way he ensured that the survivors were culpable, too, and were inextricably linked to him. Later, during the Gulf War, Hussein volunteered to step down after a series of setbacks. All of the members of the Revolutionary Command Council opposed the offer but one, the minister of health, Riaz Hussein. Saddam then took Riaz into a separate room and, after a heated argument, shot and killed him with a revolver. According to a version passed along the streets, Saddam had Riaz's dismembered body delivered to his wife in a plastic bag. Re-

gardless of the accuracy of that final detail, the gruesome image of a wife receiving the pieces of her husband's corpse served the purpose of spreading terror.

Many, if not most, of Hussein's associates during his rise to power—his friends as well as his enemies—were eventually purged from leadership positions, and several were jailed, assassinated or forced to flee. Some were assassinated after they fled. Among the close friends and associates whose murder he presumably arranged were Adnan Hussein, a deputy prime minister; Mohamed Ayesh, a top party organizer; and Khalik Samarrai, who recruited the 20-year-old Hussein into the Ba'ath Party.

Hussein also attempted to use a strategy of terror against the coalition before and during Desert Storm by threatening to use chemical weapons against Israeli civilians and allied soldiers, by dumping oil from Kuwaiti oil wells into the Persian Gulf in order to disable the desalination plants that furnished the water supply for most of Saudi Arabia and the coalition armies, by setting fire to the Kuwaiti oil fields, and by launching Scud missiles against civilian targets in Israel and Saudi Arabia.

In the 1980s, Hussein further consolidated his power during the war with Iran, and it was during this period that he began to establish his personality cult. Hussein initiated the eight-year Gulf War primarily to regain control of the Shaṭṭ al-'Arab waterway and the oil-rich, predominantly Arabic border province of Khūzistān (called *Arabistan* in Iraq). He timed his invasion to take advantage of the weakened state of the Iranian military, which had been purged when Khomeini and the Islāmic fundamentalists took power in 1979. During the first two years the Iraqis met with some success. But subsequently they were thrown on the defensive, as Iranian troops invaded Iraq in the second year of fighting. In 1982, Hussein offered to settle the war by accepting the Shaṭṭ al-'Arab as the frontier, with Iran controlling the eastern half and Iraq the western half. This settlement would have

*Source: John Bullock and Harvey Morris, Saddam's War. This work is the source for much of this biographical entry.

effectively reinstated the 1975 Algiers Accord which Hussein renounced when he inaugurated the war. However, Khomeini rejected the offer, vowing to overthrow Hussein's "ungodly" regime. The war lasted for six more years. The fighting was characterized primarily by World War I–style trench warfare, but both sides employed chemical warfare and launched long-range missile attacks against civilian populations (*see* **Iran-Iraq Gulf War**).

In conjunction with his battles against Iran, Hussein also renewed his genocidal war against the Kurds in northern Iraq. In 1988, he authorized the use of nerve and mustard gas against Kurdish civilians, a practice that killed thousands. A report commissioned by the U.S. Senate Foreign Relations Committee verified Iraq's use of chemical weapons and concluded that Hussein was trying to depopulate Kurdistan and force the Kurds to relocate elsewhere: "The end result of this policy will be the destruction of the Kurdish identity, Kurdish culture, and a way of life that has endured for centuries."

Though Hussein inflicted great harm upon the Kurds, he did, however, not succeed in subjugating or eliminating them. They rebelled again immediately after the Iraqi defeat in Desert Storm, but Hussein was able to squelch the rebellion without significant interference from the coalition, which deplored his action but officially treated it as an internal Iraqi affair outside of their U.N. mandate to intervene.

The Gulf War ended in 1988 when, aided by the Soviet Union, France, the other Persian Gulf states, and even the United States, Iraq was finally able to force Iran to accept a ceasefire. Although Hussein achieved none of his original objectives—he conceded half control of the Shaṭṭ al-'Arab to Iran in 1990—he declared victory and represented himself as the great defender of Arabs against the invading Persians.

Despite Iraq's urgent need for postwar reconstruction, Hussein used the Iraqi treasury to further build up the armed forces and to celebrate his self-proclaimed victory. At great cost he commissioned vast public monuments, and these too contributed to the sense of grandeur with which he associated himself. One 150-foot tall memorial to the war dead was reputed to cost $250 million.

After the war Iraq's economy was reeling due to Iraqi war debts, and the large number of unemployed soldiers presented a political danger. Hussein addressed the second problem by re-employing the soldiers. He built a million-man army that was reputed to be the most powerful in the Middle East aside from Israel's. He also demanded that Kuwait and Saudi Arabia forgive the approximately $40 billion in loans Iraq owed them, arguing that he had fought the war to protect their interests, and he demanded higher oil prices from OPEC and strict adherence to OPEC quotas on production. Saudi Arabia, but not Kuwait, agreed to forgive the Iraqi loans, and OPEC acquiesced to a substantial increase in oil prices and strict compliance with the quotas, which Kuwait had been exceeding.

In the summer of 1990, Hussein accused Kuwait of waging economic war against Iraq by exceeding its OPEC oil production quotas and driving down the price of crude oil—Iraq's major asset. He also accused Kuwait of stealing Iraqi oil by slant drilling across the border in the Rumaila oil field. He demanded access to two Kuwaiti islands in the Persian Gulf in order to build an Iraqi port on the Gulf. When Kuwait refused to give in to any of his demands, Hussein ordered his army to invade it (*see* **Causes of the War, Invasion and Occupation of Kuwait**).

### *The Persian Gulf War*

A week before the August 2 invasion, Hussein conferred with U.S. Ambassador April Glaspie to ascertain what the American response to an attack on Kuwait might be and to threaten against U.S. interference. According to a transcript of the meeting that Iraq leaked to the press after the invasion, Hussein represented Iraq as the victim in its dispute with Kuwait. He argued that by depressing the price of oil, Kuwait was threatening the jobs of Iraqi workers and "harming even the milk our children drink and the pension of

Saddam Hussein (photograph courtesy of AP/Wide World Photos).

the widow who lost a husband during the war and the pensions of the orphans who lost their parents."

Hussein also threatened that should the United States intervene, it would have to be willing to accept a large number of war casualties, and it could face terrorism at home. The conversation concluded with Hussein announcing that he had agreed to meet in Saudi Arabia for a meeting with high-level representatives from Kuwait. Glaspie congratulated Hussein on that development and indicated that the United States took no position on the border dispute between the two Arab countries.

Most U.S. officials believed even through the end of July that either Iraq would not invade Kuwait at all, or, if Iraq did attack, it would seize the disputed section of the Rumaila oil field and perhaps Būbiyān Island and or Warbah Island to give it a secure port on the Persian Gulf. The Bush administration was apparently prepared to accept such an outcome. But Hussein apparently failed to real-

ize that Bush was not willing to concede full control of Kuwait to Hussein or to permit the possibility that Iraq might likewise conquer Saudi Arabia.

Initially, Hussein claimed that the invasion was made at the behest of an indigenous, anti-emir revolutionary movement inside Kuwait. He also claimed that his intention was to serve warning to Kuwait, and he promised to withdraw his troops within two days. However, Hussein retracted the promise to withdraw after the Arab League and the U.N. Security Council immediately condemned the conquest, the United States increased its military presence in the Gulf, and the major banks throughout the world precluded Hussein from seizing Kuwaiti assets by freezing them. He tried to install a puppet government and declare Kuwait an independent republic, but when the government he imposed failed to achieve any international recognition, Hussein annexed Kuwait as Iraq's nineteenth province on August 8.

On August 6, the day Saudi Arabia officially requested U.S. assistance for its self-defense, Hussein summoned Joseph Wilson, the U.S. chargé d'affaires in Baghdad, and accused the United States of meddling in Arab affairs and spoiling the special relationship between Saudi Arabia and Iraq, a relationship that had helped created stability in the region. "We were brothers," he claimed, "but you [the United States] spoiled that relationship between us, and you turned the Saudis against us." Hussein subsequently assured Wilson that he had no intention of attacking Saudi Arabia: "We will not attack those who do not attack us, we will not harm those who do not harm us.... As for Saudi Arabia, that question did not even occur in my mind."

Despite his friendly assurances, Hussein refused to provide exit visas to several thousand Westerners who happened to be in Kuwait or Iraq when the invasion took place. Ignoring the Security Council's Resolution 664 calling for their release, he initially called the hostages "guests" and "heroes of peace." But on August 19, he announced that he would not release the Westerners unless the United States promised to remove its forces from the Persian Gulf region. He insisted that the Security Council fix a timetable and guarantee that the troop withdrawal would not take longer than it took to deploy the troops in the first place. The next day Hussein ordered some of the foreigners transferred to potential military targets throughout Iraq to be used as human shields, precluding allied air strikes.

Throughout the next two months Hussein tried to use the hostages as a bargaining tool, as he alternated between threats and accommodating gestures. During an internationally televised meeting with 15 British hostages he singled out a 7-year-old boy, Stuart Lockwood, and, patting him on the head, asked about his well-being and whether he was receiving his milk. Though Hussein was ostensibly exhibiting his concern and sympathy for Lockwood and another boy he addressed, most viewers regarded the broadcast as a thinly veiled threat that Hussein would use these children and the other men and women in the group as human shields if the then-forming coalition were to attack him. On the other hand, perhaps in response to negative world reaction to the broadcast, he released all of the women and children on August 29.

However, Hussein retained the male hostages and continued to use them as human shields around sensitive target areas. Finally, on November 18, perhaps in response to negative world opinion or to the additional 150,000 troops Bush ordered to the Persian Gulf, Hussein announced that Iraq would release the remaining 2,000 Western hostages between December 25 and March 25, "unless something would take place that mars the atmosphere of peace." However, Hussein's offer was not sufficient to preclude the Security Council on November 29 from authorizing war if Iraq did not free the hostages and withdraw from Kuwait by January 15. To back up the threat, the United States called up an additional 115,000 reservists on December 1. A week later, on December 6, Hussein agreed to free the hostages, who departed Baghdad between December 10 and 14 (*see* **Hostages**).

In addition to threatening the hostages, Hussein broadcast statements indicating that any attempt to forcibly remove his troops from Kuwait would result in unacceptable losses for his enemies. Hussein believed that the Western countries were unwilling to sustain heavy casualties. On the other hand, he had already demonstrated during the Gulf War that he was willing to sustain and capable of inflicting hundreds of thousands of deaths. Moreover, Hussein had also demonstrated in the Gulf War his willingness to use chemical weapons. He vowed to launch missiles with chemical warheads against Israel and against allied armies if the coalition attacked. He also promised to set fire to Kuwait's oil fields (*see* **Chemical Warfare**, **Environmental Warfare**).

Hussein's warnings were broadcast on network and cable television and were directed not only to the Western governments but also to their citizens. He believed the memory of the Vietnam War would cause Americans to resist another complicated foreign entanglement in which the United States had no direct stake, and he appealed to their aversion to heavy casualties to pressure Bush not to initiate a war. His most famous and most colorful effort at this form of psychological maneuvering came on August 21, when Hussein vowed that if the allies initiated a war against him, they would find themselves embroiled in "the mother of all battles."

Though the United Nations overwhelmingly condemned Iraq's actions, Hussein's posturing won great support among the Arab people. He described his battle against the allies as a *jihad*, a holy war, and he urged all Arabs to join him. The Palestinian Liberation Organization backed him, and popular demonstrations celebrating him sprang up in Yemen, the Sudan, Jordan, and among the Palestinians in Israel. Thus, at the cost of condemnation by the Western powers, certain Arab governments, and most of the members of the United Nations, Hussein took a large step forward in garnering the popular support throughout the Arab world that he needed to fulfill his dream of leading a new Pan-Arab state and creating a new Babylon.

Similarly, Hussein's proposal of August 12, 1990, to link an Iraqi withdrawal from Kuwaiti-occupied territory to the withdrawal of all foreign forces from all occupied territory in the Middle East was probably more a gesture to win support among Arabs than it was a serious attempt at settling the crisis through diplomacy. The proposal would have required Israeli troops to leave the West Bank and other lands seized after the 1967 Six-Day War. It would also have forced Syria, Hussein's other enemy in the region, to withdraw from Lebanon.

If accepted, the plan would have been an enormous diplomatic victory for Hussein. For one thing, he would weaken and humiliate his Syrian rival, General Hafez al-Assad. But much more importantly, as the liberator of Palestine Hussein would enormously enhance his prestige among Arabs and take a large step towards his ultimate goal of establishing himself as the leader of a Pan-Arab nation. Some members of the international community, such as France and the Soviet Union, appeared willing to consider linking the resolution of the Kuwaiti situation to a U.N. conference on the larger regional issues in the Middle East. But Bush predictably rejected Hussein's proposal, saying that it imposed preconditions and did not comply with the U.N. resolutions calling for Iraq's immediate evacuation from Kuwait, the release of foreign hostages, and annulment of Iraq's annexation of Kuwait. In addition to these stated reasons, the United States and Britain no doubt opposed the plan for precisely the same reason Hussein offered it. They were unwilling to concede such a major political victory to Hussein or to undermine Israel's position within the region. Hussein probably knew Bush would reject his peace proposal. But merely by making the offer he recast Israel and Syria, instead of Iraq, as the oppressors. Though not successful in the United States or Britain, this strategy of vilifying Israel won Hussein further support among Arabs, especially Palestinians and Jordanians. Later, even after he lost the war, Hussein retained much of his popularity among Arabs from the lower economic classes because he had attacked Israel, demanded Palestinian rights, and stood up to the Western powers and survived (*see* **Diplomacy**).

Hussein offered few other diplomatic initiatives to peacefully resolve the situation. Shortly before the air war began, Iraqi Foreign Minister Tariq Aziz met with U.S. Secretary of State James Baker, but neither side offered significant compromise. During the air campaign, the Soviets increased their efforts to find a diplomatic solution, and on February 19, a week prior to the ground campaign, Hussein indicated he would accept a Soviet peace proposal. The plan called for Iraq to begin "to withdraw its forces immediately and unconditionally" from Kuwait and complete the withdrawal within 21 days. Iraqi troops were to evacuate Kuwait City within four days and return all POWs within three days. In return, the plan called for the coalition to agree to a cease-fire and allow all U.N. resolutions against Iraq to expire once the Iraqis had withdrawn from Kuwait. However, these conditions would have annulled the U.N. condemnation of Iraq's annexation of Kuwait and eliminated the demand that Iraq repay Kuwait for the damage done by its occupation and by the oil it spilled into the Persian Gulf and the fires it set in the Kuwaiti oil fields. The Soviet proposal also failed to secure freedom for the thousands of Kuwaiti citizens being held captive in Iraq or to fulfill another major U.N. objective—to create conditions for peace and security within the region. Therefore, the coalition rejected the Soviet proposal. On February 22, the United States countered with an ultimatum that Iraq begin a large-scale withdrawal from Kuwait by noon the following day (EST) and complete the evacuation within one week, or face a ground war.

Though Schwarzkopf officially denied Hussein had been specifically targeted during the war, he did point out that the Iraqi command structure was a target and that he would have no regrets if Hussein were killed. In fact, during the air war allied planes launched over 250 strikes at positions where he was believed to be located. In response, Hussein kept a low profile during the war. He traveled around Baghdad in delivery trucks and other plain-looking vehicles, and he made few television broadcasts for fear of being bombed in a broadcast studio. According to his chief of military intelligence, Major General Wafic al-Sammarai, Hussein became depressed as the war waged on.

In late January Hussein authorized an Iraqi strike into Saudi Arabia to improve morale and force the allies into initiating their ground offensive prematurely. He also hoped to capture 4,000 or 5,000 allied POWs to use as human shields, as he had publicly threatened to do on January 21. According to General al-Sammarai, Hussein intended to have his soldiers strap American, French, and British POWs to the front of Iraqi tanks, and then have the tanks overrun the oil fields in Saudi Arabia. Hussein was convinced that to spare the hostages, the allies would refrain from bombing the invading tanks.* Consequently, on the night of January 29, Hussein ordered an attack

on the Saudi border town of Khafji. Iraqi armored divisions held the town for two days before being driven back by Saudi and Kuwaiti forces and U.S. Marines. After suffering heavy losses, the Iraqis pulled back and assumed defensive positions to await the allied ground attack. Despite large losses and the Iraqis' inability to hold Khafji, Hussein touted the battle as a victory and maintained that by capturing a Saudi town, he had shown that the allies were vulnerable, despite their air superiority and their ground forces (see **Khafji**).

On the other hand, the quick success of the allied ground offensive in late February made Hussein more deeply depressed. On February 26, Hussein announced on Baghdad Radio that Iraq was withdrawing its troops from Kuwait. In response, President Bush called the announcement "an outrage. He is not withdrawing. His defeated forces are retreating. The coalition forces will continue to prosecute the war with undiminished intensity." By the end of the day, the allies destroyed over 21 Iraqi divisions.

According to General al-Sammarai, Hussein became desperate and frightened that the allies would continue on to Baghdad and forcibly depose him. Even if they did not directly overthrow him, Hussein feared he would become too weakened by the defeat to retain power in Iraq. In an apparent move to shift the blame for the loss onto his generals, Hussein ordered the execution of five ranking officers whom he accused of betrayal. However, al-Sammarai maintains that when Bush ordered the cessation of offensive action prior to completely destroying the Republican Guard, Hussein's morale rose "from zero to one hundred," and Hussein declared, "We won! We won!" According to al-Sammarai, Hussein quickly acquiesced to the allied demands because he did not want to give them any excuse to resume the fighting. The Republican Guard, which was loyal to him personally, was a major foundation of his power base, and Hussein wanted to retain as much of it intact as possible. Eventually, about one-

---

*General al-Sammarai made this claim on the Frontline documentary The Gulf War, which aired on January 9–10, 1996.

third of his forces managed to escape from Kuwait.

Even Hussein's crushing defeat in the Persian Gulf War did little to loosen his grip on the Ba'ath Party or the Iraqi government. Indeed, in the long run it offered him another excuse to purge his internal rivals and further consolidate his control. Despite U.S. hopes that the Iraqi military would rise up against him, the generals remained loyal, apparently preferring to cast their lot with Hussein rather than risk creating a power vacuum in which rebelling Shī'ah Muslims could seize control of the government. The generals no doubt feared that if the Shī'ites came to power they would purge the military, as they had done when they took over the Iranian government in 1979. Thus, shortly after the war concluded Hussein was able to further assert his power by directing successful offensives against the Kurdish and Shī'ite populations within Iraq.

The Western powers declined to assist the rebellions, and in so doing enabled Hussein to remain in command. Bush may have tolerated Hussein's suppression of the Kurds and Shī'ites because he did not want to enmesh the U.S. military in a bloody and prolonged occupation or peacekeeping operation. This was the position of General Colin Powell, the chairman of the Joint Chiefs of Staff, and other members of the administration who pointed out that the conflict had been going on for hundreds of years, and that the United States was unlikely to resolve it. Moreover, like the Iraqi military, the Sunni-led Saudis may have preferred having a weakened Hussein in power to seeing an independent Shī'ite nation established on its border, right beside the portion of Saudi Arabia that contains the greatest oil reserves and has a large Shī'ite population. Likewise, Turkey, which had its own difficulties with Kurdish separatists on its southern border, was not anxious to see an independent Kurdish nation formed in northern Iraq. Whatever the underlying reasons, the United States officially took the position that Hussein's war against the Kurds and Shī'ites was an internal Iraqi matter for which there was no U.N. mandate to inter-

vene (*see* **Kurdish Rebellion, Shī'ite Rebellion**).

Former British Prime Minister Margaret Thatcher, one of the architects of the war, has maintained that the allies could have brought down Hussein by humiliating him before the Iraqi people and the Arab world. Thatcher stepped down in November 1990 and thus was not in power when the war concluded. In an appearance on a 1996 PBS television documentary, *Frontline*, she stated that the Iraqis should have been made to surrender all of their military equipment to further weaken Hussein and demonstrate to the Iraqi people that he was responsible for the defeat. Likewise, Bush's national security adviser, Brent Scowcroft, believes that the coalition should have required Hussein to personally negotiate the cease-fire so he would be publicly seen to be a loser. Instead, the Iraqi population identified the defeat with the generals who signed the armistice.

To date, Hussein remains securely in power, despite betrayals by two of his sons-in-law who tried to foment revolution and an assassination attempt on the life of his oldest son, Odai Hussein. He has resisted complying with the terms of the cease-fire that require Iraq to permit U.N. inspections of its biological facilities, and occasionally he has provoked military action by U.S. peacekeeping forces by attacking Kurdish safe areas and or ordering his pilots to violate no-fly zones. Because of the violations of the cease-fire agreement, the United Nations retained the embargo against Iraq through 1996. Finally, in December 1996, it voted to allow Iraq to sell $2 billion worth of oil over a 180-day period, with the provision that the revenue be used to compensate war victims, pay for U.N. weapons monitoring in Iraq, and provide food and supplies for the Iraqi populace. On the next day Hussein opened the valves to the oil pipeline leading to Turkey amid much fanfare in a public ceremony.

**Instant Thunder**—Air Force Colonel John A. Warden III and his Washington-based staff, the so-called Jedi Knights, devised a plan for an air campaign against Iraq shortly after the initial deployment of U.S. troops in early

August 1990. Based on principles Warden had articulated in his 1988 book, *Air Campaign: Planning for Combat*, the plan was first submitted to General Schwarzkopf on August 10, under the code name Instant Thunder. Its goal was to strike at strategic "centers of gravity" within Iraq in order to destroy Iraq's leadership, command and control capabilities, and ability to reinforce Iraqi ground forces in Kuwait and southern Iraq. The five major strategic centers of gravity were, in descending order, Iraqi leadership, petroleum plants and electric generation facilities, transportation infrastructure, the Iraqi population, and the Iraqi Army inside the Kuwaiti theater of operations. Warden believed that by concentrating resources against the three most important centers of gravity, the coalition could cripple Iraq's capacity to wage war. In marked contrast to the Vietnam War, Instant Thunder was, according to Warden, "a focused, intense air campaign designed to incapacitate Iraqi leadership and destroy key Iraqi military capability in a short period of time. And it is designed to leave basic Iraqi infrastructure intact. What It Is Not—A graduated, long-term campaign plan designed to provide escalation options to counter Iraqi moves." Warden believed that such a strategic air campaign could win the war and possibly compel the Iraqis to withdraw from Kuwait without the allies having to wage a costly ground attack.

Schwarzkopf and Colin Powell, the chairman of the Joint Chiefs of Staff, retained infantrymen's skepticism of air force claims about winning wars without ground troops—something that has never happened historically—and at their insistence, Warden subsequently revised the plan to inflict heavy casualties on the Iraqi Army prior to the ground offensive and destroy much of the Republican Guard's armor and artillery. After reviewing the revised plan on August 17, Schwarzkopf ordered Warden and his staff to fly to Saudi Arabia and present it to Lieutenant General Charles Horner, who commanded all allied air forces (*see* **Charles Horner**).

Horner, who distrusted Washington-based planners far removed from the scene of the action, disapproved of Warden's almost total reliance on bombing strategic targets at the expense of tactical targets on the battlefield. Warden, for instance, had prepared no contingency for responding to an Iraqi tank attack against coalition forces in Saudi Arabia. Horner consequently sent Warden back to Washington but retained Warden's deputy, Lieutenant Colonel David A. Deptula. Deptula managed to keep the basic structure of Instant Thunder as the basis of the air campaign that Horner ultimately approved and implemented during Operation Desert Storm (*see* **Air Campaign**).

**Invasion and Occupation of Kuwait**—Most Arab and U.S. officials believed even through the end of July 1990 that either Iraq would not invade Kuwait at all, or, if Iraq did attack, it would seize the disputed section of the Rumaila oil field and perhaps Bubiyan and Warbah islands to give it a secure port on the Persian Gulf. (The Israelis, on the other hand, were more suspicious of Hussein's intentions.) The Bush administration was apparently prepared to accept such an outcome. The transcripts from Hussein's July 15 conference with U.S. Ambassador April Glaspie, along with other ambiguous U.S. actions, became the basis for Bush's critics to maintain that the United States had given Hussein tacit approval to invade Kuwait. The most extreme of these critics suggest that the Americans "set up" Hussein by inducing him to invade Kuwait in order to justify an all-out war against Iraq that would either destroy Hussein or significantly curb his power within the Middle East, and simultaneously reassert the United States as the world's dominant, military superpower in the new, post–Cold War world order. However, these criticisms overlook Hussein's incentives for invading and subsequently annexing Kuwait: immediate cancellation of Iraq's massive war debt to Kuwait, acquisition of Kuwait's assets including its vast oil reserves, and Iraq's acquisition of a long-sought port on the Persian Gulf. Moreover, Hussein had reason to believe that the Saudis would not permit Western nations to base their troops in Saudi Arabia for a war against an Arab country, and

**Kuwait City after Iraqi occupation, engulfed by smoke from burning oil wells (photograph courtesy of the Department of Defense).**

he doubted whether the United States would risk incurring heavy casualties to liberate Kuwait (*see* **Causes of the War, Diplomacy**).

The conquest of Kuwait required less than a day. At 2 A.M. on August 2, 1990, Hammurabi Armored and Tawakalna Mechanized divisions from Iraq's Republican Guard overran a Kuwaiti brigade guarding the border. Meeting minimal resistance, they proceeded to Kuwait City, about 50 miles to the south. At the same time Republican Guard special forces attacked Kuwait City by helicopter, and sea commandos took command of the southern coastal road leading to it. By 5:30 A.M. the armored divisions arrived. By 2:20 P.M. the battle concluded, and Iraq controlled Kuwait's capital. The Iraqi forces then proceeded farther south to establish defensive fortifications approximately 10 kilometers from the Saudi border.

The Kuwaiti Navy played no role in the fighting. The small air force claimed it destroyed six Iraqi helicopters, two fighters, and several armored vehicles before fleeing to safe havens in Saudi Arabia. It later participated in

Operation Desert Storm, as did other members of the Kuwaiti military who escaped.

Part of Hussein's plan was to capture Kuwait's emir, Sheikh Jabir Āl Ṣabāḥ. Consequently, fighting was especially heavy at the emir's Dasman Palace. Hussein reportedly had intended to offer the captured emir the choice of cooperating with Iraq and remaining head of a puppet regime under Iraqi domination, or being shot. However, Sheikh Jabir and his cousin who was also prime minister, Crown Prince Saud Āl Ṣabāḥ, escaped in the early morning as the battle for Kuwait City started. They drove south to a police post at Kuwait's border with Saudi Arabia. As Iraqi troops approached their position they entered into Saudi Arabia, where they were later welcomed by King Fahd al Saud. Along with the other Kuwaiti government ministers, all of whom also escaped to Saudi Arabia, they set up a government-in-exile at the al-Hada Sheraton in aṭ-Ṭā'if, Saudi Arabia, near the Red Sea. Though the top government officials survived, some members of the emir's family were killed

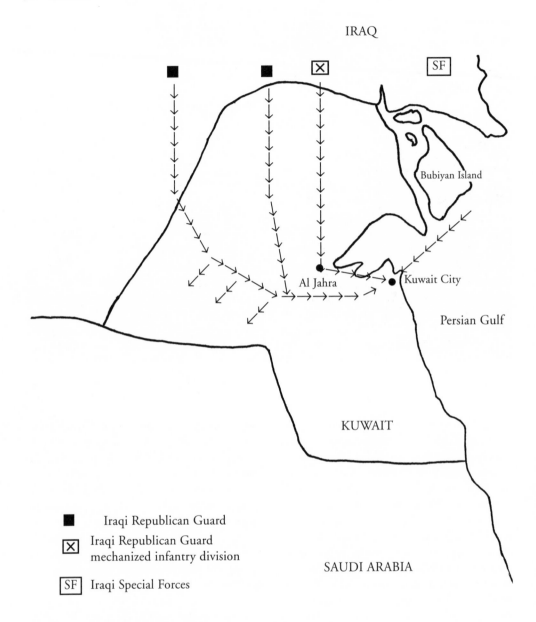

IRAQ

Bubiyan Island

Al Jahra

Kuwait City

Persian Gulf

KUWAIT

■    Iraqi Republican Guard

☒    Iraqi Republican Guard
     mechanized infantry division

SF    Iraqi Special Forces

SAUDI ARABIA

# INVASION OF KUWAIT
## (August 2, 1990)

**Boundary lines and troop dispositions are approximate.**

in the fighting, including his brother, Sheik Fahd Āl Ṣabāḥ, who died defending the palace.

During the invasion Iraqi forces took control of the Kuwait airport and captured the passengers and crew of a British Airways plane that had just landed in Kuwait City for a stopover en route to India. The men from the flight were subsequently taken to Baghdad to become "human shields" that Hussein deployed around sensitive targets in Iraq (*see* **Hostages**).

The United Nations Security Council immediately passed Resolution 660 condemning the invasion and demanding Iraq's withdrawal from Kuwait. The vote was 14–0–1, with Yemen abstaining. Moreover, the world's main banking centers froze Kuwaiti assets, thereby depriving Hussein access to Kuwait's offshore wealth. Both Cold War superpowers—the United States and the Soviet Union—condemned the invasion within one day after it took place, and as the threat to Saudi Arabia became apparent, the Bush administration quickly concluded that it was in the vital interest of the United States to protect the Saudis, who were now vulnerable to an Iraqi invasion. The fear of such an invasion was the basis for Operation Desert Shield (*see* **Operation Desert Shield**).

Hussein claimed that his troops had invaded Kuwait to support a popular insurrection opposed to the autocratic rule of the emir. Iraq announced the establishment of a provisional government on August 2, and on August 3, Hussein announced Iraq would withdraw its forces within two days if asked by the provisional government. On August 4, a cabinet was chosen, and on August 7, the Republic of Kuwait was proclaimed. However, the new government had no support among the Kuwaitis and did not receive recognition from any outside nations. On the next day Hussein disbanded it and annexed Kuwait as the nineteenth Iraqi province (*see* **Provisional Kuwaiti Government**).

Even as Hussein was declaring on August 3 that he would withdraw in two days, Iraq moved large numbers of reinforcements into Kuwait and fortified positions along the Saudi border, reinforcing apprehensions that Iraq was preparing to invade Saudi Arabia.

Some critics of the Persian Gulf War maintain that Hussein never intended to invade Saudi Arabia and that he was sincere when he claimed that he was merely teaching Kuwait a lesson and would withdraw his troops within two days, so long as it did not appear that he was being coerced. They claim that Hussein then planned to resolve his differences in negotiations with Kuwaiti leaders at a summit meeting of Arab heads of state. (Of course, Kuwait would literally have been negotiating under the gun, with the Republican Guard still massed at its border and its own armed forces destroyed.) But Kuwait rejected the summit proposal and turned to the United Nations instead. On the next day the Arab League also voted to condemn Iraq, and Hussein retracted his promise to withdraw his troops and negotiate a settlement.

A majority of the Arab League opposed the conquest and voted 12–8 on August 10 to respect U.N. sanctions against Iraq and send troops to defend Saudi Arabia. However, Jordan, Algeria, Tunisia, Yemen, Libya, Mauritania, Sudan, and the Palestinian Liberation Organization (PLO) supported Iraq. Moreover, popular sentiment within Egypt, Syria, and other Arab nations was also with Hussein, even though their governments had sided against him. The oil-rich Kuwaitis and Saudis were often envied and resented in less wealthy Arab nations, especially those like Egypt and Jordan that furnished much of Kuwait's labor force. Moreover, Hussein's stance against the United States and his threat to attack Israel won him strong support among Palestinians.[*]

The Iraqi occupation of Kuwait was brutal,

[*]*Ultimately, their support for Hussein left the Palestinians among the big losers in the war, since they lost political leverage by siding against both the other Arab governments and the western industrial powers. Moreover, Iraq's invasion halted Kuwait's considerable subsidies to the Palestinians, and it eliminated thousands of jobs for Palestinians and other Arabs and Muslims who had worked in Kuwait and sent money back home. In the first three months following the invasion, approximately one million imported laborers fled from Kuwait to their homelands in India, Pakistan, the Philippines, and the other Arab countries.*

and the severe treatment of one group of Arabs by another violated the unspoken code of conduct that the Arab countries traditionally tried to live by, with mixed success. Iraq's brutality may have been calculated to drive a large number of Kuwaitis into exile in order to annex their territory more easily. The U.N. Security Council's Resolution 677 condemned attempts by Iraq to alter the demographic composition of Kuwait by forcing out Kuwaiti citizens. It also condemned Iraq's destruction of records maintained by the legitimate government of Kuwait and required the secretary general to take custody of a copy of the population register of Kuwait, which had been certified by the Kuwaiti government (*see* **United Nations**).

Iraq's occupying soldiers were not well disciplined, and rape, pillage, and plunder were common occurrences. Much of it was officially sanctioned. Iraqi troops broke into the Central Bank of Kuwait and removed the gold and currency reserves, which were then taken in a truck convoy back to Baghdad. So, too, were holdings from the National Museum. Government records were either removed to Baghdad or destroyed. The gold and gem markets were also looted, and many consumer goods and industrial and medical equipment were shipped back to Iraq. Most private and government vehicles were confiscated. At the end of the war, many Iraqi soldiers carrying their plunder in stolen vehicles fell victim to allied bombing raids as they tried to flee Kuwait City on what became known as the Highway to Hell (*see* **Highway to Hell**).

Kuwaiti men of military age, including even 16-year-old boys, were routinely rounded up and in many cases sent to Iraq. Influential Kuwaitis and others believed to be potential troublemakers were also removed. In their place, busloads of Iraqi citizens arrived in Kuwait to occupy the abandoned homes and resettle Iraq's new, nineteenth province.

The Kuwaiti resistance sprang up immediately after the invasion and fought against the Iraqi military occupation. During Operation Desert Storm, Kuwaiti resistance fighters cooperated with the coalition. The Iraqis systematically sought out resistance fighters and dealt with them ruthlessly. In retaliatory acts, the Iraqis would inflict brutal reprisals upon entire neighborhoods.

During and immediately after the invasion, patients were ordered to leave hospitals, regardless of their health. According to some accounts, babies were taken from hospital incubators and left to die on cold floors, while the incubators and other hospital equipment were shipped back to Iraq. Other patients were likewise unhooked from respirators and other machines that Iraqis soldiers then stole. Patients too ill to flee were physically removed from their beds, while doctors were forced to abandon their patients and instead tend to Iraqi casualties. Nurses were repeatedly raped.*

A U.S. report on war crimes submitted to the U.N. Security Council on March 19, 1993, concluded that:

> The gruesome evidence confirms torture by amputation of or injury to various body parts, to include limbs, eyes, tongues, ears, noses, lips and genitalia.... Some victims were killed in acid baths. Women taken hostages were raped repeatedly.... Eyewitnesses reported Iraqis torturing a woman by making her eat her own flesh as it was cut from her body.

During the Iraqi occupation an estimated 1,082 Kuwaiti civilians were murdered, and several thousand remain missing. Moreover, the Iraqis wrought extreme environmental havoc by polluting the Persian Gulf and Kuwaiti shoreline with oil spills and setting fire to over 500 Kuwaiti wells during the war (*see* **Environmental Warfare**).

Following the Iraqi withdrawal from Kuwait, there were reports of Kuwaitis torturing

---

*\*Jean P. Sasson's* The Rape of Kuwait *presents the claims of several victims and eyewitnesses of the Iraqi abuses. Among the accounts Sasson reports is the charge that the Iraqis removed babies from incubators. An anonymous 15-year-old girl made that same accusation before a Congressional subcommittee investigating Iraqi human rights violations. However, the credibility of the charge fell into doubt when it was revealed that the girl was the daughter of the Kuwaiti ambassador to the United States, Saud Nasir Āl Ṣabāḥ.*

and committing other human rights violations as acts of vengeance against Iraqis, Kurds, Palestinians, and others believed to have collaborated with the Iraqis. The emir returned to Kuwait on March 14, and on May 18, the restored Kuwaiti government began trials of 200 alleged collaborators, most of whom were convicted and sentenced to death. However, in response to objections by human rights organizations and world governments, the sentences were commuted on June 26 to life imprisonment.

**Iran**—Though officially neutral during the Persian Gulf War, Iran, which was a fierce opponent of the United States, tacitly supported Iraq. The strained relations between the United States and Iran dated back to 1979, when Islāmic fundamentalists overthrew the U.S.-backed shah and established a Shī'ite Muslim theocracy in Iran dedicated to spreading an Islāmic revolution throughout the Middle East. Diplomatic relations between the two countries were severed after the occupants of the American embassy in Tehran were seized as hostages in November 1979. A desire to contain Iran's revolutionary goals and curb its influence within the region lay behind the U.S. decision to assist Iraq in the late 1980s, despite Iraq's Cold War alliance with the Soviet Union and its poor human rights record.

Persian Iran and Arabic Iraq were longstanding enemies. Hussein and the leaders of his regime were Sunni Muslims, whereas the Iranian government was led by Shī'ah Muslims. In fact, in 1978 Hussein had expelled Ayatollah Khomeini, the Islamic fundamentalist who became ruler of Iran in 1979. Between 1980 and 1988 Iran and Iraq fought the Gulf War, which produced between 500,000 and 1 million casualties. In the final years of the fighting, the United States supported Iraq by escorting Kuwaiti tankers carrying Iraqi oil through the Persian Gulf. Sunni-led Kuwait, Saudi Arabia, and the other Persian Gulf states also supported Iraq because they feared the spread of the Shī'ite revolution. Hussein's demand for the cancellation of his war debts to those nations, for whose interests he maintained Iraq had been fighting, was a major cause of the Persian Gulf War (*see* **Causes of the War**).

The Iran-Iraq Gulf War was fought primarily over control of the Shaṭṭ al-'Arab estuary that runs along the border of the two countries, and the fighting ended more or less in a stalemate after Iran was forced to accept a cease-fire in 1988. Although Hussein claimed victory, the final terms of a peace settlement were not reached until August 1990, after Hussein agreed to concede everything Iran was demanding so he could redeploy the Iraqi forces stationed at the Iranian border to Kuwait. Within two days of resolving the war with Iran, Hussein moved 24 divisions—some 300,000 troops—from the Iran border to Kuwait and the Saudi border areas. The peace settlement granted Iran half-control of the Shaṭṭ al-'Arab and called for the removal of Iraqi troops from Iranian territory and the immediate exchange of prisoners (*see* **Iran-Iraq Gulf War**).

On August 12, Iran President Rafsanjani condemned the presence of U.S. and other foreign troops in the Gulf. On August 15, Hussein sent a letter to Rafsanjani offering to conclude a treaty to end the Gulf War. The two nations resumed diplomatic relations on September 10, 1990. The subsequent opening of their border created a long frontier through which goods could be smuggled into Iraq in violation of the U.N. embargo (*see* **Embargo**).

On the initial night of Operation Desert Storm, the U.S. Navy secretly fired Tomahawk cruise missiles over western Iran en route to targets in Iraq. During the war Iran repeatedly threatened to shoot down coalition planes that entered its airspace. On the other hand, it offered sanctuary for more than 80 Iraqi jets that fled from their bases in Iraq to avoid destruction by allied air raids. Iranian officials assured the United States that the planes would be interned for the duration of the war, but the coalition fleet in the Persian Gulf feared a sneak attack by the Iraqi fighters from their new bases in Iran. They were also concerned that Iran might enter the war against the coalition and use its large air force and Chinese-made Silkworm missiles against their ships. In fact, the Iranians stayed out of the fighting, and the Iraqi planes remained interned throughout the war.

**Iran-Iraq Gulf War**—In 1980 Hussein initiated Iraq's eight-year Gulf War with Iran primarily to gain control of the Shaṭṭ al-'Arab waterway and Iran's oil-rich, predominantly Arabic border province of Khūzestān (called *Arabistan* in Iraq). These would have given Iraq direct shipping access to the Persian Gulf, something it had desired since 1969, when the shah of Iran unilaterally revoked a 1937 treaty that had given Iraq control over most of the Shaṭṭ al-'Arab, a deep-channel estuary at the border between the two nations.

The shah's action, which came one year after Hussein's Ba'ath Party came to power in Iraq, indicated Iran's intention to retain control of the Persian Gulf after 1971, when Great Britain would complete the evacuation of its military bases east of the Suez Canal. The newly installed Ba'ath regime objected and threatened retaliation, but was not then strong enough to take military action against Iran. However, in 1975 Iraq signed the Algiers Accord which established the middle of the Shaṭṭ al-'Arab as the border and granted Iran control over the eastern half of the estuary. Hussein, who then held the title of deputy minister of internal security but was considered the most influential leader in Iraq, reluctantly conceded control of the waterway in order to obtain Iran's agreement to stop supplying the Kurdish rebellion in northern Iraq, which Hussein had been unable to suppress. The rebellion ended, at least temporarily, soon after the agreement took effect.

In 1979 a populist rebellion in Iran forced the pro–American shah to flee the country, and Ayatollah Ruholla Khomeini came to power. Khomeini, whom Hussein had expelled from Iraq in 1978, established an anti-Western Muslim theocracy that preached Islāmic fundamentalism and called for the establishment of Islāmic rule throughout the entire Muslim world. Khomeini drew his support from the Shī'ah sect of Muslims who

constituted the vast majority of Iranians. They also outnumbered Sunni Muslims in Iraq by nearly 2–1 and had a strong presence in the oil-rich, northeastern section of Saudi Arabia. (Hussein and the ruling parties in Iraq and the Gulf states were Sunnis.)

Iran had enjoyed considerable support from the United States throughout the Cold War until Khomeini came to power. Because the United States had regarded Iran as essential for checking Soviet expansion and maintaining U.S. interests in the Persian Gulf, it helped Iran assemble the most potent and technologically sophisticated armed forces in the region. This military power fell under Khomeini's control after the shah fled in early 1979. However, after assuming power, Khomeini purged Iran's officer corps which had been loyal to the shah. The purges left the armed forces highly disorganized and depleted of many of their most competent, knowledgeable, and adept leaders.

Perceiving that Iran was suddenly weakened by Khomeini's purges and that the fledgling revolutionary government was in disarray, Hussein renounced the Algiers Accord and invaded Khūzestān in September 1980.

When Hussein initiated the Gulf War, he was pursuing Iraqi objectives, not those of the Persian Gulf states, as he later claimed (*see* **Causes of the War**). At the same time, however, he was also impeding the spread of Khomeini's Islamic fundamentalist revolution and was thereby advancing the interests of the Persian Gulf states. The leaders of Saudi Arabia, Kuwait, and the other Gulf states feared the fundamentalist Shī'ite revolution because like Hussein they were Sunni Muslims governing either majority or large minority Shī'ite populations. Moreover, their secular governments were in league with the United States, whose materialist capitalism and support of Israel were anathema to the religious fundamentalists.

Consequently, throughout the war Hussein enjoyed substantial financial support from the Persian Gulf countries. Kuwait permitted Iraqi warplanes to fly across its airspace, and it served as the main port of entry for Iraq's war supplies later in the war. Moreover, like Saudi Arabia and the other Persian Gulf states, Kuwait supplied money in the form of outright gifts and loans. It was these loans, which amounted to some $40 billion, that Hussein later insisted should be forgiven. The large debt, along with Hussein's policy of further enlarging his military, crippled Iraq's economy and inhibited its recovery from the eight-year war. Saudi Arabia agreed to forgive the $22 billion it lent Hussein, but Kuwait refused to write off the $13 billion Iraq owed.

The Gulf states were not the only ones to support Iraq against Iran. The Soviet Union, which was officially atheistic in accordance with the tenets of Communism, had a large Muslim population in its regions bordering the Middle East, and it too perceived Islāmic fundamentalism as a destabilizing threat. So, when Iranian armies crossed into Iraq in 1982, the Soviet Union resumed the weapons deliveries to Iraq it had begun in the 1970s but canceled following Iraq's invasion of Iran in 1980. France, too, provided Iraq with modern weapons. During the war the French government transferred weapons valued at $15–17 billion, including advanced Etendard jets armed with Exocet missiles, and French civilian corporations sold Hussein an additional $5 billion in munitions.

Although Iraq was a Soviet client state, the United States also implemented favorable policies toward it, since the U.S. government likewise hoped to contain the spread of Khomeini's ferociously anti–American revolution. Moreover, Khomeini had humiliated the United States when he refused for over a year to release personnel from the American embassy whom fundamentalist Iranian students had taken hostage in November 1979. In the later stages of the war, when Iran was attacking tankers carrying Iraqi oil through the Persian Gulf, U.S. warships escorted Kuwaiti tankers through the waters and U.S. helicopters attacked an Iranian ship laying mines in the Gulf. When Iraqi Exocet missiles struck the USS *Stark* and killed 37 crewmen in May 1987, the United States accepted an Iraqi apology and took no retaliatory action. But in April 1988, U.S. planes and ships destroyed two Iranian oil platforms, crippled two frigates, and sank a patrol boat in response to an Iranian attack on a U.S. ship. Finally, on July 3, 1988, an American cruiser, the USS *Vincennes*, shot down a civilian Iranian airliner, killing all 290 people aboard. President Reagan told Congress the downing was a case of mistaken identity but justifiable as an act of self-defense.

Iraq had only limited success in the first year of the war, and in the second year Iranian counteroffensives pushed the Iraqi Army back across the border and placed Iraq on the defensive for the next six years. In 1982, Hussein offered to settle the war by accepting the Shaṭṭ al-'Arab as the frontier, with Iran controlling the eastern half and Iraq the western half. This settlement would have effectively reinstated the 1975 Algiers Accord which Hussein renounced when he inaugurated the war. However, Khomeini rejected the offer, vowing to overthrow Hussein's "ungodly" regime.

The Iraqis proved adept defenders in eastern Iraq's mountainous and swampy terrain, and Khomeini tried unsuccessfully to score a decisive blow. In 1984, the first confirmed Iraqi use of poison gas was reported (*see* **Chemical Warfare**); in 1987 Iran and Iraq began attacking oil tankers in the Persian Gulf, prompting the United States to protect Kuwaiti ships carrying Iraqi cargoes. In 1988 Iraq and Iran launched long-range Scud missiles at civilian targets. Finally, on July 18, 1988, two weeks after the *Vincennes* incident, Iran accepted a UN-sponsored cease-fire and agreed to begin peace talks.

Hussein proclaimed victory and presented himself as the protector of Arabs against the Persian invaders, although the fighting ended in a virtual stalemate, with little change from before the war began. His posturing did not point out that he, not the Iranians, had initiated the war, or that Hussein had failed to obtain any of his original objectives. Notably, he failed to secure control of the Shaṭṭ al-'Arab. However, the war years did enable him to consolidate his power in Iraq and build up his armed forces, especially the elite Republican

Guard that was loyal to him personally. After the war's conclusion he continued to invest in the military instead of rebuild his war-torn country.

Although the cease-fire took effect in 1988, Iran and Iraq did not conclude a peace agreement until August 15, 1990—two weeks after the invasion of Kuwait. Anxious to eliminate an enemy on his eastern flank while preparing to defend against the international forces to the south, Hussein conceded everything Iran had been asking for since the cease-fire began. He agreed to withdraw from all occupied Iranian territory, exchange prisoners immediately, and establish the middle of the Shaṭṭ al-'Arab as the border between the countries.

But although the Gulf War failed to realize Iraq's own objectives, it did succeed in impeding the spread of revolutionary Islāmic fundamentalism. The war had depleted Iran's resources and left the economy and government in a state of disarray. Consequently, Iran could not effectively extend its fundamentalist revolution beyond its borders to overthrow the secular, Sunni regimes that controlled the Persian Gulf region. Thus the war did, in fact, achieve the goals of Saudi Arabia, Kuwait, and the other Persian Gulf states. But it also left Iraq with a well-equipped standing army of some 1 million soldiers. And with Iran at least temporarily eliminated as a major force in the Gulf, there was no other military power in the region that could challenge Hussein.

**Iraqi Fortifications** The Iraqis built extensive fortifications along a 250-kilometer line along the Saudi-Kuwaiti border, extending some 75 miles into eastern Iraq. Regular army infantry units manned these border fortifications. The better equipped, better trained Republican Guard armored divisions were deployed in reserve behind them in northwest Kuwait and in the Euphrates River Valley near Basra and Hawr Al-Ḥammār. Additional infantry positions were clustered near Kuwait City, along the coast where the Iraqis were expecting an

amphibious assault and near the Kuwait airport. The infantry defenses were based on tactics borrowed from the Soviet Union, which had been one of Iraq's chief military suppliers in the 1970s and 1980s.* The Iraqis had successfully used these tactics in their Gulf War with Iraq (see **Iran-Iraq Gulf War**).

Prior to the allied ground offensive, Iraqi soldiers laid two minefield belts paralleling the Kuwaiti-Saudi border. The first was about 10 kilometers (6 miles) inside of Kuwait, the second about 20 kilometers behind the first. The minefields were approximately 100 to 200 kilometers wide and filled with barbed wire, antitank ditches, berms, and fire trenches filled with oil. The main defensive infantry positions were behind the second minefield, though infantry teams hidden in so-called "spider holes" with antitank weapons and infantry companies housed in bunkers and slit trenches were positioned within the minefields. The overall defensive plan was to trap the advancing forces in killing zones between the two minefields and then counterattack with tanks and artillery.

Within and behind the minefields were nearly 100,000 separate defensive positions, ranging from reinforced bunkers to slit trenches and foxholes manned by infantry and armored units. Those that were not manned served as decoys for allied air and artillery strikes. Infantry brigades consisting of 2,000 to 3,000 troops apiece were responsible for defending areas of about 40 square kilometers (approximately 25 square miles), usually 8 to 12 kilometers wide and 3 to 5 kilometers deep. The brigades were deployed in strongpoints that covered about 1½ square kilometers, with about a kilometer or more of empty desert on each side. These strongpoints consisted of a triangle of berms, or ridges, of dirt and sand approximately 2 kilometers long and 3–4 meters high (9 to 13 feet). In front of the forwardmost leg of the triangle was an antitank ditch. Inside battalion-sized strongpoints, a company of infantry occupied each corner,

---

*Iraq signed a 15-year treaty of friendship and cooperation with the Soviets in 1972, when the United States was making its arsenal available to Iran, and Iraq remained a Soviet client state throughout the Cold War.

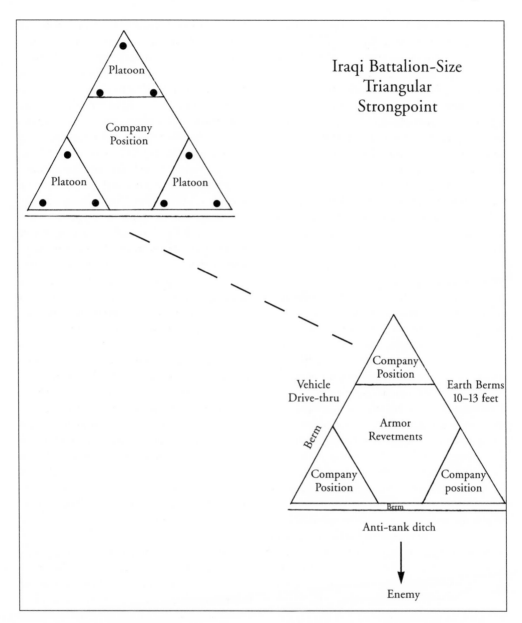

Iraqi Battalion-Size
Triangular
Strongpoint

while the tanks and other armored vehicles were dug into fixed positions in the center. Drive-through openings were built into the berms to allow the vehicles to enter and exit. Such access was necessary to permit the armored units to launch a counterattack from their defensive positions. Behind the strongpoints were mobile reserve units, usually consisting of a company of tanks or a battalion of mechanized infantry troops (see **Berms**).

The allies countered the Iraqi defenses first by heavily bombing the minefields and dug-in fortifications during the air campaign. Often helicopters and transport planes cleared the minefields by dropping fuel air explosives and igniting powerful explosions over them. They also used incendiary devices to burn off oil in the fire trenches. Though the Iraqis had more artillery pieces with longer range than the allies, they had lost virtually all of their reconnaissance capabilities at the beginning of the air campaign and were unable to effectively target their guns. Moreover, whenever Iraqi artillery pieces opened fire, allied spotters armed with Firefinder radars were able to locate their positions and call in precise retaliatory attacks. Prior to the ground offensive, allied engineers used mine plows to clear lanes through the minefields and destroy the bunkers and spider holes within them. The engineers also cleared holes through the berms to allow allied troops to pass through. In the breaching operations that opened the ground war, bulldozers often pushed dirt from the berms back into the Iraqi trenches, burying alive those defenders who did not or could not flee.

**Israel**—Though Israel was not a member of the anti–Iraqi coalition and conducted no offensive military operations against Iraq during the Persian Gulf War, it was the target of 40 Scud missile attacks by Iraq. Antagonism between Israel and Iraq dates back to the foundation of the State of Israel on May 14, 1948, when Iraqi troops joined with other Arab forces in their attempt to eradicate the Jewish state immediately after its existence was proclaimed. (The United Nations had voted in November 1947 to allow the partition of the British mandate of Palestine to include a new Jewish nation, as well as a new Palestinian state.) An armistice in January 1949 concluded the fighting, with Israel surrendering the old city of Jerusalem to Jordan but gaining about 50 percent more territory elsewhere. At the same time, Jordan annexed the remaining portions of Palestine that had been designated for the Palestinian state, and Egypt occupied the Gaza Strip. Despite the armistice, no final peace settlement was ever reached, and since 1948 Israel has technically remained in a state of war with Iraq and most of the other Arab nations—except for Egypt, which signed a formal peace treaty and granted Israel full recognition in 1979.

Since winning its independence, Israel defeated Arab forces in three additional wars (1956, 1967, and 1973). Iraq contributed troops to the 1967 and 1973 wars. During the 1967 Six-Day War, Israel conquered the West Bank of the Jordan River, the Gaza Strip, and the old city of Jerusalem, from which Jews had been excluded during the Jordanian occupation. Israel annexed the old city and occupied the Gaza Strip and West Bank, which are both predominately populated by Palestinians. The annexation of Jerusalem, which is a holy site for Jews, Muslims, and Christians alike, and the occupation of the West Bank and Gaza Strip have ever since been matters of contention between Israelis and Arabs, who are predominately Muslim.

In June 1981, Israeli bombers destroyed a nuclear power plant under construction in Osirak, Iraq, after Israeli intelligence ascertained it was to be used for producing nuclear weapons. Though Iraq and France maintained that the French-built facility was intended solely for peaceful uses, Hussein's desire to procure nuclear weapons had been widely known. Israel, which is generally believed to possess nuclear weapons of its own, was condemned by the U.N. Security Council for the raid, which was an act of war. In 1987, Palestinians began an uprising (called an *intifada*) against the Israeli occupation and demanded their own homeland in the occupied territories. Hussein championed the Palestinian cause, and throughout the Persian Gulf War he commanded the overwhelming support of most Palestinians within Jordan and Israeli-occupied lands.

During the summer of 1990, while most U.S. and Arab experts downplayed the possibility of an Iraqi attack against Kuwait, Israeli analysts warned Colin Powell, Chairman of the Joint Chiefs of Staff, that an invasion was likely. Israel was quick to condemn the invasion, but its offer to assist in Operation Desert Shield was turned down because the Bush administration feared that the participating Arab countries would leave the coalition if Israel joined. After invading Kuwait, Hussein offered to withdraw if Israel would likewise withdraw from its occupied territories and Syria would remove its troops from Lebanon. But his efforts to link the Kuwaiti occupation to the other military occupations in the region were unsuccessful, despite some efforts by the French and Soviets to appease him by calling for an international conference on the Middle East (*see* **Diplomacy**).

To simultaneously gain popular support among Arabs and undermine support by American Jews for a war against Iraq, Hussein threatened to launch Scud missiles armed with chemical warheads against Israel if the coalition attacked Iraq. (Iraq had fired such missiles against Iran during the Gulf War.) In response, all Israeli citizens and, to a lesser extent, Palestinians in the occupied territories were issued gas masks and instructed on how to seal rooms in the event of a chemical attack. On January 18, the day after the commencement of the war, Hussein ordered the first Scud launching against Israel, injuring 12 civilians. However, fearing nuclear reprisal, the Iraqis did not use chemical warheads in this or any of the other missile attacks. During the war a total of 40 Scuds were launched against Israel, all against civilian populations. Even though a few wayward missiles landed in the West Bank, the Scud attacks were widely cheered by Palestinians in the occupied territories (*see* **Scud Missiles**, **Patriot Missiles**).

Ever since its inception, Israel's policy had always been to aggressively defend itself, but Israeli Prime Minister Yitzhak Shamir acceded to President Bush's request that Israel refrain from retaliating against Iraq. Bush feared that an Israeli reprisal might force the Arab nations from the coalition, since the Arab governments would find it politically impossible to fight alongside Israel against another Arab country. Indeed one of the main reasons Iraq attacked Israel was to splinter the coalition in just this way. And though the Israelis had plans to launch aerial strikes and insert ground forces into western Iraq to destroy the Scud launchers, Shamir refrained because he did not want to jeopardize Israel's special relationship with the United States and because he feared Hussein might use an Israeli attack as an excuse to withdraw his troops from Kuwait—and thereby dissolve the coalition—and redeploy them in a holy war against Israel.

Instead, Shamir agreed to Bush's proposal to give substantial military aid to Israel and send batteries of Patriot antimissile missiles to Israel and to make destroying Scud launchers a major priority in the air campaign. Altogether, the 40 Scuds killed 4 civilians, wounded 289, and damaged or destroyed 11,727 apartments.

Though the Persian Gulf War did not have an immediate impact on Arab-Israeli relations, it contributed to the movement toward normalized relations between Israel and Jordan, Syria, and the Palestinians later in the 1990s.

**Joint Forces Command**—For political reasons the Arab and other Islamic forces serving in the Persian Gulf War did not serve under the U.S. Central Command (CENTCOM), which, under the leadership of General Norman Schwarzkopf, commanded all British, French, and U.S. troops. Instead, the Arab and Islamic forces banded together under a Joint Forces Command (JFC) that coordinated with CENTCOM through the Coalition Coordination, Communications and Control Integration Center.

Saudi Arabia's Lieutenant General Khalid Bin Sultan commanded the JFC, which was organized into two main army corps comprised of troops from 24 nations: JFC–North and JFC–East. The JFC–North consisted of an Egyptian armored division, an Egyptian mechanized division, a Syrian armored division, a Syrian mechanized division, a regiment of Egyptian Rangers, a regiment Syrian special forces, a Saudi armored brigade, a Saudi mechanized brigade, a Kuwaiti infantry brigade, and a Niger infantry battalion. The less heavily armored, more infantry oriented JFC–East included units from all six nations in the Gulf Cooperation Council: Saudi Arabia, Kuwait, Oman, Bahrain, United Arab Emirates, and Qatar, as well as battalions from Morocco, Pakistan, and Senegal. In addition to these two main army corps, a smaller Forward Forces Command was comprised of the Saudi National Guard, Saudi army units, and a Pakistani armored brigade.

The JFC–East played a major role in the battle of Khafji between January 29 and 31, 1991. In their only significant ground offensive of the war, Iraqi armored divisions initially over-ran lightly armed Saudi National Guard units close to the border, but with the support of U.S. Marines and U.S. artillery, air, and naval gun support, Saudi and Qatari forces turned back the attack and inflicted heavy damage. The Saudis suffered 29 killed and 36 wounded in action (*see* **Khafji**).

The JFC also played a significant role during the ground offensive to drive the Iraqis from Kuwait. The JFC–East flanked the U.S. Marines on their right and drove up the coast to Kuwait City. On February 27, they became the first troops to enter and liberate the city. The JFC–North flanked the Marines on their left. They breached dug-in Iraqi defenses on the first day of fighting and then likewise drove toward Kuwait City, capturing many Iraqis along the way. They, too, entered Kuwait City on February 27 as liberating heroes. Seventy-one JFC soldiers died in combat: 47 Saudis, 12 Egyptians, 10 from the United Arab Emirates, and 2 Syrians. In addition the JFC suffered 344 wounded: 220 Saudis, 95 Egyptians, 17 from the United Arab Emirates, 8 from Senegal, 2 from Bahrain, 1 from Oman, and 1 Syrian (*see* **Battle for Kuwait**).

**Jordan**—Though officially neutral during the Persian Gulf War, Jordan, which has a large Palestinian population, gave political support to Iraq, and Hussein enjoyed popular support within Jordan throughout the crisis. In compliance with the U.N. embargo against Iraq, Jordan closed the Red Sea port of Aqaba to Iraqi shipping, but otherwise it did not strictly enforce prohibitions against smuggling materials into Iraq. Following Iraq's invasion of Kuwait on August 2, 1990, Jordan was beset by some 200,000 refugees fleeing Kuwait and Iraq, most of whom were Arabs and other Muslims who had worked as laborers in Kuwait. Jordan set up refugee camps but was forced to close its border with Iraq on August 22, because it could no longer handle the influx of refugees. Despite its new policy of accepting no new refugees until those currently in Jordan had been repatriated, thousands more fled across the border. Following pleas by

the United States and other countries, Jordan reopened the border on August 24 and agreed to allow 20,000 people a day to enter. In return the United Nations, Great Britain, and the United States agreed to offer assistance, but because of Jordan's support of Iraq, that assistance was slow in coming. On January 9, 1991, Jordan again announced it was closing the border until it received international aid. However, on January 18, the day after the war began, Jordan reopened the border. The same day it and the Palestine Liberation Organization (PLO) officially condemned the air attacks against Iraq. On February 2, a misdirected Scud missile aimed at neighboring Israel landed in Jordan but caused no casualties.

**Khafji**—The Saudi coastal town of Khafji, located across the Kuwaiti border from Mīnā Saʿūd, is important to the history of the Persian Gulf War for two reasons. It was the site of the first major ground engagement of the war. It was also the site of a mysterious rocket explosion on January 20, 1991, that appears to be associated with high risk for Gulf War Syndrome.

On the night of January 29, the Iraqis launched their only ground offensive in the war, as four columns from the Iraqi 15th Mechanized Regiment and 5th Mechanized Division invaded border regions in Saudi Arabia near the coast. Marine reconnaissance aircraft detected them as they crossed the Saudi border, but inexplicably the Air Force command failed to issue an order to bomb the highly vulnerable armored units, which proceeded undeterred into Saudi Arabia. Earlier in the day, British carrier-based helicopters sank 12 of 15 Iraqi patrol boats that were apparently on their way to raid Khafji, in coordination with the ground attack.

Three of the Iraqi columns encountered allied forces and were repulsed in the early morning hours of January 30. At Al Wafrah, on the Saudi-Kuwaiti border southwest of Mīnā Saʿūd, U.S. Marines stopped an Iraqi tank battalion, and allied jets destroyed dozens of Iraqi tanks and armored vehicles. To the west, a reinforced Saudi National Guard company briefly skirmished with a mixed force of

Iraqi tanks, reconnaissance vehicles, and personnel carriers. This may have been primarily a reconnaissance mission to discover allied positions in the area. The third column attacked a U.S. Marine position at Umm Hujul. The Americans also defeated that attack, but 13 Marines from the 2nd Division's 2nd Light Armored Infantry Battalion were killed, 11 by "friendly fire"—fire from their own troops. Seven of the friendly fire deaths came when a U.S. Maverick missile struck a Marine Light Attack Vehicle. Four more Marines died when an American TOW missile struck their vehicle (*see* **Friendly Fire**).

The fourth column, consisting of 80 to 100 tanks from the Iraqi 5th Mechanized Division, comprised the main attack force. The tanks approached a Saudi National Guard outpost with their gun turrets pointed backwards—an internationally recognized sign of surrender. But as they approached the Saudi positions, which were manned by only about 20–25 soldiers in Land Rovers, the tanks turned their turrets forward and sprayed the Saudi guardsmen as they drove past. U.S. AC-130 helicopters and Cobra gunships destroyed four tanks and 13 other vehicles, but the Iraqi brigade proceeded south to occupy the abandoned Saudi town of Khafji.

The sudden arrival of the Iraqi mechanized units trapped two Marine reconnaissance teams inside the town. The 11 Marines hid in houses and cellars for almost two days and ordered in "danger close" fire support and close air support to fight off the Iraqis and stop their forward progress. Meanwhile, the Saudi National Guard from the Abdul Aziz Brigade counterattacked, supported by a Qatari tank battalion and U.S. Marines from the 1st and 2nd Marine divisions. In one of the most evenly matched tank battles of the war, four Qatari AMX-30 tanks fought five Iraqi T-55M tanks. The Qataris destroyed four of the T-55Ms; the fifth was abandoned. By 2 P.M. on January 31, the Iraqi force in Khafji was defeated. About 100 Iraqis were killed, and 430 surrendered. The Saudis and Qataris captured 85 Iraqi armored vehicles, including 11 tanks, while losing 19 soldiers killed in action. Four of those were killed by friendly fire when a mixed flight of American and Qatari planes accidentally bombed their position. More successful air strikes inflicted heavy casualties on the Iraqi armored columns, though 14 Americans were killed when their AC-130 Spectre gunship was shot down by an Iraqi missile. A total of 25 Americans were killed during the battle. After suffering heavy losses, the remaining Iraqi units involved in the offensive pulled back and assumed defensive positions to await the allied ground attack.

Khafji was a decisive military victory for the allies, as they quickly repulsed Iraq's only offensive threat and inflicted heavy losses on the enemy. Nonetheless, Hussein touted it as a victory for the Iraqis and maintained that by capturing a Saudi town, he had shown that the allies were vulnerable, despite their air superiority and their ground forces. Indeed, one of the reasons for ordering the attack may have been to bolster the morale of the Iraqi troops who had been passively enduring allied bombardments for over a week, and Hussein's declaration of victory contributed to that effort. Hussein may also have been trying to provoke the allies into initiating their ground offensive prematurely. Another reason for the attack was to gain intelligence about allied troop strength and positions, since the allies' air campaign had eradicated Iraqi reconnaissance capabilities two weeks earlier. Finally, according to the Iraqi chief of military intelligence, Major General Wafic al Sammarai, Hussein ordered the attack on Khafji in the hopes of capturing 4,000 or 5,000 allied POWs to use as human shields, as he had publicly threatened to do on January 21, only eight days before the battle. According to General al Sammarai, Hussein intended to have his soldiers strap American, French, and British POWs to the front of Iraqi tanks, and then have the tanks overrun the oil fields in Saudi Arabia. Hussein was convinced that to spare the hostages, the allies would refrain from bombing the invading tanks.*

*\*General al-Sammarai made this claim on the* Frontline *documentary* The Gulf War, *which aired on January 9–10, 1996.*

Though the Iraqis failed to take the large number of prisoners Hussein wanted, they did take the first American woman prisoner of the war when Army Specialist Melissa Rathburn-Nealy, a truck driver, inadvertently drove into Iraqi-occupied Khafji on January 29. Her companion, Specialist David Lockett, was also captured (*see* **Women in the Military**).

The battle had other consequences as well. The Saudi guardsmen reported the Iraqis' false surrender ruse, putting other allied troops on guard against subsequent Iraqi surrenders. This may in fact have been the point of the ruse, since it might discourage Iraqi soldiers in the future from surrendering to allied personnel who henceforth would be suspicious of their true intentions.

Also, the Marine friendly fire deaths brought increased attention to the problem of accidentally shooting friendly troops, and it prompted additional steps for improved recognition of friendly forces.

Finally, a 1997 University of Texas study of 249 veterans from the 24th Naval Reserve Construction Battalion suggests that personnel who were exposed to mist from a rocket explosion over Khafji on January 20 appeared to be at higher risk for Gulf War Syndrome. The Pentagon claims the mist was rocket propellant from an Iraqi Scud missile that detonated in the air above Khafji. But some veterans who were present believe the mist, which burned the skin and triggered chemical alarms, was an Iraqi gas attack. Those with the most severe ailments had taken PB, an antinerve gas tablet, and been exposed to the stinging mist from the explosion (*see* **Gulf War Syndrome**).

**Kurdish Rebellion**—During the war and following the allied victory in Operation Desert Storm, President Bush called upon the people of Iraq to depose Hussein, and two separate rebellions sprang up in southern and northern Iraq. A spontaneous uprising of Shī'ah Muslims in southern Iraq began on March 3, 1991. However, it failed to receive the support from nearby coalition troops, and the Republican Guard suppressed the Shī'ites in about three weeks (*see* **Shī'ite Rebellion**).

On March 5, Kurds in northern Iraq initiated their own revolt. The Kurds, an ethnic minority that had suffered persecution in Iraq, had been seeking autonomy virtually since the formation of Iraq after World War I, and they had already rebelled against Hussein twice before. In 1973, when Hussein was deputy chairman in charge of internal security, the shah of Iran furnished weapons and other support to the Kurdish independence movement. As long as the Kurds enjoyed Iranian support, Hussein was unable to suppress the rebellion, and in 1975 he was forced to sign the Algiers Accord with the shah in order to terminate Iranian support for the Kurds. In return, Hussein renounced Iraq's claim to total control of the Shaṭṭ al-'Arab estuary, which Iraq needed to gain shipping access to the Persian Gulf. This was no small concession: control of the Shaṭṭ al-'Arab later became the principal cause of Iraq's eight-year Gulf War with Iran in the 1980s. Once Iran stopped supplying the Kurds, Hussein was able to quickly squelch the insurrection. However, in the later years of the Gulf War, while Iranian armies were invading Iraq, Kurdish rebels renewed their rebellion. This time Hussein used nerve gas to suppress them, killing some 5,000 Kurdish civilians in a single attack at Ḥalabjah, on the Iran-Iraq border, in 1988 (*see* **Iran-Iraq Gulf War**). Following the overwhelming allied victory in Operation Desert Storm, Kurdish rebels again hoped to take advantage of Iraq's military misfortunes to gain independence.

The Kurdish insurrection began on March 5. On March 7, Hussein ordered the Republican Guard to suppress both the Kurdish and Shī'ite insurrections. The rebels, who were being attacked by Iraqi tanks and helicopters that survived the war, as well as by forces that had been held in reserve outside the Kuwaiti theater, requested assistance from the coalition. But despite Bush's earlier calls for revolt, the United States announced on March 10 that it would not actively support the rebellions because they were Iraqi internal affairs. The Kurdish leaders, in particular, had understood Bush's call for insurrection to imply U.S. support would be forthcoming, and they counted on that support when they launched their rebellion. Consequently, when Bush declared that the United States would not intervene, they felt betrayed.

Bush may have tolerated Hussein's suppression of the Kurds and Shī'ites because he did not want to enmesh the U.S. military in a bloody and prolonged occupation or peacekeeping operation. This was the position of General Colin Powell, the chairman of the Joint Chiefs of Staff and other members of the administration who pointed out that the conflict had been going on for hundreds of years, and that the United States was unlikely to resolve it. Moreover, like the Iraqi military, the Sunni-led Saudis may have preferred having a weakened Hussein in power to seeing an independent Shī'ite nation established on its border, right beside the portion of Saudi Arabia that contains the greatest oil reserves and has a large Shī'ite population. Likewise, Turkey, which had its own difficulties with Kurdish separatists on its southern border, was not anxious to see an independent Kurdish nation formed in northern Iraq. Whatever the underlying reasons, the United States officially took the position that Hussein's war against the Kurds and Shī'ites was an internal Iraqi matter for which there was no U.N. mandate to intervene.

The Kurdish rebellion lasted about five weeks, and the Kurds briefly seized control of a large portion of northern Iraq before they were squelched. On March 19, Kurdish rebels captured the oil city of Kirkūk, but on March 28 the Iraqi Army launched a major counteroffensive. It retook Kirkūk on March 30 and recaptured the Kurdish city of As-Sulaymānīyah on April 3. By April 7, approximately one to two million Kurdish refugees were fleeing from the Iraqi Army. U.S. and British pilots, who were under strict orders not to intervene, watched from the air as the Iraqi Army pursued and massacred them. On April 9, British Prime Minister John Major proposed that the United Nations establish protected enclaves as safe havens for the Kurds. Finally, on April 13 a cease-fire was declared.

As the plight of the Kurds became a featured television news story, the United States and Great Britain increased emergency aid to the refugees. On April 7, the United States inaugurated Operation Provide Comfort to send humanitarian aid and security assistance to Kurds in northern Iraq, and four days later Bush warned Hussein against using military force against the proposed safety enclaves. On April 16, Bush announced the establishment of safe havens for Kurdish refugees. The next day he and Major agreed that coalition troops would be required to protect the safety zones. Meanwhile, the Patriotic Union of Kurdistan and the government of Iraq began negotiating an agreement to permit limited Kurdish autonomy within Iraq. On April 24, they provisionally agreed on a plan, and on June 21 they concluded a draft agreement spelling out the terms of Kurdish autonomy. But on June 28, the Kurdish leaders refused to sign the agreement after Hussein imposed new conditions.

The United States and Great Britain began withdrawing from the Kurdish safe havens on June 15, leaving the peacekeeping responsibility to less well equipped U.N. security forces. However, the United States temporarily ceased its withdrawal on June 21, and on June 25 it announced plans to place a small rapid deployment force in Turkey to protect the Kurds.

In accordance with the terms of the peace agreement that ended the Persian Gulf War, coalition planes continue to enforce zones over northern Iraq where Iraqi military aircraft are forbidden to fly, and periodically Iraqi jets have been shot down. More recently, the situation has been further complicated by fighting between the two major Kurdish independence movements (*see* also **Aftermath**).

**Kuwait** *see* **Invasion and Occupation of Kuwait, Causes of the War, Diplomacy.**

**Luck, Gary E.**—Lieutenant General Luck commanded the U.S. Army 18th Airborne Corps which was responsible for the western flank of the allied invasion during the ground war. Born in 1937, Luck was commissioned as a second lieutenant of armor in 1960, after

**General Norman Schwarzkopf converses with General Gary Luck (right) (photograph courtesy of the Department of Defense).**

graduating from Kansas State University. He served in Vietnam first as a Special Forces commander and later as a troop commander. He received an MBA from Florida State University and a Ph.D. in business administration from George Washington University.

The 18th Airborne Corps was the first to deploy to Saudi Arabia during Operation Desert Shield. From August through November 1990, it was the major U.S. ground force in the region and was responsible for countering an anticipated Iraqi invasion of Saudi Arabia. That invasion did not occur, however. The Corps consisted of the 82nd Airborne Division, the 101st Airborne Division, and the 24th Mechanized Division. In addition, the 3rd Armored Cavalry Regiment, the 12th Combat Aviation Brigade, and French 6th Light Armored Division were attached to the corps and fell under Luck's command.

During Operation Hail Mary the corps secretly shifted to positions as far as 250 miles inland along the Saudi-Iraqi border in preparation for the ground war (*see* **Operation Hail Mary**). During the ground war the French 6th Light Armored Division and the 2nd Brigade of the 82nd Airborne Division captured the strategic airfield at As-Salmān (*see* **As-Salmān Airfield**), and the 101st Airborne Division made military history when its 1st Brigade conducted the largest heliborne operation ever, as over 300 helicopter sorties ferried troops, ammunition, supplies, refueling equipment, and building materials to establish Forward Operation Base Cobra 93 miles inside Iraq. The next day, 101st's 3rd Brigade conducted the deepest air assault in military history (*see* **Forward Operating Base Cobra**), and over the first four days the 24th Mechanized Infantry Division traveled faster and farther than any armored division in history, as it raced into the Euphrates River Valley to cut off the Republican Guard.

In 1993, Luck was promoted to four-star general and named commander-in-chief of the U.N. Command in Korea (*see* **U.S. Army 18th Airborne Corps**, **Battle Against the Republican Guard**).

**Media Coverage**—The Persian Gulf War was notable for its media coverage. On the one hand, satellite technology permitted instantaneous "real time" television war coverage never before available. Moreover, the Cable Satellite Public Affairs Network (C-SPAN, founded 1979) offered complete coverage of Congressional deliberations and military briefings, and the Cable News Network (CNN, founded 1980) provided virtually continuous coverage of the ongoing crisis. During the early part of the war CNN journalists were permitted to file reports from Iraq. Such live coverage from the enemy capital during wartime was unprecedented. On the other hand, strict military censorship limited U.S. reporters' access to information and the battlefield to a far greater extent than in previous wars. At the same time, Iraqi censorship skewed reporting from Baghdad. Both the Iraqis and allies were aware of the impact of television on public support for the war; both sides tried to take advantage of it; and actions of both sides were influenced by it.

Prior to the war Hussein was able to directly address the citizens of the countries that were opposing him. His ability to make his own case was unprecedented. In an effort to forestall the Bush administration from waging war, he appealed to what he believed were the greatest fears among the American public. He vowed that a war would result in huge casualties, threatened environmental warfare and missile attacks against Israel, and invoked memories of the Vietnam War. Nonetheless, Hussein's manipulation of the medium was far from masterful, and he turned many viewers against him in late August when he met with 15 British hostages during an internationally televised session. After saying he was detaining them to avoid "the scourge of war" and that they would all be "heroes for maintaining peace," Hussein singled out 7-year-old Stuart Lockwood and, patting him on the head, asked the child about his well-being and whether he was receiving his milk. Though Hussein was ostensibly exhibiting his concern for Lockwood and another boy who was present, most viewers throughout the world regarded the broadcast as a thinly veiled threat that Hussein would use these children and the other men and women in the group as human shields if the then-forming coalition were to attack Iraq. His attempt to intimidate the Western powers backfired, as world opinion denounced his implied threat against the innocent children.

President Bush, too, had access to worldwide television coverage. He justified the U.S. deployment of troops to defend Saudi by repeatedly likening Hussein to Hitler and rejecting any Munich-like appeasement of the aggressor. Though this demonizing of Hussein probably helped Bush win support for the military involvement, it later fueled sentiments that the war was unsuccessful because Hussein, the Hitler-like tyrant, remained in power even after allied forces defeated him. On September 16, 1990, a videotaped message from Bush to the Iraqi people was broadcast over Iraqi television. Bush denounced the invasion of Kuwait as monstrous and declared, "Nobody wants war, but if the military option is imposed on us, we will have to take it." Afterward, an Iraqi official accused Bush of trying to fool the Iraqi people. In televised addresses during the air war Bush encouraged the Iraqi people to end the war by overthrowing Hussein. On February 15, 1991, about one week before the ground war began, he called for "the Iraqi military and the people of Iraq to take matters into their own hands to force Saddam Hussein the dictator to step aside." This statement and later ones after the conclusion of Desert Storm suggested to Iraqi Kurds and Shī'ites that the United States would support their postwar insurrections against Hussein, though that support was never given.

For the first time in history, viewers throughout the world were able to watch a war commence when reporters in Baghdad broadcast live video coverage of the first air raids on the morning of January 17, 1991. Likewise, viewers from coalition nations could see the immediate destruction caused by their countries' air raids, including damage to civilians and nonmilitary structures. One of the effects of

this immediate access to visual documenta-
tion of the horrors of war was to create unprecedented sympathy for the enemy while
the fighting was ongoing. In this respect, television coverage influenced the conduct of the
war. For instance, when an American raid on
February 13 destroyed an Iraqi bomb shelter,
Iraq pointed to the 204 noncombatants killed
in the bombing as proof that the allies were selecting civilian targets, despite their proclaimed policy of limiting civilian casualties.
Cable News Network (CNN) broadcast images
of the ruined bunker and the casualties, and
its on-the-spot reporter, Peter Arnett, reported
to the entire world that the Iraqi government
claimed the facility had been used solely as a
civilian bomb shelter and that he could see no
evidence that it had been employed for any
military use. Despite the fact that CNN soon
presented military experts who reviewed the
videotape and pointed out considerable evidence to suggest that the bunker had indeed
also been a military command and control
facility as the United States claimed, Iraq
won a big public relations victory. Moreover,
the allies thereafter restricted their targets in
Baghdad as a result. The incident also increased the pressure to end the air campaign
in Iraq and begin the ground war more
quickly (see **Al-Firdos Bunker**). Similarly, anticipation of the public response to televised
carnage on the Highway to Hell, in which
hundreds of Iraqis were killed while fleeing
Kuwait on February 26 and 27, influenced
President Bush's decision to call an end to the
fighting at midnight on the 27th (EST), before
the Iraqi forces were entirely destroyed (see
**Highway to Hell**).

Throughout the war, administration officials and military officers briefed the public,
and by its end several generals emerged as admired media figures who held their own
against a sometimes combative press corps.
Among these were General Schwarzkopf, the
commander-in-chief in the Kuwaiti theater of
operations, Lieutenant General Thomas Kelly,
the Joint Chiefs of Staff operations officer, and
Marine Brigadier General Richard Neal. In
addition to providing basic information, these
briefings were intended to sustain public
confidence and support. For this reason, the
advanced technology used against the Iraqis
received considerable attention. In one of the
most impressive briefings General Schwarzkopf presented video footage showing a video-
guided "smart bomb" entering the headquarters of his Iraqi counterpart. On the other
hand, care was taken to "sanitize" the war by
not showing dead bodies or providing the
body counts that had been a daily feature of
Vietnam War reporting. The day before the
war ended Schwarzkopf gave a clear, effective
presentation of the allied battle plan and the
progress of the ground offensive. Dubbed "the
mother of all briefings"—an ironic reference to
Hussein's vow to wage "the mother of all battles"—Schwarzkopf used charts to show how
the Republican Guard was trapped with no
route of escape: "The gate is closed." In fact,
however, the gate had been left ajar, and a large
portion of the Republican Guard did manage
to escape into the Iraqi city of Basra.

U.S. military censorship was controversial
because of the American tradition of a free
press. In Iraq that tradition did not exist, and
Iraqi censorship was typically taken for
granted. CNN reporters were not permitted to
show or discuss military damage in Iraq or to
freely interview Iraqi citizens without a government escort. Israeli officials also imposed
restrictions on television coverage of the Scud
attacks.

One of the most controversial aspects of the
media coverage was the U.S. military's re-
striction of reporters' movement and access to
information. These policies were the result of
the Sidle Commission that followed the 1983
Grenada invasion in which press access to military operations was also highly restricted. It
is generally believed that these restrictions resulted from a widespread perception within
the military that negative reporting had been
responsible for turning the public against the
Vietnam War. Instead of having open access to
the battlefield, as they had during the Vietnam
War, journalists reporting on Grenada and the
Persian Gulf War were restricted to limited-
sized press pools. The rules governing the

pools were established in a January 14 memo that stated:

> Prior to or upon commencement of hostilities, media pools will be established to provide initial combat coverage of U.S. forces.... News media personnel who are not members of the official CENTCOM [Central Command] media pools will not be permitted into forward areas. Reporters are strongly discouraged from attempting to link up on their own with combat units.... In the event of hostilities, pool products will be subject to review before release to determine if they contain sensitive information about military plans, capabilities, or vulnerabilities.... Material will be examined solely for its conformance to the attached ground rules, not for its potential to express criticism or cause embarrassment. The public affairs escort officer on scene will review pool reports, discuss ground rule problems with the reporter, and ... when no agreement can be reached with a reporter ... immediately send the disputed materials to JIB Dhahran [Job Information Bureau in Dhahran] for review.

Of the approximately 1,000 accredited reporters and technicians covering the air war from Saudi Arabia, only 126 were ever assigned to pools. Only about 250 journalists were chosen to cover the ground war. Each pool was accompanied by a military escort who was ostensibly present to assist the reporters but could also limit their access to people and places and censor their reports.

On February 14, the Pentagon issued guidelines for covering the war. Among the rules was the admonition that "the following information should not be reported because its publication or broadcast could jeopardize operations and endanger lives."

> 1) For U.S. or coalition units, specific numerical information on troop strength, aircraft, weapons systems, on-hand equipment, or supplies (e.g. artillery, tanks missiles, trucks, water), including amounts of ammunition or fuel moved by or on hand in support and combat units. Unit size may be described in general terms such as "company size," "multibattalion," "multidivision," "naval task force," and "carrier battle group." Number or amount of equipment and supplies may be described as "large," "small," or "many."

> 2) Any information that reveals details of future plans, operations, or strikes, including postponed or canceled operations.

> 3) Information, photography, and imagery that would reveal the specific location of military forces or show the level of scrutiny at military installations or encampments. Locations may be described as follows: all Navy embark stories can identify the ship upon which embarked as a dateline and will state that the report is coming from the "Persian Gulf," "Red Sea," or "North Arabian Sea." Stories written in Saudi Arabia may be datelined "Eastern Saudi Arabia," "Near the Kuwaiti Border," etc. For specific countries outside Saudi Arabia, stories will state that the report is coming from the Persian Gulf region unless that country has acknowledged its participation.

> 4) Rules of engagement details.

> 5) Information on intelligence collection activities, including targets, methods and results.

> 6) During an operation, specific information on friendly force troop movements, tactical deployments, and dispositions that would jeopardize operational security or lives. This would include unit designations, names of operations, and size of friendly forces involved, until released by CENTCOM.

> 7) Identification of mission aircraft points of origin, other than as land- or carrier-based.

> 8) Information on the effectiveness or ineffectiveness of enemy camouflage, cover, deception, targeting, direct and indirect fire, intelligence collection or security measures.

> 9) Specific identifying information on missing or downed aircraft or ships while search and rescue operations are underway.

> 10) Special operations task forces methods, unique equipment, or tactics.

> 11) Specific operating methods and tactics (e.g.. air angles of attack or speeds, or naval tactics and evasive maneuvers). General terms such as "low" or "fast" may be used.

> 12) Information on operational or support vulnerabilities that could be used against U.S. forces, such as details of major battle damage or personnel losses of specific U.S. or coalition units, until that information no longer provides tactical advantage to the enemy and is, therefore, released by CENTCOM. Damage and casualties may be described as "light," "moderate," or "heavy."

Many members of the press found the pool arrangement unsatisfactory. For instance, opportunities to interview pilots were extremely limited, and no reporters were allowed to fly on bombing missions, as Edward R. Murrow had during World War II. Moreover, the pool reporting on the battle of Khafji was not permitted to travel to the site of the fighting. Instead, it was forced to rely on official military reports that indicated the fighting had been solely between Iraqis and Saudis. The role of U.S. Marines was not made public until several reporters violated the press rules and went to Khafji on their own (*see* **Khafji**). Elsewhere, military escorts often insisted on changing words or facts that had no relation to matters of military security but that affected the slant of the story. For instance, a description of pilots as "giddy" was changed to "proud," and references to Navy pilots watching sex films were deleted, as were potentially embarrassing revelations of Christian church services being held in Saudi Arabia. Also frustrating for reporters was the military's practice of delaying their stories until they were no longer timely. On the other hand, military security was rarely, if ever, compromised during the war. Of special importance, nothing about Operation Hail Mary, the secret western redeployment of the bulk of the coalition ground forces—thousands of soldiers, trucks, and tanks—was prematurely revealed.

**Mother of All Battles**—On August 21, 1990, Hussein vowed that if the allies initiated a war against him, "the mother of all battles" would follow. The colorful language caught the popular imagination and provoked many spin-off expressions. The best known spin-off was the one used to describe General Schwarzkopf's February 27 press conference in which he described to reporters how the allied ground forces had trapped the Republican Guard in northern Kuwait. Some wittily described Schwarzkopf's performance as "the mother of all briefings."

**Naval Action**—Iraq has a very small shoreline, and only one limited port at Umm Qaṣr. In fact, its desire to gain unimpeded shipping access to the Persian Gulf was a major cause of both its Gulf War with Iran and its invasion of Kuwait (*see* **Iran-Iraq Gulf War, Causes of the War**). Because Iraq has less than 50 miles of coastline, its navy is minimal. Therefore, most of the naval action during Operations Desert Shield and Desert Storm involved enforcing the military and economic embargo against Iraq. Beginning on August 16, 1990, coalition ships intercepted some 7,673 merchant ships in the Persian Gulf, North Arabian Sea, the Red Sea, and the Gulf of Aden and boarded 964 of them. Fifty-one ships were turned back for trying to violate the embargo, and 11 warning shots were fired. There was no disabling fire. Though 78 percent of the interceptions occurred in the Persian Gulf and North Arabia Sea, 91 percent of the boardings and 88 percent of the diversions took place in the Red Sea and Gulf of Aden. U.S. ships accounted for 57 percent of the boardings. U.S. Navy personnel were responsible for conducting most of the searches, but teams from the U.S. Coast Guard also participated (*see* **Coast Guard**). The other searches were conducted by ships from Australia, Belgium, Canada, France, Great Britain, Greece, Italy, the Netherlands, Saudi Arabia, and Spain. Altogether, coalition navies patrolled nearly 250,000 miles of sea lanes (*see* **Embargo**).

Some 243 ships comprised the coalition navy. Most were used for enforcing the embargo or sweeping mines, though the U.S. Navy and Great Britain's Royal Navy actively participated in Operation Desert Storm. Those navies also furnished the most ships: the United States provided 160 vessels and Britain 26. Other contributors were France (14), Italy (10), Belgium (6), Germany (5), Spain (4), Australia (3), Canada (3), Netherlands (3), Argentina (2), Turkey (2), Denmark (1), Greece (1), Norway (1), Poland (1), and Portugal (1). Though not part of the coalition, the Soviet Union contributed 4 ships for enforcing the embargo. Members of the Gulf Cooperation Council patrolled in areas near their territorial waters (*see* **Gulf Cooperation Council**).

During the early part of the air campaign objectives for naval war were articulated: "1)

**Naval action (photograph courtesy of the Department of Defense).**

Destroy all Iraqi surface combatants and minelayers; 2) Deny Iraq the use of oil platforms for military purposes; 3) Move back Iraqi surface forces in the northern Persian Gulf from the south to north; and 4) Prevent attacks or threats against coalition forces and countries in the Gulf."

The Iraqi Navy was targeted during the air campaign, mostly by helicopters firing laser-guided missiles. The British Royal Navy played a major role in the war against the Iraqi fleet. On January 29, 1991, British carrier-based helicopters sank or severely damaged 12 of 15 Iraqi patrol boats that were apparently en route to attack the Saudi port of Khafji, which was then falling under Iraqi ground attack (*see* **Khafji**). On the next day several Iraqi missile boats and amphibious ships were heavily damaged during a 13-hour battle off Būbiyān Island (*see* **Battle of Būbiyān**). By February 2, 1991, all of Iraq's 13 naval vessels capable of delivering antiship missiles were damaged or destroyed. The Iraqi navy was thereafter judged to be no longer an effective combat force, and as of February 8, the coalition claimed sea control of the northern Persian

Gulf. Thereafter, the remaining Iraqi ships conducted only minor, isolated operations.

Iraqi water mines caused more problems for the allies than their navy did. The Iraqis placed over 1,200 mines into the Persian Gulf. Most were older contact mines which are typically anchored to the bottom of the ocean, with the mine itself residing just below the surface. These are relatively easy to clear, but the Iraqis cut a number of them loose, creating "free-floating" mines that are harder to detect or anticipate, because they are constantly moving and do not conform to any strategic pattern. Eventually, it is expected that free-floating mines left over from the Persian Gulf War will find their way through the Persian Gulf and into the Indian Ocean. On February 18, a contact mine blew a large hole in an American amphibious aircraft carrier, the USS *Tripoli*. Though severely damaged and initially in some danger of sinking, the *Tripoli* was able to continue its mission for several days before sailing to Bahrain for repairs.

The Iraqis also planted numerous bottom mines that rest on the seabed. These more sophisticated mines are detonated by the sound, water pressure, and/or change in magnetic field created by a passing ship. On February 18, a few hours after the *Tripoli* incident, a bottom mine damaged the USS *Princeton* so severely that the cruiser had to be towed from service and subjected to extensive repairs.

In addition to damaging two ships, the mines offshore from Saudi Arabia prevented the battleships USS *Missouri* and USS *Wisconsin* from supporting allied forces in the battle of Khafji. Mines also created a substantial obstacle to an amphibious landing on the Kuwaiti coast. Indeed, they were a contributing reason why the allies did not attempt to assault the Kuwaiti shore (*see* **Amphibious Landing**).

The allies did, however, use the threat of an amphibious assault to divert large numbers of Iraqi defenders to the coast and away from the actual sites of the ground attack. Prior to the ground war, General Schwarzkopf publicly alluded to an amphibious attack, and the Navy and Marines staged several practice landings— code-named Sea Soldier I–IV—to convince the Iraqis that one was forthcoming. On the evening before the ground offensive began, a 14-man team of Navy SEALs simulated an attack at Mīnā Saʿūd, Kuwait, to convince Iraqi defenders that an attack against the Kuwaiti coastline had begun. They detonated high explosives and shot at the beach with .50-caliber machine guns and grenade launchers, which they fired from four special warfare speedboats. They continued to simulate attacks throughout the ground war (*see* **Deceptions, Feints, and Ruses**). In other action before the ground war, SEALs gathered intelligence information along the Kuwaiti coast.

Offensive naval actions during Desert Storm included air attacks by carrier-based planes and offshore artillery fire from battleships. Overall, Navy and Marine aircraft flew about 24,000 sorties during the war. Thirty-two Tomahawk cruise missiles were also launched from ships against inland targets; twelve of these were fired from nuclear submarines, which had never previously fired the missiles in combat. The submarine launches were considered successful. Moreover, the bat-

tleships *Missouri* and *Wisconsin* fired over 1,000 tons of shells against land targets during Desert Storm. They primarily used their large 16-inch guns, which had a maximum range of 40 kilometers (24 miles). These were especially effective in supporting the forces from the Joint Arab Command–East as they proceeded up the coast toward Kuwait. Overall, the two ships combined to fire 1,083 16-inch shells during 80 artillery missions.

Coalition maritime forces also conducted raids on Iraqi-held islands offshore from Kuwait. On January 24, Navy SEALs recaptured the first piece of Kuwaiti territory when they assaulted Qaruh Island after taking fire from Iraqi forces there while trying to rescue Iraqi sailors from a sunken minesweeper. The SEALs took 67 prisoners and raised the Kuwaiti flag on the island. On January 29, Marines raided Umm Al-Maradim. Though they expected to find an Iraqi company occupying the island, they found it abandoned. The Marines captured documents detailing Iraqi mine locations in the northern Persian Gulf, and they destroyed heavy equipment that the Iraqis had left behind. From February 20 to February 22, helicopters raided Faylakah Island as part of the deception that an amphibious landing against Kuwait was imminent. On February 24, the first day of the ground war, a raid against the Kuwaiti port facility at Ash-Shuʿaybah was feigned to keep Iraqi defenders in place along the coast instead of sending reinforcements inland. Ash Shuʿaybah had been the planned site of the canceled amphibious landing. Similar feints took place the next day at Al-Faw and Faylakah islands and on February 26 at Būbiyān Island.

**Nuclear Warfare**—In addition to targeting Iraq's chemical and biological warfare facilities, the coalition also made it a top priority to destroy Iraq's facilities for developing nuclear weapons. By 1990, Hussein had made the production of a nuclear device one of his top goals, and Iraqi nuclear researchers had reached the first stages of producing enriched uranium. Prior to the war, the Iraqis were trying to illegally import U.S.-built nuclear triggering devices, but their efforts were foiled by a joint U.S.-British sting operation. At the time of its invasion of Kuwait, Iraq did not yet have a nuclear capability, though after the war experts examining their facilities estimated that the Iraqis may have been able to assemble a crude nuclear device within six months or one year. Thus, had the coalition waited one to two years for sanctions to succeed, there is a strong possibility Iraq would have been able to produce a nuclear device during that period (*see* **Embargo**).

According to Iraqi Foreign Minister Aziz, Iraq refrained from using chemical weapons against Israel or the coalition forces because it feared nuclear retaliation. (Though it has never acknowledged having a nuclear arsenal, Israel was believed to possess one. Of the coalition nations, the United States, France, and Great Britain had nuclear weapons.)

Although the United States never seriously contemplated the use of nuclear weapons, it did not entirely rule out the possibility of their use in the event of extreme provocation—presumably an Iraqi nuclear attack or a devastating chemical or biological attack. In early October, on the command of Defense Secretary Richard Cheney, and against his own wishes, Colin Powell, the chairman of the Joint Chiefs of Staff, ordered an assessment of nuclear strike options against the Iraqi Army. Cheney told Powell that he was not seriously considering the nuclear possibility, but that he wanted to be thorough and was curious about what it would entail. The team Powell assembled concluded that a large number of small, tactical nuclear weapons would be necessary just to damage a single division. Powell showed the results to Cheney and then destroyed them. When Powell commanded the 5th Corps in Germany in the 1980s, he formed great reservations over the practicality of tactical nuclear weapons. After seeing the results of this study he concluded, "If I had had any doubts before about the practicality of nukes on the field of battle, this report clinched them."

The U.N. Security Council's Resolution 687 (April 3, 1991) called for Iraq to notify the International Atomic Energy Agency (IAEA) within 15 days of all of the locations, amounts, and types of nuclear material it possessed and to place all of its nuclear material and facilities under the custody of the IAEA and the special U.N. commission. Iraq was also required to agree to on-site inspections and future ongoing monitoring and verification of its compliance. Because Iraq failed to comply fully with these provisions, the United Nations has since maintained the embargo against it (*see* **United Nations**).

**Objectives**—The Persian Gulf War achieved all the objectives President Bush articulated on September 13, 1990, before a joint session of Congress. The first goal was Iraq's withdrawal from Kuwait, the small, oil-rich neighbor located on the Persian Gulf which Iraq had conquered on August 2, 1990, and annexed on August 8. Bush also called for the restoration of the legitimate Kuwaiti government, security and stability in the Persian Gulf, and the safety of Americans abroad. The victory accomplished all of those goals. It pushed the Iraqi Army back into Iraq, made the Persian Gulf region secure, and enabled Kuwait's pro–Western emir, Sheikh Jabir Āl Ṣabāḥ, and his family to return to power. The Western hostages Hussein had used as human shields around sensitive military targets were returned before the fighting began.

Moreover, the war eliminated the ominous threat that Iraq might continue on to invade Saudi Arabia after conquering Kuwait. Like Kuwait, Saudi Arabia was rich in oil and had military and economic ties to the United States and other NATO powers. An Iraqi conquest of Saudi Arabia, coupled with its annexation of Kuwait, would have taken the world's most abundant oil reserves from conservative, pro–West Arab regimes and placed them instead under the sole control of Saddam Hussein, Iraq's anti–Western, anti–Israeli dictator. Operation Desert Storm ensured that this did not happen (*see* **Causes of the War**).

The results of the coalition's unstated and less universally shared objectives were more mixed. Though the allies inflicted heavy casualties on the Iraqi Army and eliminated it as an immediate threat within the region, they did not destroy it entirely, even though they had an opportunity to do so on February 28, when Bush called for an immediate suspension of offensive combat operations. Bush's much-criticized decision to end the fighting after the Iraqi Army had retreated from Kuwait, but while its war machine was still intact but highly vulnerable, remains the most controversial aspect of the war.

Neither did the allies succeed in another unstated goal: removing Hussein from power, either by killing him outright through missile and bombing attacks against his suspected residences in Baghdad, or by so weakening him politically at home that the disaffected Iraqi military would overthrow him in a coup or citizen uprisings would overthrow his regime. Though uprisings among Iraqi Kurds and Shī'ah Muslims broke out soon after Hussein's defeat in Operation Desert Storm, the military remained loyal, and the Western powers declined to assist the rebellions. Thus, even while his troops were collapsing on the battlefield, Hussein managed to consolidate his power by executing top generals who might oppose him, blaming them for the defeat. Shortly after the war concluded he further asserted his power by directing successful offensives against the Kurdish and Shī'ite populations within Iraq (*see* **Saddam Hussein**, **Kurdish Rebellion**, **Shī'ite Rebellion**).

Nor did the Persian Gulf War succeed in completely destroying Iraq's capacity to produce chemical and biological weapons. Most of the rest of the world had long since outlawed these forms of warfare, but between 1984 and 1988 Iraq employed deadly gas attacks in its Gulf War with Iran and in assaults against the Kurds, and Hussein had threatened to use chemical and biological weapons against the allies if they attacked his forces in Kuwait. He also threatened to use them in missile attacks against civilian population centers in Israel. Though Iraq did, in fact, launch 40 Scud missiles at Israel, and about 40 more at targets in Saudi Arabia, none carried chemical or biological warheads. Despite agreeing

to allow U.N. teams to inspect its chemical, biological, and nuclear research and production facilities and to destroy its stockpiles of materials, Iraq has refused to cooperate fully since the war. Consequently, the United Nations has refused to lift the economic embargo against Iraq (*see* **Biological Warfare**, **Chemical Warfare**, **Nuclear Warfare**).

**Occupation of Kuwait** *see* **Invasion...**

**Offensive War Preparations for Liberating Kuwait**—Even before the United Nations authorized it, the allies had begun preparing to take the offensive to remove the Iraqi Army from Kuwait. On September 24, 1990, General Norman Schwarzkopf, commander-in-chief of the U.S. Central Command, presented to General Colin Powell, chairman of the Joint Chiefs of Staff, a four-phase plan to liberate Kuwait. President Bush was briefed on the plan, which became the basis for Operation Desert Storm, on October 11. It called for a strategic air campaign within Iraq whose goal was, according to General Schwarzkopf, "to decapitate his [the enemy's] leadership, command and control, and eliminate his ability to reinforce Iraqi ground forces in Kuwait and southern Iraq." The plan would also establish air supremacy over Kuwait, inflict heavy casualties on the Iraqi Army prior to the ground offensive, and provide air support during the ground campaign. The initial plan for a ground campaign, which was based on a coalition force of only 200,000 troops, was unsatisfactory, but by the end of October a new plan based on more than twice as many troops called for allied armored divisions to exploit the Iraqis' vulnerable western flank.

On October 1, most of the U.S. naval ships in the area participated in Operation Camel Sand off the shore of Oman. This was the first rehearsal for a possible amphibious attack. In response to the allies' increasingly bellicose words and actions, Hussein threatened to attack Saudi Arabia and Israel with long-range Scud missiles if a war broke out. And in late October, the Iraqi Army began placing explosives on Kuwaiti oil wells to destroy them if the allies attacked, thereby depriving Kuwait of its greatest financial asset and permanently depriving the West of an important source of oil (*see* **Environmental Warfare**).

On November 8, immediately after the mid-term Congressional elections, Bush enabled Schwarzkopf and his staff to prepare for Desert Storm by ordering an additional 150,000 air, sea, and ground troops to the Persian Gulf. The massive buildup was predicated on Schwarzkopf and Powell's conviction, based in part from their experiences in Vietnam, that the best military and political strategy would be one that allowed the allies to employ all of their resources against the enemy, without restrictions. This contrasted the Vietnam War policy of gradual escalation in response to new enemy actions. Bush concurred, preferring to take the short-term political lumps for calling up reserve units and sending hundreds of thousands of Americans overseas, to the long-term political consequences of a limited and protracted war. Moreover, Schwarzkopf and Powell accurately contended that by using their full force, the allies could minimize their casualties and bring the war rapidly to a close.

The generals were anxious to start the offensive in January or February, since the desert conditions would be optimal during that period. In late February and March, seasonal rain and dust storms could impede maneuvers and threaten to jam the sophisticated machines and technology that gave the allies their advantage.* After March, the fierce summer heat would be too intense for fighting. So, if Desert Storm did not commence in January or February, the coalition would have to wait until the following autumn, and that would entail many political risks, domestically and within the coalition.

On the other hand, the argument against the January-February timetable was that it did not give ample time for a diplomatic solution to be worked out. Indeed, one of the main criticisms of Bush's handling of the crisis was that he did not try hard enough—or not very hard at all, according to some critics—to resolve the conflict by diplomatic means, or give the economic embargo sufficient time to change the political climate inside of Iraq and force Hussein to relent (*see* **Diplomacy**).

However, Bush's defenders maintain that prospects for a negotiated settlement appeared slim right from the beginning, especially as the allies were unwilling to compromise on their basic demands: release of all hostages, complete withdrawal from Kuwait, renunciation of the annexation of Kuwait and of aggressive intentions against it, and reparations to Kuwait. And each new aggressive step Hussein took made it more difficult for him to back down without losing face and harder for the coalition to accept solutions that would permit the Iraqis simply to walk away from Kuwait unpunished. Plus, waiting for sanctions to work would require Bush to take the unpopular step of maintaining hundreds of thousands of troops in Saudi Arabia, many of whom were reservists who had been called away from families and jobs.

Moreover, a prolonged U.S. military presence in Saudi Arabia would have been politically unpalatable to the Saudis, who had heretofore resisted having foreign bases on their soil. And the coalition troops would have to passively stand by in their defensive positions, while Hussein would still be free to plunder Kuwait, abuse the human rights of its citizens, and threaten new bellicose actions against Israel and elsewhere. At the same time, his stature would increase among working class Arabs who admired his ability to stand up to the West. Plus, the American diplomats and citizens held in Iraq and Kuwait would have remained hostages to Hussein, who released them in December 1990, only after the United Nations voted to permit an offensive war against Iraq. Furthermore, Hussein would gain time to crack the unnaturally united front against him and eventually undermine the coalition and the sanctions themselves.

---

*No doubt Schwarzkopf was cognizant of the desert sandstorm that crippled U.S. helicopters and ruined a commando effort to rescue the American hostages in Iran on April 25, 1980.*

Waiting for sanctions to succeed would also have given the Iraqis more time to develop their nuclear, biological, and chemical weapons programs. After the war experts estimated that at the time of its invasion of Kuwait, Iraq was six months to one year away from being able to assemble a crude nuclear device. Thus, had the coalition waited one to two years for sanctions to succeed, there is a strong possibility Iraq would have been able to produce a nuclear device during that period.

Consequently, both as a means of putting more pressure on Hussein to leave Kuwait and as a prelude to waging war if he did not, the Bush administration continued to strengthen the U.S. forces in Saudi Arabia. At the same time, Iraq, which had begun conscripting 17-year-old boys, was estimated to have deployed 35 divisions, consisting of 542,000 troops, 4,300 tanks and 3,100 pieces of artillery in the Kuwaiti theater of operations. On November 29, the U.N. Security Council voted to authorize the use of force to eject the Iraqis from Kuwait if they did not withdraw by January 15. Talks on January 9 between U.S. Secretary of State James Baker and Iraq's Foreign Minister Tariq Aziz failed to yield results, and on January 12 Congress voted to authorize war.

**Oman**—A member of the Gulf Cooperation Council and the Arab League, Oman is located on the southeast coast of the Arabian peninsula. In 1979, it entered into negotiations with the United States to provide port and airport facilities to the U.S. military; these became available in 1983. In 1980, Oman participated in Bright Star, a joint military exercise conducted with the United States. During the Gulf crisis Oman provided air bases, ports, and other facilities to the coalition and established a major hospital staffed by U.S. Army personnel. Its ships helped enforce the naval embargo against Iraq, and several vessels carrying illegal materials to Iraq were diverted to its port of Muscat. Omani troops participated in the diversionary amphibious exercises intended to convince the Iraqis that a coalition landing would take place on the Kuwaiti shore. During Operation Desert Storm, Oman contributed a motorized infantry battalion to the Arab Joint Forces Command-East that liberated Kuwait City on February 27, 1991. One Omani soldier was wounded in combat (*see* also **Gulf Cooperation Council, Joint Forces Command**).

**101st Airborne Division** *see* **Battle Against the Republican Guard**, **U.S. Army 18th Airborne Corps**.

**Operation Desert Shield**—After the invasion of Kuwait on August 2, 1990, Iraq's subsequent intentions were not clear. With its armored divisions massed at the border of Saudi Arabia and Kuwait, Iraq was in a position either to consolidate its victory in Kuwait or to proceed onto Saudi Arabia, where the oil-rich northern provinces were essentially undefended and vulnerable to the Iraqi forces. Iraq's modern, well-equipped armed forces were not only the largest and most formidable in the region—apart from Israel's—they were also mobilized and in position. On the other hand, the sudden conquest of Kuwait had taken the Saudis and their allies by surprise, and the comparatively small Saudi armed forces were not at a high state of readiness. Consequently, Saudi Arabia was highly vulnerable to attack, and much of the world feared an invasion might be imminent.*

An Iraqi conquest of Saudi Arabia, coupled with its annexation of Kuwait, would have taken the world's most abundant oil reserves from conservative, pro–West Arab regimes

---

*Some commentators argue that had Hussein indeed continued the invasion and at least seized the ports and oil fields in eastern Saudi Arabia, he might have fared better in the war that followed. Not only would he have had most of the Middle East's oil under his direct control—about 40 percent of the world's proven oil reserves—he could also have denied the allies any Saudi port of entry on the Persian Gulf, thereby considerably impeding their ability to land troops and supplies in the contested regions.

One possible explanation for his failure to take this course of action is that Saddam may not have expected a military response to his seizure of Kuwait and did not want to provoke one by invading Saudi Arabia.

Some of Bush's critics maintain that the Bush administration deliberately overstated the threat to Saudi Arabia because

and placed them instead under the sole control of Saddam Hussein, Iraq's anti–Western, anti–Israeli dictator. This contingency was clearly neither in the best interests of the United States, the Western industrialized nations, or Saudi Arabia itself. Therefore, on August 6, after meeting with Defense Secretary Richard Cheney and being briefed by General Schwarzkopf, Saudi Arabia's King Fahd took the unprecedented step of allowing the United States military to send troops to his country in order to defend it against a possible Iraqi invasion. The agreement stipulated that the U.S. military presence would be temporary, and U.S. personnel would respect the Saudis' traditions and religious customs. In return, Saudi Arabia agreed to increase its oil production by 2 million barrels a day to help compensate for the 4.1 million barrels lost when Iraq stopped exporting its own oil and Kuwait's. The Saudis later also agreed to pay for all American contracts and for 4,800 tents, 20 million meals, and 20.5 million gallons of fuel a day. The defense of Saudi Arabia was conducted under the code name Operation Desert Shield.

Immediately after receiving King Fahd's permission to station troops in Saudi Arabia, President Bush began deploying troops to the region. Bush defended the action by invoking the 1979 Carter Doctrine, in which President Carter had declared following the Soviet invasion of Afghanistan that any attempt to gain control of the Persian Gulf would be treated as "an assault on U.S. vital interests and such an assault will be repelled by any means necessary, including military force." (*See* **Carter Doctrine**.)

On the day after the Saudis requested U.S. assistance in their defense, Egypt consented to permit U.S. warships to use the Suez Canal, and that day a carrier battle group headed by the USS *Dwight D. Eisenhower* passed through it from the Mediterranean Sea into the Red Sea. Egypt's severe condemnation of Iraq in the Arab League and its early cooperation with the Saudis and United States were important first steps in forming an international coalition against Iraq that included other Arab states (*see* **Egypt**, **Joint Forces Command**).

On August 7, preparations to send an American rapid deployment force to defend the Saudis and their oil fields began, and on August 8, elements of the 82nd Airborne Division and the 101st Airborne Division departed for Saudi Arabia, where they arrived the next day in the port of Dhahran. They traveled fully armed in anticipation of the possibility that they might enter combat immediately upon debarking, though this proved unnecessary. The possibility of war remained, however. On August 10, Hussein called for a "holy war" to liberate Mecca and Medina, Islām's holiest cities in Saudi Arabia.

Hussein gave credence to the threat by moving more troops into Kuwait and strength-

[continued] *Bush wanted to go to war all along, and he manipulated Hussein, the press, the American public, and world leadership into waging war so he could destroy Iraq's power and reassert the United States' position in the emerging post–Cold War world order.*

*Martin Yant's* Desert Mirage *presents the extreme case against Bush. One of Yant's most significant claims is that Bush and the military community deliberately inflated the number of Iraqi troops, tanks, and offensive weapons massed in Kuwait in order to convince the Saudis and the rest of the world that Saudi Arabia was at risk.*

*Yant cites an article in the* St. Petersburg Times *from January 6, 1991, in which two satellite imaging experts who reviewed satellite photos from September 11, 1990, stated that they could not see anything to indicate an Iraqi force in Kuwait even 20 percent as large as the Bush administration was claiming. According to one of the analysts, Peter Zimmerman, who had formerly served with the U.S. Arms Control Disarmament Agency, although he could clearly make out the U.S. troops congregating near Dhahran, in Iraqi-occupied Kuwait, "We don't see any tent cities [in the satellite photos], we don't see congregations of tanks, we don't see troop concentrations, and the main Kuwaiti air base appears deserted."*

*According to Yant, the* St. Petersburg Times *purchased the photos from a commercial Soviet service. The discrepancy between Pentagon claims of an Iraqi buildup and those made in the newspaper was never resolved. The major news services declined to pick up the story and report it nationwide, either because, as Yant suggests, by January most people had made up their mind to support the president, and editors did not wish to challenge their complacency, or the news services found the story flawed or unreliable.*

*The Iraqi's experience in their eight-year war with Iran had made them adept at camouflaging the troops and equipment from aerial surveillance. However, U.S. military reconnaissance had sophisticated sensors that allowed nonvisual means of detection. They could, for instance, detect the heat radiating from camouflaged tanks and trucks at night. It is possible that these sensors allowed military analysts to discern an Iraqi buildup, even though it was masked from the commercial Soviet satellite.*

**Soldier patrolling the desert in a Blackhawk helicopter during Operation Desert Shield (photograph courtesy of the Department of Defense).**

ening the Iraqi defenses along the Saudi border. The Iraqis also began mining Kuwait's harbors to impede an amphibious invasion. On August 8, Hussein declared that Iraq had annexed Kuwait as its nineteenth province, and on August 15, he offered to settle the final terms of Iraq's Gulf War with Iran. Anxious to eliminate an enemy on his eastern flank while preparing against the international forces to the south, Hussein conceded everything Iran had been asking for since the 1988 cease-fire. Iran accepted the offer, and Iraq began dismantling its field fortifications there on August 18. On August 19, some 300,000 Iraqi ground troops began withdrawing from Iranian territory they had occupied since the conclusion of the Gulf War. Within two days of resolving the war with Iran, the Iraqis began moving 24 divisions from the Iran border to the Kuwaiti and Saudi border areas. By September 30, Iraq had stationed 22 divisions in the Kuwait theater of operations. These included some 433,000 soldiers, 3,350 tanks, 2,340 armored personnel carriers, and 2,140

pieces of artillery. Iran and Iraq resumed diplomatic relations on September 10 (*see* **Diplomacy, Iran-Iraq Gulf War**).

Hussein also tried to enhance his position against the allies by taking hostage Westerners who had been caught in Kuwait during the invasion. Hussein subsequently released all women and children but retained the men and continued to use them as human shields around sensitive target areas until December (*see* **Hostages**). The United Nations condemned this and other Iraqi actions against Kuwaitis and foreign nationals trapped in Kuwait and Iraq. During Operation Desert Shield it passed 12 resolutions directed against Iraq (*see* **United Nations**).

Meanwhile, the coalition continued to assemble. On August 9, Britain and France agreed to deploy their air forces in the Persian Gulf, and Turkey consented to allow U.S. planes to use its airbases and permitted the United States to expand its military presence in Turkey. By August 10, the Royal Saudi Air Force, the U.S. Air Force and U.S. Navy had begun exercises to coordinate air operations over the Persian Gulf. On August 11, the first Egyptian troops joined the defensive forces. On August 12, the first American was killed when an Air Force sergeant was struck by a military truck. On August 15, Syria announced it would deploy troops to Saudi Arabia, and on the next day warships from the Italian Navy were deployed to the eastern Mediterranean, south of Cyprus.

On August 21, Hussein threatened that if the allies initiated a war against him, "the mother of all battles" would ensue. The next day, Bush called up 200,000 members of reserve units for up to 180 days. The build-up of defensive forces, primarily from the United States but also from other coalition countries, continued through January.

The nascent coalition defenses remained vulnerable to an Iraqi assault throughout August and September. During that period, when it was believed that an invasion could come at any time, the heavily outnumbered coalition forces were too small and underequipped to stop an attack, and their mission would have been to fight a delaying action until reinforcements could be assembled and deployed. But the U.S. logistical effort was more efficient than even its planners had envisioned. By September 30, the U.S. Transportation Command had airlifted to Saudi Arabia 115,826 tons of cargo and 127,739 military and other support personnel, and the 24th Mechanized Infantry Division's M-1A1 tanks were beginning to arrive. Moreover, Great Britain, the Netherlands, France, and Italy had begun patrolling the Persian Gulf and Strait of Hormuz. France committed 4,000 troops on September 10, and eventually contributed 14,000. After the beginning of October the defense of Saudi Arabia was considered relatively secure.

On September 30, the United States sustained additional deaths in Operation Desert Shield when two crewmen were killed after a U.S. F-15E jet crashed while on a training mission in Oman. On October 8, the first fatal accident involving U.S. Marines occurred when two helicopters crashed in a night training mission, killing eight Marines.

Operation Camel Sand, the first amphibious rehearsal in Desert Shield, took place in Oman on October 1. Most of the U.S. naval ships in the area participated. Two days later, the U.S. Senate supported the deployment of troops to the Gulf region by a 96–3 vote. On October 9, Hussein announced that he would attack Saudi Arabia and Israel with long-range missiles if a war broke out.

Though many in the Bush administration, including Secretary of State James Baker and Chairman of the Joint Chiefs of Staff Colin Powell, initially wanted to allow the U.N.-sponsored economic and military embargo against Iraq to force Hussein to withdraw, by early October plans were already being prepared for an offensive action to drive the Iraqis out of Kuwait. On October 11, Powell briefed Bush on plans for the air campaign and on an initial plan for a ground attack based on the 200,000 troops then at Schwarzkopf's disposal. The plans for the ground attack were unsatisfactory, but at the end of October a new plan was submitted. Based on more than twice as many troops, it called for allied armored divisions to exploit the Iraqis' vulnerable western flank. If there was to be a war, Schwarzkopf was anxious to start it in January or February, since the desert conditions would be optimal during that period. In late February and March, seasonal rain and dust storms could impede maneuvers and threaten to jam the sophisticated machines and technology that gave the allies their advantage. After March, the fierce summer heat would be too intense for fighting. So, if Desert Storm did not commence in January or February, the coalition would have to wait until the following autumn, and that would entail many political risks, domestically and within the coalition.

Consequently, both as a means of putting more pressure on Hussein to leave Kuwait and as a prelude to waging war if he did not, the Bush administration continued to strengthen the U.S. forces in Saudi Arabia. On November 8, two days after the midterm Congressional elections, Bush ordered an additional 150,000 air, sea, and ground troops to the Per-

An Air Force tent city in Qatar during Operation Desert Shield (photograph courtesy of the Department of Defense).

sian Gulf. On November 14, Cheney authorized the call-up of 80,000 more Army reserves and 15,000 Marine Corps reserves.

Bush spent the Thanksgiving holiday in Saudi Arabia with the troops. A week later, on November 29, the U.N. Security Council authorized war against Iraq when it passed Resolution 678. The resolution permitted U.N. members to employ "all means necessary" to enforce the previous resolutions if Iraq did not withdraw from Kuwait by January 15, 1991. (Cuba and Yemen opposed the resolution, and China abstained). The following day, Bush offered for the first time to negotiate directly with Iraq and suggested a meeting between Secretary of State James Baker and Iraqi Foreign Minister Tariq Aziz. However, on December 18, a tentative meeting in Washington was canceled when the two sides could not agree upon terms for a reciprocal visit in Iraq. The meeting was eventually held on January 9, but it produced no results.

On December 1, Cheney increased to 115,000 the number of Army reservists called to active duty. Two days later he increased the Marine call-up to 23,000 and the call-up of an additional 63,000 National Guard reservists. By December 20, 280,000 U.S. troops were in the Middle East. By January 1, the number rose to 325,000, and by January 17, the beginning of Desert Storm, 425,000 U.S. troops were in the region, along with ground forces from 18 additional countries and ships from 13 others. The total number of coalition troops was about 720,000. At the same time Iraq, which had begun conscripting 17-year-old boys, was estimated to have deployed 35 divisions, consisting of 542,000 troops, 4,300 tanks and 3,100 pieces of artillery in the Kuwaiti theater of operations.

On January 12, the U.S. Congress voted to permit the use of military force to remove Iraq from Kuwait. The Senate vote was 52–47; the House voted 250–183. This was the first time since the Vietnam War that Congress voted directly to approve an offensive U.S. military action. After the failure of last-minute negotiations by France, Operation Desert Shield ended and Operation Desert Storm began on January 15.

Desert Shield stirred some controversy, both in the United States and Saudi Arabia. In particular, the matter of respecting the Saudi's Islāmic customs was a sensitive and somewhat complicated issue. Throughout Desert Shield and Desert Storm the U.S. Central Command tried to isolate American troops from the Saudi population to avoid cultural clashes. General Schwarzkopf made respecting Saudi customs the subject of his first general order in Saudi Arabia, which he issued on August 30. Schwarzkopf forbade alcohol and banned all printed material the Saudis might consider sexually explicit, such as body-building magazines, swimsuit editions of periodicals, lingerie and underwear advertisements, and any other visual material that "infer but do not directly show human genitalia, women's breasts or human sexual acts."

Moreover, because in Saudi Arabia women must wear *abayas* (robes that conceal all of their body and part of their head) and are not permitted to drive, Schwarzkopf ordered that female U.S. soldiers should dress modestly at all times. They were not allowed to wear shorts, short sleeves or certain bright colors, and in some companies they were not allowed to drive.

The deference to Saudi custom, at the expense of the personal freedoms of U.S. personnel—especially female soldiers—highlighted the fact that American troops were being sent to protect a nondemocratic monarchy that deprived its citizens of many of the personal and political freedoms Americans have traditionally cherished. The disenfranchisement of Saudi women and the imposition of stringent limitations on their behavior, in accordance to Islāmic tradition, struck an especially raw nerve among many Americans who had celebrated the expanded rights and opportunities that U.S. women had acquired during the Cold War era. Paradoxically, American women played a much larger role and were given far greater responsibilities in the Persian Gulf War than in any previous war, but they were constrained by the coalition's desire and need to respect Islāmic culture.

The Saudis, in turn, were concerned that the American presence might provoke Saudi citizens to emulate the behavior of American soldiers, in violation of Islāmic tradition. A highly publicized demonstration of Saudi women who drove cars around Riyadh demanding driving privileges was the most visible example of the effect of the American influence on Saudi citizens during Operation Desert Shield.

**Operation Desert Storm**—The offensive war against Iraq was called Operation Desert Storm. Officially, it lasted from January 17 through the cease-fire on March 3, 1991, though the major fighting ceased at 8 A.M. on February 28, when President Bush ordered the termination of offensive actions. At the beginning of the war Iraq had deployed an estimated 42 divisions in the Kuwaiti theater of operations, consisting of more than 540,000 troops, 4,700 tanks and 3,100 pieces of artillery. The total number of coalition troops in the Kuwaiti theater was about 720,000, with about 3,500 tanks. Another 150,000 Turkish troops were stationed at the border between Turkey and Iraq, but these did not participate in the war. The allies had fewer tanks and artillery pieces, but overall their equipment was better and their soldiers were better trained. They also enjoyed overwhelming air and naval superiority.

Desert Storm had two major phases: an air campaign and a ground offensive. Coalition navies provided air support and offshore artillery support, and Special Forces performed reconnaissance behind enemy lines, hunted for Scud launchers, served as liaisons with Arab forces, and performed other special operations (*see* **Naval Action** and **Special Operations Forces**). Meanwhile, psychological units dropped leaflets and broadcast messages over radio and loudspeakers encouraging Iraqi soldiers to desert or surrender and instructing them how to do it (*see* **Psychological Operations**).

### *The Air Campaign: January 17–February 28*

The air campaign began at 1 A.M. on January 17, 1991 (local time, 5 P.M. January 16, EST), one day after the U.N. deadline for an Iraqi withdrawal from Kuwait (*see* **Air Campaign**).

It continued throughout Operation Desert Storm. Based on an early plan submitted by Colonel John A. Warden III called Instant Thunder, the goal of the air campaign was to destroy Iraq's leadership and command and control capabilities and to eliminate its ability to reinforce Iraqi ground forces in Kuwait and southern Iraq (*see* **Instant Thunder**). The plan also established air supremacy over Kuwait, inflicted heavy casualties on the Iraqi Army prior to the ground offensive, and provided air support during the ground campaign.

Though it was the U.S. planes that flew most of the missions (about 85 percent), warplanes from Great Britain, France, Canada, Italy, Saudi Arabia, Qatar, and Kuwait contributed to the air war. The campaign made use of state-of-the-art aircraft, laser-guided "smart bombs" and high velocity antiradiation missiles (HARM missiles), sophisticated electronics, remote-piloted drones, and satellite data (*see* **Weapons Systems and Advanced Technology**).

The allies achieved air superiority in the first day and air supremacy by January 27. Their quick mastery of the air allowed the allies to safely bomb subsequent targets, it also deprived Iraq of reconnaissance capabilities. This proved crucial to the success of the ground war. Deprived of their aerial reconnaissance capabilities, the Iraqis frequently had no idea where the allied ground forces were. Meanwhile, the allies often had very good intelligence about Iraqi locations. Moreover, eliminating Iraqi reconnaissance enabled Schwarzkopf to secretly set up the surprise flanking attack that ultimately trapped and destroyed most of the Republican Guard. Schwarzkopf initiated the westward redeployment, which he called Operation Hail Mary, when he launched the air campaign on January 17, 1991 (*see* **Operation Hail Mary**).

The air campaign passed through several phases as it accomplished successive objectives. After destroying Iraqi air defenses it concentrated on destroying the Iraqi Air Force by shooting their planes from the sky, destroying them in their hangars, and destroying their airfields and runways.

With the Iraqi air force effectively eliminated from the fighting, the allies were able to concentrate on strategic bombing missions. Between January 19 and February 15, Iraqi strategic command and communication centers emerged as primary targets for Stealth bombers and F-15E fighter-bombers using laser-guided smart bombs. Without their command and communication centers, the Iraqi high command could not effectively direct and deploy their forces, arrange for supplies, or communicate important information.

After Iraq launched its first Scud missile against Israel on January 18, President Bush promised to make destroying Scud launchers a top priority in order to convince the Israelis not to retaliate. Bush feared that Israeli participation in the war would cause the coalition to splinter, as the participating Arab countries might refuse to fight alongside Israel against another Arab nation.

Despite General Schwarzkopf's objections that Scuds were not a major military target, Bush insisted that destroying Scud launchers become a top priority. "Scud hunting" thus accounted for as much as 40 percent of all air sorties in late January. The allies quickly destroyed the Iraqis' fixed-position Scud launchers, but destroying mobile Scud launchers was far more difficult, and Scud hunting remained a top priority throughout the war, as allied jets were assigned to crisscross over some 28,000 square miles of desert searching about for mobile launchers (*see* **Scud Missiles**). Iraqi chemical, biological, and nuclear facilities were also major targets (*see* **Chemical Warfare**, **Biological Warfare**, **Nuclear Warfare**).

By January 26, the Iraqi Army and its logistical and support facilities emerged as new priorities for the allies. General Colin Powell, the chairman of the Joint Chiefs of Staff, had stated that the allies would cut off the Iraqi Army and kill it. Destroying its source of supplies enabled them to cut it off, and bombing Iraqi troops on the ground played a major role in killing it. Thus, prior to the beginning of the ground war, allied planes and helicopters attacked Iraqi fortified positions, fieldworks, bunkers, tanks, and artillery pieces. Their goal was to reduce Iraqi ground strength by 50 percent before the beginning of the offensive. Coalition planes also targeted the trucks and railroads necessary for delivering food, water, fuel, ammunition, medical supplies, replacement parts, clothing, and other materials essential to the Iraqi Army. They also struck at Iraq's electric power generators to further cripple the army's ability to sustain itself. By the time the ground war began on February 24, the Iraqi ground troops suffered from a severe lack of food and water, and many were ill. Consequently, both their stamina and morale were low. Once the ground war began, Iraqi troops and armored vehicles became targets for allied bombers and helicopters as they deployed from their concealed positions into the open desert.

The allies suffered 42 combat losses and 33 noncombat losses during the air campaign at a rate of 31 losses per 100,000 sorties. Iraq lost 40 planes in the air (confirmed) and several hundred on the ground. An additional 80 or more planes fled to Iran, where they were impounded. Though the allies tried to keep civilian casualties to a minimum, noncombatants were inevitably killed in the air war. Altogether, Iraq reported some 2,300 civilian casualties and 6,000 wounded by allied air attacks.

### The Battle of Khafji:
### January 29–31

The only Iraqi offensive action of the war took place about two weeks after the air campaign began. On the night of January 29, four columns from the Iraqi 15th Mechanized Regiment and 5th Mechanized Division invaded border regions in Saudi Arabia near the coast. Marine reconnaissance aircraft detected the mechanized columns as they crossed the Saudi border, but inexplicably the Air Force command failed to issue an order to bomb them, and the Iraqi forces proceeded undeterred into Saudi Arabia. One column attacked a U.S. Marine position at Umm Hujul. The Americans stopped the attack, but 13 Marines were killed, 11 by "friendly fire"—fire from their

own troops. Two of the other Iraqi columns were also repulsed in the early morning of January 30, as allied jets destroyed dozens of Iraqi tanks and armored vehicles. But the fourth column, consisting of 80 to 100 tanks accompanied by other armored vehicles, overran a thinly manned Saudi National Guard outpost and proceeded to occupy the abandoned Saudi coastal town of Khafji. The Iraqis apparently attempted to coordinate a naval raid on Khafji with the ground assault, but it was frustrated when British planes damaged 12 of the 15 participating patrol boats on January 29 (*see* **Naval Action**).

Two Marine reconnaissance teams trapped inside the town hid in houses and cellars for almost two days, while ordering in "danger close" fire support and close air support to fight off the Iraqis. Meanwhile, Saudi troops counterattacked, supported by Qatari tank units and elements of the U.S. 1st and 2nd Marine divisions. By 2 P.M. on January 31, the entire Iraqi force in Khafji was either killed or captured. After suffering heavy losses, the remaining Iraqi units involved in the offensive pulled back and assumed defensive positions to await the allied ground attack (*see* **Khafji**).

### The Ground Offensive:
### February 24–February 28

The ground war was the final phase of Operation Desert Storm. It incorporated the Air-Land battle doctrine developed in the 1980s to combat a potential Soviet invasion of Europe, and it relied on surprise, rapid thrusts deep inside enemy territory, and coordination among the different military services (*see* **AirLand Battle Doctrine**). The initial plan had been to commence in early– to mid–February, but Schwarzkopf postponed the ground offensive for about two weeks to allow the air campaign to continue weakening Iraqi positions on the battlefield. Schwarzkopf believed he could reduce allied casualties this way.

On February 9, Schwarzkopf recommended beginning the ground attack between February 21 and 25, and Bush approved. They set 4 A.M. on February 22 (local time, 8 P.M. on February 21, EST) as the starting time, though that

**M-1A1 Abrams tanks from the 1st Armored Cavalry Division (photograph courtesy of the Department of Defense).**

was later delayed for two days to allow for last-minute repositioning of the 1st Marine Expeditionary Force.

About 730,000 allied personnel were available for the offensive—(530,000 of those served in the U.S. armed forces)—while over 500,000 Iraqi troops were entrenched in defensive positions inside Kuwait. The Iraqis possessed more tanks than the allies (4,700 to 3,500) and more artillery pieces, but the allied tanks were superior and their crews were better trained. Plus, the allies enjoyed total air dominance. The allied commanders expected the ground offensive to require approximately ten days to four weeks and produce 10,000 or more allied casualties. (Estimates ranged from 3,000 to 20,000.) As it turned out, the ground war lasted 100 hours—a little more than four days. The allies suffered 190 killed in action,

including 88 Americans, 71 members of the Arab Joint Forces Command, 29 British, and two French troops. The Iraqis lost 20,000–30,000 dead. The allies captured over 70,000 POWs; the Iraqis took 41.*

On February 19, four days after the countdown for the ground assault had begun, Hussein agreed to a Soviet-brokered plan which called for him to withdraw from Kuwait within 21 days, in return for a cease-fire and the coalition's agreement to cancel the trade embargo and nullify all of the U.N. resolutions against Iraq. But the United States and the other coalition members rejected those conditions when the Security Council discussed the proposal and countered with an ultimatum that Iraq begin a large-scale withdrawal from Kuwait by 8 P.M. on Saturday, February 23 (local time, noon EST), or face a

---

*Source for allied KIA: Kevin Don Hutchinson, Operation Desert Shield/Desert Storm. Source for Iraqi KIA and POWs: Roger Cohen and Claudio Gatti, In the Eye of the Storm. The Iraqis did not keep close records, so the figure is approximate. In addition to these combat deaths, perhaps as many additional Iraqi soldiers died of diseases and other desert-related afflictions.*

ground war. Iraq failed to meet the deadline for withdrawing, and Schwarzkopf launched the offensive eight hours after the deadline expired, at 4 A.M. on February 24 (local time, 8 P.M. on February 23, EST).

Prior to the offensive, Schwarzkopf ordered several actions designed to fool the Iraqis into believing the attack would come at sites different from where it actually took place. Between February 15–20, the U.S. Army 1st Cavalry Division and artillery units from the 7th Corps initiated a series of feints designed to convince the Iraqis that the main assault would come up through the Wadi al-Bātin at the Saudi-Kuwaiti border. (A wadi is a river or stream bed that is usually dry, except during the rainy season. It makes a natural invasion route in desert terrain.) Moreover, Schwarzkopf issued public statements about an amphibious assault on the Kuwaiti shore and ordered several practice assaults to encourage the Iraqis to move their defensive units to the coast. On the evening before the ground offensive began, Navy SEALS simulated an attack at Mīnā Saʿūd, Kuwait to convince Iraqi defenders that an amphibious attack against the Kuwaiti coastline had begun. In fact, the amphibious attack never came because Schwarzkopf feared that water mines and other obstacles along the heavily defended Kuwaiti coast would make an amphibious landing too costly. But the preparations had been a successful ruse to convince the Iraqi commanders to deploy some 3,000 troops, artillery, and other resources away from the actual targets on the Iraqi western flank (*see* **Amphibious Landing**, **Deceptions, Feints, and Ruses**).

The offensive had two principle components: the Battle for Kuwait and the Battle Against the Republican Guard (*see* **Battle for Kuwait**, **Battle Against the Republican Guard**). The Battle for Kuwait concentrated on the liberation of Kuwait. It involved an assault against fortified Iraqi positions straight across the border into Kuwait and north toward Kuwait City on the coast. The Iraqis were expecting this attack and had prepared for it by building fortified bunkers, laying ex-

tensive minefields, and digging fire trenches (*see* **Iraqi Fortifications**). This part of the offensive was conducted primarily by the U.S. 1st Marine Expeditionary Force (1st and 2nd Marine divisions and the U.S. Army's armored Tiger Brigade) and the Arab and Islāmic Joint Forces Command (JFC). The JFC was broken into two forces. The heavily armored JFC-North flanked the Marines on the west and was comprised of armored divisions from Egypt, Syria, and Saudi Arabia. The mechanized and more mobile JFC–East flanked the Marines on the east and proceeded up the Kuwaiti coast. It was comprised of units from the Gulf Cooperation Council nations: Saudi Arabia, Kuwait, the United Arab Emirates, Qatar, Oman, and Bahrain. Other Islāmic countries such as Pakistan, Morocco, and Afghanistan also contributed small units to the JFC, which was under the overall command of Saudi Arabia's General Khalid bin Sultan (*see* **U.S. Marine 1st Expeditionary Force**, **Joint Forces Command**).

Prior to the main assault, Marine ground patrols reconnoitered the Iraqi minefields, and four Marine battalions advanced into Kuwait to provide fire support and mark lanes through the minefields for the ground attack. In what Schwarzkopf later called a textbook example of how to breach minefields, fire trenches, and entrenched fortifications, the Marines attacked at 4 A.M. on February 24 and quickly overcame the Iraqi defenses and moved north and east toward the coast and Kuwait City, which was their ultimate objective. The forces from the JFC began their attacks later in the day. On February 25, the JFC–North completed breaching the Iraqi fortifications, and the JFC–East began progressing up the coast toward Kuwait City. Meanwhile, the 1st Marine Division fought the largest tank battle in Marine Corps history in the Burqan oil field, where visibility was severely limited by oil well fires the Iraqis had set a few days earlier (*see* **Environmental Warfare**). Also, the 2nd Marine Division fought off an Iraqi counterattack. That night a large number of Iraqi trucks and armored vehicles were detected fleeing Kuwait City towards Iraq. Over the next two days these were subjected to intense allied air attacks, and thousands of vehicles were destroyed on the so-called "Highway to Hell" or "Highway of Death." (*See* **Highway to Hell**.) On February 26, the Tiger Brigade approached Kuwait City and destroyed a large number of enemy tanks at Mutla Ridge, high ground southwest of the capital that commands all of the highways leading into and away from Kuwait City. The 2nd Marine Division captured the suburb of al-Jahrah after encountering stiff resistance. Meanwhile, the JFC–East continued its movement up the coast toward Kuwait City, and the JFC–North approached its last objective, the ʿAlī as-Salīm airfield west of the city. On the night of February 26 and early morning of February 27, the 1st Marine Division destroyed approximately 250 Iraqi tanks while clearing the Kuwait airport, south of the city. This action enabled the Kuwait forces and other armies from the JFC–East to enter and officially liberate Kuwait City on February 27. Likewise, after capturing the ʿAlī as-Salīm airfield in the morning, the Egyptian, Syrian, and Saudi forces from the JFC–North passed through the 2nd Marine Division to enter the city from the west.

The campaign's second—and primary component, the battle against the Republican Guard—involved tank battles in northern Kuwait and in Iraq's Euphrates River Valley and the desert south of it. This was the main allied attack, and it surprised the Iraqis. Its objective was to destroy the Republican Guard, and it largely succeeded (*see* **Republican Guard**).

During Operation Hail Mary, the U.S. Army's heavily armored 7th Corps and highly mobile 18th Airborne Corps secretly shifted hundreds of miles to the west before the ground war began. Under their operational control were the British 1st Armoured Division and the French 6th Light Armored Division (the Daguet Division) (*see* **U.S. Army 7th Corps, U.S. Army 18th Airborne Corps, British 1st Armoured Division, French 6th Light Armored Division**).

On February 24, the mechanized forces that had deployed to the west during Operation Hail Mary pushed northward from Saudi Arabia into Iraq, before turning east. During the first two days, the 7th Corps proceeded approximately halfway to the Euphrates River Valley before executing its "left hook" as it rotated clockwise to send two American armored divisions and a mechanized infantry division eastward against the Republican Guard's flank near the northwestern border of Kuwait. Starting farther west, the 24th Mechanized Infantry Division raced north to the Euphrates Valley and then turned east to attack from the rear. It traveled faster than any mechanized ground force in history, averaging about 55 miles a day over four days. At the same time the British 1st Armoured Division crossed into Iraq and pushed east, paralleling the American attack above it and protecting the southern flank of the allied assault. Meanwhile, on the first day of battle farther west, the 1st Brigade of the 101st Airborne Division established a forward operating base 93 miles inside Iraq in the largest heliborne operation in military history. On the second day, the 101st's 3rd Brigade conducted the deepest air assault in military history as it airlifted 150 miles into the Euphrates River Valley, then marched an additional 20 miles through rain and mud to capture Highway 8, a key Iraqi supply route (*see* **Forward Operating Base Cobra**). During the first days of battle the French 6th Light Armored Division, accompanied by the 2nd Brigade of the U.S. 82nd Airborne Division, advanced to and captured the Iraqi airfield at As-Salmān to eliminate Iraqi air support from the ensuing tank battles and protect the western flank (*see* **As-Salmān Airfield**). Thus, within two days 7th Corp, the British 1st Armoured Division, and the 24th Mechanized Infantry Division had trapped the Republican Guard within a pocket outside of Basra, and the 101st Airborne Division had cut it off from reinforcements and supplies.

On February 26, Hussein announced on Baghdad Radio that Iraq was withdrawing its troops from Kuwait. President Bush called the announcement "an outrage. He is not withdrawing. His defeated forces are retreating. The coalition forces will continue to prosecute the war with undiminished intensity." By the end of the day, the allies destroyed over 21 Iraqi divisions, and the 24th Mechanized Infantry Division sealed off the Euphrates River Valley by cutting off the strategic Highway 8.

Moreover, 7th Corps and the British 1st Armoured Division began their assaults against the Republican Guard's armored divisions in what became the largest tank battle since World War II. It began when the 2nd Armored Cavalry Regiment encountered dug-in Iraqi tanks and soldiers along a ridge east of the map designation 73 Easting. The six-hour Battle of 73 Easting produced some of the fiercest fighting of the war, as the Republican Guard sent waves of tanks and motorized infantry against the 2nd Armored Cavalry's 2nd Squadron. The Americans took advantage of their M-1A1 tanks that had longer range, thicker armor, and thermal gun sights that enabled them to see through the rain and sandstorms that drastically reduced visibility (*see* **Weapons Systems and Advanced Technology**). The unsuccessful Iraqi tank attack was one of the few Iraqi offensive operations of the war. To the south at Wadi al-Bāṭin, the British 1st Armoured Division cut behind two dug-in Iraqi infantry divisions that had been opposing the U.S. 1st Cavalry Division. The British forces overran the infantry's rear positions and attacked Iraqi mechanized troops, who began to surrender.

On the following day, British and American forces trapped approximately three divisions of Republican guards in the Euphrates Valley and destroyed approximately 200 tanks, 50 armored vehicles, and 20 artillery pieces in what General Schwarzkopf described as a classic tank battle. Meanwhile, the U.S. 1st Armored Division destroyed 300 Republican Guard tanks and armored vehicles in the 40-minute Battle of Medina Ridge. To the north and west, the 101st Airborne Division cut off Highway 6, the Republican guard's final avenue of escape.

The allied forces were positioned to destroy most of the Republican Guard on February 28, when Bush ordered all coalition offensive combat operations to cease at 8 A.M. local time (midnight February 27, EST), because Kuwait had been liberated and Iraq defeated. The President, his civilian advisers, and generals Powell and Schwarzkopf all agreed that Iraq's offensive capabilities had been destroyed and continuing to slaughter Iraqi troops would be pointless and inhumane. Bush's order remains the most controversial decision of the war, because by terminating the fighting early it allowed much of the Republican Guard to survive and retreat back into Iraq, where it remained loyal to Hussein personally and helped him retain his absolute power within the defeated country (*see* **Cease-fire, Aftermath, George Bush**).

However, in the early morning of March 1, U.S. armored vehicles destroyed a convoy of 1,000 Iraqi vehicles moving north of the Rumaila oil field, after the Iraqis fired on them. Likewise, on the following day elements of the U.S. 24th Mechanized Infantry Division encountered fire from infantry, and a battle ensued in which two battalions of Republican Guards were destroyed. The fighting, which lasted several hours, led to the destruction of 177 Iraqi tanks and armored personnel carriers and the deaths of several hundred Iraqi soldiers. In addition, several civilians were killed, included a group of children whose school bus was struck in an air attack.

On March 2, the U.N. Security Council passed Resolution 686 setting down the conditions for a cease-fire, and on March 3, Iraqi generals met with Schwarzkopf and other coalition military leaders in a tent at Safwān airfield in southern Iraq, where they formally accepted the cease-fire and worked out the details for enforcing it. The Iraqis agreed to show their good faith by immediately releasing some POWs, which they began to do the following day. On March 8, Operation Desert Farewell began as the first 5,000 American troops left for home.

The Iraqi infantry and Republican Guard armored division were not entirely destroyed, but they were rendered an ineffective threat to other nations in the region, although they were still able to inflict heavy damage on Shī'ite and Kurdish rebels within Iraq (*see* **Kurdish Rebellion, Shī'ite Rebellion**).

According to the U.S. Air Force, the Iraqi Army lost about 76 percent of its tanks, 55 percent of its armored personnel carriers, and 90 percent of its artillery. About 1,430 Iraqi personnel carriers and 700 tanks managed to escape back into Iraq. On the other hand, the allies destroyed about 3,700 tanks, took over 70,000 prisoners, and rendered 33 Iraqi divisions ineffective. Approximately 20,000–30,000 Iraqis were killed from bombings and ground combat, and many others died from diseases and other desert-related illness. Moreover, an estimated 100,000 soldiers deserted during the air campaign. Approximately 2,300 civilians were killed and 6,000 were wounded during the air campaign.

U.S. casualties in Desert Storm were 124 killed in action, 357 wounded in action, and 21 taken prisoner. There were an additional 102 noncombat fatalities. During the ground war, 88 Americans were killed. The Arab Joint Forces Command lost 71, and 29 British, and 2 French soldiers died in combat. Eleven British, nine Saudi, two Italian, and one Kuwaiti soldiers were taken prisoner.

**Operation Hail Mary**—On January 17, 1991, along with launching the air campaign, the allies began their secret redeployment to points west of Ḥafar al-Bāṭin. Made in preparation for the surprise ground attack against the Republican Guard's western flank that took place between February 24 and 28, this western redeployment was called Operation Hail Mary. The name is a football expression to describe a play where the fastest receivers all line up on one side and race towards the end zone. Though often considered a desperation play—which the western redeployment was not—the play also connotes speedy movement and a quick strike. And Operation Hail Mary provided those.

Their quick mastery of the air allowed the allies to safely and secretly redeploy, free from Iraqi reconnaissance and Iraqi bombers or armored divisions that might try to destroy the vulnerable convoys or disrupt their move-

ment. Deprived of their aerial reconnaissance capabilities, the Iraqis were unable to detect the enormous movement of allied troops, armored vehicles, and supplies. Thus the 82nd and 101st Airborne divisions from the Army 18th Airborne Corps and the French 6th Light Armored Division traveled undetected as far as 530 miles to positions 250 miles inland along the Saudi-Iraqi border. The 24th Mechanized Division took up positions just east of them, and the Army 7th Corps and the British 1st Armoured Division redeployed about 300 miles to positions 150 miles inland in order to set up the surprise flanking attack that ultimately trapped and destroyed most of the Republican Guard. The western redeployment played a huge role in the overwhelming success of Operation Desert Storm.

Operation Hail Mary was one of the great logistical achievements in the history of warfare. As Schwarzkopf later noted, never had so large an army moved so far and then gone immediately and successfully into battle. Prior to the beginning of the ground offensive, 117,844 troops, 5,145 tanks and other tracked vehicles, 22,884 wheeled vehicles, and sufficient food, water, fuel, and ammunition to sustain them in the desert for 60 days of heavy combat were secretly transported as far as 530 miles. At the end of the first day, the initial convey was 120 miles long. For almost three weeks, columns of troops, weapons, and supplies moved continuously through difficult desert conditions, day and night, to their new, offensive positions west of Hafar al-Batin. By February 20, the 7th Corps, the 18th Airborne Corps, the French 6th Light Armored Division, and the British 1st Armoured Division were positioned to attack, with enough forward supplies to sustain the assault for 29 days (*see* **Operation Desert Storm**).

**Patriot Missiles** Known as "Scud Busters," Patriot antimissile missiles were the allies main defense against Iraqi Scud missile attacks. The U.S. Army Air Defense Artillery deployed 29 Patriot batteries to the Middle East to shoot Iraqi Scud missiles from the sky: 21 to Saudi Arabia, 6 to Israel, and 2 to Turkey. Initially,

**Patriot missile (photograph courtesy of Raytheon Corporation).**

the Patriots were believed to be very accurate, intercepting over 90 percent of the Scuds they were targeted for. (Official Army figures were 45 hits in 47 launches, with two accidental launchings; others counted 49 hits in 51 launches.) However, after the war it was revealed that the Patriots' rate of success was far lower, and it is now believed that the success rate for the Patriots was 20 percent or less, perhaps as low as 9 percent, though the exploding Patriots did sometimes deflect the Scud warheads from their targets. The discrepancy occurred because Scuds frequently broke-up in the air before striking their targets. The Scuds' self-destruction was originally attributed to the Patriots, which often mistakenly targeted the rocket boosters or other rocket debris and left the warhead intact. In either case, falling debris from disintegrating Scuds was also responsible for a number of military and civilian casualties. Towards the end of the war, Raytheon, the Patriot's manufacturer, improved the computer software to address this problem, but the fighting concluded before it could be widely implemented.

Each Patriot battery, or "fire unit," consisted of a radar that controlled eight launchers. Each launcher had four missiles. A Patriot battalion contained six batteries, for a total of 48 launchers and 300–400 missiles (including reloads).

The Patriot missile was originally designed in the early 1960s for antiaircraft, not antimissile, purposes. It was not put into full production, though, until the 1980s. In the intervening years designers continually upgraded the missile, especially its fire-control computers which, by the early 1980s, were fast enough to enable the Patriot to detect and destroy incoming missiles. Beginning in 1986, the Patriot was tested as an antimissile missile, and its fire-control computer software continued to be upgraded. In 1990, the Patriot received a new warhead that made it more effective.

On February 25, 1991, debris from a Scud exploding over Dhahran killed 28 U.S. Army Reserve personnel and wounded 100. No other single incident in the war accounted for more allied casualties. Neither of the two Patriot batteries assigned to protect the area was operating at the time of the attack. One was closed down for maintenance, the other failed to detect the incoming missiles because it was long overdue for maintenance and its fire-control system had lost accuracy. Each Patriot battery requires maintenance every 14 hours, but during the war some batteries, including the one at Dhahran, had to operate for over 100 hours between maintenance services.

Despite their shortcomings, the Patriots played an important political role by helping to keep Israel out of the war. On January 18, the day after the allies inaugurated the air war, Hussein countered by launching Scuds against Israel. His main intention was to draw Israel into the war in hopes that Israeli participation would cause the Arab partners to leave the coalition. In order to forestall this sequence of events, the United States convinced Israel not to retaliate, despite the unprovoked attacks on its main civilian centers. To keep the Israelis from retaliating, the Bush administration agreed to make the destruction of Scuds a top military priority and to supply batteries of Patriot missiles for Israel's defense. On January 20, after Patriot missiles ostensibly destroyed three of four Scuds aimed at the Saudi port of Dhahran, Israel requested a Patriot missile defense, and within 27 hours six Patriot batteries were established within Israel. Israelis manned two of the batteries; Americans operated the other four. The Patriots were credited with intercepting virtually all of the subsequent Scud attacks, and the Americans who manned the Patriot batteries were treated like heroes in Israel. The apparent success of the Patriot reduced public pressure on the Israeli government to retaliate against Iraq and helped make it politically possible for Prime Minister Yitzhak Shamir to exercise the restraint the United States requested, even though Israeli intelligence quickly ascertained that the Patriots were not working. Thus, even if their success later proved illusory, the Patriots played a critical role in keeping the coalition together.

On February 15, President Bush toured the Raytheon plant in Massachusetts that produced the Patriot missiles. Declaring, "We are going to prevail, and our soldiers are going to come home with their heads high" and "Thank God for the Patriot missile," he received a standing ovation and loud applause.

**Popular Support in the U.S. for the War**— Immediately following Iraq's conquest of Kuwait, the Bush administration began vilifying Hussein, calling him a brutal dictator and likening his seizure of Kuwait to Hitler's 1939 invasion of Poland at the start of World War II. For the West, the lesson of the 1938 Munich agreement that conceded Czechoslovakia's Sudetenland to Hitler was that bullying regimes must never be appeased. According to the analogy, the world could not afford to appease Hussein by permitting Iraq to retain Kuwait. (In the 1960s, the same analogy had been applied to North Vietnam's aggressive actions against South Vietnam to justify U.S. intervention there, though North Vietnam's claim that it was fighting a civil war of reunification had considerably more credibility than Hussein's claim that Kuwait was historically part of Iraq.) The intention of efforts to demonize Hussein was to make Americans perceive Iraq as a dangerous, aggressive power, presumably so they would be willing to support the administration's efforts to drive him from Kuwait. Indeed, Iraq was a dangerous and aggressive power, and Bush's rhetorical strategy was largely successful.

On the other hand, while most Americans approved of sending troops to defend Saudi Arabia, support for offensive military action to drive Hussein from Kuwait was less complete. Many believed that Bush was too eager to fight; they wanted to give diplomacy and economic sanctions more time to compel Hussein to withdraw (*see* **Embargo**). Others believed American soldiers were being sent to risk their lives primarily for the economic interests of the oil industry, with which Bush had close political and personal connections. Others had qualms about sending U.S. troops to restore a nondemocratic monarchy that deprived its citizens of many of the basic freedoms that Americans traditionally cherish. Supporters of women's rights found it especially problematic to go to war to restore a regime that, in accordance with Islāmic law, denied its women prerogatives and freedoms that are considered basic in the West. Still other citizens objected to Americans being used essentially as hired guns to fight for Saudis and Kuwaitis who had done preciously little to protect themselves. Some Jewish Americans, and other Americans as well, feared that Hussein would carry out his threat to attack Israel with chemical weapons if the allies started a war, and they did not think Kuwait was worth that risk. Moreover, the largely pro–Iraqi U.S. foreign policy up to the moment of the invasion made the administration's anti–Hussein rhetoric appear hypocritical. If Hussein was another Hitler, critics asked, why had presidents Reagan and Bush supported him for the past several years?

The fight for public support for the war was further complicated by satellite-based television news coverage which included live reporting from Baghdad. Thus Hussein was able to completely bypass government intermediaries and present his case directly to the American public. This was the first time in history that an enemy leader had the capability to make direct appeals to the American people prior to the outbreak of war. Very much aware of the psychological impact of the Vietnam War on the American psyché, Hussein warned that the United States faced a war "more terrible than Vietnam" (*see* **Media Coverage**).

The Bush administration had been able to proceed with Desert Shield primarily through executive orders which did not require Con-

gressional approval. Desert Storm was another matter, since the Constitution requires the consent of Congress to wage war. Various presidents had managed to work around that requirement during the Cold War, but in the post–Cold War political environment, where the United States was not being directly threatened by a nuclear-armed enemy, more stringent adherence to the Constitution was demanded.

But support for an offensive action was far from unanimous. Even Sam Nunn (D–Georgia), the respected conservative head of the Senate Armed Services Committee, opposed going to war, primarily because military intelligence had predicted 10,000–20,000 casualties.* Former Defense Secretary Robert McNamara, the architect of the Vietnam War, likewise warned of thousands of casualties and spoke out against war. So did Admiral William Crowe, a former chairman of the Joint Chiefs of Staff who implored Congress to give the embargo time to work. Throughout the country antiwar activists held vigils and organized peace rallies reminiscent of those which had protested the Vietnam War 25 years earlier.

A January 9 meeting in Geneva between Secretary of State Baker and Iraq's Foreign Minister Aziz yielded no results, nor had anyone seriously expected it to. But the conference enabled Bush to claim his administration had taken every extra step possible to negotiate an acceptable resolution, only to receive "a total stiff-arm" for its efforts. And on January 12, Congress voted that if Iraq did not withdraw from Kuwait by the United Nation's January 15 deadline, President Bush was authorized to use military force to remove Iraq from Kuwait. The Senate vote was 52–47; the House voted 250–183. This was the first time since the Vietnam War that Congress voted directly to approve an offensive U.S. military action.

---

*In December 1996, Nunn declared that he had been wrong to oppose the war, because "if I had voted that way [for the war], it would have given a more solid authorization of the war, which I thought was justified." Nunn had advocated giving economic sanctions more time to work before initiating military action. In his 1996 statement he added, "That assumption was wrong, and I think because the assumption was wrong, the delay in the war would not have accomplished the purpose that I thought it would, which was to cut the casualty rate down." He also observed that his vote against the war ruined any chances he might have had to become president.

**Powell, General Colin**—Chairman of the Joint Chiefs of Staff during the Persian Gulf War, Colin Powell was born April 5, 1937. An African American son of immigrants from Jamaica, he grew up in a multiethnic neighborhood in Harlem where, among other things, he learned the smattering of Yiddish that later served him well on his diplomatic assignments to Israel. He attended the City College of New York, where he majored in geology and joined the Reserve Officers' Training Corps (ROTC). Upon graduating in 1958, he joined the Army as a lieutenant and underwent Ranger and paratrooper training at Fort Benning, Georgia. Subsequently, he was assigned to the 3rd Armored Division in West Germany, whose Cold War mission was to stop a Soviet attack if one were launched. He served in Germany for two years. After a peacetime assignment in Fort Devens, Massachusetts, and five weeks at Fort Bragg's Unconventional Warfare Center, where he was promoted to captain, Powell served as a military adviser in Vietnam from December 1962 to November 1963. He was wounded in the foot by a poisoned punji stick while on patrol. After completing his tour of duty in Vietnam, he took the advanced Pathfinders course of airborne Ranger training and graduated first in his class. Powell then attended the Infantry Officers Advanced Course at Fort Benning, Georgia, which he completed in 1965. In 1966, he joined the faculty at Fort Benning and was promoted to major. In 1967, he attended the Army Command and General Staff College at Fort Leavenworth, Kansas, where he graduated second in his class.

In 1968, Powell returned to Vietnam for a second tour of duty. After serving as a battalion executive officer, he was chosen to serve temporarily as a division staff officer in charge of operations and planning. He suffered a broken ankle in a helicopter crash but remained on the job. He later received the Legion of Merit for his work and the Soldier's Medal for his rescue efforts following the helicopter crash.

After completing his tour of duty in 1969, Powell enrolled in George Washington University's Master's of Business Administration program. He was promoted to lieutenant colonel that year and received his MBA in 1971. Upon graduating he joined the staff of Lieutenant General William E. DePuy, who was restructuring the Army command in hopes of reducing the careerism and bureaucratic mentality that had been plaguing the military during the Vietnam War. In 1972, Powell was accepted into the White House Fellows Program designed to prepare future government leaders. During his year as a White House Fellow he worked at the Office of Management and Budget, where he met future national security adviser and secretary of defense, Frank Carlucci. He also visited the Soviet Union, Bulgaria, Poland, and China.

In 1973, Powell returned to the Army and was assigned to Korea, where he served as battalion commander for a year. In 1974, he worked in the Pentagon and dealt with interservice rivalries while preparing annual manpower projections for Congress.

The following year he enrolled in the National War College, the training school for generals. There Powell studied the writings of the 19th century Prussian general and military strategist Carl von Clausewitz, whose book *On War* influenced him significantly. In particular, Powell latched onto von Clausewitz's assertions that no one should start a war "without first being clear in his mind what he intends to achieve by that war and how he intends to achieve it"; that political leaders must set the war's objectives while armed forces achieve them, and that wars must retain popular support. For Powell, the United States' failure to adhere to these principles led to the debacle of Vietnam, and as chairman of the Joint Chiefs of Staff during the Persian Gulf War he remained very cognizant of them.

In 1976, while at the War College, Powell was promoted to full colonel. Subsequently, he joined the 101st Airborne Division as commander of the 2nd Brigade, but in 1977 he accepted an assignment to serve as executive assistant to John Kester, who was special assistant to the secretary and the deputy secretary of defense in the Carter administration.

In that capacity Powell visited Saudi Arabia and Iran shortly before the fall of the shah. He was promoted to brigadier general in December 1978, and made military assistant to Charles Duncan, the deputy secretary of defense. When Duncan was named head of the Department of Energy in 1979, Powell accompanied him as part of his transition team. However, after the transition was effected, Powell returned to the Department of Defense as military assistant to the new deputy secretary, W. Graham Claytor.

After Ronald Reagan became president in 1981, Powell remained in his position, but Frank Carlucci assumed the post of deputy secretary. Powell worked well with Carlucci but requested reassignment back to active military service. He served as assistant division commander for operations and training for the 4th Infantry Division from 1981 to 1982 and as deputy commanding general of the Combined Arms Combat Development Activity at Fort Leavenworth from 1982 to 1983. He was promoted to major general in 1983, shortly before returning to Washington as senior military assistant to Defense Secretary Caspar Weinberger. Powell served in that capacity until 1986, when he was promoted to lieutenant general and named commander of the Army's 5th Corps, which was stationed in Germany. However at the end of that year he returned to Washington at the personal behest of President Reagan to assume the post of deputy national security adviser during the shakeup within the administration following the Iran-Contra scandal. Carlucci, the new national security adviser, was his boss. Together, they helped devise U.S. policy during the later stages of the Iran-Iraq Gulf War in which the U.S. Navy escorted Kuwaiti oil tankers through the Persian Gulf under U.S. flags in order to assure the continued flow of oil from the Middle East (*see* **Iran-Iraq Gulf War**).

In November 1987, Reagan appointed Powell national security adviser when Weinberger stepped down and Carlucci replaced him as secretary of defense. Powell helped negotiate the INF treaty with the Soviet Union that re-duced the presence of intermediate-range nuclear missiles in Europe, and he participated in the Washington and Moscow summit meetings between Reagan and Soviet Premier Mikhail Gorbachev. Powell also played an indirect role in selecting Norman Schwarzkopf as commander-in-chief of the military's Central Command, which was responsible for areas of the Middle East and Southwest Asia, including Saudi Arabia and Kuwait.

Following the election of George Bush in 1988, Powell declined opportunities to head the CIA or serve as deputy secretary of state. Instead, following Bush's inauguration in January 1989, Powell returned to the Army and assumed the post of commander-in-chief of the Forces Command, which was responsible for all Army field forces based in the United States, including the National Guard and reserve units. He was simultaneously promoted to the rank of four-star general, the highest military rank in the nation. In August, Bush appointed him chairman of the Joint Chiefs of Staff over 14 four-star generals with seniority.

Four months later, after a U.S. Marine was killed and civilians were threatened, Powell recommended that the United States invade Panama, remove the dictator Manuel Noreiga from power, destroy his military power base, and restore the elected Endara government. He then oversaw Operation Just Cause, the U.S. invasion of Panama which achieved those objectives. Eventually Noreiga, who was then under indictment in the United States for drug trafficking, surrendered and was brought back to the United States, where he was convicted for his drug-related activities.

During July 1990, as Saddam Hussein began to issue bellicose charges and mass troops at the Kuwaiti border, Powell received regular briefings on the situation. Early in the month he traveled to the Middle East and met with leaders of Tunisia, Egypt, Jordan, Libya, and Israel. The Arab leaders told him an Arab-brokered diplomatic solution would be found, though the Israelis were less optimistic and more suspicious of Hussein's ultimate intentions. On July 24, Powell ordered Schwarzkopf to draw up plans for a U.S. military response in the event of two different possible developments: a minor border incident or a full-scale Iraqi invasion of Kuwait. On July 31, after it became evident that the Iraqis were indeed planning to attack, Powell ordered Schwarzkopf to come to Washington and brief Defense Secretary Richard Cheney and the Joint Chiefs of Staff. On the following day Schwarzkopf gave the briefing and offered his opinion that the Iraqis would probably attack but limit their objectives to seizing the Kuwaiti portion of the Rumaila oil field and Warbah and Būbiyān islands in the Persian Gulf. Dick Kerr, the deputy director of the CIA, expressed a similar assessment.

Immediately following Iraq's conquest of Kuwait on August 2, Powell briefed the president on his military options and stated his opinion that Hussein had not yet decided to invade Saudi Arabia and that the Iraqis did not want to fight a war against the United States. Nonetheless, Powell took the position that "it's important to plant the American flag in the Saudi desert as soon as possible, assuming we can get their okay." He also asked whether it was worth going to war to liberate Kuwait, but that question was deemed inappropriate for the chairman of the Joint Chiefs, who was a military adviser and not a policymaker, and it went unanswered. Though later reprimanded for raising the issue, in his memoirs Powell justified overstepping his authority by recalling how, as a midlevel officer in the field, he had been appalled at how the Joint Chiefs had pursued the Vietnam War "without ever pressing the political leaders to lay out clear objectives for them." Throughout the Persian Gulf crisis Powell tried to remain clearly focused upon the country's objectives.

On August 3, Powell and Cheney met with the Saudi ambassador, Prince Bandar, who was an old friend of Powell's. After Cheney expressed the United States' willingness to help the Saudis defend themselves, Powell overcame Bandar's early skepticism by informing him that the initial U.S. response would involve approximately 100,000 troops. After Cheney and Schwarzkopf secured King Fahd's approval on August 6 to base U.S. troops in Saudi Arabia, Powell began to oversee Operation Desert Shield.

On August 15, he briefed the president and his top advisers and provided a timetable for the U.S. buildup in Saudi Arabia. He predicted that by the end of the month enough troops would be in place to deter an Iraqi attack, and that by early December there would be 184,000 troops in the Middle East, a sufficient force to defend Saudi Arabia. The costs would be $1.2 billion through September 30, and $1 billion per month thereafter. Powell also advised that Bush would have to decide within about one week whether to call up the reserves. He further clarified the need for clear objectives by pointing out how different goals would entail different military requirements. "If your goal is only to defend Saudi Arabia and rely on sanctions to pressure Hussein out of Kuwait, then we should cap the troop flow probably sometime in October." But if Bush was planning a military operation to evict the Iraqis from Kuwait, the Joint Chiefs would need to know some time in October in order to sustain and increase the buildup. They would also need to know if the objective would be only to liberate Kuwait or destroy Iraq's warmaking capabilities, since those potential objectives would require different forces, different military planning, and a different schedule. During the meeting Bush indicated his doubts that sanctions would work, and afterward he publicly articulated the U.S. goal of achieving "the immediate, complete, and unconditional withdrawal of all Iraqi forces from Kuwait; [and] the restoration of Kuwait's legitimate government."

By early September plans for the defense of Saudi Arabia were fairly complete, and Powell instructed Schwarzkopf and his subordinates to begin preparing for an air and ground campaign to force the Iraqis from Kuwait. He approved the basic structure for the air campaign, initially called Instant Thunder, which was to strike deep inside Iraq and destroy its command and control installations, transportation systems, production and storage facilities, and air defense networks (*see* **Instant Thunder, Air Campaign**).

Powell visited Saudi Arabia on September 12. He inspected the troop deployments and met with Saudi leaders. Among other things, he helped defuse problems caused by cultural and religious differences between the Saudis and Americans. With tacit approval from the top Saudi leadership, he helped formulate a plan to bypass Saudi customs officials by shipping Christian Bibles directly to U.S. bases. Otherwise, the customs officers would have been required to confiscate the Bibles. Soldiers were ordered to wear crucifixes inside their shirts so they would not be in public view. Powell also arranged for Jewish personnel to be helicoptered to ships offshore, where religious services could be conducted outside of Saudi territory.

On September 24, Powell again advised Bush of his options. In the event that the president sought an offensive to eject the Iraqis from Kuwait, the military would be prepared to initiate a war in January 1991. On the other hand, they could maintain a defensive force in Saudi Arabia and wait for the economic sanctions that the United Nations had imposed to force Hussein to pull out. Without advocating either position, Powell noted that sanctions would require considerable time to work, if they would work at all, and they would leave the initiative with the Iraqis "to decide when they had had enough." He concluded by pointing out that the president still had several weeks to decide what he would do. Though Powell's own initial preference had been to give the sanctions time to work—according to some sources he was willing to wait up to two years—Bush expressed his opinion that there was insufficient time for the sanctions to produce results. Powell's early preference for sanctions over an offensive war later became a matter of some controversy, as some commentators maintained that he had actively opposed the president and created a rift within the administration. However, in his memoirs Powell plays down the extent of his opposition and points to Bush's continued support of him during and after the Gulf crisis.

In early October, on Cheney's command and against his own wishes, Powell ordered an

General Colin Powell (photograph courtesy of the U.S. Army).

assessment of nuclear strike options against the Iraqi Army. Cheney stated that he was not seriously considering the nuclear possibility, but that he wanted to be thorough and was curious about what it would entail. The team Powell assembled concluded that a large number of small tactical weapons would be necessary just to damage a single division. He showed the results to Cheney and then destroyed them. When he commanded the 5th Corps in Germany in the 1980s, he had formed great reservations over the practicality of tactical nuclear weapons. After seeing the results of this study he concluded, "If I had had any doubts before about the practicality of nukes on the field of battle, this report clinched them."

Also in early October, Powell asked Schwarzkopf to show him his initial plans for an offensive to force the Iraqis from Kuwait. Schwarzkopf replied, "I got no goddamn offensive plan because I haven't got the ground forces." Nonetheless, Powell insisted that Schwarzkopf send his chief of staff to Washington to brief Bush, Cheney, and the president's chief advisers on what Schwarzkopf could do with the 200,000 coalition troops at his disposal. By contrast, the Iraqis had over 400,000 defenders in fortified positions. Plans for an air campaign were satisfactory, but everyone who reviewed Schwarzkopf's initial plans for a ground offensive deemed them unsatisfactory because they called for an assault into the heart of the Iraqi defenses and would have resulted in an extremely high number of casualties.

Though Powell regarded the early plans as a "work in progress," others in the administration considered them an effort to forestall a war, and there was some talk that Cheney might bypass Powell and Schwarzkopf and assemble a different team within the Pentagon to map out a war strategy. In retrospect, it appears that Schwarzkopf's obviously unsatisfactory plan may have been a ploy to compel the political leaders to commit more troops for the war. A massive troop increase would require calling up additional reserves, diverting resources from NATO and elsewhere, and incurring other unsavory political liabilities. Many within the administration were hoping that the Iraqis could be bombed into submission without the United States having to pay those political costs. But Schwarzkopf was adamant that the 200,000 troops currently stationed in the Middle East were a defensive force, insufficient for attacking the more than 400,000 entrenched Iraqis, even if the allies had complete air superiority.

His ploy of presenting untenable assault plans guaranteed to yield high casualties succeeded, if indeed it was a ploy, as Bush ultimately agreed to provide whatever was needed for the offensive. On October 21, Powell again flew to Saudi Arabia and met with Schwarzkopf and his planners. At the end of their meeting they decided to more than double the number of U.S. troops, bring in armored divisions from Germany, and add additional fighter squadrons, aircraft carriers, and Marine units. The greater force would enable the allies to exploit the Iraqis' vulnerable western flank instead of relying upon a head-on attack into heavily fortified positions. According to Powell, "The Iraqi's disposition of forces practically wrote the plan for us." Upon leaving Saudi Arabia, Powell assured Schwarzkopf that

"the President and Cheney will give you anything you need to get the job done. And don't worry, you won't be jumping off until you're ready." This position reflected Powell's belief that the United States should strike with its full force to achieve a fast and overwhelming victory. He believed this strategy would produce the fewest casualties and retain greater political support at home.

On October 30, Powell briefed Bush and his key advisers on his and Schwarzkopf's new, more satisfactory plans for an offensive action. Then he informed them of the vast number of troops and resources necessary to implement it. The extent of the additional buildup took most of his advisers aback, but Bush decided at that meeting to increase the troop strength accordingly and to issue an ultimatum to Hussein to withdraw from Kuwait or face a war. However, he decided to wait to announce the decision in order to avoid making it an issue in the midterm Congressional elections slated for November 6.

On December 3, four days after the United Nations voted to authorize a war if Iraq did not withdraw by January 15, 1991, Powell appeared before the Senate Armed Services Committee to testify on the progress of Operation Desert Shield. He reviewed the progress of the coalition buildup and described the Iraqi forces opposing them: 450,000 soldiers, 3,800 tanks, 2,500 artillery pieces, an arsenal of chemical and biological weapons, and the possibility of some nuclear capacity.

Congress voted to authorize war on January 12, and on January 15, Powell faxed Schwarzkopf the order to begin the air campaign on January 17. The order began, "The Secretary of Defense has directed that offensive operations begin on 17 January 1991. This direction assumes Iraqi failure to comply with relevant U.N. resolutions and that the President will make the determination required by Section 2 (B) House Joint Resolution 77."

During the war Powell oversaw the fighting. On February 13, U.S. jets bombed a Baghdad bunker believed to house Iraqi intelligence units. Instead of, or in addition to being an intelligence facility, the bunker proved also to be an air raid shelter, and over 200 civilian were killed in the air raid. Powell told Schwarzkopf, "The amount of additional damage we might inflict compared to the consequences of that damage takes on more policy and political overtones.... We don't want to take a chance on something like this happening again." Subsequently, Powell assumed personal responsibility for approving targets within Baghdad (see **Al-Firdos Bunker**).

Powell also held occasional press conferences. His most notable appearance came on January 23, when he described the allied plan for dealing with the Iraqi Army. "First, we're going to cut it off, and then we're going to kill it." Powell visited the war zone between February 8 and 10, when Schwarzkopf stated that he would be ready to initiate the ground war by February 21. Schwarzkopf later delayed the offensive for three more days to give the Marines more time to prepare their frontal assault against dug-in Iraqi fortifications at the Saudi-Kuwaiti border. On February 20, however, Schwarzkopf asked to delay the assault two more days to wait for better weather. Bush and Cheney had been anxious to start the ground war sooner and were concerned that a last-minute Soviet initiative would enable Hussein to withdraw with his army largely intact. Consequently, Powell, who had supported Schwarzkopf's earlier requests, insisted on beginning the attack on February 24. After a heated conversation in which Schwarzkopf complained that he was being pressured to put aside his military judgment for political considerations, Powell reassured him, "At the end of the day you know I'm going to carry your message, and we'll do it your way." However, 30 minutes later Schwarzkopf called back to report that the weather was clearing and the attack would begin on February 24, after all.

On February 19, Hussein accepted a Soviet peace proposal that called for Iraq to begin to withdraw its forces "immediately and unconditionally" from Kuwait and complete the withdrawal within 21 days. Iraqi troops were to evacuate Kuwait City within four days and return all POWs within three days. In return, the plan called for the coalition to agree to a cease-fire and allow all U.N. resolutions against Iraq to expire once the Iraqis had withdrawn from Kuwait. This development caused problems for Bush, who was by then anxious to destroy Hussein's warmaking power and not allow him simply to walk away from Kuwait. At the same time, however, he did not want to undermine the improved relationship with Gorbachev and the Soviet Union. Powell suggested that instead of rejecting Gorbachev's plan outright, they set a deadline for the Iraqi withdrawal for noon, February 23. If the Iraqi forces did not withdraw, then the war would proceed as planned. Bush accepted the proposal, the Iraqis did not withdraw, and the ground war began on the morning of February 24 (see **Diplomacy**).

The ground war went exceedingly well, and when Powell briefed Bush on February 27, he told the president, "We're within the window of success. I've talked to General Schwarzkopf. I expect by sometime tomorrow the job will be done, and I'll probably be bringing you a recommendation to stop the fighting." Bush replied, "If that's the case, why not end it today." Powell had no objections, and he submitted the suggestion to Schwarzkopf, who agreed to a cessation of offensive hostilities at 8 A.M. local time on February 28 (midnight, February 27, EST).

Bush's decision to end the fighting before completely destroying the Iraqi armed forces or deposing Hussein remains the most controversial aspect of the war. Powell has consistently defended the action by pointing out that the war's objectives had been achieved and all of the U.N. mandates fulfilled. Iraq's warmaking capabilities were largely destroyed, and the Iraqi Army no longer posed a military threat to the region. Furthermore, by ending the fighting as soon as possible, no additional coalition soldiers were killed and the allies avoided charges of massacring an essentially defenseless army. Moreover, the United States had no U.N. mandate to overthrow Hussein, and an invasion of Iraq would possibly have provoked the participating Arab nations to leave the coalition. If Iraq was entirely decimated, or even partitioned into separate Sunni,

Shī'ite, and Kurdish states, it would cease to serve as a buffer against Syria and Iran, other nations that were quite capable of destabilizing the region. Finally, an American occupation of Iraq would have lasted for years and been quite costly in terms of money, military resources, and lives (*see* **Cease-fire, Aftermath**).

Bush reappointed Powell to a second term as chairman of the Joint Chiefs of Staff on May 22, four months before his first term was due to expire. The early reappointment was made in part to squelch speculation voiced in Bob Woodward's book, *The Commanders*, that Powell had privately opposed the president on the war and caused a major rift within the administration. In Powell's second term he oversaw the reduction of the U.S. military force in the post–Cold War era, a restructuring he had supported for several years under a plan called Base Force. He tried unsuccessfully to eliminate battlefield artillery-fired nuclear shells, which he believed were "trouble-prone, expensive to modernize, and irrelevant in the present world of highly accurate conventional weapons." However, in late 1991 Bush demanded new proposals for nuclear disarmament, and Powell helped formulate policies that eliminated short-range nuclear weapons from the U.S. arsenal, grounded the nuclear-armed bombers from the Strategic Air Command that for 32 years had been prepared to strike inside the Soviet Union, removed nuclear weapons from all ships except Trident submarines, eliminated multiple-warhead intercontinental missiles (MIRVs), and closed down many Minuteman missile silos.

Powell was approached by both the Democratic and Republican parties to run for vice-president in 1992, but he declined. He oversaw the U.S. expedition to Somalia that Bush initiated and his successor, Bill Clinton, concluded, and he advised the new president on the intensifying situation in Bosnia and on the issue of permitting gays and lesbians to serve in the military. Powell opposed allowing homosexuals to serve, since he felt it would cause many disruptions within the military and create problem situations where heterosexuals and homosexuals would be sharing barracks. As a

compromise position, he suggested the "Don't ask, don't tell" solution that eventually became the policy of the Clinton administration.

Powell retired after completing his second term as chairman of the Joint Chiefs of Staff in September 1993. In 1994, he accompanied former President Jimmy Carter to Haiti, where, at the last minute, they convinced the military dictator Raoul Cedras to surrender power and leave the country prior to an imminent American invasion whose purpose was to restore the elected government of Jean-Bertrand Aristide. In 1995, Powell published his memoirs, *My American Journey*.

**Provisional Kuwaiti Government**—On August 2, 1990, immediately following its successful invasion of Kuwait, which Hussein claimed was made in support of a popular movement against the emir, Iraq announced the existence of a new, transitional free government in Kuwait. On August 4, the Iraqi news agency announced the government's new cabinet, claiming all of the members were middle ranking Kuwaiti army officers. Kuwaiti diplomats maintained, however, that they were all Iraqi army officers.

The cabinet's prime minister was Alaa Hussein Ali, who was actually an Iraqi military officer and the former head of Iraq's antimissile program. Ali, who had written a book on the Gulf War between Iran and Iraq, was also named defense minister, interior minister, and commander-in-chief of all armed forces. Walid Saud Mohammed Abdullah was named foreign affairs minister; Fuad Hussein Ahmad was oil minister and acting finance minister; Fadil Haidar al Wafiqi was information minister and communications minister; Mishal Saad al-Hadab was health minister; Hussein Ali al-Shammari was minister of social affairs and labor; Nasser Mansour al-Mandil was minister of education and acting minister of higher education; Issam Abdul Majeed Hussein was minister of justice and acting minister of Islāmic affairs; and Yacoub Mahmoud Shallal was minister of trade and acting minister of planning.

On August 7, the provisional government

declared the Republic of Kuwait and linked Kuwaiti currency to Iraqi currency at parity. The new republic failed to win any support among Kuwaitis or to receive recognition from any foreign governments, and the pretense of an independent Kuwaiti government lasted only one day. On August 8, Hussein announced that Iraq had annexed Kuwait as its nineteenth province. Iraq had opposed the formation of Kuwait as a sovereign state in 1961, and Hussein justified the annexation by claiming that Kuwait had historically always been part of Iraq.

**Psychological Operations**—During the war the allies employed various psychological operations (PSYOP) to intimidate Iraqi troops, destroy their morale, diminish their faith in their leadership, and or encourage them to surrender or desert. After the cease-fire, one Iraqi division commander declared that second to the coalition bombings of his ground forces, PSYOP created the greatest threat to his soldiers' morale. Allied planes dropped leaflets instructing Iraqi troops how to surrender and assuring them that POWs would be treated humanely. In some cases they also provided advanced warnings of impending air strikes to encourage desertion. Radio broadcasts and loudspeakers also encouraged surrender and disaffection with Iraqi leadership.

Psychological operations were coordinated by a planning group drawn from the U.S. Central Command (CENTCOM), the Special Operations Command (SOCOM), and the 4th Psychological Operations Group (POG). Planning began at MacDill Air Force Base in Florida in early August. In late August the planning group redeployed to Saudi Arabia.

Leaflets were the most widely used method of communicating with Iraqi personnel. Some 29 million leaflets containing 33 different messages were dropped by planes or shot by artillery over the Kuwaiti theater of operations. The first leaflets were issued during the early days of Operation Desert Shield. These promoted themes of peace and brotherhood. However, as events moved closer to war subsequent leaflets emphasized the impending

January 15, 1991, deadline for Iraqi withdrawal from Kuwait. Once the air war began on January 17, the leaflets advised soldiers to abandon their equipment and desert.

Beginning January 19, broadcasts from the coalition's "Voice of the Gulf" radio were transmitted from the ground and from planes to Iraqi troops. The transmissions lasted 18 hours a day, for 40 days. A new script was prepared each day to counter Iraqi propaganda and disinformation and encourage defection and surrender.

Each U.S. Army tactical maneuver brigade had loudspeaker PSYOP teams attached. These 66 teams accompanied the military units into Iraq and Kuwait, broadcasting tapes of surrender messages in Arabic. The messages, similar to those used on the leaflets, were prepared by cross-cultural teams.

In general, feedback from surrendering Iraqis indicated that PSYOP had a significant impact in demoralizing troops and promoting surrenders. In particular, many Iraqi POWs claimed they surrendered because they feared the additional bombings warned of in the leaflets and loudspeaker tapes.

**Qatar**—A member of the Gulf Cooperation Council and the Arab League, Qatar occupies a peninsula that extends from Saudi Arabia into the Persian Gulf. During the Gulf crisis it permitted U.S. troops access to its territory and provided support to coalition medical units. It also furnished storage facilities. Qatar's navy helped enforce the embargo against Iraq, and its air force participated in the air campaign during Operation Desert Storm. Qatar also contributed a mechanized battalion to the Arab Joint Forces Command–East. That unit participated in the battle of Khafji in January, 1991, and during the ground war it drove up the coast and participated in the liberation of Kuwait City on February 27, 1991. Qatari troops suffered no casualties in the war (*see* **Khafji**, **Joint Forces Command**, **Gulf Cooperation Council**).

**Republican Guard**—An elite armored fighting unit, the Republican Guard was the best trained and best equipped force in the Iraqi military. It was formed in 1963 following the military coup that deposed the first Ba'ath Party government in Iraq and installed Abdel 'Aref as president. To protect himself against subsequent coups, 'Aref formed the Republican Guard as a military unit loyal to the president personally. Following the 1968 coup that returned the Ba'athists to power, it retained its function as a sort of palace guard, and Hussein, too, relied on it as a key component of his personal base of power.

When Hussein first became president in 1979, the Republican Guard consisted of only two brigades, both dedicated exclusively to defending the Ba'ath regime. But Hussein expanded it during the Gulf War against Iran and employed it against the Iranians. The Guard acquitted itself well and earned its reputation as a highly effective fighting force. By the war's end in 1988, it contained 28 brigades.

During the Persian Gulf War the Republican Guard consisted of eight armored and mechanized divisions: Hammurabi (1st Armored Division with 350 tanks), Medina (2nd Armored Division with 350 tanks), Tawakalna (3rd Mechanized Division with 220 tanks), Al Faw (4th Motorized Division with 100 tanks), the Baghdad Division (5th Motorized Division with 150 tanks), Nebuchadnezzar (6th Motorized Division with 100 tanks), Adnan (7th Motorized Division with 100 tanks), and a Special Forces Division. The Baghdad Division was specifically dedicated to preventing military coups, and though parts of it were assigned to the Iraq-Kuwait border area during the war, at least one brigade remained in Baghdad to protect Hussein. It oversaw the Special Forces Division, which served as a security force for the rest of the Republican Guard. The Republican Guard, in turn, kept the Regular Army in check.

The Republican Guard units occupied dug-in defensive positions in northern Kuwait and the area between the Iraqi city of Basra and the Kuwaiti border. Their mission was two-fold: to act as a mobile reserve against an allied attack and to ensure that the Regular Army did not retreat back to Iraq from its forward positions in Kuwait.

During the air campaign the Republican Guard became the target of intense bombing attacks (*see* **Air Campaign**). In the ground offensive, U.S. and British armored divisions decimated the Republican Guard in the surprise flanking action that enabled them to attack the Guard unexpectedly from the west. The British 1st Armoured Division came up from the southwest; the potent U.S. 7th Corps slammed into it from the west, and the 24th Mechanized Infantry Division cut off its escape routes from the north. The Republican Guard was on the verge of complete destruction when President Bush called for the cessation of offensive actions on February 28. However, some units did manage to escape through Basra, and they and the forces that had remained in Iraq during the war were instrumental in suppressing the Kurdish and Shī'ite rebellions that followed the war (*see* **Battle Against the Republican Guard**, **Kurdish Rebellion**, **Shī'ite Rebellion**).

**Ruqi Pocket**—A strategic position in Saudi Arabia near the Kuwaiti border, the triangular-shaped Ruqi Pocket was bounded by the Kuwaiti border on the north, the Ruqi Road on the east, and a dried up river bed known as the Wadi al-Bāṭin on the west. The eastern and western legs of the triangle converge at Ḥafar al-Bāṭin, a strategic junction where the Ruqi Road, the Tapline Road, and the road to Riyadh converge.

The Ruqi Pocket was the scene of a series of feints by the U.S. Army 7th Corps that began a week and a half prior to the beginning of the ground war. Like the preparations for an amphibious assault that never occurred, the feints were part of an overall plan to deceive the Iraqis and provoke them to fortify positions that the allies would not invade at the expense of their defenses at the actual allied targets. More specifically, the feints were intended to convince the Iraqis that the main coalition ground attack would proceed through the natural invasion route formed by the Wadi al-Bāṭin, when in fact it took place much farther to the west (*see* **Wadi al-Bāṭin**; **Deceptions, Feints, and Ruses**).

**Saddam** *see* **Saddam Hussein**.

**Saudi Arabia**—A member of the Arab League and Gulf Cooperation Council, Saudi Arabia is the world's major oil-producing nation (*see* **Gulf Cooperation Council**). It accounts for over 20 percent of the world's known oil reserves, and at the time of the Persian Gulf War it was producing about 1.3 billion barrels per year. Like Kuwait, Saudi Arabia supported Iraq during its Gulf War with Iran, because it feared that an Iranian-backed Islāmic fundamentalist revolution might cause a rebellion among the majority Shī'ah Muslim population in Saudi Arabia's oil-rich northern provinces. (For similar reasons the Saudis were not anxious for the United States to support the Shī'ite rebellion in southern Iraq after the Persian Gulf War (*see* **Iran-Iraq Gulf War**, **Shī'ite Rebellion**).

Unlike the Kuwaitis, after the Iran-Iraq war the Saudis chose to appease Hussein by canceling his $22 billion war debt. Nor did they incur Hussein's wrath by exceeding their OPEC oil production quotas and driving down the price of oil, as the Kuwaitis had. In fact, at the meeting of OPEC ministers in Geneva, Switzerland, on July 27 and 28, 1990, Saudi Arabia agreed to raise prices and impose more stringent quotas on oil production in order to satisfy Hussein's demands. Nonetheless, despite their desire to maintain smooth relations with their powerful neighbor to the north, the Saudis condemned Iraq when it invaded Kuwait on August 2, 1990, and Saudi Arabia offered asylum to the emir of Kuwait and most of his family and government officials, as well an additional 400,000 Kuwaiti refugees. The emir established his government-in-exile in the Saudi city of aṭ-Tā'if, close to the Red Sea near the holy city of Mecca.

On August 6, U.S. Defense Secretary Richard Cheney and General Norman Schwarzkopf flew to Riyadh to convince King Fahd that Saudi Arabia was facing the possibility of an imminent Iraqi invasion and to express U.S. willingness to send a major force to defend it. After being assured that the U.S. military presence would be substantial but would remain only as long as the crisis endured and that American soldiers would respect local and Islāmic customs, Fahd agreed to allow the United States to establish bases in Saudi Arabia. This was a necessary first step for Operation Desert Shield. In return, Saudi Arabia agreed to increase its oil production by 2 million barrels a day to help compensate for the 4.1 million barrels lost when Iraq stopped exporting its own oil and Kuwait's. The Saudis later also agreed to pay for all American contracts and for 4,800 tents, 20 million meals, and 20.5 million gallons of fuel a day (*see* **Operation Desert Shield**).

Schwarzkopf's first general order of Desert Shield was for U.S. troops to respect Saudi laws and Islāmic customs. No alcohol was permitted on Saudi territory, and sexually suggestive or explicit videos and pictures, including those in advertisements, were censored. In a tacit arrangement later worked out between Chairman of the Joint Chiefs of Staff Colin Powell and top Saudi officials, Jewish personnel were ferried by helicopter to ships in the Persian Gulf so they could attend religious services off shore; Bibles were sent directly to U.S. bases in order to avoid confiscation by Saudi customs officials, and soldiers were ordered to wear crucifixes inside their shirts, so they would not be in public view. Despite these and other efforts to minimize the impact of the U.S. presence on Saudi culture, the sight of women soldiers driving military vehicles prompted a highly publicized "drive-in" in which Saudi women drove around the capital protesting laws that forbade them from operating cars. The cultural differences also fueled arguments of U.S. critics of Desert Shield and Desert Storm, since American soldiers were being asked to protect a nondemocratic kingdom that did not respect the same basic liberties that Americans cherish.

The Saudis did not want their troops to serve under the U.S. military and insisted on a joint command for military forces. While most of the coalition forces served under the

U.S. Central Command (CENTCOM) headed by Schwarzkopf, the Saudi and other Arab and Islāmic ground troops fell under the Joint Forces Command (JFC) headed by Saudi Lieutenant General Khalid Bin Sultan (*see* **Joint Forces Command**). The two commands were coordinated by the Coalition Coordination, Communications and Control Integration Center. However, the Royal Saudi Air Force—the second largest air force after that of the United States—was integrated into the U.S. Air Force Component Central Command. During Operation Desert Storm, Saudis flew more than 12,000 sorties, second only to U.S. pilots. A Saudi pilot shot down two Iraqi jets, and two Saudi planes were shot down by ground defenses.

During the battle of Khafji in late January 1991, the Saudi National Guard and other elements of the JFC–East, along with U.S. Marines, beat back the only Iraqi ground offensive of the war. Nonetheless, Hussein declared a victory because his troops penetrated and briefly held a portion of Saudi territory close to the Kuwait border (*see* **Khafji**). Saudi forces served in both corps of the Joint Forces Command—the JFC–East and JFC–North. These flanked the U.S. Marine Expeditionary Force on the east and west, respectively. During the ground war the heavily armored JFC–North, which also contained Egyptian and Syrian units, breached dug-in Iraqi fortifications on the Kuwaiti border, while the mechanized JFC–East, which contained troops from the other Gulf Cooperation Council nations, drove up the coast and liberated Kuwait City. Forty-seven Saudis were killed in action and two hundred twenty were wounded (*see* **Battle for Kuwait**).

During the war Iraq launched over 40 Scud missiles at targets inside Saudi Arabia. Presumably Hussein's reasons for launching Scuds against Saudi Arabia were to damage military targets, such as the port of Dhahran where the allies had reserves and supply depots, to disrupt the Saudi government in Riyadh, and to terrorize the Saudi population—perhaps to provoke them to pressure their rulers to stop the war or simply to be vindictive, or both.

The allies suffered their single greatest losses in the war on February 25, when a Scud landed at a U.S. base in Dhahran, killing 28 U.S. Army Reserve personnel and wounding 100. In other attacks, civilian casualties were reported in Riyadh and elsewhere (*see* **Scud Missiles**).

After the war Saudi Arabia restored its diplomatic ties with Egypt. It had severed them in 1979, when Egypt established diplomatic relations with Israel.

**Schwarzkopf, General H. Norman**—As commander of the Army's Central Command (CENTCOM), Schwarzkopf was the supreme military commander of the U.S. forces during the Persian Gulf War. He was born in Trenton, New Jersey, on August 22, 1934, the son of a German American father and a West Virginian mother who was a distant relative of Thomas Jefferson. His father, General Herbert Norman Schwarzkopf, was a West Point graduate who organized the first New Jersey state police force and headed the investigation of the kidnapping of Charles Lindbergh's baby. His experiences in that highly sensational and politicized case created in his son an aversion for politics that remained with the future general into adulthood.

Schwarzkopf grew up in Lawrenceville, a small town between Trenton and Princeton. He attended military school when he was 11. However, when he was 12 years old he, his mother, and two sisters joined his father in Tehran, where the elder Schwarzkopf had been assigned during World War II to train and reorganize the Iranian national police force, which the United States underwrote to help stabilize the regime of the shah. (The elder Schwarzkopf later played a small role in the CIA-backed coup that removed Prime Minister Mossadegh and restored the shah to power in 1953.) The younger Schwarzkopf spent a year in Iran, where he developed an interest in and appreciation of Islāmic culture. The following year he attended a private school in Geneva, Switzerland, and the year after that he joined his parents in Germany, where his father had been reassigned. In 1950, the family moved to Rome, but Schwarzkopf attended Valley Forge Military Academy in Pennsylvania later that year. In 1952, he enrolled in the U.S. Military Academy at West Point, where he graduated 42nd out of 485 students in 1956.

Upon graduating from West Point and receiving the rank of lieutenant, Schwarzkopf opted to join the infantry and attended the Airborne School at Fort Benning, Georgia. He earned his paratrooper badge in 1957 and joined the 187th Infantry Regiment of the 101st Airborne Division as a platoon leader. In July 1960, he transferred to Berlin. He served there for one year as the ongoing Berlin crisis between the United States and Soviet Union intensified, and he was reassigned just prior to the erection of the Berlin Wall in August 1961.

Upon returning to the United States, Schwarzkopf enrolled in the career officer course at the Infantry School at Fort Benning. Subsequently, he attended the University of Southern California, where he received his master's degree in mechanical and aerospace engineering in 1964. He then received a three-year appointment to teach at West Point, but volunteered to serve as a military adviser in Vietnam in 1965. Promoted to captain, Schwarzkopf served as an adviser to the South Vietnamese Army's elite Airborne Division from June 1965 to 1966. He received two Silver Stars for bravery under fire and earned a reputation for avoiding casualties among his troops and tending wounded soldiers. He also received a Purple Heart for wounds sustained in battle, as well as a promotion to major.

When his tour of duty ended, Schwarzkopf returned to West Point to complete his teaching assignment from 1966 to 1968. He attended Command and General Staff College from 1968-69, and returned to Vietnam as a lieutenant colonel in the American division, where he commanded a battalion from December 1969 to June 1970 and earned another Silver Star, three Bronze Stars and a Purple Heart.

After his second tour of duty in Vietnam, Schwarzkopf worked at the Pentagon in the

**General H. Norman Schwarzkopf (photograph courtesy of the U.S. Army).**

Officer Personnel Directorate of the Infantry. In November 1970, he was accepted into the Army War College, but he deferred his enrollment for a year to undergo surgery for a hairline fracture in his back. He attended the War College from 1972 to 1973, studying international defense and national security issues, with a special emphasis on China and the Soviet Union. His thesis, *Military Merit: How to Measure Who Measures Up*, was inspired by his frustration with the bureaucratization and careerism that characterized the officer corps during the Vietnam War era. Anxious to get away from Washington and back to a military assignment, in 1974 Schwarzkopf volunteered for assignment in Alaska as deputy commander of the 172nd Infantry Brigade. Two years later he was promoted to colonel and appointed brigade commander with the 9th Infantry Division at Fort Lewis in Washington State. In 1978, Schwarzkopf was named deputy director for plans at the U.S. Pacific Command in Hawaii, where he had to deal with the Navy, Air Force, Marines, as well as the Army, and serve as a liaison with other countries in the Pacific.

Shortly after accepting that assignment he was promoted to brigadier general.

From 1980 to 1982 Schwarzkopf served as the assistant commander of the 8th Mechanized Infantry Division, which was stationed in Germany. There, he worked to improve conditions for the soldiers and enhance relations with the host German communities, and he was promoted to major general at the end of his tour in July 1982. On his return to the United States, Schwarzkopf served as director of Military Personnel Management. One of his chief objectives was to upgrade the quality of new recruits in the new, all volunteer army.

In June 1983, Schwarzkopf was named commander of the 24th Mechanized Infantry Division, the unit that later distinguished itself in Operation Desert Storm. In October 1983, he was brought in at the last moment to serve as a liaison officer among the Army, Navy, and Marine Corps during Operation Urgent Fury, the invasion of the Caribbean island of Grenada which had been taken over by Marxists. Schwarzkopf distinguished himself in that chaotic operation, improvising a helicopter landing that enabled Marines to rescue the American medical students whose well-being was the primary justification for the action.

In 1985, he was named assistant deputy army chief of staff. He was promoted to lieutenant general and commanded I Corps in 1986 and 1987. Schwarzkopf then served as deputy army chief of staff from 1987 to 1988. In 1988, he received promotion to four-star general, the highest rank in the Army, and in November he assumed the position of commander-in-chief (CINC) of the U.S. Central Command, whose responsibilities included portions of the Middle East and Southwest Asia, including Saudi Arabia and Kuwait.

Schwarzkopf's familiarity with Islāmic customs and Arabic culture helped him establish smooth relationships with Arab military and political leaders. During a visit to Saudi Arabia in October 1989, Schwarzkopf met with Ambassador Freeman to assess the dangers to U.S. interests in the region. Previously, the possibility of an Iranian-backed Shī'ite uprising in the oil-rich northeastern provinces had been considered the biggest potential danger to Saudi Arabia. But since the conclusion of the Iran-Iraq Gulf War in 1988, Hussein had chosen to build up his army to over 1 million soldiers and had procured advanced weaponry, instead of rebuilding his war-torn economy. They therefore concluded that Hussein now posed the greatest regional threat.

On February 8, 1990, Schwarzkopf reported his concerns to the Senate Armed Services Committee, which was conducting a hearing on "threat assessment, military strategy, and operational requirements" throughout the world. Nonetheless, though wary of Hussein, Schwarzkopf supported the position generally held throughout the Bush administration: that Iraq offered a counterbalance to the regional threat posed by Iran. He recommended that "the U.S. should continue to develop its contacts with Iraq by building selectively on existing political and economic relationships."

At the same time that he supported efforts for improving relations with Iraq, Schwarzkopf began to prepare CENTCOM for the possibility of military action in response to an Iraqi invasion of Kuwait or Saudi Arabia. He returned to Saudi Arabia in mid–June, as Hussein was intensifying his bellicose rhetoric. This trip reinforced his suspicions that Hussein might invade Kuwait, though Schwarzkopf's guess was that it would be a limited border action in which Iraq would seize the Kuwaiti portion of the disputed Rumaila oil field and perhaps Būbiyān and Warbah islands in the Persian Gulf. Nonetheless, on July 23, as the Iraqis were massing troops on the Kuwaiti border, Schwarzkopf initiated Internal Look '90, a five-day exercise at Hurlburt Field and Eglin Air Force Base in Florida that anticipated a U.S. rapid response to an Iraqi invasion of Kuwait.

Immediately following the invasion, Schwarzkopf flew to Washington to brief President Bush and the National Security Council about available military options. He described the Iraqi military and stated that their main strengths were the size of their army and their chemical weapons, which the Iraqis had used in the Gulf War and against Kurdish rebels. He characterized their major weaknesses as their highly centralized command and control, their dependence upon foreign nations for spare parts, and their inexperience in defending against deep operations far behind the main battlefront. These were the same weaknesses he later exploited in his battle plan, which was predicated on the AirLand doctrine (*see* **AirLand Doctrine**). Schwarzkopf also said that he would require 17 weeks to deploy the full deterrent force in the region — 200,000–250,000 troops from the four branches of the armed services. Assembling an offensive force would require an additional 150,000 troops and 8–12 months of preparation. In either case, reserves would have to be called up. Schwarzkopf expressed his belief that an air war against Iraq could be highly effective, but like Chairman of the Joint Chiefs of Staff Colin Powell and Defense Secretary Richard Cheney, he cautioned against relying solely on air power to defeat Iraq.

On August 6, four days after the invasion, Schwarzkopf traveled to Saudi Arabia with Cheney to offer U.S. assistance for the defense of that country and to gain permission for U.S. troops to establish bases on Saudi soil. Schwarzkopf briefed King Fahd on U.S. plans to send more than 200,000 troops to deter a possible Iraqi attack. Following the briefing the king accepted the American offer with the understanding that the U.S. presence would not be permanent and that the U.S. military would respect Saudi traditions and Islāmic law. Schwarzkopf readily agreed, and his first general order in Operation Desert Shield required American troops to be sensitive to Saudi religious and cultural practices.

Preparations for the rapid deployment of the 101st and 82nd Airborne divisions began immediately. Declaring that he was "drawing a line in the sand," Bush ordered U.S. armed forces to Saudi Arabia on August 8, and the first units arrived in Dhahran the following day. This marked the beginning of Desert Shield (*see* **Operation Desert Shield**).

Despite the rapid deployment of the first troops, it took several weeks to build up a sufficient force to inhibit an Iraqi attack. During that period of vulnerability Schwarzkopf tried to intimidate Hussein. One of his methods was to provide the press with ample opportunities to film the soldiers deploying with their equipment, in order to give the impression that the force was more substantial than it was.

On August 26, Schwarzkopf moved from his Florida headquarters to the Saudi capital of Riyadh, where he established headquarters in the basement of the Saudi Ministry of Defense and Aviation. He chose the heavily guarded building both for security reasons and because it had been furnished with modern equipment in 1987 during Operation Earnest Will, in which the U.S. Navy protected Kuwaiti tankers passing through the Persian Gulf. Schwarzkopf resided in a small room within the headquarters facility and he set up a Joint Operations Center that worked on 12-hour shifts, seven days a week for the duration of Operations Desert Shield and Desert Storm. He had direct telephone access to both Bush and Powell.

Schwarzkopf's initial job was to prepare for an Iraqi invasion of Saudi Arabia which, during the last days of August, appeared imminent to many serving in the country. The rapid deployment forces were heavily outnumbered, and they would have had to fight a delaying action in the event of an invasion. Schwarzkopf had his commanders draw up impromptu plans each night for how they would respond if an attack came the following day. He also began coordinating with the other coalition forces that were beginning to arrive and were under his command, he coordinated with Saudi military and political leaders.

By the end of September, enough troops and equipment had arrived that Schwarzkopf believed he could successfully defend Saudi Arabia from an Iraqi attack. It was expected that by December Schwarzkopf would have 200,000 U.S. troops under his command. However, the Iraqis had over 400,000 on the other side of the Saudi border, and Schwarzkopf considered his force purely defensive. Thus, when Powell asked Schwarzkopf in early October to show him his initial plans for an offensive to force the Iraqis from Kuwait, Schwarzkopf replied, "I got no goddamn offensive plan because I haven't got the ground forces."

Nonetheless, Powell insisted that Schwarzkopf send his chief of staff to Washington to brief Bush, Cheney, and the National Security Council on what he could do with the 200,000 troops at his disposal. The plan for an initial air campaign was well received and was eventually implemented during the war. It called for allied planes to strike at Iraqi command and control centers, impede their ability to move supplies and reinforcements, take out chemical, biological, and nuclear facilities, establish air supremacy over the Kuwaiti theater, and inflict heavy casualties on the Iraqi Army prior to the ground offensive. But everyone who reviewed Schwarzkopf's initial plans for a ground offensive deemed them unsatisfactory because they called for an assault into the heart of the Iraqi defenses that would have resulted in massive casualties.

Though Powell regarded the early plans for the ground offensive as a "work in progress," others in the administration considered them an effort to forestall a war, and there was some talk that Cheney might assemble a different team within the Pentagon to map out a war strategy and bypass Powell and Schwarzkopf, who were known to favor giving sanctions time to force Hussein from Kuwait. Schwarzkopf, in fact, later stated in an interview, "If the alternative to dying is sitting out in the sun for another summer, that's not a bad alternative."

In retrospect, it appears that Schwarzkopf's obviously unsatisfactory plan may have been a ploy to compel the political leaders to commit more troops for the war. A massive troop increase would require calling up more reserves, diverting resources from NATO and elsewhere, and incurring other unsavory political liabilities. Many within the administration were hoping that the Iraqis could be bombed into submission without a ground war, so the administration could be spared having to pay those political costs. Boasts by ranking Air Force generals reinforced their hope. But both Powell and Cheney rejected total reliance on air power, which historically had never solely been able to defeat an enemy, and Schwarzkopf was adamant that the 200,000 troops currently stationed in the Middle East were a defensive force, insufficient for attacking the more than 400,000 entrenched Iraqis, even if the allies had complete air superiority. His ploy of presenting untenable assault plans guaranteed to yield high casualties succeeded, if indeed it was a ploy, as Bush ultimately agreed to provide whatever was needed for the offensive.

In late October Powell again flew to Saudi Arabia and met with Schwarzkopf and his planners. At the end of their meeting they decided to more than double the number of U.S. troops, bring in armored divisions from Germany and the 1st Mechanized Infantry Division from Fort Riley, Kansas, and add additional fighter squadrons, aircraft carriers, and Marine units. The greater force would enable the allies to exploit the Iraqis' vulnerable western flank instead of relying upon a head-on attack into heavily fortified positions. According to Powell, "The Iraqis disposition of forces practically wrote the plan for us." Upon leaving Saudi Arabia, Powell assured Schwarzkopf that "the President and Cheney will give you anything you need to get the job done. And don't worry, you won't be jumping off until you're ready." According to Powell the tension lifted from Schwarzkopf's face for the first time and Schwarzkopf later stated, "If felt as though he [Powell] had lifted a great load from my shoulders." Throughout the crisis Schwarzkopf, who was deeply concerned with keeping allied casualties to a minimum, operated under constant, intense pressure, and he was known for losing his temper and berating subordinates. His frequent outbursts account for one of the meanings of his nickname, "Stormin' Norman." A second, more positive meaning alludes to his military aggressiveness against the enemy.

Between the end of October, when Bush

committed to an offensive action to force the Iraqis from Kuwait, and January 17, 1991, when Operation Desert Storm began, Schwarzkopf worked on preparations for the offensive, coordinated with the other coalition military leaders, most of whose forces where ultimately at his disposition, and met with Saudi officials to smooth relations between the host country and the coalition armies. During this period his staff worked out plans for Operation Hail Mary, the secret westward shift of the U.S. 18th Airborne Corps, the highly mechanized U.S. 7th Corps, the French 6th Armored Division, and the British 1st Armoured Division. This shift enabled the allies to strike a "left hook" into the Republican Guard's vulnerable western flank (*see* **Operation Hail Mary, Operation Desert Storm**).

Schwarzkopf oversaw the air campaign from the War Room in his fortified bunker, though he gave Air Force Lieutenant General Charles A. Horner, the commander of the Air Force Component of the Central Command, an almost totally free hand in conducting the campaign (*see* **Air Campaign, Charles A. Horner**). Nonetheless, Schwarzkopf did intervene in special rare circumstances. For instance, after he was assured that it would not cause excessive damage to the Kuwaiti oil field, Schwarzkopf personally approved the air strike that destroyed the pump house feeding the oil spill into the Persian Gulf that the Iraqis intentionally created on January 25. On several occasions Schwarzkopf told Powell, "I can't destroy Kuwait in the process of saving Kuwait," alluding to the Vietnam War practice of destroying villages in order to save them (*see* **Environmental Warfare**). He also personally approved Special Forces Operations, which he authorized very selectively, and he encouraged the use of psychological operations, discounting reservations expressed by some of his subordinates who doubted their effectiveness (*see* **Special Operations Forces, Psychological Operations**).

Schwarzkopf also took several steps to confuse the Iraqis so they would deploy their troops and heavy weapons ineffectively during the upcoming ground offensive. For instance, five days prior to the air campaign he ordered the construction of a fake military base. The phony base, named Forward Operating Base Weasel, was manned by about 150 people who used inflatable helicopters and tanks and maintained a steady flow of radio traffic to make Iraqi intelligence believe that the 18th Airborne Corps was still in place south of Kuwait. In fact, it had moved hundreds of miles to the west (*see* **Deceptions, Feints, and Ruses**).

He also ordered the Marines to practice amphibious landings to convince the Iraqis that they were planning to assault the Kuwaiti coast, even though on February 2 he had canceled Operation Desert Saber—the plan for the amphibious attack—because he feared it would incur too many casualties, cause too much damage to Kuwaiti property, and delay the commencement of the ground war. In his remarks to the press he repeatedly emphasized the importance of the amphibious landings. The day before the ground war began he had teams of Navy SEALs simulate an assault against the beach, and he continued such feints throughout the first days of the ground war. As a result of the deception, the Iraqis stationed at least three divisions and hundreds of artillery pieces along the coast, far from the actual attack sites (*see* **Amphibious Landing**).

Also prior to the ground offensive, Schwarzkopf ordered the U.S. Army 1st Cavalry Division and artillery units from the 7th Corps to initiate a series of feints to suggest that the main allied attack would come up through the Wadi al-Bāṭin, a natural invasion route where Iraq, Kuwait, and Saudi Arabia converge (*see* **Wadi al-Bāṭin**).

Hussein responded to the first air attacks by launching Scud missiles against Israel. He ordered these attacks in hopes of provoking Israel to strike back and thereby cause the allied coalition to splinter, since the Arab countries in the coalition would find it unacceptable to fight alongside Israel. To convince Israel not to retaliate, Bush and Cheney agreed to provide the Israelis with Patriot missiles for defense and to make Scud launchers a top priority on their list of bombing targets. Schwarzkopf objected to the diversion of his bombers to a target whose military value was comparatively low, but whose political value was quite high. However, his objections were overruled, and Scud-hunting remained a priority throughout the air campaign (*see* **Scud Missiles**).

By February 3, Operation Hail Mary was complete and the troops were in place for the ground offensive. Originally Schwarzkopf had anticipated beginning the ground war about two weeks after initiating the air campaign. Because they were concerned about holding the coalition together and maintaining public support as television broadcasts showed Iraqi casualties, administration officials pressured him to keep to that schedule. However, Schwarzkopf believed that he could minimize casualties by prolonging the bombing attacks against the Iraqi ground forces, and, with Powell's support, he resisted the pressure to begin the ground war according to the original schedule. On February 8, Powell and Cheney came to Riyadh to discuss the timing of the ground offensive with Schwarzkopf and his commanding generals. The consensus was that the ground war would require ten days to two weeks to complete, though supplies were readied for six weeks of fighting. His field commanders required seven days advance notice to complete preattack operations, and Schwarzkopf agreed to commence operations to "soften" enemy positions and clear minefields and other obstacles on February 15 and initiate the ground attack on the early morning of February 22. A last-minute request by Walt Boomer, the commander of the Marine 1st Expeditionary Force, for more time to reposition his troops for the assault delayed the offensive for two days. However, on Schwarzkopf's command the Marines launched the allied offensive at 4 A.M. on Sunday, February 24.

The initial plan called for the Marines to begin the attack by assaulting the Iraqi fortifications on the Kuwaiti border. This would provoke the Republican Guard armored divisions to move forward from their dug-in positions in northern Kuwait to meet the attack (*see* **Battle for Kuwait**). On the following day the main thrust of the assault would follow as the coalition armored divisions west of Kuwait would cross into Iraq and execute their left hook into the Republican Guard's flank. However, when the Marines met with greater success than anticipated, Schwarzkopf moved up the armored attack by more than 15 hours to 3 P.M. on the 24th (*see* **Battle Against the Republican Guard**).

Both phases of Operation Desert Storm continued to exceed expectations. On the first day the Marines breached and overran the Iraqi minefields, fire trenches, and other fortifications (*see* **Iraqi Fortifications**). In fact, Schwarzkopf had to order the Marines to hold up temporarily so they would not run ahead of the Pan-Arab forces on their flank and leave themselves exposed to a counterattack. To the west the 101st Airborne Division established a forward base deep inside Iraq (*see* **Forward Operating Base Cobra**). The French 6th Light Armored Division took hundreds of prisoners after defeating an Iraqi force on the way to its objective, the As-Sālman airfield (*see* **As-Sālman Airfield**). Meanwhile, the 24th Mechanized Division raced forward to the Euphrates Valley to cut off the Republican Guard's escape route.

However, the 7th Corps, which comprised the main muscle of Schwarzkopf's attack, was slow to engage the enemy, and Schwarzkopf became angered when he learned that its commander, Lieutenant General Frederick Franks, Jr., had ordered his troops to stop for the night. Schwarzkopf wanted to attack the Republican Guard's armored divisions as quickly as possible, while they remained off-balance from the initial attack and before they could retreat back into Iraq. Fearing that the enemy tanks might escape, he repeatedly ordered Franks to engage them and threatened to replace Franks if he did not. Franks, who was still well ahead of the original schedule, wanted to move more slowly so he could strike with his full force, instead of with sparring jabs. Franks was also concerned that his troops might accidentally shoot each other in the dark, and he wanted to maintain resupply lines for fuel. Ultimately, the 7th Corps did engage the Republican Guard with its full force and inflicted extremely heavy casualties (*see* **Frederick Franks, Jr.**).

By February 27, three days after the commencement of the ground war, the coalition forces had cut off the Republican Guard armored divisions and were prepared to enter Kuwait City. In deference to the Kuwaitis, Schwarzkopf allowed the Pan-Arab force to enter the capital city first. Later that day Schwarzkopf appeared before the press and gave what was dubbed as "the mother of all briefings," a sarcastic reference to Hussein's earlier vow to wage "the mother of all battles" against the coalition. Schwarzkopf straightforwardly described Operation Hail Mary and illustrated how the fighting had proceeded on the various fronts over the past three days. He announced that 29 of the 42 Iraqi divisions in the Kuwaiti theater had been rendered completely ineffective: "We've almost completely destroyed the offensive capability of the Iraqi forces in the Kuwaiti theater." Schwarzkopf added, "As far as Saddam Hussein being a great military strategist, he is neither a strategist, nor is he schooled in the operational arts, nor is he a tactician, nor is he a general, nor is he a soldier. Other than that he's a great military man." Schwarzkopf then went on to criticize the Iraqi military leadership. "They committed them [their troops] to a cause they did not believe in. They [the Iraqi POWs] are all saying they didn't want to be there, they didn't want to fight their fellow Arabs, they were lied to when they went into Kuwait, and then after they got there, they had a leadership that was so uncaring that they didn't properly feed them, didn't properly give them water, and in the end, kept them there only at the point of a gun."

Schwarzkopf then proceeded to describe how the Republican Guard was cut off with no avenue of escape: "The gates are closed." In fact, however, a route into the Iraqi city of Basra did exist, and several hundred tanks and armored personnel carriers were able to escape into the city and avoid destruction.

On the same day Bush decided to terminate the fighting as of 8 A.M. February 28 (local time). Powell consulted Schwarzkopf before the decision was made and reported back to the President. Schwarzkopf reportedly told him, "I am prepared to stop. But with time I could do more." In a later interview with David Frost he added, "Frankly, my recommendation had been, you know, continue the march…. We could have completely closed the doors and made it in fact a battle of annihilation. And the President made the decision that we should stop at a given time, at a given place, that did leave some escape routes open for them to get back out, and I think this was a very humane decision and a very courageous decision on his part also. Because it's one of those ones that historians are going to second-guess forever." Some members of the press seized on the Frost interview to suggest that Schwarzkopf had actively opposed the decision and that a rift existed between him and Bush. However, Schwarzkopf denied both charges and later apologized to Bush for his poor choice of words. He insisted that he had not objected to the cessation of hostilities and pointed out that all of the war's objectives had been achieved: the U.N. mandate had been fulfilled, Iraq had been removed from Kuwait and eliminated as a regional threat. Moreover, by terminating the war when he did Bush had doubtlessly saved lives, American as well as Iraqi.

On March 3, Schwarzkopf and other coalition military leaders met with Iraqi generals in a tent at Safwān airfield in southern Iraq. The Iraqis accepted the U.N.'s terms for a ceasefire, and they and Schwarzkopf worked out the details for enforcing it. They prepared to exchange POWs (the Iraqis held 41; the allies had taken over 70,000) and exchanged information about missing soldiers, and the Iraqis provided details about the positions of their land mines. Prior to this meeting Schwarzkopf had retained his standing order to shoot down any Iraqi warplanes flying over Iraqi airspace. But after the Iraqis pointed out how the allies had destroyed most of their strategic bridges and roads, he acceded to a request to permit helicopter flights so they could implement the cease fire and begin to restore order in the country. This seemed like a reasonable request to Schwarzkopf. But soon afterward, the Iraqi Army employed its helicopters to suppress the Shī'ite uprising in southern Iraq near Basra and the Kurdish rebellion in northern Iraq that had sprung up during Desert Storm. In the Frost interview Schwarzkopf stated, "I think I was suckered because I think they intended—right then, when they asked that question—to use those helicopters against the insurrections that were going on." (*see* **Kurdish Rebellion, Shī'ite Rebellion**).

Elsewhere, Schwarzkopf took pains to point out that overthrowing Hussein and stopping the brutal suppression of those uprisings had never been part of the war's objectives or the U.N. mandate and that Hussein's continued rein did not imply a failure of the Persian Gulf War. "It's important to remember that this [Kurdish] rebellion has been going on for many, many years. There's no question about the fact that the Kurds probably saw an opportunity to take advantage of a major defeat of the Iraqis.... But to somehow imply that because we did not continue for one more day the attack, that the rebellion did not succeed, is bogus.... I don't think we should ever say that ... what's happening to the Kurds now means that our mission failed ... it does not affect the accomplishment of our mission one way or another."

On April 20, the day he departed the Middle East to return to the United States, Schwarzkopf became the first foreigner to receive the Saudi's Order of King Abdul Aziz, First Class decoration. He returned home to a hero's welcome, and after his retirement from the Army shortly thereafter, after 35 years of service, he was mentioned as a possible Republican candidate for vice-president, but he declined to run for that or any other office. He published his memoirs, *It Doesn't Take a Hero*, in 1992.

**Scud Missiles**—Among Iraq's arsenal at the beginning of the war were several hundred So-

viet-made SS-1 missiles, more popularly called Scuds. Hussein had procured the surface-to-surface missiles in the 1980s during Iraq's Gulf War with Iran. The original Scuds could carry a 2,000 pound warhead and fly about 300 kilometers (185 miles). However, during the Gulf War the Iraqis modified some of the Soviet Scuds to give them longer range. This enabled them to launch missiles against Tehran, the Iranian capital. The modified Al Abbas Scuds could carry a 770 pound warhead and travel some 900 kilometers (560 miles), and the Al Hussein Scuds could carry a 1,100 pound warhead and strike targets 650 kilometers (400 miles) away. The Iraqis also possessed short-range Laith missiles, a variant of the Russian Frog-7 that could carry a 500 pound warhead and travel 60 kilometers (35–40 miles). Apparently the Iraqis used Al Hussein Scuds during the Persian Gulf War. They deployed four Laith regiments with five to six launchers per regiment and several hundred missiles. They also had five Scud brigades, each with ten to eleven launchers, as well as several dozen fixed launch sites, most of which were destroyed at the beginning of the air campaign. Moreover, during the war the Iraqis improvised additional mobile Scud launchers by placing launchers on flatbed trucks. These Mobile Erector Launchers (MELs) were especially difficult to identify through aerial reconnaissance.

The Soviets had designed the Scud to deliver nuclear warheads; consequently, its capacity to carry a heavy warhead was more important to the designers than its accuracy, since nuclear-armed missiles to do not have to be very precise to take out their targets. Though the Iraqis had no nuclear warheads, they did possess chemical warheads for the Scuds, and on several occasions prior to the outbreak of the war Hussein threatened to use these against the Israeli civilian population and coalition soldiers if the allies attacked. Ultimately, Hussein did not employ the chemical warheads,* but he did use the unreliable Scuds as a tool for terrorizing civilians in Saudi Arabia and Israel,

*According to Major General Wafic al-Sammarai, Hussein's chief of military intelligence, Hussein refrained from using the chemical warheads because he feared nuclear retaliation.

much as the Nazis had used its earliest prede-cessor, the V-2 rocket, to punish and terrorize British civilians during World War II.

The Iraqis launched at least 83 Scuds dur-ing the Persian Gulf War, 40 of them against Is-rael. The Scuds killed four Israeli civilians, wounded 289, and damaged or destroyed 11,727 apartments. Israel was not part of the coalition and had taken no military action against Iraq since 1981, when Israeli bombers destroyed an Iraqi nuclear power plant that the Israelis believed was being used to develop nu-clear weapons. Hussein ordered the Scud at-tacks against Israel because he hoped to provoke Israel to strike back and thereby cause the al-lied coalition to splinter, since the Arab coun-tries in the coalition might find it unacceptable to fight alongside Israel. If the coalition dis-solved, then the United States and its NATO al-lies would find it politically difficult to con-tinue to wage the war. However, Israel forewent retaliation at the urgent request of the United States, which agreed to make destroying Scuds a military priority, to send Patriot antimissile batteries to Israel, and to give the Israelis ex-tensive military aid and other concessions. Thus, Hussein's Scud policy against Israel failed to achieve its most important immediate ob-jective—the disintegration of the coalition.

On the other hand, the Scud attacks against Israel cost Hussein little and won him some significant benefits. First, they forced the allies to divert their bombers to Scud hunting in-stead of attacking more strategic military tar-gets. (Scud hunting accounted for as much as 40 percent of all air sorties in late January.) Moreover, the unanswered missile attacks on Israel enhanced Hussein's already-immense popular support among Palestinians, Jordani-ans, and much of the rest of the Arab world, even in those countries whose governments had sent troops to fight against Iraq. Thus Hussein increased the political price the gov-ernments of Egypt and Syria paid at home for their unpopular participation in the coalition. At the same time, by winning greater popular

support throughout the Arab nations, Hussein advanced his goal of eventually establishing himself as the leader of a Pan-Arab, anti-Israeli political entity that would unite the Arab world under the leadership of a new Babylon.

The Iraqis launched the remaining Scuds at targets inside Saudi Arabia. Presumably Hus-sein's reasons for launching Scuds against Saudi Arabia were to damage military targets, such as the port of Dhahran where the allies had re-serves and supply depots, to disrupt the Saudi government in Riyadh, and to terrorize the Saudi population, perhaps to provoke them to pressure their rulers to stop the war or simply to be vindictive, or both. The Scud attacks he launched against Tehran during the Gulf War are believed to have helped prompt Iran to ac-cept the 1988 cease-fire that ended that war.

On February 25, the allies suffered their largest number of causalities from a single in-cident when debris from a Scud exploding over Dhahran killed 28 U.S. Army Reserve personnel and wounded 100. In other attacks, civilian casualties were reported in Riyadh and elsewhere. Also, the Pentagon attributed a mysterious explosion above Khafji, Saudi Ara-bia, on January 20 to a Scud missile that det-onated in the air. The explosion produced a mist that burned the skin of personnel on the ground and triggered chemical alarms. The Pentagon claimed the mist was rocket propel-lant from the Scud. But some veterans who were present believe the mist came from a chemical warhead. A 1995 study by the Uni-versity of Texas indicated that veterans who were at Khafji during or soon after the explo-sion and who also took PB, an anti-nerve gas tablet, were at especially high risk for Gulf War Syndrome (*see* **Gulf War Syndrome**).

The allies were quite successful at taking out Iraq's fixed Scud launchers, but they had difficulty locating camouflaged mobile missile launchers and MELs. By January 21, "Scud hunting" became a top military priority in the air campaign, despite Schwarzkopf's objec-tions,* and allied jets were assigned to criss-

*Schwarzkopf opposed making Scud hunting a top priority because he believed Scuds were an "insignificant" military tar-get. However, Defense Secretary Cheney overruled him because of the political necessity of appeasing Israel.

Remains of warehouse in Dhahran, Saudi Arabia, struck by an Iraqi Scud missile on February 25, 1991. One hundred twenty-eight U.S. Army Reserve personnel were killed or wounded (photograph courtesy of the Department of Defense).

cross over some 28,000 square miles of desert searching for about 14 mobile launchers. On January 31, Major General Wayne Downing deployed a special operations task force in the Iraqi desert specifically to knock out the Scud launchers and prevent further attacks. U.S. Special Forces and British SAS commandos patrolled "Scud alley" in the Iraqi desert closest to Israel for 43 days, destroying the radar sites, microwave towers, and communications systems the Scuds required. They also attacked Scud convoys when they encountered them and directed air strikes against Scud launchers. The Americans operated northwest of Highway 10 near the Syrian border, and British commandos operated south of the highway to the Saudi border (*see* **Special Operations Forces**). Despite their achievements, however, neither the air patrols nor the Special Operations Task Force was able to destroy all of the mobile Scud launchers, and Scud attacks on Israel continued well into February. On February 26, U.S. Air Force pilots discovered and attacked a Scud launching site

containing approximately 25 missiles at Al-Qā'im, near the Syrian border. According to a CIA operative in Baghdad, these missiles had been held in reserve for a possible desperation attack.

To defend against the Scud attacks, the United States employed Patriot antimissile missiles, which the troops called "Scud busters." Initially, the Patriots were believed to be very accurate, intercepting over 90 percent of the Scuds they were targeted for. However, after the war it was revealed that the Patriots' rate of success was far lower, perhaps 20 percent or less, though the exploding Patriots did sometimes knock the Scuds off target. The discrepancy occurred because Scuds frequently disintegrated over their targets before striking them. The Scud's self-destruction was originally attributed to the Patriots, which in fact frequently targeted the rocket boosters or other rocket debris and left the warhead intact. In either case, falling debris was also responsible for a number of Scud casualties (*see* **Patriot Missiles, Israel**).

**2nd Armored Cavalry Regiment** *see* **Battle Against the Republican Guard, U.S. Army 7th Corps**.

**2nd Marine Division** *see* **Battle for Kuwait, U.S. 1st Marine Expeditionary Force**.

**Shī'ite Rebellion**—During and immediately after the war, President Bush called upon the people of Iraq to depose Hussein, and two separate rebellions sprang up in southern and northern Iraq after the conclusion of Operation Desert Storm. In the north, Kurdish rebels initiated an organized insurrection that was part of a series of rebellions dating back to the formation of Iraq (*see* **Kurdish Rebellion**). In southern Iraq, a spontaneous uprising of Shī'ah Muslims began on March 3, 1991, the day that coalition and Iraqi military leaders formalized the cease fire. The disaffected rebels attacked government buildings and Ba'ath Party offices and for a short while took control of much of southern Iraq. But the rebellion was not well organized, and it received no outside support. Consequently, Hussein's Republican Guard units were able to suppress it within three weeks. They used troops and tanks that survived when Bush ended the war before the Republican Guard was entirely destroyed, as well as forces that had been held in reserve in Iraq and did not fight in the war. The Iraqis also employed helicopters to suppress the rebellion after General Schwarzkopf agreed in the cease-fire negotiations to permit the Iraqis to fly them. Schwarzkopf agreed to let the Iraqis use helicopters so they could implement the cease fire and begin to restore order in the country. He later stated in a television interview with David Frost, "I think I was suckered because I think they intended—right then, when they asked that question—to use those helicopters against the insurrections that were going on."

Bush had hoped that Iraqi military officers would take advantage of Hussein's weakened state to stage a coup. However, the officers reasoned that if the majority Shī'ite population overthrew the government, they would prob-ably purge the military, as the Shī'ites had done when they came to power in Iran in 1979. Consequently, the Shī'ite uprising posed an even greater danger to the officers than Hussein did, and it essentially compelled the military to remain loyal to Hussein.

The Shī'ites had expected to receive support from the United States and coalition forces, since Bush had urged them to revolt. Although military plans existed for providing support, they were not implemented because Bush and his advisers feared being drawn into a prolonged occupation from which the United States would not be able to easily extract itself. They also feared that a Shī'ah state might emerge and ally itself with Iran, one of the United States's fiercest enemies. Moreover, the Sunni-led Saudis may have preferred having a weakened Hussein in power in Iraq to seeing an independent Shī'ite nation established on its border, right beside the portion of Saudi Arabia that contains the greatest oil reserves and a large Shī'ite population. Consequently, units of the 18th Airborne Corps, which were only ten miles from the fighting in An-Nāṣirīyah, were ordered not to intervene as the Republican Guard brutally suppressed the revolt. Unlike the Kurds, who received some protection and support, the Shī'ites did not obtain much significant assistance, though in March and April, the U.S. 3rd Armored Division provided some humanitarian aid to 35,000 refugees in the Safwān area, which was part of the security zone established at the end of the war.

In August 1992, after fighting erupted again, the United States, France, and Great Britain established a no-fly zone in the area of Iraq south of the 32nd parallel in order to protect Shī'ites from further attacks. But Hussein's troops continued to use tanks, artillery, and ground troops to suppress the renewed revolt. In July 1993, U.S. planes bombed Iraqi air defenses in the area. At the beginning of 1998, the no-fly zone remains in effect (*see* also **Aftermath**).

**Smart Bombs** *see* **Weapons Systems and Advanced Technology**.

Soviet Union—Though it did not join the coalition, the Soviet Union played an important role by not impeding coalition action against Iraq, which had been a Soviet client state during the Cold War. During the late 1970s and 1980s the Soviets and French were the main weapons suppliers for Iraq. For instance, the Iraqis had thousands of advanced Soviet T-72 tanks (though these were not the top-of-the-line models that the Soviets retained for their own army), and the Iraqi Scud missiles were modified Soviet SS-1 missiles. Soviet advisers trained the Iraqi military, and many of the Iraqi defensive strategies were based on Soviet models. Since the U.S. forces in the Persian Gulf War had been trained during the Cold War to fight against the Soviets—especially the heavily armored 7th Corps which had been based in Germany—they entered the war prepared to encounter the tactics employed by the Iraqis. One ironic consequence of the Soviet presence in Iraq was that following the Iraqi invasion of Kuwait, many Soviet civilians were in the country, and these, along with other foreign nationals, became hostages when Hussein refused to permit them to depart (*see* **Hostages**).

The invasion of Kuwait came just as the Cold War was ending, and a "new world order" was beginning to emerge. During the Cold War most of the world had been polarized into two opposing camps—one led by the United States and the other by the Soviet Union. The Soviets would almost certainly have defended their ally against U.S.-led retaliation, and they would also have used their permanent seat on the U.N. Security Council to veto resolutions calling for action against Iraq. But in the new world order the Soviet Union was more interested in cultivating closer ties with the United States than in supporting a renegade ally. Consequently, even the Soviet Union and its allies in the Warsaw Pact joined in condemning the invasion, occupation, and annexation of Kuwait, and the Soviet Union voted for all of the Security Council resolutions directed against Iraq, including Resolution 678 which authorized war against Iraq if it did not withdraw from Ku-

wait and comply with all of the earlier U.N. resolutions by January 15, 1991. This Soviet cooperation made it possible for President Bush to obtain the U.N. endorsement he needed to assemble his broad-based anti–Iraqi coalition. (*See* **Coalition**.)

Prior to the commencement of the war in January 1991, Soviet Premier Mikhail Gorbachev and his envoy Yevgeni Primakov tried unsuccessfully to convince Hussein to withdraw his troops from Kuwait and avoid almost certain destruction by the coalition forces. On February 12, Primakov traveled to Baghdad to meet with Hussein and Iraqi Foreign Minister Tariq Aziz, and on February 18, Aziz went to Moscow to discuss a peace proposal with Gorbachev. The following day, a week prior to the ground campaign, Hussein indicated he would accept a Soviet peace plan. It called for Iraq to begin "to withdraw its forces immediately and unconditionally" from Kuwait and complete the withdrawal within 21 days. Iraqi troops were to evacuate Kuwait City within four days and return all POWs within three days. In return, the plan called for the coalition to agree to a cease-fire and allow all U.N. resolutions against Iraq to expire once the Iraqis had withdrawn from Kuwait. However, these conditions would have annulled the U.N. rejection of Iraq's annexation of Kuwait and eliminated the demand that Iraq repay Kuwait for the damage done by its occupation and by the oil it spilled into the Persian Gulf and the fires it set in the Kuwaiti oil fields. The Soviet proposal also failed to secure freedom for the thousands of Kuwaiti citizens being held captive in Iraq or to fulfill another major U.N. objective—to create conditions for peace and security within the region. Therefore, Bush rejected the Soviet proposal. On February 21, Gorbachev and Aziz negotiated a new eight-point plan, but the modified plan still did not satisfy allied and U.N. requirements. On February 22, the United States countered with an ultimatum that Iraq begin a large-scale withdrawal from Kuwait by noon the following day (EST) and complete the evacuation within one week or face a ground war. Iraq did not comply, and the ground offensive commenced on February 24 (local time) (*see* **Diplomacy**).

Though not part of the coalition, the Soviet Union contributed four ships for enforcing the U.N.'s military and economic embargo against Iraq (*see* **Embargo**).

**Special Operations Forces**—Special Forces fell under the Special Operations Command Central Command (SOCCENT), which reported directly to the U.S. Central Command (CENTCOM) headed by General Schwarzkopf. Units included U.S. Army Special Forces (Green Berets), Delta Force, Army Rangers, Navy SEALs, Air Force special forces, British Special Air Service (SAS) and Special Boat Service (SBS) commandos, and French and Kuwaiti special forces. By the end of the war, some 7,700 special operations soldiers served in Kuwait and Iraq. An additional 1,050 based in Turkey rescued airmen downed over northern Iraq. Though initially disinclined towards special operations, Schwarzkopf relied on them more in wartime than he had anticipated. Nonetheless, throughout the war he exercised personal approval over most special forces operations and authorized them very selectively.

Details of Special Forces operations remain classified, but in general special forces were responsible for serving as liaisons with the Arab ground forces, calling in helicopter strikes and coordinating air strikes, performing strategic reconnaissance inside Kuwait and Iraq, rescuing downed allied pilots, and locating and destroying Scud missiles. On January 31, 1991, Major General Wayne Downing organized a Special Operations Task Force of British and American commandos to prevent Scud launches in western Iraq. That force eventually grew to approximately 400 soldiers, including members of Delta Force, Rangers, Navy SEALs, and British SAS commandos. On January 24, 1991, Navy SEALs recaptured the first piece of Kuwaiti territory when they assaulted Qaruh Island, captured 67 prisoners, and raised the Kuwaiti flag (*see* **Naval Action**). On the evening before the ground offensive began, a 14-man team of Navy SEALs simu-

lated an attack at Mīnā Sa'ūd, Kuwait, to convince Iraqi defenders that an attack against the Kuwaiti coastline had begun. They detonated high explosives and shot at the beach with .50-caliber machine guns and grenade launchers, which they fired from four special warfare speedboats. They continued to simulate attacks throughout the ground war (*see* **Deceptions, Feints, and Ruses**, **Amphibious Landing**). Navy SEALs also performed intelligence operations throughout Desert Storm.

The single greatest loss of personnel during the air campaign occurred when a helicopter carrying 14 Americans crashed on January 31 while supporting a Special Forces operation in Kuwait. The crash claimed the second-largest number of American combat deaths during the war.

**Stealth fighters** *see* **Weapons Systems and Advanced Technology**.

**Syria**—Despite having been regarded by the U.S. State Department as a supporter of international terrorism, Syria was welcomed into the anti–Iraq coalition. The Ba'ath Party was founded in Syria in 1943, and it first came to power there in 1963. In 1952, Fuad al-Rikabi founded the Iraqi branch of the Ba'ath Party, which Hussein joined in 1957. Though the Iraqi and Syrian branches initially supported one another, a rift ensued in 1966 after a military *junta* in Syria purged Hussein's mentor, Michel 'Aflaq, and other more moderate members of the party (*see* **Ba'ath Party**).

The new government strengthened Syria's ties with the Soviet Union, and throughout the remainder of the Cold War Syria received weapons and other forms of military aid from the Soviets. In 1970, Hafez al-Assad led another coup, and in 1971 he became president of the ruling military regime. Despite the fact that both were Ba'athists who shared strong anti–Israeli convictions, Hussein and Assad emerged fierce rivals, and Syria supported Iran during its Gulf War with Iraq in the 1980s (*see* **Iran-Iraq Gulf War**). Syria was one of the first nations to condemn Iraq's invasion of Kuwait, and it supported important motions in the

Arab League calling for action against Iraq. In return, Hussein tried to link an Iraqi withdrawal from Kuwait to a Syrian withdrawal from Lebanon and an Israeli withdrawal from territories it occupied (*see* **Diplomacy**).

In October 1990, Syria sent to Saudi Arabia the first of about 20,000 troops that served in the Persian Gulf War. The heavily armored Syrian troops served under the Saudi-led Joint Forces Command–North, which flanked the U.S. Marines on the west, and during the ground war they participated in the Battle for Kuwait and helped liberate Kuwait City. Two Syrian soldiers were killed and one was wounded in the fighting (*see* **Joint Forces Command, Battle for Kuwait**).

**3rd Armored Cavalry Regiment** *see* **Battle Against the Republican Guard, U.S. Army 18th Airborne Corps.**

**3rd Armored Division** *see* **Battle Against the Republican Guard, U.S. Army 7th Corps.**

**3rd Army** *see* **U.S. 3rd Army.**

**Tiger Brigade (1st Brigade of the U.S. Army 2nd Armored Division)** *see* **Battle for Kuwait, U.S. 1st Marine Expeditionary Force.**

**Turkey**—Though Turkey did not contribute forces to the coalition against Iraq, it nonetheless played an important role in the war. President Turgut Ozal helped provide the political support necessary for building the coalition, and a week after Iraq conquered Kuwait, Turkey consented to allow U.S. planes to use its airbases and permitted the United States to expand its military presence in Turkey. Moreover, by closing off Iraqi oil pipelines running through the country to the port of Ceyhan, Turkey played a major role in enforcing the economic embargo against Iraq. The pipelines were not reopened until December 1996, and their closing cost Turkey billions of dollars in lost revenues. (The United States took steps to help compensate

for these losses, including trade concessions for Turkish textiles.) By massing some 150,000 troops on its border with Iraq, Turkey threatened Hussein with a second front and tied down large numbers of Iraqi troops who had to deploy against the possibility of an invasion from the north. On January 2, 1991, NATO sent 42 aircraft to Turkey to protect against an Iraqi attack, and during the war coalition special forces based in Turkey performed missions in northern Iraq to rescue downed pilots (*see* **Special Operations Forces**). Turkey may also have played a role in Bush's decision not to intervene more actively in the Kurdish rebellion following the war. Turkey had long-standing problems with the large Kurdish minority within its own border, and it was not anxious to see the establishment of a Kurdish state in northern Iraq (*see* **Kurdish Rebellion**).

**24th Mechanized Infantry Division** *see* **Battle Against the Republican Guard, U.S. Army 18th Airborne Corps.**

**United Arab Emirates** (UAE)—A member of the Arab League and the Gulf Cooperation Council, the UAE provided the coalition with port facilities, facilities for aircraft, hospitals, lodging, food, and fuel. It also contributed billions of dollars to the war effort. The UAE's navy helped enforce the naval embargo against Iraq, and the UAE Air Force participated in the air campaign. Other coalition aircraft also took off from bases in the UAE. The UAE contributed a motorized infantry brigade to the Arab Joint Forces Command–East which drove up the coast during the ground war and liberated Kuwait City. Ten UAE troops were killed in action and seventeen were wounded (*see* also **Gulf Cooperation Council, Joint Forces Command**).

**United Nations**—The authority to wage war against Iraq came from the United Nations Security Council, which passed a number of resolutions condemning the invasion of Kuwait, the seizure of foreign hostages, and the annexation of Kuwait (*see* **Invasion and Occupation of Kuwait, Hostages**). It also imposed an economic and military embargo on Iraq in hopes of pressuring Iraq to withdraw from Kuwait (*see* **Embargo**). In addition, U.N. Secretary General Perez de Cuellar tried unsuccessfully to negotiate a diplomatic solution to the crisis. He met with Iraqi Foreign Minister Tariq Aziz on August 31, 1990, but they failed to make any progress towards an acceptable resolution. President Bush addressed the General Assembly on October 1 and asserted that the United States was still seeking a diplomatic solution (*see* **George Bush**). France also submitted peace proposals to the Security Council calling for linkage between the situation in Kuwait and other issues in the Middle East, but these were rejected (*see* **Diplomacy, France**).

On November 29, 1990, two days before the presidency of the Security Council was scheduled to rotate from the United States to pro–Iraqi Yemen, Resolution 678 authorized member nations "to use all necessary means" to extract Iraqi forces from Kuwait and compel Iraq to comply with the other U.N. demands. This language gave the coalition the U.N.'s endorsement to wage war against Iraq.

After the war Resolution 686 set the terms for the cease-fire, and Resolution 687 established the more comprehensive terms for the formal cessation of hostilities. These included the verified destruction of all Iraqi chemical, biological, and nuclear weapons and all facilities for developing and producing such weapons. The resolution also called for the repatriation of Kuwaitis who had been abducted to Iraq and required Iraq to pay reparations for the losses incurred by the invasion and occupation. Iraq's failure to comply fully with these requirements resulted in a continued embargo on Iraqi oil exports after the war.

The Security Council* resolutions were as follows:

**Resolution 660** (August 2, 1990) condemned the invasion of Kuwait and demanded an immediate and unconditional Iraqi withdrawal to positions held prior to the attack. It also called for immediate, intensive negotiations between Iraq and Kuwait, and it endorsed the efforts of the Arab League to help negotiate a settlement. The vote was 14–0. Yemen did not cast a vote.

**Resolution 661** (August 6, 1990) imposed a complete military and economic embargo against Iraq and occupied Kuwait, except for food, medical supplies, and other goods intended for humanitarian purposes. It also froze all Kuwaiti and Iraqi assets, except for payments made exclusively for medical or humanitarian purposes. The resolution also established a committee of the Security Council, composed of all the members of the council, to oversee the implementation of the embargo. The vote was 13–0, with Cuba and Yemen abstaining.

**Resolution 662** (August 9, 1990) condemned Iraq's annexation of Kuwait. It specifically called for Iraq to rescind the annexation and for all states not to recognize it. The vote was unanimous.

**Resolution 664** (August 18, 1990) called for the release of all foreign nationals held in Iraq and Kuwait and demanded that Iraq take no action to jeopardize their safety. The vote was unanimous.

**Resolution 665** (August 25, 1990) authorized member states to enforce the embargo against Iraq by stopping ships in the Persian Gulf and inspecting and verifying their cargoes. The vote was 13–0 with Cuba and Yemen abstaining.

**Resolution 666** (September 13, 1990) reiterated earlier demands for the release of the foreign nationals held in Kuwait and Iraq and reaffirmed Iraq's responsibilities under the Fourth Geneva Convention to provide for their safety. The resolution also called for close monitoring of the human deprivation in Iraq and Kuwait caused by the embargo, especially in terms of the availability of food, and

---

*Seated on the Security Council were Austria, Belgium, China, Cuba, Ecuador, France, Great Britain, India, the Ivory Coast, Romania, the Soviet Union, the United States, Yemen, Zaire, and Zimbabwe.*

*The complete texts of the resolutions, the proceedings, and supporting documents are available in M. Weller, ed.,* Iraq and Kuwait: The Hostilities and Their Aftermath *(Cambridge International Documents Series, Vol. 3, 1993).*

it called upon the secretary general to use his good offices to facilitate the delivery and distribution of food to Kuwait and Iraq through the Red Cross and/or other appropriate humanitarian agencies. The vote was 13–2 with Cuba and Yemen opposing the resolution.

**Resolution 667** (September 16, 1990) condemned Iraq's abduction of foreign diplomats and personnel from embassies in Kuwait and demanded their immediate release. It also reiterated the demand that all foreign nationals be well treated and permitted to leave. The vote was unanimous.

**Resolution 669** (September 24, 1990) authorized the Committee of the Security Council established in Resolution 661 to examine requests for humanitarian shipments to Iraq and Kuwait and make recommendations for appropriate action. The vote was unanimous.

**Resolution 670** (September 25, 1990) extended the embargo to apply to air shipments and flights into and out of occupied Kuwait and Iraq. The vote was 14–1 with Cuba opposing the resolution.

**Resolution 674** (October 29, 1990) demanded that Iraq assure that all Kuwaitis and foreign nationals in Kuwait receive immediate access to food, water, and basic services. It also reminded Iraq that it was liable under international law for any losses, damages, or injuries resulting from the invasion and occupation, and it invited all nations to collect information necessary for obtaining compensation from Iraq. The resolution reiterated demands that Iraq cease taking foreign hostages, release those already in custody, and permit all diplomats and embassy personnel to leave. Finally, it called on the secretary general to pursue diplomatic solutions to the crisis. The vote was 13–0 with Cuba and Yemen abstaining.

**Resolution 677** (November 28, 1990) condemned attempts by Iraq to alter the demographic composition of Kuwait by driving out Kuwaiti citizens. It also condemned Iraq's destruction of records maintained by the legitimate government of Kuwait and required the secretary general to take custody of a copy of the population register of Kuwait, which had been certified by the Kuwaiti government. The vote was unanimous.

**Resolution 678** (November 29, 1990) authorized war against Iraq if it did not withdraw from Kuwait and comply with all of the earlier U.N. resolutions by January 15, 1991. The vote was 12–2 with Cuba and Yemen opposed and China abstaining.

**Resolution 686** (March 2, 1991) provided the terms for a cease-fire after the success of Operation Desert Storm. It demanded that Iraq accept the 12 previous U.N. resolutions, specifically insisting that Iraq rescind its annexation of Kuwait, accept liability for losses incurred by its invasion and occupation of Kuwait, release all Kuwaiti and foreign nationals it had detained, and return all Kuwaiti property it had seized.

The resolution also required Iraq to cease all military actions including missile attacks and flights of combat aircraft, meet with military commanders from the coalition to arrange for the military aspects of the cessation of hostilities, release all prisoners of war, return the remains of those killed in action, and provide information and assistance in identifying mines and chemical and biological weapons in the war zone. The vote was 11–1 with Cuba opposed and China, India, and Yemen abstaining.

### Postwar Resolutions

After the war, the Security Council passed additional resolutions establishing the terms of the formal cessation of hostilities and addressing Iraq's attacks against its Kurdish population, its failure to comply fully with the terms of the cease-fire, and its violations of the 1925 Geneva Protocol prohibiting biological and chemical warfare and of the 1968 Nuclear Non-Proliferation Treaty.

**Resolution 687** (April 3, 1991) set the terms for the formal cessation of hostilities. It required Iraq and Kuwait to respect the borders agreed upon on October 4, 1963, and it established an observer unit to monitor the Khōr 'Abdullah and a demilitarized zone extending 10 kilometers into Iraq and 5 kilometers into Kuwait. It also invited Iraq to unconditionally reaffirm the 1925 Geneva Protocol prohibiting biological and chemical warfare and to ratify the 1972 treaty banning the stockpiling of chemical and biological weapons and calling for their destruction. It further required Iraq to unconditionally accept the destruction of all chemical and biological weapons, their related subsystems and components, and all research, development, support, and manufacturing facilities, and to destroy all ballistic missiles with a range greater than 150 kilometers. It created a special commission to implement and verify this requirement.

Resolution 687 further required Iraq not to acquire or develop nuclear weapons or nuclear weapons usable material or any related research, development, support, and manufacturing facilities. It called for Iraq to notify the International Atomic Energy Agency (IAEA) within 15 days of all of the locations, amounts, and types of nuclear material it possessed and to place all of its nuclear material and facilities under the custody of the IAEA and the special U.N. commission. Iraq was also required to agree to onsite inspections and future ongoing monitoring and verification of its compliance.

Resolution 687 further held Iraq liable for all direct losses and damages—including environmental damages and the depletion of natural resources—incurred by its conquest and occupation of Kuwait. The resolution created a fund from which Iraq would meet its financial liabilities, based on a percentage of the value of Iraq's petroleum exports. It continued the arms embargo against Iraq and linked the lifting of the economic embargo to Iraq's compliance with the other demands of the resolution.

Finally, Resolution 687 required Iraq to repatriate Kuwaitis and other foreign nationals and to cooperate fully with the efforts of the Red Cross to locate individuals who were unaccounted for. It also demanded that Iraq promise not to commit or support any acts of international terrorism or allow terrorist organizations to operate from Iraqi territory.

The vote was 12–1 with Cuba opposed and Yemen and Ecuador abstaining.

**Resolution 688** (April 5, 1991) condemned Iraq's repression of Kurdish civilians and insisted that Iraq cease its repression, respect the human and political rights of all Iraqi citizens, and give international humanitarian organizations immediate access to all those in need of assistance in all parts of Iraq. The resolution cited the threat to international peace and regional security posed by the massive flow of Kurdish refugees from Iraq. The vote was 10–3 with Cuba, Yemen, and Zimbabwe opposed and China and India abstaining (*see* **Kurdish Rebellion**, **Shīʿite Rebellion**).

**Resolution 689** (April 9, 1991) approved the secretary general's plan to implement a U.N. monitoring team at the Iraq-Kuwait border. The vote was unanimous.

**Resolution 692** (May 20, 1991) implemented the fund from which Iraq would repay losses caused by its conquest of Kuwait. It further decided that if Iraq failed to comply with the requirements of the fund, the Security Council would reimpose an embargo on Iraqi petroleum. The vote was 14–0 with Cuba abstaining.

**Resolution 699** (June 17, 1991) approved the secretary general's plan to have the IAEA and the special U.N. commission oversee the destruction of Iraq's nuclear materials and facilities. The vote was unanimous.

**Resolution 700** (June 17, 1991) reiterated the Security Council's commitment to an arms embargo against Iraq. The vote was unanimous.

**Resolution 705** (August 15, 1991) asserted that Iraq's contribution to the fund for reparations should not exceed 30 percent of its annual petroleum revenues. The vote was unanimous.

**Resolution 706** (August 15, 1991) permitted Iraq to export oil for six months, provided that the revenues not exceed $1.6 billion, and that they be used for humanitarian relief for the Iraqi population and to contribute to the fund for reparations. The vote was 13–1 with Cuba opposed and Yemen abstaining.

**Resolution 707** (August 15, 1991) noted

Iraq's failure to comply with provisions from Resolution 687 calling for inspection of its nuclear facilities. It reiterated demands calling for Iraq to disclose all aspects of its weapons program and allow the U.N. special commission and IAEA to unconditionally inspect its nuclear facilities. It also called for Iraq to cease its efforts to conceal its programs for nuclear, chemical, biological weapons and long-range ballistic missiles. The vote was unanimous.

**Resolution 712** (September 19, 1991) made provisions for humanitarian relief for the civilian population of Iraq. The vote was 13–1 with Cuba opposed and Yemen abstaining.

**Resolution 715** (October 11, 1991) demanded that Iraq unconditionally meet all of its obligations to permit inspection of its nuclear facilities and destruction of materials intended for the production of nuclear weapons. It further held Iraq liable for defraying the full costs of the inspection program. The vote was unanimous.

**United States Army 18th Airborne Corps—** The 18th Airborne Corps was responsible for the western flank of allied ground operations during Operation Desert Storm. Under the command of Lieutenant General Gary Luck, the corps was comprised of the U.S. 82nd Airborne Division, the U.S. 101st Airborne Division, and the U.S. 24th Mechanized Infantry Division (*see* **Gary Luck**). During Operation Desert Storm the U.S. 3rd Armored Cavalry was under its operational command, as were the 12th Combat Aviation Brigade and the French 6th Light Armored Division (*see* **French 6th Light Armored Division**). Together, the 18th Airborne Corps and the heavily armored 7th Corps, which was deployed east of it, comprised the U.S. 3rd Army, which was under the command of Lieutenant General John Yeosock (*see* **John Yeosock, U.S. Army 7th Corps**). Thus Luck reported to Yeosock, and Yeosock reported to General Schwarzkopf, the commander-in-chief of the U.S. Central Command (*see* **Norman Schwarzkopf, U.S. Central Command**).

A main constituent of the U.S. rapid deployment force, the 18th Airborne Corps was the first allied force to deploy to Saudi Arabia after the initiation of Operation Desert Shield. Units from the 82nd and 101st Airborne divisions left the United States on August 8, 1990, and arrived in Dhahran the next day, fully armed and prepared to defend against an anticipated Iraqi attack. Throughout the autumn of 1990, the 18th Airborne Corps constituted the main defense against an Iraqi invasion.

Prior to the ground offensive, the 18th Airborne Corps took part in Operation Hail Mary, in which units secretly traveled over 500 miles to redeploy to positions up to 250 miles inland (*see* **Operation Hail Mary**). To convince the Iraqis that the corps was still in its original position south of Kuwait, a phony command post was established in the abandoned sector, in which false radio communications were broadcast, dummy tanks and helicopters were assembled, sounds of moving tanks and other vehicles were broadcast over loudspeakers, and other deceptions were employed (*see* **Deceptions, Feints, and Ruses**).

During the ground war, the French Sixth Light Armored Division, accompanied by the 2nd Brigade of the 82nd Airborne Division, captured the strategic As-Salmān airfield to anchor down the allies' western flank (*see* **As-Salmān Airfield**). The rest of the 82nd Airborne Division captured a major supply road leading north into Iraq and later moved into the Euphrates Valley. On the first day of battle, the 1st Brigade of the 101st Airborne Division established a forward resupply base some 93 miles inside Iraq. Over 300 helicopter sorties ferried troops, ammunition, supplies, refueling equipment, and building materials to FOB Cobra in the largest heliborne operation in military history. On the next day, the 101st's 3rd Brigade airlifted over 150 miles and then marched 20 miles farther in the rain and mud to capture the strategic Highway 8 in the Euphrates River Valley. The assault on Highway 8 was the deepest air assault in military history. On February 27, the 101st's 2nd brigade and the 12th Combat Aviation Brigade airlifted over 90 miles east from FOB Cobra to establish a new forward operating base, FOB Viper (*see* **Forward Operating Base Cobra**).

Meanwhile, the 24th Mechanized Infantry Division, which was spearheaded by the 3rd Armored Cavalry, also made military history by traveling faster than any other mechanized ground force had ever done. It raced north from the Saudi border to the Euphrates River Valley and then turned east to attack Republican Guard armored units. In four days it covered almost 220 miles. Along the way it overran two airfields, collected numerous prisoners, and blocked the path of Iraqi forces retreating back toward Baghdad. (For a more detailed account of the fighting, *see* **Battle Against the Republican Guard.**)

**United States Army 7th Corps**—The heavily armored 7th Corps constituted the backbone of the allied assault against the Republican Guard. Lieutenant General Frederick Franks, Jr., commanded the corps (*see* **Frederick Franks, Jr.**). Prior to being sent to the Middle East, the corps was stationed in Germany, where its Cold War assignment had been to repulse a possible Soviet-led tank attack against Western Europe. The 7th Corps was comprised of the 1st and 3rd Armored divisions, the 2nd Armored Cavalry Regiment, the 1st Infantry Division (Mechanized), and the 11th Aviation Brigade. The 1st Cavalry Division fell under the command of the U.S. Central Command (CENTCOM), which oversaw most of the allied action in the Kuwaiti theater of operations (*see* **U.S. Central Command**). The 1st Cavalry was held back as the theater reserve during the first two days of the ground war, but in the last days of the fighting General Schwarzkopf, the commander-in-chief of CENTCOM, released it to the operational control of the 7th Corps. The British 1st Armoured Division was also under its operational control (*see* **British 1st Armoured Division**). Together, the 7th Corps and the 18th Airborne Corps comprised the U.S. 3rd Army, which was under the command of Lieutenant General John Yeosock (*see* **U.S. Army 18th Airborne Corps**). Thus Franks reported to Yeosock and Yeosock reported to Schwarzkopf (*see* **John Yeosock, Norman Schwarzkopf**).

Along with the 18th Airborne Corps, which deployed west of it, the 7th Corps secretly shifted almost 200 miles inland during the first weeks of the air campaign (*see* **Operation Hail Mary**). It was originally scheduled to launch its attack on the morning of February 25, 1991, but after the Marines passed through the Iraqi defenses in Kuwait much more rapidly than anticipated, Schwarzkopf advanced the attack by 15 hours, and the 7th Corps began moving into Iraq at 3 P.M. on February 24.

The 2nd Armored Cavalry Regiment spearheaded the assault on the corps' western flank, with the 1st and 3rd Armored divisions following on either side behind it. Encountering virtually no resistance, they advanced almost 50 miles into Iraq on the first day. Meanwhile, the 1st Infantry Division breached dug-in Iraqi defenses at the center of the Corps. It advanced some nine miles into Iraq by nightfall. Rather than risk attempting further breaching operations in the dark and fearful that the western flank might outpace the center, Franks held up the corps' advance that evening, much to Schwarzkopf's displeasure.

The next day, the British 1st Armoured Division passed through the breaches opened by the 1st Infantry Division and moved east to cut off any Iraqi counterattack. It then attacked and destroyed the Iraqi 52nd Armored Division and proceeded east. The 1st Infantry Division continued its breaching operations straight ahead up the middle, as the forces on the western flank advanced to a point about 70 miles deep into Iraq and, after encountering and destroying several Iraqi armored units, turned east near the Iraqi town of Al-Buṣayyah.

On the next day, February 26, the entire corps rotated clockwise to the east to begin the corps' surprise "left hook" against the Republican Guard's western flank. The most intense tank battles since World War II followed. The 1st Armored Division, which captured Al-Buṣayyah earlier in the day, formed the northernmost line of attack. Below it was the 3rd Armored division, followed by the 2nd Armored Cavalry Regiment and the 1st Infantry Division. Below them, also moving east, was the British 1st Armoured Division.

In the afternoon the 2nd Armored Cavalry Regiment fought the decisive Battle of 73 Easting while screening in front of the 1st Infantry Division, which had just arrived after clearing the mine belt by the Saudi border. The 2nd Cavalry destroyed at least 29 Iraqi tanks and 24 armored personnel carriers and took 1,300 prisoners.

That night the 1st Infantry Division passed through the 2nd Armored Cavalry Regiment and pushed the attack farther east. At the same time, to the north the 3rd Armored Division attacked through heavy wind, rain, and sandstorms into the Republican Guard's Tawakalna Division, that was entrenched in westward-facing defensive positions. After intense fighting, the Tawakalna Division was destroyed as a coherent fighting unit. Later, as the weather cleared, an Apache helicopter attack battalion, guided by intelligence from a JSTARS airplane, spotted an Iraqi mechanized infantry task force and destroyed eight tanks and nineteen armored vehicles.

At Wadi al-Bāṭin to the south, the British 1st Armoured Division cut behind two dug-in Iraqi infantry divisions that had been opposing the U.S. 1st Cavalry Division. The British forces overran the infantry's rear positions and attacked Iraqi mechanized troops, who began to surrender in mass. The British destroyed 40 tanks and captured an Iraqi division commander.

On February 27, the 7th Corps began a coordinated assault against the Republican Guard's mechanized Tawakalna, Medina, and Hammurabi divisions and won several decisive actions. The Republican Guard made its last significant defensive stand when its Medina Division pivoted to the west and dug in behind a desert ridge in northwest Kuwait. Forming a battle line six to seven miles long, the Iraqis hoped to ambush the approaching U.S. 1st Armored Division. However, the thermal gunsights on the American tanks were able to detect the enemy tanks two miles away. As in the Battle of 73 Easting, the Americans began firing while still out of range of the Iraqi T-72 tanks. Artillery units and Apache helicopters soon joined the battle, and within about 40 minutes the 1st Armored Division destroyed approximately 300 Iraqi tanks and armored vehicles while suffering only one combat death. According to Major General Wafic al-Sammarai, Hussein's chief of military intelligence who was with him, Hussein fell into a state of despair after learning of the destruction.

The 7th Corps joined up with the 24th Mechanized Infantry Division in the Euphrates River Valley to the north and was on the verge of completing a double encirclement to destroy what was left of the Republican Guard when President Bush ordered a ceasefire for 8 A.M. on February 28. (For a more detailed account of the fighting, see **Battle Against the Republican Guard**.)

**United States Central Command** (CENTCOM) — Based at MacDill Air Force Base in Tampa, Florida, the U.S. Central Command (CENTCOM) is responsible for coordinating U.S. military activities in the Arabian Peninsula. An offshoot of the Rapid Deployment Force conceived during the Carter administration, CENTCOM was in charge of operations Desert Shield and Desert Storm. During the Persian Gulf War its commander-in-chief was four-star general Norman Schwarzkopf (see **Norman Schwarzkopf**). Lieutenant General Calvin Waller was deputy commander-in-chief (see **Calvin Waller**). The 18th Airborne Corps and 24th Mechanized Armored Division are permanently assigned to it, but during the war CENTCOM's operational command included the U.S. 3rd Army (whose operational command included the U.S. 7th Corps, the U.S. 18th Airborne Corps, the British 1st Armoured Division, and the French 6th Light Armored Division), the 1st Marine Expeditionary Force, and the coalition air and naval forces (see **U.S. Army 7th Corps, U.S. Army 18th Airborne Corps, U.S. 1st Marine Expeditionary Force, British 1st Armoured Division, French 6th Light Armored Division, Naval Action, Air Campaign**). The Arab and Islāmic forces served under the Saudi-led Joint Forces Command (see **Joint Forces Command**). The two coalition commands were coordinated by the

Coalition Coordination, Communications and Control Integration Center.

**United States 1st Marine Expeditionary Force**—The U.S. 1st Marine Expeditionary Force had most of the responsibility for assaulting the entrenched and well fortified Iraqi defenses in Kuwait. Lieutenant General Walt Boomer commanded the force, which comprised the 1st and 2nd Marine divisions. The U.S. Army's 1st Brigade of the 2nd Armored Division—the Tiger Brigade—was also under his operational command (*see* **Walt Boomer**).

Positioned between 50 and 70 miles inland, on either side of the boot heel where the Saudi border turns from horizontal to diagonal, the 1st Marine Expeditionary Force was flanked on the west by the heavily armored Arab Joint Forces Command (JFC)–North and on the east by the more mobile, mechanized JFC–East (*see* **Joint Forces Command**). An additional 17,000 Marines were offshore, prepared to launch an amphibious assault against the Kuwaiti coast at Ash-Shu'aybah, about 20 miles south of Kuwait City. They were originally going to provide a resupply base and protect the land-based Marines against an Iraqi counterattack. However, General Schwarzkopf, the commander-in-chief in the Kuwaiti theater of operations, canceled the landing because it threatened to be too costly, do too much damage to Kuwaiti property, and delay the commencement of the ground offensive (*see* **Amphibious Landing**). However, Schwarzkopf ordered the sea-based marines to continue practicing their assaults in case the land-based forces required help and to fool the Iraqis into deploying their troops needlessly to the coast to defend against the anticipated amphibious attack (*see* **Deceptions, Feints, and Ruses**).

The Marine and Arab invasion of Kuwait was itself something of a diversion. Its primary task was to convince the Iraqi high command that the main allied attack would strike straight at the dug-in Iraqi defenses in Kuwait, when in fact the primary assault was a surprise attack in the desert to the west, directed against the Iraqi flank (*see* **Battle Against the Republican Guard**). Nonetheless, the Marine

and Arab attack proved overwhelmingly successful and rapidly achieved its secondary goal of liberating Kuwait City.

The ground offensive had been scheduled to begin on the early morning of February 22, 1991 (local time), but Schwarzkopf delayed it until February 24, so Boomer could redeploy his Marine force in more advantageous positions. The 2nd Marine Division and the armored Tiger Brigade, which together comprised the main attack unit, moved north and west of the tip of the boot heel, while the 1st Marine Division deployed just east of it. Prior to the commencement of the ground war, advanced teams from both divisions moved into Kuwait to mark lanes through the Iraqi mine fields and provide spotters for Marine artillery. Marine bombers dropped napalm and fuel-air explosives to burn off the oil in the fire trenches that the Iraqis had dug to impede an invasion.

The Marines initiated the coalition's ground war at 4 A.M. on February 24. Advanced units moved through artillery fire, wearing protective clothing for a chemical counterattack that did not materialize. 1st Division attacked first and after a few hours passed through the Iraqi defenses and into the Al-Burqan oil field in southern Kuwait. It bypassed the Al-Jaber airfield, opting to clear it later with infantry. The 2nd Division attacked at 5:30 A.M. and required nine hours to pass through the minefields and fortifications, but by midafternoon lead units had penetrated the second mine belt and assumed defensive positions. They also opened 20 attack lanes for forces behind them. By midnight most of the division had passed through the enemy lines. Combined, the two divisions took some 8,000 prisoners and advanced about 20 miles into Kuwait. The Marine assault on the first day of battle was so successful that Schwarzkopf decided to move up the main attack in the west by 15 hours, from the morning of February 25 to the afternoon of February 24.

On the next day, assisted by Marine air support, both divisions fought tank battles. Fighting at close range, the 2nd Division and Tiger Brigade repulsed a fierce Iraqi armored counterattack in their sector, as the 1st Division likewise engaged the enemy for three hours near the Burqan oil field, destroying 30 to 35 Iraqi tanks in the largest tank engagement in Marine Corps history. Altogether, the two divisions destroyed more than 100 Iraqi armored vehicles and captured at least 1,500 prisoners. That night Marine aircraft spotted a large number of Iraqi vehicles fleeing Kuwait City and began bombing them. The attack lasted for the next 48 hours, as Marine, Navy, and Air Force pilots destroyed thousands of vehicles on the so-called Highway to Hell (*see* **Highway to Hell**).

The 1st Division proceeded toward the Kuwaiti International Airport, south of Kuwait City, where it engaged over 300 Iraqi tanks and armored personnel carriers on February 26. Fighting late into the night, the division destroyed most of the Iraqi armor and captured the airport in the early morning of February 27. On February 26, the Tiger Brigade advanced on the strategic Mutla Ridge that commanded the roadways leading into and out of Kuwait City. After capturing the ridge, the Tiger Brigade contributed its firepower to the destruction on the Highway to Hell. Meanwhile, the 2nd Division moved toward the western suburb of al-Jahrah, which it captured on February 26. On February 27, the Marines joined up with the Arab forces and allowed them to pass through their lines to liberate Kuwait City (*see* **Battle for Kuwait**).

**United States 3rd Army**—Along with French and British forces under its operational command, the U.S. 3rd Army fought the Battle Against the Republican Guard (*see* **Battle Against the Republican Guard**). Lieutenant General John Yeosock commanded the 3rd Army, which was comprised of the 18th Airborne Corps and the heavily armored 7th Corps (*see* **John Yeosock, U.S. Army 7th Corps, U.S. Army 18th Airborne Corps**). The British 1st Armoured Division was under the operational control of the 7th Corps, and the French 6th Light Armored Division was under the operational control of the 18th Airborne Corps (*see* **British 1st Armoured Division, French 6th**

**Light Armored Division**). The 3rd Army fell under the command of the U.S. Central Command, whose commander-in-chief was General Norman Schwarzkopf (*see* **U.S. Central Command, Norman Schwarzkopf**).

**Wadi al-Bāṭin**—The Wadi al-Bāṭin is a river bed at the convergence of the Iraqi, Kuwaiti, and Saudi borders. It runs northeast to southwest from western Kuwait into southern Iraq and northern Saudi Arabia. Except during the rainy season it is usually dry, making it a natural invasion route through the desert. Prior to the ground offensive, the Wadi al-Bāṭin was the site of several feints by the U.S. Army 1st Cavalry Division designed to deceive the Iraqis into believing the main allied attack would come up through the dried-up river bed.

Between February 15 and February 20, the 1st Cavalry Division launched three diversionary raids into Iraqi-held territory at the Wadi al-Bāṭin: Operation Berm Buster, Operation Red Storm, and Operation Knight Strike. On February 15, engineers participating in Operation Berm Buster blew a hole in the Smugglers' Berm separating Saudi Arabia and Iraq to convince the Iraqis that the allies were opening up an invasion route. A psychological unit provided taped recordings of tracked vehicles to enhance the deception.

Operation Red Storm took place on February 16. Ground artillery and air bombing raids on the Wadi al-Bāṭin were intended to deceive the Iraqis into believing that the region was being prepared for the main offensive. Involved were the 11th Aviation Brigade, the 1st Cavalry Division Artillery, and elements of the 7th Corps Artillery, as well as Air Force jets that attacked deeper targets.

Operation Knight Strike was a reconnaissance-in-force mission that the 1st Cavalry Division's 2nd Brigade conducted on February 19-20. The first sustained ground action on Iraqi-held territory during the war, its purpose was to determine the strength, composition, and disposition of Iraqi forces in the area and to convince the Iraqis that the allies were definitely intending to launch a major attack up through the Wadi al-Bāṭin.

On the night of February 19, elements of the 1st Cavalry Division probing for land mines encountered an Iraqi battalion ten kilometers into the Wadi al-Bāṭin, and a brief firefight ensued. The next evening, after 1st Cavalry units discovered an elaborate bunker complex in the wadi, they were ambushed by Iraqi infantry, armor, and artillery. In the ensuing ten-minute battle, three U.S. soldiers were killed and seven were wounded when two Bradley tanks and a Vulcan half-track that had stopped to pick up surrendering Iraqi soldiers were struck by enemy antitank weapons. The 1st Cavalry destroyed the Iraqi bunker before breaking off the engagement and pulling back to Saudi Arabia.

Overall, the 1st Cavalry Division's feints at Wadi al-Bāṭin diverted four Iraqi divisions and convinced the Republican Guard that the allies' main ground attack would come up the wadi into Kuwait. This deception helped prepare for the so-called "left hook"—the unexpected thrust into Iraq by the U.S. Army 7th Corps, the Army 18th Airborne Corps, and the French 6th Light Armored Division.

During the ground war, the British 1st Armoured Division fought a major battle at Wadi al-Bāṭin about 50 miles north of the Saudi border. They cut in behind two dug-in Iraqi infantry divisions that had been facing the U.S. 1st Cavalry Division to the north. The British force overran the Iraqis' rear areas and destroyed the mechanized forces in front, prompting a large number of Iraqi surrenders (*see* **Battle Against the Republican Guard, Ruqi Pocket, Deceptions, Feints and Ruses**).

**Waller, Calvin**—Lieutenant General Calvin H. Waller was the deputy commander-in-chief of the U.S. Central Command (CENT-COM) during the Persian Gulf War. Born in Baton Rouge, Louisiana, in 1937, Waller received his commission as a second lieutenant in the Army chemical corps in 1959, after completing the Reserve Officers Training Program at Prairie View A&M University in Texas. He served in Vietnam from 1969 to 1970. In 1978, he received an M.S. in public administration from Shippensburg State University in Pennsylvania. Prior to his assign-

**General Calvin Waller (photograph courtesy of the U.S. Army).**

ment as deputy commander-in-chief of CENT-COM in November 1990, Waller served as assistant division commander of the 82nd Airborne Division, commanding general of the 8th Mechanized Infantry Division, and commanding general of I Corps.

On December 19, 1990, Waller created a media stir when he declared that the ground troops would not be ready to begin an offensive by the January 15 deadline President Bush had given Iraq for withdrawing from Kuwait. Waller stated that the ground troops would not be ready until February. The remark, though accurate, provoked the ire of Colin Powell, the chairman of the Joint Chiefs of Staff, who felt it undermined the administration's efforts to pressure Hussein.

Schwarzkopf had declared that destruction of at least half the Iraqi ground troops, fortifications, artillery, and armored vehicles was necessary for the success of the ground war, and during the middle stages of the air campaign, the Army began complaining that the Air Force was assigning too many of its sorties to strategic targets in Iraq and not enough to bombing the Iraqi ground troops on the battlefield in Kuwait. Schwarzkopf concurred, and in early February he assigned Waller to approve the daily bombing targets to ensure that adequate effort went into "shaping" the battlefield.

Waller temporarily assumed command of the 3rd Army on February 15, 1991, when Lieutenant General John Yeosock was hospitalized. Waller's more active, hands-on command style contrasted with Yeosock's more withdrawn approach. But Yeosock resumed command on February 23, the day before the ground offensive began (*see* **John Yeosock**).

After the war, Waller was among the more vocal critics of a proposal by Secretary of State James Baker to establish a demilitarized zone (DMZ) across southern Iraq, to be patrolled by U.N. troops. According to Baker, the DMZ would provide a buffer against future Iraqi aggression, but the military command opposed the plan. Waller claimed it would serve no useful purpose and asked, "How are you going to man the thing? We don't want another Korea, do we?" Schwarzkopf, too, denounced the proposal, and Baker dropped it. Echoing Waller, President Bush declared, "We are not going to permit this to drag on in terms of [a] significant U.S. presence á la Korea."

Soon after the war's conclusion, Waller resumed command of I Corps in Fort Lewis, Washington. He retired in November 1991 as one of the highest ranking African American officers ever to serve in the Army. Waller died of natural causes on May 9, 1996.

**Weapons Systems and Advanced Technology**—The Persian Gulf War was remarkable for the level of high technology and numerous advanced weapons systems that were employed. These range from the use of fax machines on the battlefield to allow field commanders to exchange information with their superiors to laser-guided "smart bombs."

The Iraqis had been clients of the Soviet Union, and they possessed many sophisticated systems, including a radar-based air defensive system that the allies made a point of de-

stroying as their first target in the air campaign. These were heavily defended by surface-to-air missiles and antiaircraft batteries. The Iraqis also possessed advanced, Soviet-made T-72 tanks, MiG-25 jets, and French-made Mirage jets armed with Exocet missiles, and they possessed Chinese-made Silkworm missiles used to attack ships. Moreover, they had Soviet-made Scud missiles which were modified to increase their range and used to attack Israel and Saudi Arabia. To defend against these the United States deployed Patriot antimissile systems (*see* **Scud Missiles, Patriot Missiles**).

Overall, the coalition forces led by the United States were able to utilize even more advanced technologies, many of which had never before been used in combat. Moreover, coming from Western societies, the coalition soldiers were more accustomed to using computers and other forms of high technology as a part of everyday life, and they were much better trained in the use of their sophisticated weaponry. As a result, the coalition's advanced weaponry and high technology gave it a decisive edge over the Iraqis, and these systems played a considerable role in the one-sided victory that the coalition achieved.

### *Weaponry—Aircraft*

Aircraft had several functions. Some planes were designed solely to detect enemy aircraft and defense systems. Others provided reconnaissance, supported ground troops, attacked enemy planes, or bombed strategic targets. Some planes performed several of these functions; others were more highly specialized (*see* **Air Campaign** for details of which planes were used for specific missions).

Though not new technology, E-3 AWACS (Airborne Warning & Control System) aircraft were modified Boeing 707s filled with computers, radars, and other electronic devices. They could track several hundred aircraft simultaneously, and they served as both an early warning system to detect enemy jets and as a flying control tower to direct friendly planes. Their radars could track air traffic within a range of 370 miles. At least three

AWACS were in the air at all times, and each could remain airborne for 11 hours without refueling. Their computers were in close communication with those from the other AWACS and with ground stations. The Navy's E-2 Hawkeye was a smaller version of the E-3 with shorter range.

Joint Surveillance Target Attack Radar System (E-8 JSTARS) served both the Air Force and Army and primarily tracked ground activity. It was not scheduled to go into production until 1993, but two prototypes that had been undergoing tests when Iraq invaded Kuwait in August 1990 were brought up to operational status and used in the war. Like the AWACS, the JSTARS were Boeing 707s that had been fitted with special radar systems. But whereas the AWACS controlled air traffic, the JSTARS were used to locate enemy targets on the ground and coordinate attacks against them. Its radar could take wide-angle views of a 500 square kilometer area or detailed views of 20 square kilometers. In addition to the display monitors on board the plane, 15 Army units on the ground could also display data from the JSTARS radar. This allowed field commanders to track the movement of friendly and enemy ground troops and to ascertain the positions of fortifications, buildings, and vehicles. For the first time in history, the JSTARS also gave field commanders the ability to view mechanized forces in real time and control them over wide areas. The two JSTARS flew 49 missions and performed well. They were particularly well suited to the AirLand Battle doctrine that called for coordination between the Army and Air Force (*see* **AirLand Battle**).

Pioneer RPV (Remote Piloted Vehicles) were small, unmanned propeller planes used for reconnaissance. Equipped with video cameras for daytime use and infrared cameras at night, they were guided by pilots on the ground using remote control devices. About 40 were used during the war, mostly by the Marines who employed them to spot enemy troop movements, fortifications, and artillery positions. They were also used for spotting Scud missile launchers and enemy planes on the ground and were especially desirable in situations where helicopters were vulnerable to ground fire. Difficult to hear or spot on radar, RPVs could remain in the air for four hours and fly as high as 15,000 feet—out of the range of small antiaircraft guns. During the war they flew 533 missions. Only two were shot down, but ten more were lost in accidents and another 14 were damaged. Though their loss rate was relatively high, no pilots were killed because the flights involved no humans. Moreover, they were about 90 percent less expensive than the cheapest manned reconnaissance planes. A shorter-range version, the Pointer RPV, was also employed but with less success. The French and British also had remote piloted aircraft used for artillery fire control.

In addition to reconnaissance aircraft, the Air Force employed "Wild Weasels" to detect and jam enemy radar and other electronic systems. Filled with sophisticated electronic equipment, these planes could determine the type of enemy radar in operation, its distance, and whether it had detected the aircraft. Wild Weasels were used to guide attack planes against enemy radars and antiaircraft emplacements. They could also fire their own high velocity antiradiation missiles (HARM missiles) and drop cluster bombs. The most common type of Wild Weasel was the F-4G jet, which was a variant on the F-4 Phantom fighter. The best equipped Wild Weasels were EF-111 Ravens. The Navy's EA-6 Prowler and S-3B antisubmarine aircraft also served to detect and confuse enemy radar.

A-10 Thunderbolt IIs provided ground support on the battlefield. Affectionately called "Warthogs," the A-10s fired armor-piercing shells that were used against tanks. They also employed guided bombs against enemy bunkers. These bombs had a sensor and small computer attached to the front of the bomb and fins at the rear to guide it and make corrections in flight. Some A-10s fired longer-range, laser-guided Maverick missiles which were used against vehicles and fortifications. The Warthog's chief virtue for ground support was its ability to fly low. Because it was built to sustain hits from enemy ground fire, it could remain longer over the battlefield.

Stealth F-117A fighter-bomber (photograph courtesy of the Department of Defense).

Air support was conducted by various fighter-bombers, the most advanced of which were the F-15 Eagle, the F-15E Strike Eagle, the F-16 Falcon, the British Tornado, and the French Mirage jet. Their primary job was to escort bombers and shoot down enemy aircraft, though they also had bombing capabilities of their own. The Navy's F-14 Tomcats were used to defend ships in the Persian Gulf against Iraqi air attacks.

F-117A Stealth fighters and large B-52 Stratofortresses conducted the heavy bombing missions. The Stealth fighter, also known as "Nighthawk," was capable of delivering laser-guided bombs and conducting bombing raids at night, in any kind of weather. Difficult to detect on radar, it was also hard to hear because its jets were quieter than those of conventional aircraft. Thus it could fly closer to targets. It had a state-of-the-art fire-control system that used two infrared radars to detect the target and activate a laser designator to guide "smart bombs" to it. It could carry two 2,000-pound bombs or four 500-pound bombs. Stealth fighters were used in the first days of the air war to knock out Iraqi radar and antiaircraft systems, and they did most of the bombing over Baghdad and elsewhere deep inside Iraq. Because of their stealth capabilities, the Iraqis rarely knew the planes were overhead until the bombs exploded, after which jets were already out of range of the air defense systems. Consequently, no Stealth aircraft were lost during the war.

The massive B-52s were used mostly for carpet bombing—saturating large areas with bombs. An older plane designed for the Cold War, it typically carried either 51 500-pound iron bombs or 18 2,000-pound iron bombs. Despite their age, the B-52s had been updated and possessed advanced fire-control systems and highly effective electronic countermeasures systems for defense. Only about 65 B-52s were available for use during Operation Desert Storm, since the rest of the fleet was outfitted for delivering cruise missiles with nuclear warheads. Nonetheless, the Stratofortresses dropped about 30 percent of the total bomb tonnage during the war. They also dropped millions of leaflets on Iraqi ground troops encouraging them to surrender or desert and sometimes warning them when new attacks were going to come, in order to heighten their terror (*see* **Psychological Operations**).

### *Weaponry—Bombs and Missiles*

Iron bombs, also known as Bomb Live Units (BLUs) were metal casings filled with explosives. Typically dropped from B-52s, they exploded in the air and rained shrapnel down on everything below. They were capable of killing any unprotected person within about two-and-a-half miles of the explosion and were therefore especially effective against Iraqi ground troops. In addition to destroying equipment and killing soldiers, the BLUs also terrorized the Iraqi forces who were subjected to repeated bombings. The iron bombs thus served the additional function of demoralizing the enemy.

"Smart bombs" made their debut in the Persian Gulf War. These were bombs or missiles guided by lasers, infrared detection, or video cameras attached to the weapon. Laser-guided bombs proved the most successful. A laser beam directed from the aircraft would strike the target and reflect from it. The missile or bomb had a laser detector built into its nose cone, and it homed in on the reflected beam. Once dropped, the weapon did not need to communicate with the plane. Thus the laser signal was impervious to jamming. Often a lead airplane directed the laser beam while others dropped the bombs. If the target was too heavily defended for the lead plane to remain until all the bombs had struck, the pilot could program the bombs to set their course for the last position where the laser beam was detected. This was effective against fixed sites but not against moving targets.

Infrared systems sought out the warmest object on the ground. For instance, tanks and other vehicles in the desert radiated more heat at night than their surroundings, even if they were camouflaged and not visibly detectable. The advantage to infrared-guided weapons was that they were self-guided. On the other

Launching of a Tomahawk cruise missile (photograph courtesy of the Department of Defense).

hand, an already struck target that was burning would radiate more heat than unscathed targets. The pilot could confirm whether the bomb should seek out a particular target, but there was still considerable room for error. During the war a video component was sometimes added to these bombs to provide greater precision.

Video-guided bombs were the most precise but most complicated. A television camera in the nose of the bomb communicated with a weapons officer on board the plane. As the officer watched the bomb progress towards the target on his video screen, he could direct it by placing a cross-hair symbol over where he wanted it to strike. This was the most precise form of smart bomb, and it was the kind General Schwarzkopf featured in a press conference when he showed a video-guided bomb strike with great precision against the headquarters of his Iraqi counterpart. However, because it relied on continued communication with the plane that dropped it, the bomb was subject to enemy jamming and other such problems.

Tomahawk cruise missiles were fired from ships in the Persian Gulf and Red Sea against distant targets. They were usually employed against targets surrounded by heavy air defenses and were thus used primarily against Iraqi command and control, airfields, and air defense systems. In addition to Tomahawks, B-52s fired 35 air-launched cruise missiles against eight separate targets on the first night of the air campaign. Later in the war, the use of cruise missiles against targets in Baghdad was discontinued to avoid civilian casualties. The Tomahawk traveled at high subsonic speeds ranging from Mach 0.5 to Mach 0.75. It had a range of greater than 500 miles and was guided by a terrain-contour matching system (TERCOM). A radar altimeter used by TERCOM produced terrain profiles at preselected points in flight. That data was compared with reference maps in the missile's guidance computer, which programmed midflight course corrections as needed. The Tomahawks carried either 1,000 pounds of high explosives or 166 bomb live units (BLUs). During the Per-

sian Gulf War, 288 Tomahawk cruise missiles were launched, and 282 successfully achieved cruise flight, yielding a 98 percent success rate. Damage assessment was inconclusive because analysts were unable to distinguish between damage caused by the cruise missiles and that caused by other munitions. Because the flat desert terrain made contour recognition difficult, some missile flights were programmed to take indirect routes over mountainous areas. At the beginning of the war, some of the first flights secretly passed over the mountains of western Iran.

### Weaponry—Helicopters

The Apache AH-64 helicopter gunship had been criticized for its peacetime record, but it performed quite well during the war, especially in support of ground troops. It maintained a 90 percent level of operational readiness and, armed with laser-guided Hellfire missiles, the Apache was highly effective against enemy tanks. In one battle alone, a helicopter battalion from the 101st Airborne Division destroyed 50 Iraqi tanks, and overall Apaches were credited with destroying 500 tanks, 120 armored vehicles, 10 radar sites, and 10 fixed-wing aircraft. They were also used to take 4,500 prisoners. In addition, Apaches destroyed antiaircraft installations on oil platforms in the Persian Gulf and attacked enemy bunkers and trucks. The Hellfire missile, which was first used in combat during the Persian Gulf War, could strike targets over three miles away, which enabled the helicopters to remain out of range of enemy fire. Moreover, the Apache had sophisticated defensive systems that warned when radar-guided missiles had locked onto them and heat-suppression devices to confuse heat-seeking surface-to-air missiles. Pilots also used a sophisticated "look and shoot" helmet for aiming the helicopter's cannon. As the pilot turned his head, the gun automatically moved along with it and targeted whatever was in the cross hairs of a special visor attached to the helmet. So the pilot had only to look at his target in order to aim his weapon.

The Kiowa Warrior OH-58D helicopter

served as a scout vehicle to provide laser targeting for Apache Hellfire missiles and artillery-fired, laser-guided Copperhead 155mm shells.

### Weaponry—Artillery

Advances in artillery technology enabled the allies to fire more accurately, more quickly, and more comprehensively. The M270 MLRS multiple long-range rocket launcher could hit targets as far as 40 kilometers (25 miles) away. Each rocket launcher contained two canisters which carried six rockets apiece. Moreover, each rocket contained 644 DPICM "bomblets" which were released in mid-air, and a single salvo of 12 rockets could saturate an area approximately 700 by 100 meters. These were tremendously effective against enemy ground troops because soldiers had so little time to protect themselves after hearing the first explosion. The allies launched MLRS strikes at all hours of the day and thus terrorized Iraqi soldiers who feared leaving their bunkers lest they be caught in the open when a rocket attack might suddenly subject them to a downpour of what they called "steel rain." The MLRS was also used against Iraqi artillery, antiaircraft emplacements, staging areas for troops and vehicles, and command-and-control and logistics facilities. The U.S. Army deployed 181 MLRS rocket launchers and fired over 10,000 rockets during the war, at a cost of $16,000 apiece. The launcher, which was housed on a tracked chassis of an M-2 tank, could also be used to fire ATACMS rockets that had a range of 100 kilometers (60 miles) and contained 950 bomblets apiece. These could be fired only two at a time, however.

In addition to MLRS missiles, the Army employed its tactical missile system (ATACMS) for the first time during the Persian Gulf War. One hundred five of these systems were deployed in Saudi Arabia, and they struck at distant targets up to 150 kilometers away, usually antiaircraft emplacements, logistical sites, tactical bridges, and rocket and howitzer batteries. Each missile contained 950 baseball-sized bomblets. The missiles were reprogrammed against fixed targets located by JSTARS aircraft

and were capable of adjusting their altitude and direction while in flight. About 35 AT-ACMS were fired during the war, and initial reports showed that all struck their targets.

Allied artillery units also employed laser-guided 150mm Copperhead shells. Ninety Copperhead rounds were fired during the war, and at least seventy-five scored direct hits.

In addition to its own highly effective artillery, the allies employed advanced Firefinder radar to spot enemy artillery in use. Computers would then pass the information about enemy artillery positions to MLRS units even before the incoming shells landed. Consequently, if the Iraqi guns did not move after firing their first round, they were often targeted and destroyed by allied artillery. This system was so effective that Iraqi artillery units often abandoned their guns rather than subject themselves to return fire from an MLRS rocket. The Firefinder radar was supported by electronic warfare equipment to prevent enemy radars from locking onto it and similarly directing return fire against it.

Computers also provided artillery fire control systems with constantly updated information about temperature, winds, humidity and other local weather conditions that affect artillery fire. Global Positioning Satellite (GPS) receivers enabled allied artillery units to accurately locate their own positions on a map and better calculate how to hit enemy targets.

### Weaponry—Tanks

The U.S. Army deployed 1,837 M-1A1 tanks, its latest model, and 116 older M-1 tanks. These were accompanied by the British Challenger, a high performance tank of comparable quality to the M-1A1. The Iraqis' Soviet-built T-72 tanks were no match. (These were not the top-of-the-line models, which the Soviets did not export.) The M-1A1 had been criticized during peacetime, primarily for its tendency to break down, but it performed remarkably well during the Persian Gulf War. During a 125-mile nighttime move by the 3rd Armored Division, none of the 320 tanks broke down. The M-1A1 tanks performed equally as well in the 24th Mechanized Infantry Division's unprecedented four-day, 220-mile push to the Euphrates River Valley. The M-1A1 enjoyed heavy armor that allowed it to survive hits from as close as 400 meters and a highly accurate 120mm tank gun that could destroy enemy tanks as far as 3,500 meters away (two miles). In one instance an armor-piercing shell fired from an M-1A1 passed through the turret of an Iraqi tank and destroyed a second tank behind it. The M-1A1 used a thermal gunsight to see targets as "hot spots" up to 5,000 meters away and to positively identify targets at ranges between 1,000 and 1,500 meters. It was effective even in conditions of poor visibility, such as in Kuwait where thick smoke from burning oil wells made visual contact particularly difficult, or in desert sandstorms and driving rain storms that also limited visibility. The British Challenger was not as maneuverable, but it could hit targets from even greater distances. One Challenger destroyed an Iraqi tank 5,100 meters away—over three miles. The allied tanks were thus able to strike at the enemy while remaining out of range of the Iraqi tanks, an advantage that contributed considerably to their success.

### Satellite Technology

The Persian Gulf War was the first in history to make extensive, coordinated use of space technology. In particular, allied war planners and troops used data collected from weather satellites controlled by the Defense Meteorological Satellite Program, multi-spectral imagery satellites operated by US LANDSAT, the Defense Support Program's early warning satellites, satellites from the Tactical Information Broadcast Service, and the Global Positioning System (GPS) that enabled troops to accurately ascertain their position in the desert without having to rely on compasses. The multispectral imagery satellites were used to provide updated maps of the region, track Iraqi troop movements, and prepare military operations. The multispectrum provided data beyond what was available in the visual light spectrum. Its infrared capabilities of detecting heat radiation were especially useful for locat-

ing camouflaged vehicles in the desert. The hand-held GPS receivers could ascertain locations within 25 meters. This was crucial not only for troops traveling in the desert, but also for soldiers performing reconnaissance or calling in artillery strikes. About 4,5000 GPS receivers were used in the war.

**Western Redeployment** *see* **Operation Hail Mary**.

**Women in the Military**—During the Persian Gulf War women played more active roles in U.S. military and were more fully integrated into the armed services than at any other time in history. Women comprised about 6.8 percent of the total U.S. forces in the Middle East. Many were on active duty when the crisis began; others were reservists who were called up during Operation Desert Shield. Approximately 37,000 women served in the war: 26,000 in the Army, 3,700 in the Navy, 2,200 in the Marine Corps, and 5,300 in the Air Force. Whereas in previous wars women had traditionally served as nurses and in administrative positions, for the first time in U.S. military history the majority of female service personnel were not nurses. During the Persian Gulf War their roles expanded to include helicopter pilots, radio operators, electronic warfare repair technicians, truck drivers, chaplains, and crew members aboard noncombat military vessels such as supply and ammunition ships. Some women commanded combat support and combat service support companies, platoons, brigades, and battalions. On September 5, 1990, the first combined crew of American men and women shipped out in wartime conditions when the USS *Acadia* departed San Diego for the Persian Gulf with 360 women among its crew of 1,260. Six women were killed in action; seven died from accidents and other noncombat causes; twenty-one were wounded in action and two were captured.

Traditionally, front line positions were more dangerous than support assignments in the rear. Consequently, women had been limited to serving behind the front lines. During the

Persian Gulf War the rear areas were no longer safe, since the Iraqis fired Scud missiles into the staging and supply areas behind the front lines. In fact, the single largest number of coalition casualties occurred on February 25 in the port of Dhahran, when 28 U.S. Army Reserve personnel from the 14th Quartermaster Detachment were killed and 100 were wounded. The enemy's ability to penetrate behind the front lines blurred the distinction between combat and noncombat areas, and this ultimately broadened the scope of places where women were permitted to serve. Fourteen women received the Combat Action Ribbon for crossing minefields during the ground war or receiving and returning enemy fire.

Most unit commanders and focus group participants cited in "Women in the Military," a July 1993 report by the General Accounting Office to the Secretary of Defense, gave positive assessments of women's performance during the war. The Defense Department reviewed the draft of the report and concurred with its findings. The report notes that men and women endured similar harsh encampment facilities, but that health and hygiene problems did not have a significant impact on the performance or well-being of either group. Nor did the participants in the study indicate substantial differences in women's and men's ability to cope with the stress of the deployment. Cohesion in mixed gender units was generally considered to be effective during deployment, and there were few complaints that women benefited from favoritism or escaped unpleasant tasks because of their gender. Though many participants interviewed in the study stated that men felt a need to protect women, they did not believe that this feeling distracted men from performing their jobs or meeting their responsibilities. Overall, perceptions of women's performance were positive. Though some people expressed concern over limitations to women's physical strength, participants frequently indicated that teamwork was used to overcome strength limitations of both women and men. Several focus groups stated that some women returned early from deployment or were not deployed at all

because they were pregnant, but the participants could cite few specific cases to substantiate this perception. As of the time of the report, the Defense Department had not tabulated hard data on the reasons why assigned military personnel were not deployed or returned early.

Following the Persian Gulf War, combat opportunities for women increased even further. The National Defense Authorization Act for fiscal years 1992 and 1993 repealed the statutory limitations on assigning women to aircraft flying combat missions. The rule forbidding women from serving in combat areas was rescinded on October 1, 1994. Women can now serve as pilots of combat aircraft and helicopters and as crew members on warships.

**Yeosock, John**—Lieutenant General John Yeosock commanded the U.S. 3rd Army during the Persian Gulf War (*see* **U.S. 3rd Army**). His command included all of the troops that secretly shifted west during Operation Hail

**Lieutenant General John Yeosock (photograph courtesy of the Department of Defense).**

Mary and fought the Battle Against the Republican Guard: the U.S. 7th Corps, the U.S. 18th Airborne Corps, the French 6th Light Armored Division, and the British 1st Armoured Division. Altogether some 330,000 coalition troops served under him. Yeosock reported directly to General Schwarzkopf, the commander-in-chief of the U.S. Central Command (CENTCOM) (*see* **Operation Hail Mary, Battle Against the Republican Guard**).

Born in 1937, Yeosock was commissioned as a second lieutenant in 1959 after completing the Reserve Officer Training Program at Pennsylvania State University, where he received his B.S. degree in industrial engineering. He served in Vietnam as a senior advisor and later earned a M.S. degree in operations research/systems analysis at the Navy Postgraduate School in Monterey, California. In March 1989, Yeosock was made commanding general of the 3rd Army and deputy commander of the U.S. Forces Command.

During the early 1980s Yeosock served as project manager for the Saudi National Guard's modernization program. His familiarity with the Saudi military proved useful during the Persian Gulf War, when Yeosock assembled the Coalition Coordination, Communications and Control Integration Center that coordinated between CENTCOM and the Saudi-led Joint Forces Command, under which the Arab and Islāmic forces served (*see* **U.S. Central Command, Joint Forces Command**). Yeosock was also responsible for all aspects of Army combat operations, rear operations and logistical support within the Kuwaiti theater of operations. He was hospitalized for pneumonia and gallbladder surgery on February 15, 1991, but returned to duty on February 23, one day before the ground offensive began. Lieutenant General Calvin Waller replaced him during his absence (*see* **Calvin Waller**).

During the ground war General Schwarzkopf, perhaps unfairly, became angered by the comparatively slow pace of the 7th Corps. Although it was ahead of the original schedule, the 7th Corps did not proceed as rapidly as the 24th Mechanized Infantry Division or other units, and its commander, Lieutenant General Frederick Franks, had stopped during the first night to avoid confusion and friendly fire casualties in the dark. Schwarzkopf wanted the 7th Corps to strike swiftly against the retreating Republican Guards, but Franks chose to move more cautiously and to concentrate his troops so that when he did attack, he could strike in full force (*see* **Frederick Franks**). At one point Schwarzkopf threatened to replace both Franks and Yeosock, who was Franks's commander, if the pace of the attack did not quicken. However, shortly thereafter the 7th Corps did engage the enemy and achieved overwhelming success.

Yeosock returned with the 3rd Army to the United States later in March. He subsequently retired from active duty.

# Chronology

## I. Events leading to the rise of Saddam Hussein and the Persian Gulf War

### 1958

*July 14:* A military coup led by Brigadier General Abdul Karim Kassem's Free Officers Movement overthrows the monarchy and establishes the Republic of Iraq. King Faisal, Crown Prince Abd al-Ilah, and Prime Minister Nuri al-Said are killed in the coup. Supported by the Communists, Kassem emerges as prime minister and head of state. He dissolves Iraq's Arab Union with Jordan, which Iraq had formed earlier in February to counter the formation of the United Arab Republic that merged Syria and Egypt.

### 1959

*March 24:* Iraq withdraws from the 1955 Baghdad Pact, a Cold War treaty among Turkey, Iran, Pakistan, Great Britain, and, in 1957, the United States. The treaty intended to counter the threat of Soviet expansion into the oil-producing regions of the Middle East.

*October 7:* Along with a team of other members from Iraq's revolutionary Ba'ath Party, which is dedicated to secular Pan-Arabism, Saddam Hussein tries unsuccessfully to assassinate General Kassem. He flees first to Syria and then to Egypt, where he stays until the Ba'ath Party's successful coup in February, 1963.

### 1961

*June 19:* Kuwait receives its independence from Great Britain and becomes an emirate under the leadership of Emir Abdul Āl Ṣabāḥ.

*June 25:* Iraq publicly declares that it owns Kuwait and begins to mass troops along the border.

*July 3:* British forces land in Kuwait to defend it against Iraq.

*July 20:* The Arab League refutes Iraq's claim and admits Kuwait as a new, sovereign member. Iraq removes its troops from the border but does not formally withdraw its claim to Kuwait until October 1963.

### 1963

*February 8:* Ba'ath military officers in the Iraqi Army oust General Kassem in the Ramadan Revolution (so named because it took place during the holy month of Ramadan.) Abdel Salem 'Aref is named provisional president and Ali Saleh Saadi, the head of the left-wing faction of Iraq's Ba'ath Party, becomes deputy premier. Kassem is executed on February 9 (*see* **Ba'ath Party**).

Hussein returns from his exile in Egypt shortly after the coup. During the power struggles within the Ba'ath Party that follow, Hussein serves as personal bodyguard to his relative, Aḥmad Ḥassan al-Bakr, leader of the centrist faction that dominates the government. Hussein is elected to the general council of the Ba'ath Party's command after he criticized and privately offered to assassinate Saadi, the leader of the leftists. Hussein subsequently allies himself with Michel 'Aflaq, the founder of the Ba'ath Party in Syria who becomes Hussein's chief mentor and promoter.

'Aflaq came to Baghdad to resolve the internal conflicts within the Iraqi Party, and he ordered the expulsion and exile of Saadi and his leftist followers. In response, Saadi's supporters organized the massive public demonstrations that prompted the military to conclude that the Ba'athists could not govern effectively and needed to be removed from power.

*November 18:* President 'Aref, with the support of the Iraqi military, engineers a coup that removes Ba'athists from positions of power within the government. The coup comes in response to excesses by the Ba'ath-led National Guard and to the major split between leftists and nonleftists within the Ba'ath Party that sparked severe civil unrest and rendered the party unfit to rule.

After the Ba'ath Party is removed from office, Hussein, who had been attached to the National Guard, takes command of the underground Jihaz Hunain, an intelligence or assassination unit that becomes his power base within the party and eventually enables him to dominate it (*see* **Saddam Hussein**).

## 1967

*June 5–10:* Israel wins a decisive victory in its Six-Day War against Egypt, Syria, Jordan, Lebanon, and Iraq. Israel takes possession of the Old City of Jerusalem and occupies the West Bank of the Jordan River and the Gaza Strip, both of which were predominately populated by Palestinians. (The Israeli occupation remains a point of contention between Arabs and Israelis. In 1990, Hussein tried unsuccessfully to link Iraqi withdrawal from Kuwait to an Israeli withdrawal from the occupied territories.)

## 1968

*January 16:* Prime Minister Harold Wilson announces that by December 1971, Great Britain will withdraw all of its military forces currently stationed east of the Suez Canal. The removal of British bases and the inability of the United States to assert a strong military presence in the region due to its involvement in the Vietnam War creates a power vacuum that greatly influences subsequent events in the Middle East.

*July 17:* A group of senior military officers and members of the Ba'ath Party, including Hussein, seize control of the government in a bloodless coup.

*July 30:* The second coup in two weeks gives the Ba'athists indisputable control over the government. Hussein's relative and patron, Hassan al-Bakr, emerges as chairman of the ruling Revolutionary Command Council. Hussein is named deputy chairman in charge of internal security. Bakr was a former army officer who had participated in the 1958 coup that overthrew the monarchy; he later served as prime minister during the brief Ba'ath reign in 1963. By the middle 1970s Hussein becomes the most powerful figure within the government, though he is not officially made chairman of the Revolutionary Command Council and President of Iraq until 1979.

## 1969

*April 19:* The shah of Iran unilaterally revokes the 1937 treaty between Iran and Iraq that had given Iraq sole sovereignty over most but not all of the Shatt al-'Arab estuary. The newly installed Ba'ath Party objects and threatens retaliation, but is not strong enough to take military action against Iran. The waterway is Iraq's primary shipping access to the Persian Gulf, and the shah's action indicates Iran's intention to retain control of the Gulf after Great Britain completes the evacuation of its military bases east of the Suez Canal in 1971. Control over the Shatt al-'Arab and Iraqi access to the Persian Gulf are major causes of both the Gulf War Iraq fought with Iran from 1980 to 1988 and the Persian Gulf War (*see* **Iran-Iraq Gulf War**).

## 1972

*April 8:* Iraq and the Soviet Union sign a 15-year treaty of friendship and cooperation.

*May 30:* President Nixon promises to cooperate with Iran and authorizes the shah to purchase any nonnuclear American weapons system he requires.

*June 1:* Iraq nationalizes its oil industry.

## 1973

*March 20:* Iraqi troops cross into Kuwait and take possession of two border posts. However, they soon withdraw in response to international condemnation.

*October 6:* Egypt and Syria launch coordinate attacks against Israel to initiate the Yom Kippur War. Although Iraq does not border Israel, it sends troops to fight the Israelis. After initial setbacks, Israel regains its lost territory and advances into both Syria and Egypt. A cease-fire is signed on October 24.

After the war, Egypt and the United States restore diplomatic relations which had been severed following the 1967 Six-Day War in which Israel also scored a decisive victory. Egypt's movement toward the pro–Israeli United States and away from the anti–Israeli Soviet Union profoundly impacts subsequent Middle East politics.

Another important byproduct of the war was the Arab oil embargo, in which members of the Organization of Petroleum Exporting Countries (OPEC) almost quadrupled the price of oil within one year and temporarily stopped shipping oil to the United States in order to punish it for supporting Israel and pressure it to change its pro–Israeli Middle Eastern policies. Between October 19 and 21, Libya, Saudi Arabia, Kuwait, Bahrain, Qatar, and Dubai implement an oil embargo against the United States, and that month Iraq nationalizes the holdings of U.S.-owned corporations Exxon and Mobil. The embargo causes an energy crisis that leaves Americans profoundly aware of the importance of oil to its economy and way of life, as prices quadruple and long lines for gasoline become commonplace. Moreover, the higher prices greatly enrich the oil-producing countries and enable Iran, Iraq, Saudi Arabia, and other states to purchase advanced weap-

ons systems and vastly upgrade their military capabilities. In Iraq, the increased income from higher prices amounts to over $80 billion between 1973 and 1980, doubling the nation's gross national product (GNP) and greatly enriching Hussein's ruling Ba'ath Party.

## 1974

*October 10:* The U.N. General Assembly recognizes the Palestinian Liberation Organization (PLO) as the official representative of the Palestinians. On October 28, 20 Arab countries, including Iraq, call for the creation of an independent Palestinian state in territory currently occupied by Israel. On November 22, the PLO receives observer status in the United Nations.

## 1975

*September 17:* Iran and Iraq ratify the Algiers Accord which grants Iran control of the eastern half of the Shatt al-'Arab in return for its agreement to end support to Kurdish rebels inside Iraq. Conflicting claims to the waterway later become a key issue in their 1980–88 Gulf War.

## 1978

*September 5–17:* At the presidential retreat in Camp David, Maryland, U.S. President Jimmy Carter hosts talks between Egyptian Premier Anwar Sadat and Israeli Prime Minister Menachem Begin in which the two countries agree to fix a schedule for peace negotiations and conclude a formal treaty within three months. On November 5, the Arab League denounces the Camp David Accords and offers Egypt $50 billion in aid to renounce them, but Sadat and Begin sign a formal peace treaty on March 26, 1979.

*October 11:* Iraq expels the Ayatollah Khomeini, the Islāmic fundamentalist who became ruler of Iran in 1979.

## 1979

*January 16:* Following months of demonstrations and riots, the shah of Iran flees to Egypt. On February 1, Ayatollah Khomeini returns after a 15-year exile. In March the Iranian people vote to establish an Islāmic Republic (*see* **Iran**).

*March 26:* Egyptian President Sadat and Israeli Prime Minister Begin sign a peace treaty that ends a 31-year state of war. The Arab League promptly censures Egypt and on March 31 breaks diplomatic ties and imposes an economic boycott.

*July 16:* Hussein becomes president of Iraq. He is simultaneously named chairman of the Revolutionary Command Council and commander-in-chief of the armed forces. After an unsuccessful coup attempt against him, Hussein purges the Ba'ath Party of many of its old-guard leaders and much of its leftist membership.

*November 4:* Militant Iranian students storm the U.S. embassy in Tehran and take 66 hostages from the delegation, staff, and Marine guard. The students demand that the deposed shah, who was then receiving medical treatment in a U.S. hospital, be returned to Iran for prosecution. The Iranian hostage situation, which lasts until January 20, 1981, the day Ronald Reagan is inaugurated, debilitates the administration of President Carter. It also prompts America's subsequent anti–Iran foreign policy and its support of Iraq during the Iran-Iraq Gulf War.

*December 2:* Ayatollah Khomeini is elected Iran's absolute leader for life.

*December 25:* The Soviets invade Afghanistan in order to prop up the regime they had installed there. In response, President Carter issues the Carter Doctrine, declaring that the United States regards the Persian Gulf as vital to U.S. interests and will take any means necessary to repel efforts by an outside force to gain control of it (*see* **Carter Doctrine**).

## 1980

*September 4:* Iraq declares that war with Iran has begun. Iraq nullifies the 1975 Algiers Accord on September 17 and invades Iran on September 22, inaugurating the eight-year Gulf War that lasts until July 18, 1988, and results in 500,000 to 1 million casualties (*see* **Iran-Iraq Gulf War**).

## 1981

*June 7:* Israeli bombers destroy Iraq's Osirak nuclear reactor, which Israel claimed was going to be used to produce nuclear weapons.

## 1982

*June 30:* Iraq withdraws unilaterally from Iranian territory and assumes a defensive posture throughout most of the rest of the war.

*October 26:* Hussein announces that he will end the war with Iran and accept the middle of the Shaṭṭ al-'Arab as their border, as agreed upon in the 1975 Algiers Accord. His renunciation of that agreement had led directly to his invasion of Iran in September 1980. However, Iran's Ayatollah Khomeini rejects Hussein's peace offer. Khomeini's rejection allows Hussein to represent Iran as the aggressor and Iraq as victim of a foreign attack. The Soviet Union resumes arms sales it had suspended after Iraq first invaded Iran; France also supplies large numbers of sophisticated weapons, including Mirage jets and Exocet missiles. Hussein is thus able to consolidate his power while rallying the country around an external aggressor.

## 1984

*February, 1984:* Iran captures Iraq's oil-rich Majnoon Island.

*March 1:* Iraq's first use of poison gas in the war with Iran is confirmed.

## 1986

*November 13, 1986:* In a televised speech, President Reagan admits that the United States and Iran had entered into a deal in which Iran would be permitted to purchase American weapons in return for using its influence to free Western hostages held in Lebanon. The profits from those weapons sales were then illegally diverted to assist Nicaraguan contras in their revolution against the Marxist Sandinista regime. Known as the Iran-Contra affair, the arms-for-hostages deal gave Iran limited access to U.S. advanced weaponry for the first time in the Iran-Iraq war. Revelation of the deal strains U.S.-Iraqi relations, but the setbacks are only temporary as the United States later intervenes more forcefully on Iraq's side during the war.

## 1987

*July 20:* The United Nations Security Council passes Resolution 598 calling for a cease-fire between Iran and Iraq. However, Khomeini rejects the cease-fire and continues to prosecute his offensive war against Iraq.

*July 22:* The U.S. Navy begins Operation Earnest Will in which it escorts Kuwaiti tankers carrying Iraqi oil through the Persian Gulf. Kuwait is Iraq's ally during the war, and Iran had widened the war by attacking Kuwaiti oil tankers. In addition to securing its vital supply of oil from the Persian Gulf, the U.S. protection offered indirect support to Iraq, which the United States, other Western countries, and the Sunni-led nations of the Persian Gulf hoped would stem the spread of Iran's Shī'ite-led Islāmic revolution. On September 21, U.S. helicopters kill five Iranians when they fired on an Iranian ship laying mines in the Persian Gulf.

## 1988

*February 29:* For the first time Iraq uses long-range Scud missiles to strike at distant Iranian cities.

*March 28:* An Iraqi gas attack on Halabja, at the Iran-Iraq border, kills some 5,000 Kurdish civilians. This is part of an ongoing Iraqi attempt to suppress the independence of Kurds living in northern Iraq.

*July 3:* In the Persian Gulf the U.S. warship *Vincennes* shoots down a civilian Iranian airliner, apparently mistaking it for an attacking jet. All 290 passengers are killed. President Reagan tells Congress that the downing was a regrettable but justified act of self-defense. Iran apparently interprets the act as a signal that the United States is planning to launch a major offensive against it, and it accepts a cease-fire with Iraq two weeks later.

*July 18:* Iran formally accepts U.N. Resolution 598 calling for a cease-fire. The Gulf War between Iran and Iraq ends on August 8, and direct peace talks begin in Geneva on August 25. However, final settlement does not occur until September 1990. Though Hussein claims victory, and uses those claims to argue that the other Persian Gulf states are beholden to him for their protection, the war ended in a virtual stalemate with little change in the prewar status quo. Hussein concludes the war without obtaining any of his original objectives. Notably, he fails to secure control of the Shaṭṭ al-'Arab waterway that runs along the border.

## 1989

*August 17:* A missile-development plant in Al-Ḥillah, Iraq, explodes. The plant had been designed by Dr. Gerald Bull, the inventor of the supergun, a huge artillery piece with long-range nuclear capacity that Iraq was trying to assemble. Bull is assassinated in Belgium on March 22, 1990, possibly by Israeli agents.

*September 15:* Farzad Bazoft, an exiled Iranian journalist writing for the London *Observer*, is arrested for spying after visiting the site of the missile plant that had exploded at Al-Ḥillah. Daphne Parish, a British nursing administrator who accompanied him, is arrested on September 19. In a televised interview, apparently made under duress, Bazoft admits to spying for Israel. He is executed on March 15, 1990. Parish is sentenced to a 15-year prison term but is released on July 16, 1990, in what British and American officials then regard as a gesture of good will.

**December 5:** Iraq announces that it has successfully tested a three-stage rocket capable of launching a satellite into space. It also claims that it has tested two missiles with ranges of 1,200 miles—sufficient to strike Israel.

# 1990

**March 15:** Following a one-day trial, Farzad Bazoft is executed in Iraq as a spy. After the execution Iraq leaks a forged confession in which Bazoft purportedly admits to spying for British and American intelligence and to having connections with Dr. Gerald Bull, the inventor of the supergun and the designer of Iraq's Al-Ḥillah missile plant. Most Westerners believe Bazoft is innocent and that Hussein forced a false confession for political reasons. No hard evidence demonstrating Bazoft's guilt was presented at the trial. The incident sparks protests from the United States, Britain, and other Western countries.

**March 28:** Great Britain announces that customs officials have uncovered an Iraqi plan to smuggle American-made triggers for detonating nuclear bombs to Iraq. Two weeks later, customs confiscates a shipment of high precision steel piping bound for Iraq. The piping was to be used for a supergun designed by Dr. Gerald Bull, who had been assassinated on March 22. These developments give additional credence to the belief that Iraq was trying to develop nuclear weapons and an effective delivery system for them. In 1989, British and American agents had likewise foiled an Iraqi plot to illegally import krytrons, high voltage switches used for triggering nuclear bombs.

## II. Prelude to the Invasion of Kuwait and Operation Desert Shield

**May 3:** Iraqi Foreign Minister Tariq Aziz criticizes unnamed OPEC members who exceed their oil production quotas.

**May 28:** In Baghdad, Hussein hosts an emergency summit meeting of the Arab League. The ostensible reason for the meeting is the threat implied by the expected immigration of an additional 150,000 Soviet Jews to Israel. But Hussein also uses the forum not only to denounce Israel and the United States but also to justify his military buildup, assert himself as leader and protector of the Arab community, and threaten Kuwait for driving down the price of oil and stealing oil from Iraq's Rumaila field at the Kuwaiti border. This is Hussein's first public denunciation of Kuwait.

**July 16:** In an open letter to the Arab League, Hussein accuses Kuwait of stealing $2.4 billion in oil by drilling into the Rumaila oil field which Iraq claimed sole ownership, despite the fact that the southernmost five kilometers lay in Kuwait. Hussein further accuses Kuwait of military aggression because the Kuwaitis had advanced their border and customs posts northward. Kuwait points out that the posts, which remained in its territory, had been redeployed for practical and administrative reasons. It further accuses Iraq of trying to intimidate it and other countries into canceling Iraq's war debts, something Kuwait refused to do (*see* **Causes of the War**).

On this day Iraq also frees Daphne Parish, the British nursing administrator who was convicted of spying along with Farzad Bazoft, the journalist whom Iraq executed on March 15.

**July 17:** Iraq publicly denounces Kuwait and the United Arab Emirates and threatens to go to war with them for driving down the price of oil by producing more oil than the OPEC production quotas permit. Around this time Hussein also orders Lieutenant General Ayad Futayih al-Rawi, commander of the elite Republican Guard, to prepare his troops to invade Kuwait. In response to Hussein's threat, Kuwait places its armed forces on high alert.

*July 18:* Hussein accuses Kuwait of preparing to invite foreign countries (i.e., the United States and ones in Western Europe) to intervene in their dispute. His additional comment that Kuwait had given up the possibility of an Arab-brokered solution to the problem is interpreted as a signal that Hussein is seeking such a solution. Consequently, in the following days Egyptian President Mubarak confers in Cairo with foreign ministers from various Arab nations and then flies to the capitals of Iraq, Kuwait, and Saudi Arabia to speak with the leaders of those countries. According to Mubarak, on July 24 Hussein indicated that Iraq has no intention of attacking Kuwait while talks are going on.

*July 19:* The improved prospects for a diplomatic solution prompt Kuwait to drop its state of military alert.

*July 21:* The U.S. Central Command learns that about 3,000 military vehicles are moving from Baghdad toward Kuwait and that an Iraqi armored division has deployed to an area just across the border. The next day Iraq masses some 30,000 troops at the Kuwaiti border, and Kuwait soon reinstates its military alert. By July 26, 120,000 Iraqi troops were in position to attack Kuwait.

*July 25:* Hussein confers with U.S. ambassador April Glaspie to learn what the U.S. response might be to an Iraqi military action and to threaten against U.S. interference. According to a transcript of the meeting that Iraq leaked to the press after the invasion, Glaspie tells Hussein, "We have no opinion on Arab-Arab conflicts, like your border disagreement with Kuwait." She also adds that "President Bush is an intelligent man. He is not going to declare an economic war against Iraq."

Hussein threatens that should the United States intervene, it would have to be willing to accept a large number of war casualties, and it could face terrorism at home (*see* **Diplomacy**).

*July 27–28:* As Iraq continues to mass troops on the Kuwaiti border, it wins major concessions at the OPEC conference in Geneva, Switzerland, where it has insisted on elevating

the price of oil from $18 per barrel to $25. The Saudis, who favor more moderate prices, finally compromise and consent to a $3 increase to $21 per barrel, which OPEC accepts. OPEC also agrees to limit daily production to 22.5 million barrels and to enforce the quotas. These policies represent a slap against Kuwait and the United Arab Emirates, who had been exceeding their quotas. Their overproduction is one of Iraq's major complaints.

*July 31:* U.S. Central Command informs the Joint Chiefs of Staff that Iraq appears ready to invade Kuwait.

*July 31–August 1:* Saudi Arabia's King Fahd hosts a meeting in Jiddah between high-level Iraqi and Kuwaiti officials, in hopes of peacefully resolving the differences between the two countries. But after making intractable demands that the Kuwaitis do not accept, the Iraqis walk out of the meeting in protest. Iraq commences the invasion in the early hours of the next morning.

## III. The Invasion of Kuwait and Operation Desert Shield

*August 2:* At 2 A.M. (local time, 6 P.M. on August 1, EST) armored divisions from Iraq's Republican Guard overrun a Kuwaiti brigade guarding the border. The armored divisions then continue on to the capital, Kuwait City, about 50 miles to the south. At the same time Republican Guard special forces attack Kuwait City by helicopter, and sea commandos take command of the southern coastal road leading to the capital. By 5:30 A.M. the armored divisions arrive and the battle for the city begins. By 2:20 P.M. the battle concludes and Iraq controls the capital city. The Iraqi troops then continue on to the Saudi border, where they establish defensive positions (*see* **Invasion and Occupation of Kuwait**).

Iraq announces that it had sent its troops to support a popular coup, and it will withdraw when the situation in Kuwait becomes stable and the new, provisional government asks it to remove its troops. The "transitional free government" announces on Kuwaiti radio that the emir has been deposed and the National Assembly dissolved.

The emir, Crown Prince Saad as-Sabah (who was also the prime minister), and the other Kuwaiti ministers escape ahead of the invading Iraqi forces into Saudi Arabia.

During the invasion Iraqi forces take control of the airport and capture the passengers and crew on British Airways flight 149 that had just landed in Kuwait City for a stopover en route to India. The men from the flight are subsequently taken to Baghdad to become "human shields" that Hussein deploys around sensitive targets in Iraq.

In response to the invasion, France, Britain, and the United States condemn the invasion and call for an immediate Iraqi withdrawal, the freezing of Iraqi and Kuwaiti assets, and a moratorium on weapons deliveries to Iraq. The Soviet Union also calls for a prompt withdrawal and announces that it will immediately cease its arm sales to Iraq.

The Arab League foreign ministers convene an emergency meeting in Cairo. The Iraqi ambassador walks out of the session, which adjourns until the next day.

Bush meets in Aspen, Colorado, with British Prime Minister Thatcher, who encourages him to take a hard line against Hussein.

That evening the U.N. Security Council passes Resolution 660 condemning the invasion and demanding Iraq's withdrawal from Kuwait. The vote is 14–0–1, with Yemen abstaining (*see* **United Nations**).

*August 3:* Iraq announces that it will withdraw from Kuwait on August 5, in accordance with an agreement with the new, provisional government. But at the same time it continues to send reinforcements into Kuwait and mass troops five to ten miles from the Saudi Arabia border, prompting fears that Iraq plans to invade Saudi Arabia.

The Arab League resumes its meeting in Cairo and condemns the invasion. The 12–8 vote calls for Iraq to withdraw its troops and warns against further incursions into any Arab country.

President Bush is briefed at a National Security meeting. After reviewing several options he concludes that force against Iraq might be required.

Iraq begins jamming BBC Arabic and Voice of America broadcasts.

*August 4:* Claiming that the invasion of Kuwait was made at the behest of an indigenous, antiemir revolutionary movement, Iraq installs a puppet government under the leadership of Alaa Hussein Ali. Ostensibly a colonel in the Kuwaiti Army, Ali is actually an Iraqi military officer and the former head of Iraq's antimissile program (*see* **Provisional Kuwaiti Government**).

Bush learns that U.S. land and carrier-based aircraft can arrive in the region within days, but that it will require several weeks to establish a ground defense and 17 weeks to launch a ground attack.

The European Community freezes Iraqi and Kuwaiti assets.

*August 5:* In a public speech Bush describes the Iraqis as "international outlaws and renegades" and declares, "I view very seriously our determination to reverse this aggression…. This will not stand." (*See* **George Bush**.)

U.S. warships begin to deploy in the Persian Gulf and Red Sea to defend Saudi Arabia.

Japan announces a ban on oil imports from Kuwait and Iraq.

*August 6:* The U.N. Security Council passes Resolution 661 imposing a worldwide embargo on Iraq. Cuba and Yemen abstain. The British Royal Navy begins enforcing the embargo on August 14. On August 16 the USS *John L. Hall* becomes the first U.S. warship to intercept a vessel sailing from Iraq to Kuwait. However, the United Nations does not vote to permit military enforcement of the embargo until August 25. The first Iraqi merchant vessel is boarded by a team from the USS *Biddle* on August 31 (*see* **Embargo**, **Naval Action**).

Operation Desert Shield begins after U.S. Defense Secretary Richard Cheney and General Norman Schwarzkopf meet with King Fahd in Saudi Arabia, where they agree that the United States will send troops and other military assistance to help defend against a possible Iraqi attack. In return, Saudi Arabia agrees to increase its oil production by 2 million barrels a day to help compensate for the 4.1 million barrels lost to the world market when Iraq stopped exporting its own oil and Kuwait's. A purely defensive mission, Desert Shield was so-named because its purpose was to shield Saudi Arabia from an Iraqi invasion across the desert (*see* **Operation Desert Shield, Saudi Arabia, Richard Cheney, Norman Schwarzkopf**).

Israel offers to assist in defending Saudi Arabia if requested, but no request ever comes. Throughout the war the United States encourages Israel to maintain a low profile, since many coalition partners, especially the Arab countries, would find it politically unacceptable to fight on the same side as Israel.

A group of British, American, and German nationals, including some from British Airways Flight 149, are taken by bus from Kuwait to Baghdad. These are the first of Hussein's hostages (*see* **Hostages**).

*August 7:* Preparation for the deployment of American ground troops in Saudi Arabia begins.

Cheney arrives in Cairo for talks with Egyptian President Mubarak. He requests and receives permission for U.S. warships to pass through Egypt's Suez Canal. Later that day, a carrier battle group headed by the USS *Dwight D. Eisenhower* passes from the Mediterranean Sea through the Suez Canal into the Red Sea.

The puppet government in Kuwait, installed by Iraq and led by Alaa Hussein Ali, declares itself the Republic of Kuwait. However, no outside country recognizes it.

*August 8:* In a televised address to the American people, Bush announces that he is ordering U.S. armed forces to Saudi Arabia. Bush calls for the complete withdrawal of Iraq from Kuwait, the replacement of the puppet regime installed by Iraq in Kuwait, stability in the Gulf region, and the protection of U.S. citizens. Elements of the 82nd Airborne Division and the 101st Airborne Divisions depart for Saudi Arabia within hours and arrive the next day (*see* **Objectives**).

In a Radio Baghdad broadcast Hussein announces the annexation of Kuwait, which he maintains is now Iraq's nineteenth province.

Britain announces its plan to contribute to a multinational force to defend Saudi Arabia. It indicates that it will immediately send aircraft and reinforce its naval fleet in the Persian Gulf.

*August 9:* The U.N. Security Council unanimously passes Resolution 662 rejecting Iraq's annexation of Kuwait.

Britain and France agree to deploy their air forces in the Persian Gulf, and Turkey consents to allow U.S. planes to use its airbases and permits the United States to expand its military presence in Turkey (*see* **Great Britain, France, Turkey**).

Hussein sends a message to Bush declaring that Iraq has no plans to invade Saudi Arabia.

Mexico and Venezuela announce they will increase their oil production to help compensate for oil controlled by Iraq.

Iraq closes its borders and forbids foreign nationals from leaving either Iraq or Kuwait. It further demands that all foreign embassies in Kuwait close by August 24 and their diplomatic staff be transferred to Baghdad.

*August 10:* The Arab League votes 12–8 to support U.N. sanctions against Iraq and send troops to help the United States defend Saudi Arabia. Opposed are Jordan, Algeria, Tunisia, Yemen, Libya, Mauritania, Sudan, and the Palestinian Liberation Organization. This same division is repeated on August 30, when the league votes to transfer its headquarters from Tunisia to Egypt. The deep split caused by the war leads to the demise of the Arab League as an effective, Pan-Arab body, and both its secretary general and ambassador to the United States resign as a result of the internal differences.

The Royal Saudi Air Force, the U.S. Air Force, and U.S. Navy begin Exercise Arabian Gulf to coordinate air operations over the Persian Gulf.

Hussein calls for a *jihad*, a "holy war," to liberate Mecca and Medina, Islam's holiest cities that are located in Saudi Arabia.

*August 11:* Demonstrations in Yemen and Sudan call for support of Hussein. Throughout Desert Shield and Desert Storm, Saudi Arabia is concerned about the possibility of attack from Sudan and Yemen. All member organizations of the Palestinian Liberation Organization also support Hussein, except for the Popular Front for the Liberation of Palestine-General command.

Under the code name Operation Granby, the first British forces leave for the Middle East when 12 Jaguar fighter-bombers deploy to Oman.

The first Egyptian troops arrive in Saudi Arabia, where they serve under the Saudi-led Joint Forces Command.

A British citizen, Douglas Thomas Croskery, is shot and killed near the Saudi border while attempting to flee from Kuwait.

*August 12:* Hussein offers peace negotiations to resolve "all issues of occupation" in the Middle East, including Israel's occupation of Palestinian-inhabited territories conquered in 1967 and Syria's occupation of Lebanon. Hussein repeatedly tries to join his occupation of Kuwait to these other issues, but the United States emphatically refuses to accept this linkage as a precondition for Iraqi withdrawal from Kuwait and compliance with the other U.N. demands. Whether or not Hussein ever seriously expected this demand for linkage to succeed diplomatically, he nonetheless derives political benefit by posturing as a protector of the Palestinians and a leader concerned for all Arabs. This image contributes to his effort to emerge as the head of a new Pan-Arab nation supported by lower and working class Arabs throughout all of the current Arab nations.

The first American fatality of Operation Desert Shield occurs when an Air Force sergeant is struck by a military truck in Saudi Arabia.

Anti-Western demonstrations are held in support of Hussein in Jordan, Yemen, southern Lebanon, and Somalia.

Iranian President Rafsanjani condemns the presence of U.S. and other foreign troops in the Gulf.

*August 13:* King Hussein of Jordan condemns the presence of Western troops on Arab lands and claims that the West is more interested in preserving its access to oil than in helping people in the region. Later that day King Hussein holds talks with Saddam Hussein in Baghdad (*see* **Jordan**).

Holland announces that it will send two frigates to the Persian Gulf to help enforce the embargo against Iraq.

France claims that the British and U.S. naval policy amounts to a blockade and exceeds the measures authorized by the Security Council. France declares that it will not participate in operations to intercept ships in the Persian Gulf.

Pakistan announces that it will send troops to assist in the defense of Saudi Arabia.

Yemen offers to help Iraq deal with the effects of the embargo.

The British Royal Navy begins intercepting shipping in the Gulf to enforce the trade embargo.

*August 15:* Hussein sends a letter to Iranian President Rafsanjani offering to conclude a treaty to end the Gulf War. Anxious to eliminate an enemy on his eastern flank while preparing against the international forces to the south, Hussein concedes everything Iran had been asking for since the 1988 cease-fire. He agrees to withdraw from all occupied Iranian territory, exchange prisoners immediately, and establish the middle of the Shaṭṭ al-'Arab waterway as the border between the countries. Iraq begins dismantling its field fortifications on the Iranian front on August 18, and on August 19, Iraqi ground troops begin withdrawing from Iranian territory they had occupied since the conclusion of the Gulf War. Within two days of resolving the war with Iran, Hussein begins moving 24 divisions—some 300,000 troops—from the Iran border to Kuwait and the Saudi border areas. Iran and Iraq resume diplomatic relations on September 10 (*see* **Iran**).

Colin Powell, the chairman of the Joint Chiefs of Staff, briefs Bush and his top advisers and provides a timetable for the U.S. buildup in Saudi Arabia. Powell predicts that by the end of the month enough troops will be in place to deter an Iraqi attack, and that by early December there will be 184,000 troops in the Middle East, a sufficient force to defend Saudi Arabia. The costs would be $1.2 billion through September 30, and $1 billion per month thereafter. Powell also advises that Bush decide within about one week whether to call up the reserves. He further clarifies the need for clear objectives by pointing out how different goals would entail different military requirements. During the meeting Bush indicates his doubts that sanctions would work, and afterward he publicly articulates the U.S. goal of achieving "the immediate, complete, and unconditional withdrawal of all Iraqi forces from Kuwait; [and] the restoration of Kuwait's legitimate government." (*See* **Colin Powell, George Bush.**)

Iraq requires all Westerners in Kuwait—some 4,000 British and 2,500 U.S. citizens—to report to three hotels.

Syria announces the deployment of troops to Saudi Arabia (*see* **Syria**).

Morocco sends troops to Saudi Arabia.

Bangladesh announces its plans to send a small force to join in the defense of Saudi Arabia.

Palestinians hold a general strike in the Israeli-occupied territories in protest to the U.S. presence in Saudi Arabia.

The Soviet Union begins evacuating citizens from Iraq, but only women and children are permitted to leave.

*August 16:* Warships from the Italian navy depart from Italy to join Desert Shield. They are deployed to the eastern Mediterranean, south of Cyprus.

British and U.S. citizens in Kuwait are ordered to assemble in hotels.

British, French, and U.S. citizens are among a large group that crosses from Iraq into Jordan. They are the first Westerners to depart from Iraq since the border was closed on August 9.

The United States warns that it will respond in kind if Iraq uses chemical weapons.

Bush meets with Jordan's King Hussein, who later denies delivering a message from Hussein. Hussein states that Jordan will respect the U.N. sanctioned embargo and will close its Red Sea port of Aqaba to goods bound for Iraq.

The U.S. Defense Department announces the deployment of 45,000 Marines to the Gulf.

*August 17:* Bush orders the U.S. Navy to begin enforcing U.N. trade sanctions against Iraq. In response U.N. Secretary General Javier Perez de Cuellar states that the use of military force to impose sanctions violates the U.N. charter. On August 25, however, the Security Council votes for military enforcement of the embargo.

*August 18:* The speaker of the Iraqi parliament announces that Iraq would "play host" to foreign citizens as long as there is the threat of war against Iraq. Iraq will "provide accommodation at military bases and key civilian installations" in Iraq and Kuwait. Later that day, the first Westerners are moved from hotels to such installations, where they become "human shields" to discourage allied attacks. Some 4,000 British and 2,500 U.S. citizens are in Kuwait, as well as Europeans from other countries trapped in both Kuwait and Iraq.

The U.N. Security Council unanimously passes Resolution 664 demanding the release of foreign nationals being held as hostages or human shields in Iraq. The resolution also addresses thousands of Kuwaitis who were forcibly removed to Iraq, as well as several thousand Westerners caught in Kuwait and Iraq at the time of the invasion.

In the first direct U.S.-Iraqi confrontation, a U.S. Navy ship fires warning shots across the bow of an Iraqi tanker that refuses to stop.

*August 19:* Hussein announces that he will not release foreign hostages unless the United States promises to remove its forces from the Persian Gulf region.

*August 20:* Iraq announces that it has made human shields of the Western men it seized as hostages during the invasion of Kuwait. The hostages are placed at sensitive targets in Iraq, so any allied air attack against those targets would kill the hostages. The intention is to discourage attacks against those sites.

*August 21:* Hussein vows that if the allies initiate a war against him, "the mother of all battles" will ensue.

Iraq begins deploying medium range missiles in Kuwait and completes mining Kuwait's harbors.

Spain announces the deployment of four ships to the Gulf.

*August 22:* Bush signs Executive Order 12727 authorizing the mobilization of 200,000 members of reserve units for up to 180 days.

Overwhelmed by some 200,000 refugees fleeing Kuwait and Iraq, Jordan temporarily closes its borders with Iraq. Most of the refugees are Arabs and other Muslims who have worked as laborers in Kuwait prior to the invasion. Jordan reopens the border two days later after receiving offers of assistance from the United Nations, Great Britain, and the United States.

The Soviet Union suspends all economic ties with Iraq and Kuwait.

*August 23:* In a televised meeting Hussein tells a group of 15 British hostages he is detaining them to avoid "the scourge of war" and that will all be "heroes for maintaining peace." He then singles out a 7-year-old boy, Stuart Lockwood, and, patting him on the head, asks the child about his well-being. Most viewers regard the broadcast as a thinly veiled threat that Hussein would use these children and the other men and women in the group as human shields if the then-forming coalition were to attack Iraq. The broadcast leads to worldwide condemnation of Hussein, who announces five days later that all foreign women and children will be allowed to leave Kuwait.

Afghan rebels in Pakistan announce that they are sending 2,000 mujahideen soldiers to protect holy shrines in Saudi Arabia.

The Security Council agrees to provide short-term financial aid for refugees in Jordan.

*August 24:* The U.S. Embassy in Kuwait is ordered closed and approximately 100 U.S. officials, Marine guards, and civilians are moved to Baghdad. There are now 1,000 American hostages in Iraq. The other remaining embassies in Kuwait are also shut down. The male diplomats become hostages, but their dependents are freed.

*August 25:* The U.N. Security Council passes Resolution 665 calling on member nations to enforce the sanctions against Iraq. The resolution approves the use of military force to maintain the embargo. Cuba and Yemen abstain.

Austrian President Kurt Waldheim arrives in Baghdad and holds talks with Hussein that secure the release of 96 Austrian hostages. Austria declines to join the coalition against Iraq.

*August 27:* Qatar allows coalition troops to be based on its soil.

Denmark's Parliament votes to send a ship to the Gulf to help enforce the embargo.

France announces it will send a small force of combat helicopters to Saudi Arabia, the first French military unit to join Operation Desert Shield.

*August 28:* Belgium sends two minehunters to the Gulf.

An American citizen dies while being detained in Iraq, apparently from a heart attack.

*August 29:* Hussein announces that all women and children hostages will be released. He retains the male hostages and continues to use them as human shields around sensitive target areas, though he states that he will free them if the United States promises not to attack Iraq.

Japan agrees to provide $1 billion to help finance Operation Desert Shield and to furnish additional food and medical supplies.

Bush agrees to sell $2.2 billion in weapons to Saudi Arabia.

Chairman of the PLO Yasser Arafat proposes a peace plan for the Gulf at a conference on Palestine in Geneva. His plan calls for a U.N. peacekeeping force to replace U.S. and coalition troops and for the lifting of all sanctions against Iraq. The plan is to be part of a broader solution to all outstanding problems in the Middle East. Later in the day Arafat meets with French Premier Michel Rocard.

*August 30:* The U.S. Central Command issues its first general order of Desert Shield, a command requiring American troops to be sensitive to Saudi religious and cultural practices.

*August 30:* Iraq announces that it will launch attacks against Israel and Saudi Arabia if war breaks out.

U.S. politician Jesse Jackson meets in Baghdad with Iraqi Foreign Minister Tariq Aziz.

*August 31:* U.N. Secretary General Perez de Cuellar meets with Foreign Minister Aziz, but no progress is made.

The United States agrees to advance Israel $1 billion in military equipment.

*September 1:* Iraq continues to strengthen its defensive positions inside Kuwait. The U.S. command estimates that the Iraqi Army could launch an offensive ground attack within one day of receiving the order.

*September 4:* A convoy of seven buses from Kuwait carrying 300 British women and children arrive in Baghdad.

*September 5:* The USS *Acadia* departs San Diego for the Persian Gulf with 360 women among its crew of 1,260. This is the first time a combined crew of American men and women serve in wartime conditions.

Senegal sends a small military force to Saudi Arabia.

Hussein reiterates his call for a holy war and calls upon Arabs to revolt against their leaders who are supporting the coalition. He maintains that Iraqi children are dying because of food and medical shortages.

*September 6:* The British Parliament meets in an emergency session and after a two-day debate strongly endorses the Desert Shield operations.

*September 7:* Iranian President Rafsanjani warns the United States not to establish permanent bases in Saudi Arabia, vowing that Islāmic forces will eject them.

*September 8:* Kuwaiti Defense Minister Sheikh Nawaf al-Sabah announces that 5,000 soldiers have regrouped and joined the multinational force. They bring with them the tanks, heavy weapons, and combat aircraft that escaped from the invasion.

*September 9:* Bush and Soviet President Mikhail Gorbachev issue a joint declaration condemning Iraq and threatening repercussions if it does not withdraw from Kuwait.

*September 10:* Iran restores diplomatic relations with Iraq, and Hussein offers free oil to any nation that ships goods to Iraq in violation of the U.N. embargo.

*September 13:* The U.N. Security Council passes Resolution 666 reaffirming that Iraq is responsible for ensuring the well-being of foreign hostages and establishing guidelines for mercy shipments of medical supplies to Iraq. Cuba and Yemen oppose the resolution.

The U.S. House of Representatives passes legislation requiring the allies to assume more of the costs of Operation Desert Shield.

Syria announces it will send more troops to Saudi Arabia.

The Moslem League passes the "Mecca Declaration" approving Saudi Arabia's request for U.S. assistance and condemning Hussein for violating the Tenets of the Faith of Islām when he invaded Kuwait.

*September 14:* Iraqi soldiers break into the remaining Western embassies in Kuwait and take several diplomats hostage.

Britain announces it is sending additional arms and troops to Saudi Arabia.

Canada announces that it will send a squadron of fighter jets and 450 military personnel to the Gulf.

Italy announces that it is sending a fourth warship and eight fighter planes to the Gulf.

British, Dutch, French, and Italian officials designate areas in the Persian Gulf and Strait of Hormuz where their navies patrol.

*September 15:* France announces that it will send 4,000 troops to Saudi Arabia. French light armor and helicopters are already deployed. Eventually France commits some 14,000 troops, 40 fighter planes, and 14 ships.

Following talks between U.S. Secretary of State James Baker and West Germany Chancellor Helmut Kohl, West Germany announces that it will contribute $2 billion in military and financial aid. The money is designated for the U.S. military and for aid to

Egypt, Jordan, and Turkey to help compensate for losses incurred by the embargo.

**September 16:** The U.N. Security Council unanimously passes Resolution 667 condemning Iraqi actions against diplomats and demanding the immediate release of hostages.

A videotaped message from Bush to the Iraqi people is broadcast over Iraqi television. Bush denounces the invasion of Kuwait as monstrous and declares, "Nobody wants war, but if the military option is imposed on us we will have to take it." Afterward, an Iraqi official accuses Bush of trying to fool the Iraqi people.

**September 17:** Saudi Arabia and the Soviet Union restore diplomatic relations after a 52-year hiatus, and they agree to work together to achieve Iraq's withdrawal from Kuwait.

Defense Secretary Cheney fires Air Force Chief of Staff Michael J. Dugan for making public statements about U.S. plans in the event of a war with Iraq. General Merill "Tony" McPeak succeeds him.

**September 18:** Sweden contributes $15 million to a U.N. refugee fund. Denmark contributes $2 million and Holland $1 million.

Argentina becomes the first Latin American country to join the coalition when it announces it will send naval and air force units to the Gulf.

**September 22:** Bush states that he will hold Hussein responsible for Iraqi-sponsored terrorism against U.S. interests.

**September 24:** The U.N. Security Council unanimously passes Resolution 669 to examine requests for humanitarian shipments to Iraq and Kuwait and make recommendations for appropriate action.

Iraq withdraws the Kuwaiti dinar from circulation. Kuwaiti dinars can be exchanged for Iraqi currency until October 6.

South Korea announces it will contribute $220 million toward the coalition efforts.

Taiwan announces it will send financial and material aid worth $30 million to help Jordan, Turkey, and Egypt deal with refugees and economic problems occasioned by the embargo.

Czechoslovakia says it will send 200 chemical weapons defense specialists, doctors and medical personnel to Saudi Arabia, if requested by the Saudis.

In a speech before the United Nations, French President Mitterrand presents a four-stage plan calling for free elections in Kuwait, the restoration of Kuwait's sovereignty, and an international conference on all major issues in the Middle East.

**September 25:** The U.N. Security Council passes Resolution 670, establishing an air blockade of Iraq and calling for Iraqi ships to be detained. Cuba opposes the resolution.

Romania offers to let Western forces use some of its holiday resorts while in transit to and from the Gulf.

**September 27:** The emir of Kuwait addresses the U.N. General Assembly and praises the world community for standing up to Iraq. The Iraqi delegation walks out in protest.

The Iraqi Interior Ministry confirms that after October 1, foreign nationals within Iraq will no longer have access to certain rationed foods.

**September 28:** The first British ground troops embark for Saudi Arabia. Eventually some 9,000 soldiers and 120 tanks join the coalition force.

**September 30:** The Soviet Union announces that it will support the coalition, but that its troops will serve only under U.N. auspices (i.e., not under the United States or NATO). Soviet ground troops never actually serve in either Desert Shield or Desert Storm, though the Soviet navy contributes a small number of ships for enforcing the embargo.

Two crewmen die when a U.S. F-15E jet crashes while on a training mission in Oman. They are the first Americans killed while on military maneuvers during Desert Shield.

As of this date the U.S. Transportation Command has airlifted 115,826 tons of cargo and 127,739 military and other support personnel in 3,541 flights.

Iraq has stationed 22 divisions in the Kuwait theater of operations, including some 433,000 soldiers, 3,350 tanks, 2,340 armored personnel carriers, and 2,140 pieces of artillery.

***October 1:*** The U.S. House of Representatives votes 380–29 to support Bush's actions in the Middle East. The House underscores its desire for a diplomatic resolution of the crisis.

Bush addresses the U.N. General Assembly and states that the United States is still seeking diplomatic solutions to the crisis.

British Prime Minister Margaret Thatcher insists on American television that Iraq must pay compensation for the damages inflicted on Kuwait.

British Defense Secretary Tom King announces that Sir Peter de la Billiere will command the British forces in the Gulf and that, though ultimately under British control, these troops will serve under American field command when appropriate.

Operation Camel Sand, the first amphibious rehearsal in Desert Shield, takes place in Oman. Most of the U.S. naval ships in the area participate.

***October 2:*** The U.S. Senate votes 96–3 to endorse Bush's efforts to "deter Iraqi aggression."

The Saudis dismiss a French peace initiative linking the Palestinian issue to the occupation of Kuwait.

Iraq offers to eliminate its weapons of mass destruction if other Middle East countries, including Israel, do likewise. (Israel is generally believed to possess nuclear weapons.)

A report by Amnesty International accuses Iraqis of widespread killings and human rights violations in Kuwait.

***October 3:*** The U.S. Senate supports the deployment of troops to the Gulf region. The vote is 96–3.

Hussein makes his first known visit to Kuwait since the invasion.

Iran declares it will not participate in any military action to force Iraq from Kuwait.

***October 5:*** Soviet envoy Yevgeni Primakov meets in Baghdad with Hussein. Afterward, Hussein states that a large group of Soviet citizens will be permitted to leave Iraq.

***October 7:*** Israeli authorities begin distributing gas masks to civilians.

***October 8:*** The first fatal accident involving U.S. Marines occurs when two helicopters crash in a night training mission. Eight Marines are killed.

***October 9:*** Hussein announces that he will attack Saudi Arabia and Israel with long-range missiles if a war breaks out.

***October 10:*** A chief adviser to President Mubarak says that Egypt's forces are purely defensive and they will not participate in an offensive attack against Iraq.

A U.S. F-111 fighter-bomber crashes in the Saudi desert, killing both crew members.

***October 11:*** Bush is briefed on plans for Operation Desert Storm, the offensive to drive Iraq from Kuwait. It calls for a strategic air campaign within Iraq whose goal is, according to General Schwarzkopf, "to decapitate his [the enemy's] leadership, command and control, and eliminate his ability to reinforce Iraqi ground forces in Kuwait and southern Iraq." The plan will also establish air supremacy over Kuwait, inflict heavy casualties on the Iraqi Army prior to the ground offensive, and provide air support during the ground campaign. The plan for the air campaign remained essentially unchanged, but the initial plan for a ground campaign, which was based on a coalition force of only 200,000 troops, was unsatisfactory because it would require a head-on assault into Iraqi fortified positions and result in excessive casualties. However, by the end of October a new plan based on more than twice as many troops calls for allied armored divisions to exploit the Iraqis' vulnerable western flank (*see* **Offensive War Preparations for Liberating Kuwait**).

***October 17:*** A team from the U.S. Defense Department leaves to meet with Saudi officials to negotiate an arrangement to defray the costs of Desert Shield. The Saudi government agrees to pay for all American contracts and for 4,800 tents, 20 million meals, and 20.5 million gallons of fuel a day.

Soviet envoy Primakov holds talks in Paris with French President Mitterrand. He meets the following day with U.S. Secretary of State James Baker in Washington and on October 19 with Bush. On October 20, he meets in London with British Prime Minister Thatcher and Foreign Secretary Douglas Hurd.

*October 20:* The first large protests against the American military involvement take place within the United States, notably in New York, Boston, San Francisco, and Los Angeles. Other protests take place in Paris (*see* **Popular Support for the War**).

*October 21:* Chairman of the Joint Chiefs of Staff Colin Powell flies to Saudi Arabia to meet with Schwarzkopf. Over the next two days they discuss plans for a ground offensive and decide to more than double the U.S. military force in the region. The new plans for an offensive involve two army corps and focus on destroying the Republican Guard. It includes the surprise "left hook" flanking movement. According to Powell, "The Iraqi's disposition of forces practically wrote the plan for us." Upon leaving Saudi Arabia, Powell assures Schwarzkopf that "the President and Cheney will give you anything you need to get the job done. And don't worry, you won't be jumping off until you're ready." (*See* **Colin Powell, Norman Schwarzkopf**.)

*October 23:* After meeting with Hussein, former British Prime Minister Edward Heath leaves Iraq with 38 British hostages. They arrive in London the next day. Heath reports that Hussein seemed sympathetic to the plight of the sick and elderly and that the Iraqis did not want war but would fight to the death if attacked. He urges more diplomacy to end the crisis.

*October 26:* A senior engineer for the Kuwait Oil Company claims that Iraq has placed explosives on 300 Kuwaiti oil wells to destroy them if necessary.

Soviet envoy Primakov meets with Egyptian President Mubarak in Cairo.

*October 27:* The eight antiballistic Patriot missile systems in Saudi Arabia are fully operational by this date. The Patriot missiles are charged with shooting down Iraqi Scud missiles directed at targets within Saudi Arabia. They are later also deployed within Israel. Though they were credited with considerable success during the war, studies made after the war concluded that they were much less effec-

tive than originally believed (*see* **Patriot Missiles**).

*October 28:* Soviet envoy Primakov meets in Baghdad with Hussein and delivers a message from Soviet Premier Gorbachev. Primakov later meets with PLO Chairman Arafat, who was also in Baghdad for meetings with Hussein.

*October 29:* The U.N. Security Council passes Resolution 674 demanding Iraq cease its mistreatment of Kuwaitis and foreign nationals and reminding Iraq that it is liable for damages. Cuba and Yemen abstain.

Primakov meets in Saudi Arabia with King Fahd. The next day he meets with the emir of Kuwait. After returning on October 31 from his tour of Europe and the Middle East, Primakov states that he detects an important shift in the Iraqi position.

*October 30:* Bush decides that if Hussein does not withdraw from Kuwait by early 1991, the coalition will wage a war to evict the Iraqis. He waits to announce his corresponding decision to increase the number of troops in the Middle East until after the midterm elections on November 6.

Ten crew members aboard the USS *Iwo Jima* die from a massive steam leak in the engine room.

*November 3:* The speaker of the Iraqi National Assembly states that Iraq is now prepared to free all hostages in return for assurances of nonaggression by the coalition.

*November 4:* Secretary of State Baker travels to Bahrain and Saudi Arabia as he begins a new mission in the Middle East.

*November 5:* U.S. officials announce an agreement on military command should a war break out. In the event of an attack on Saudi Arabia, action would be controlled by a joint Saudi-U.S. command. But an offensive action against Iraqi forces in Kuwait would be under sole U.S. command.

*November 6:* Midterm Congressional elections take place in the United States. The build-up in the Persian Gulf is not a major issue, but Bush delays announcing the deployment of more troops until after the elections pass.

*November 7:* Former West German Chancellor Willy Brandt meets in Baghdad with Hussein, Aziz, and PLO Chairman Yasser Arafat. Subsequently, Hussein orders the release of 120 hostages, mostly Germans.

*November 8:* Bush orders an additional 150,000 air, sea, and ground troops to the Persian Gulf. This build-up introduces a second phase in Desert Shield and enables General Schwarzkopf and his staff to prepare for Desert Storm.

*November 13:* General Schwarzkopf tells his subordinate commanders that the key targets in the air war will be the Iraqi command and control, the Iraqi capacity to wage nuclear, biological, and chemical warfare, and the elite Republican Guard.

An RAF pilot who was killed when his Jaguar fighter-bomber crashed during a training flight becomes the first British serviceman to die in the crisis.

*November 14:* Defense Secretary Cheney authorizes the call-up of 80,000 Army reserves and 15,000 Marine Corps reserves.

*November 18:* Iraq announces that it will release the remaining 2,000 Western hostages between December 25 and March 25, "unless something would take place that mars the atmosphere of peace." U.S. officials dismiss the announcement as a propaganda ploy.

*November 20:* Fifty-three Representatives and one Senator file suit in U.S. Federal District Court seeking an injunction to prevent Bush from going to war without first gaining Congressional approval. The judge turns down the request but said he will consider granting it if the full Congress requests it.

*November 20:* British Prime Minister Thatcher, French President Mitterrand, and Soviet Premier Gorbachev hold talks in Paris. At the same time, the foreign ministers of Britain, France, the Soviet Union, and the United States hold a series of bilateral talks in Paris.

*November 21:* Bush arrives in Saudi Arabia and meets with King Fahd and the emir of Kuwait. The leaders reiterate their call for an unconditional Iraqi withdrawal.

*November 22:* Bush and Congressional leaders spend the Thanksgiving holiday with U.S. troops in Saudi Arabia.

British Prime Minister Margaret Thatcher resigns. John Major, a fellow Conservative, succeeds her.

Jean-Marie Le Pen, leader of the French National Front, returns from Baghdad with approximately 50 European hostages, including several British citizens. Another 36 hostages are released to a Swiss parliamentary delegation headed by Edgar Oehler.

*November 23:* Bush meets with Egyptian President Mubarak in Cairo. Prior to their meeting Mubarak rules out any Egyptian military operations within Iraq. Later in the day Bush flies to Geneva and meets with Syrian President Assad in the first U.S.-Syrian summit in 13 years.

*November 27:* The Senate Armed Services Committee opens the first Congressional hearing on the Persian Gulf crisis (*see* **Popular Support for the War**).

*November 28:* The U.N. Security Council passes Resolution 677 condemning Iraq's destruction of Kuwait's civil records and its attempt to absorb Kuwait demographically.

*November 29:* The U.N. Security Council authorizes war against Iraq when it passes Resolution 678. The resolution permits U.N. members to employ "all means necessary" to enforce the previous resolutions if Iraq does not withdraw from Kuwait by January 15, 1991. Cuba and Yemen oppose the resolution; China abstains.

*November 30:* For the first time, Bush offers to negotiate directly with Iraq and suggests a meeting between Secretary of State James Baker and Iraqi Foreign Minister Tariq Aziz. However, on December 18, a tentative meeting in Washington is canceled when the two sides cannot agree upon terms for a reciprocal visit in Iraq. The meeting is eventually held on January 9, but it produces no results.

*December 1:* Defense Secretary Cheney increases to 115,000 the number of Army reservists to be called to active duty. Two days later he increases the Marine call-up to 23,000 and the call-up of an additional 63,000 National Guard reservists.

*December 6:* Hussein announces that Iraq will free the remaining Western hostages. On December 7, the Iraqi National Assembly votes to release the hostages. The first American hostages are released on December 10. The last group leaves Baghdad on December 14.

*December 11:* Czechoslovakia deploys a chemical decontamination battalion. This is the first detachment of Warsaw Pact troops to join the coalition forces in the Gulf.

*December 16:* The four phases of Operation Desert Storm are articulated. These are the strategic air campaign against targets inside Iraq, the campaign to achieve air dominance over the Kuwaiti theater of operations, the battlefield preparation involving bomb attacks against the Iraqi Army, and the ground attack.

*December 20:* By this date 280,000 U.S. troops are in the Middle East.

In an interview on German television Hussein asserts that Iraq will not withdraw its troops before the January 15 deadline. He adds that once 5,000 U.S. troops had been killed in the conflict Bush will be forced to call off the war.

*December 21:* Twenty-one sailors from the USS *Saratoga* die while returning from liberty when their ferryboat capsizes off of Haifa, Israel.

*December 23:* Two American sailors die and five are injured in an automobile accident in the United Arab Emirates.

*December 24:* In an interview on Spanish television Hussein declares that Israel will be Iraq's first target in a war, whether or not it participates in action against Iraq.

Egyptian President Mubarak again calls for Hussein to withdraw from Kuwait and declares that Hussein is living in a fantasy world if he believes he can defeat the United States and its allies.

*December 28:* The Defense Department announces that for the first time in history U.S. troops will be vaccinated against chemical and biological weapons.

*December 30:* An Iraqi spokesman declares that any attempt to force Iraqi troops from Kuwait will result in an Islamic holy war and that American targets throughout the world will be subject to terrorist attacks.

*December 31:* Iraq issues its first orders conscripting 17-year-old boys for military training.

# 1991

*January 1:* By this date 325,000 U.S. troops are stationed in the Middle East. By January 8, the number exceeds 360,000, and by January 17, the beginning of Desert Storm, 425,000 U.S. troops are in the region, along with ground forces from 18 other countries and ships from 13 others.

On January 7, U.S. intelligence estimates that Iraq has deployed 35 divisions, consisting of 542,000 troops, 4,300 tanks and 3,100 pieces of artillery in the Kuwaiti theater of operations.

*January 2:* Forty-two aircraft are sent by NATO to Turkey to protect against an Iraqi attack.

A British soldier is killed in an accident while helping transport tanks.

The Voice of Free Iraq, a clandestine radio station, begins broadcasting. It calls for the overthrow of Hussein, a new constitution, and free elections. The station is jammed on the following day.

*January 6:* The U.S. 1st Armored Division begins training for Operation Desert Storm, using "service" instead of "training" ammunition.

*January 7:* Israeli Foreign Minister David Levy states that Israel is willing to enter a comprehensive Middle East peace process after the Gulf crisis has been resolved.

*January 9:* A meeting in Geneva between Secretary of State Baker and Iraqi Foreign Minister Aziz yields no results. No one had seriously expected the conference to succeed, but it enables Bush to claim his administration had taken every extra step possible to negotiate an acceptable resolution, only to receive "a total stiff-arm" for its efforts (*see* **Diplomacy**).

Jordan again announces it is closing its border to non–Jordanian refugees until it receives international assistance for helping them.

*January 10:* French Defense Minister Jean-Pierre Chevenement calls for the United States to agree to an international peace conference on the Middle East as a face-saving mechanism that would enable Hussein to withdraw from Kuwait before the January 15 deadline. However, the United States turns down the proposal on January 12.

*January 11:* Hussein again calls for an Islāmic holy war and for Islāmic leaders to prepare their followers for the Great Mother of All Battles.

Saudi Arabia agrees to pay up to half the cost of deploying U.S. forces in the Gulf.

*January 12:* The U.S. Congress votes to permit the use of military force to remove Iraq from Kuwait. The Senate vote is 52–47, and the House vote is 250–183. This is the first time since the Vietnam War that Congress voted directly to approve an offensive U.S. military action.

In the North Arabian Sea the largest amphibious task force since the Korean War forms around the aircraft carrier USS *Ranger*.

*January 13:* After being kept waiting for several hours, U.N. Secretary General Perez de Cuellar meets with Hussein in Baghdad but achieves no results.

Israel announces that it will distribute another 1 million gas masks to people in rural areas.

*January 15:* France proposes that the U.N. Security Council hold an international conference on the Palestinian situation if Iraq agrees to withdraw from Kuwait. However, the United States and Great Britain strongly oppose the proposal, since it fails to guarantee all of the conditions demanded by the United Nations. The Soviet Union also objects to the timing of the plan and its linkage of the Gulf crisis to a Middle East peace conference (*see* **Diplomacy**).

*January 16:* An hour before Desert Storm commences, Secretary of State Baker notifies Soviet Premier Gorbachev. Gorbachev, in turn, warns Hussein to withdraw from Kuwait immediately because the war was about to begin. Hussein disregards the warning.

## IV. Operation Desert Storm

### 1991

*January 17:* Operation Desert Storm begins at 1 A.M. local time (5 P.M. on January 16, EST), when allied missiles strike at early warning radar sites in Iraq. By 2:30 A.M. Baghdad is under heavy attack. The air assault is broadcast live from Baghdad by CNN camera crews and correspondents Bernard Shaw, John Holliman, and Peter Arnett (*see* **Operation Desert Storm, Media Coverage**).

These attacks inaugurate the first phase of Desert Storm, an air campaign directed against Iraqi command and control (including Hussein, personally), Iraqi chemical and biological warfare production plants, and Iraqi ground forces in the Kuwaiti theater of operations. The air forces of the United States, Britain, France, Canada, Italy, Saudi Arabia, Qatar, and Kuwait participate in this phase of the war, which involves strikes from land, air, and sea-launched missiles, jets, and helicopters (*see* **Air Campaign, Weapons Systems and Advanced Technology**).

Coordinated with the air attack, the U.S. Army 18th Airborne Corps, the French 6th Light Armored Division, the Army 7th Corps and the British 1st Armoured Division begin secretly moving supplies and equipment in preparation for their westward redeployment. Troops, tanks and other armored vehicles, weapons, ammunition, food, and water are transported as far as 530 miles over the desert to points west of Ḥafar al-Bāṭin, 250 miles inland along the Saudi-Iraqi border. The redeployment, which required continuous movement day and night for about three weeks, remained a secret because the air campaign had eradicated Iraqi aerial reconnaissance and the press was not permitted to observe it. Called Operation Hail Mary after a football play designed to achieve a quick offensive strike, the redeployment was one of the great logistical achievements in modern warfare. The shift to the west allowed Schwarzkopf to surprise the Republican Guard by striking unexpectedly at its flank, and it was the decisive maneuver of the ground war (*see* **Operation Hail Mary**).

Three Marines and one Navy corpsman are killed by Iraqi artillery fire near the Kuwait border. These are the first U.S. ground casualties of Desert Storm.

After destroying Iraqi surface-to-air missiles across the border in Kuwait, the U.S. launches its first long-range precision tactical missile strike in history. Captain Jon K. Kelk shoots down the first Iraqi warplane in the war, a Soviet-made MiG-29; Captain Robert E. Graeter downs the second and third, French-made Mirage F-1s.

*January 18:* Iraq launches its first Scud missile attack against Israel, injuring 12 civilians. In response American jets attack the missile launching sites. During the war a total of 40 Scuds were launched against Israel. Four civilians were killed, 289 wounded, and 11,727 apartments were damaged or destroyed (*see* **Israel**, **Scud Missiles**).

Jordan and the PLO officially condemn the attack against Iraq. Jordan reopens its border with Iraq to allow refugees to enter.

The coalition suffers its first air casualties as eight aircraft are destroyed, including four U.S. planes. Four U.S. airmen are taken prisoner, and four are killed.

*January 20:* A battery of antiballistic Patriot missiles ostensibly destroys three of four Iraqi Scud missiles aimed at the Saudi port of Dhahran. Israel requests a Patriot missile defense, and within 27 hours American air defense batteries are established within Israel.

Schwarzkopf reports that coalition bombers have "thoroughly damaged" Iraq's nuclear research reactors.

Hussein asks other Arabs to join in a *jihad* (holy war) against the allies.

Iraqi television shows a group of captured coalition pilots who were shot down. These include airmen from the United States, Britain, Italy, and Kuwait. Two are badly bruised, causing Britain to request a Red Cross investigation. Several state that they do not approve of the war.

A mysterious explosion above Khafji, Saudi Arabia, produces a mist that burns the skin of personnel on the ground and triggers chemical alarms. The Pentagon claims the mist was rocket propellant from an Iraqi Scud missile that detonated in the air. But some veterans who were present believe the mist came from an Iraqi gas attack. A 1995 study by the University of Texas indicated that veterans who were at Khafji during or soon after the explosion and who also took PB, an antinerve gas tablet, were at especially high risk for Gulf War Syndrome (*see* **Gulf War Syndrome**).

President Mitterrand announces that France would attack Iraq if necessary.

*January 21:* Iraq announces that prisoners of war (POWs) will be used as human shields around strategic targets inside Iraq, and Iraqi television displays five American, two British, one Italian, and one Kuwaiti POWs. In response, the United States warns that after the war Iraq will be held accountable for the mistreatment of POWs, and the International Red Cross denounces the plan to use the POWs as hostages as a violation of the Geneva convention.

Destroying Scud missile sites becomes the new focus of the air campaign, as Iraq continues to launch long-range missiles against Israel and some of the coalition Gulf states.

Objectives for the naval war are articulated: "1) Destroy all Iraqi surface combatants and minelayers, 2) Deny Iraq the use of oil platforms for military purposes, 3) Move back Iraqi surface forces in the northern Persian Gulf from the south to north; and 4) Prevent attacks or threats against Coalition forces and countries in the Gulf." (*See* **Naval Action**.)

*January 22:* An Iraqi Scud missile attack kills two people in Ramat Gan, Israel.

Iraq ignites oil storage tanks in Kuwait at

Mīnā' 'Abd Allah, Ash-Shu'aybah, and Al Wafrah. By the end of the war, some 450 oil wells were ignited. These required seven months to extinguish (*see* **Environmental Warfare**).

*January 23:* Raids by U.S. B-52s, F-111s, and F-15Es unsuccessfully attempt to kill Hussein in a bunker he is believed to be using northwest of Basra. Though Hussein was not officially an allied target, the allies launched some 250 air raids against him.

Otherwise, the primary targets in the air war shift from incapacitating Iraqi runways to destroying hardened aircraft shelters and hunting for Scud missile launching sites.

Japan agrees to increase its support for the war by $9 billion.

*January 24:* Navy SEALs reclaim the first piece of Kuwaiti territory when they capture Qaruh Island, take 67 prisoners, and raise the Kuwaiti flag.

In the only attempted Iraqi offensive air strike of the war, a Saudi fighter shoots down two Iraqi Mirage jets attacking allied ships in the Persian Gulf.

Stealth fighters attack hardened shelters north of Baghdad, where many Iraqi fighters are seeking refuge. Over the next two weeks the Air Force seeks to destroy Iraqi planes on the ground, before they can flee to Iran.

The Canadian Air Force participates in its first combat mission—its first since World War II.

*January 25:* Iraq begins releasing millions of barrels of oil from Kuwait's Sea Island oil tanker terminal into the Persian Gulf. Hussein's objective is to damage and pollute Saudi Arabia's desalinization plants that furnish fresh water for much of the kingdom. Within two days the oil slick is 35 miles long and 10 miles wide, and is estimated to contain 460 million gallons of oil (*see* **Environmental Warfare**).

An Iraqi Scud missile strikes in Tel Aviv, Israel, killing one.

*January 26:* Having already launched over 20,000 sorties primarily against Iraqi command and control, chemical weapons plants, Scud missile launchers, and runways and hardened aircraft shelters, the air campaign now begins to focus on preparing the battlefield for the attack. Targets include military storage facilities and Republican Guard troop fortifications.

Over 20 Iraqi warplanes flee to Iran, where Iranian officials impound them. Eventually, over 80 planes—10 percent of the Iraqi Air Force—manage to escape to Iran, where they are impounded.

*January 27:* Schwarzkopf declares the coalition has achieved air supremacy. This was accomplished against some of the most heavily defended airspace in the history of warfare.

U.S. Air Force jets use laser-guided bombs to sever the manifold pipelines feeding the oil spill from Kuwait's Sea Island oil tanker terminal.

*January 29:* At night, the Iraqis launch their only ground offensive in the war, as four columns from the Iraqi 15th Mechanized Regiment and 5th Mechanized Division invade border regions in Saudi Arabia near the coast. Marine reconnaissance aircraft detect the mechanized columns as they cross the Saudi border, but inexplicably the Air Force command fails to issue an order to bomb them, and they proceed undeterred into Saudi Arabia. One column attacks a U.S. Marine position at Umm Hujul. The Americans stop the attack, but 13 Marines are killed, 11 by "friendly fire"—fire from their own troops. Two of the other Iraqi columns are also repulsed in the early morning of January 30, as allied jets destroy dozens of Iraqi tanks and armored vehicles. But the fourth column, consisting of 80 to 100 tanks accompanied by other armored vehicles, overruns a thinly manned Saudi National Guard outpost and proceeds to occupy the abandoned Saudi town of Khafji. Two Marine reconnaissance teams trapped inside the town hide in houses and cellars for almost two days, while ordering in "danger close" fire support and close air support to fight off the Iraqis. Meanwhile, Saudi troops counterattack, supported by Qatari tank units and elements of the U.S. 1st and 2nd Marine divisions. By 2 P.M. on January 31, the entire Iraqi force in Khafji is either killed or captured. After suffering heavy losses, the remaining Iraqi units involved in the offensive pull back and assume defensive positions to await the allied ground attack (*see* **Khafji**).

British carrier-based helicopters sink 12 of 15 Iraqi patrol boats apparently on their way to raid Khafji, in coordination with the ground assault.

Iraqis capture Army Specialists Melissa Rathbun-Nealy and David Lockett when they inadvertently drive their truck into Iraqi-occupied Khafji. Rathbun-Nealy, the driver, is the first female POW (*see* **Women in the Military**).

The 13th Marine Expeditionary Unit recaptures Umm Al-Maradim and raises the Kuwaiti flag. The island, located 12 miles from shore, is the second reclaimed for Kuwait.

Iraqi Radio announces that a captured pilot was killed during a bombing attack on the Ministry of Industry building in Baghdad.

In its continuing effort to prepare the battlefield for the ground war by bombing Iraqi ground troops, U.S. planes drop leaflets written in English and Arabic advising Iraqi soldiers to surrender or face death. Subsequently, B-52s drop 470 bombs on Republican Guard positions. Both the leaflets and the bombings continue through the beginning of the ground campaign in February (*see* **Psychological Operations**).

*January 30:* Several Iraqi missile boats and amphibious ships are damaged or destroyed in the 13-hour Battle of Bubiyan (*see* **Battle of Bubiyan**).

Oil from the Sea Island terminal stops flowing into the Persian Gulf.

*January 31:* Using intelligence gained from the Kuwaiti Resistance, a U.S. Marine jet drops a laser-guided "smart bomb" on a building near Ash-Shu'aybah where high-ranking Iraqi generals are said to be meeting. U.S. intelligence believes that the commander of Iraq's 3rd Corps was killed in the attack.

In a separate operation over Kuwait, 14 Americans are killed when their helicopter remains in the target area too long while supporting a special forces operation and crashes into the Persian Gulf. This is the greatest number of U.S. casualties from a single inci-

dent during the air campaign and the second-largest cause of U.S. combat deaths in Operation Desert Storm.

A Scud missile strikes Israel's West Bank, but no casualties are reported. The West Bank was mostly populated by Palestinians who, as a group, supported Iraq during the war. In response to the recent Scud attacks, the coalition deploys a Special Operations Task Force specifically to knock out the missile launchers and prevent further attacks (*see* **Special Operations Forces**).

After the failure of its offensive into Saudi Arabia the day before, Iraqi troops assume defensive positions and await the allied ground attack.

*February 1:* The U.S. State Department claims that 70 terrorists attacks have been conducted against coalition countries.

*February 2:* One Iraqi Scud missile targeted for Tel Aviv, Israel, lands in Jordan; another falls on the West Bank, causing no injuries. A Patriot missile apparently destroys a third Scud aimed at Riyadh, Saudi Arabia, but the debris from the falling missile fragments injures 29 people.

By this date all of Iraq's 13 ships capable of firing antiship missiles and all of its patrol boats are damaged or destroyed, except for one that escaped to Iran. The Iraqi Navy is judged to be no longer effective in combat.

Schwarzkopf decides to cancel Desert Saber, the plan to launch a Marine amphibious landing at the Kuwaiti port of Ash-Shu'aybah, because he fears it will cause too many casualties, do too much damage to Kuwaiti coastal properties, and take too long to prepare. But he orders the ship-based Marines to continue practicing amphibious assaults, in case one is necessary to reinforce the land-based 1st Marine Expeditionary Force pushing into Kuwait from the Saudi border. Those preparations also serve as a ruse to convince the Iraqis to commit troops and weapons to coastal defenses, away from the sites of the actual attack (*see* **Amphibious Landing; Deceptions, Feints, and Ruses**).

*February 3:* The U.S. Army 7th Corps completes its shift 150 miles inland and the

18th Airborne Corps completes its western redeployment 250 miles inland; they now assume their positions for the ground offensive. Logistics troops continue to bring forward supplies and ammunition through February 20. The redeployment had begun at the beginning of the air war, on January 17 (*see* **Operation Hail Mary**).

The battleship USS *Missouri* begins bombarding Iraq's bunkers on the Kuwaiti coast with its 1.25 ton 16-inch shells, each of which contains 18,000 pounds of high explosives. This is the first combat bombardment by the *Missouri* since the Korean War. For the first time, a Remotely Piloted Vehicle (RPV) is used in combat to spot gunfire.

*February 5:* The U.S. Secretary of the Navy authorizes the call-up of 2,000 retired Marines under the age of 60.

*February 6:* British commandos operating inside Iraq destroy a communications facility used for Scud missile operations. On the next day U.S. Special Forces also begin infiltrating into Iraq to destroy or debilitate Scud missiles. A Ranger platoon destroys a microwave tower and its communications facility, then safely escapes.

*February 8:* Defense Secretary Richard Cheney, Under Secretary Paul Wolfowitz, and Chairman of the Joint Chiefs of Staff Colin Powell fly to Saudi Arabia to meet with Schwarzkopf in order to set the date for commencing the ground offensive. The next day Schwarzkopf briefs them thoroughly on his plans and indicates that he will be ready to begin on February 21, with perhaps three or four days latitude to deal with unexpected contingencies.

A Patriot missile apparently intercepts a Scud over Tel Aviv. The debris from the disintegrating Scud causes several injuries.

*February 9:* General Schwarzkopf recommends commencing the ground attack between February 21 and 24. Bush approves.

*February 11:* Three hundred Mujahideen soldiers from Afghanistan join the coalition against Iraq.

By this date 510,000 U.S. troops are committed to the war.

By this date the Iraqis have ignited over 50 Kuwaiti oil wells. The Iraqi Army uses the thick clouds of smoke from the fire to hide troop movements from allied air reconnaissance and attack planes.

*February 12:* Soviet diplomat Yevgeni Primakov meets with Hussein and tries unsuccessfully to convince him to withdraw from Kuwait before the allies commence the ground offensive.

While assisting in the rescue of a Special Forces team, Air Force captains Tim Bennett and Don Bakke bomb and destroy an Iraqi helicopter. They become the first pilots in Air Force history to down an enemy aircraft with a bomb.

*February 13:* Two U.S. precision, laser-guided bombs strike a target in Baghdad that the United States maintains is a camouflaged, fortified command and control facility. Iraq, however, claims the site was a bomb shelter that had been filled with civilians. Iraq points to the 204 noncombatants killed in the bombing as proof that the allies are selecting civilian targets, despite their proclaimed policy of limiting civilian casualties (*see* **Al-Firdos Bunker**).

*February 15–20:* At the Wadi al-Bāṭin the U.S. Army 1st Cavalry Division and artillery units from the 7th Corps initiate a series of feints designed to convince the Iraqis that the main allied attack will come up through the wadi. (A wadi is a river or stream bed that is usually dry, except during the rainy season. It serves as a natural invasion route in desert terrain).

*February 15:* Bush calls for the Iraqi military and the people of Iraq to "take matters into their own hands to force Saddam Hussein the dictator to step aside." This statement and later ones after the conclusion of Desert Storm suggest to Iraqi Kurds and Shī'ites that the United States will support their postwar insurrections against Hussein, though that support was never given (*see* **Kurdish Rebellion, Shī'ite Rebellion**).

*February 18:* Iraqi Foreign Minister Aziz arrives in Moscow to discuss a peace plan with Soviet President Gorbachev.

Two U.S. warships, the USS *Tripoli* and USS *Princeton*, are severely damaged by water mines.

*February 19:* Iraq announces that it will accept a Soviet peace proposal. The plan calls for Iraq to begin "to withdraw its forces immediately and unconditionally" from Kuwait and complete the withdrawal within 21 days. Iraqi troops are to evacuate Kuwait City within four days and return all POWs within three days. In return, the plan calls for the coalition to agree to a cease-fire and allow all U.N. resolutions against Iraq to expire once the Iraqis withdraw from Kuwait. Bush rejects the proposal. Aziz flies back to Moscow on February 21 and negotiates a new eight-point plan with Gorbachev (*see* **Diplomacy**, **Soviet Union**).

*February 20:* Three soldiers from the U.S. Army 1st Cavalry Division are killed and seven are wounded during Operation Knight Strike when their Bradley tanks and Vulcan halftrack are ambushed in the Wadi al-Bāṭin. The reconnaissance-in-force mission was the first sustained ground action on Iraqi-held territory during the war. Its purpose was to determine the strength, composition, and disposition of Iraqi forces in the area and to convince the Iraqis that the allies were definitely intending to launch a major attack up through the Wadi al-Bāṭin (*see* **Deceptions, Feints, and Ruses**). The U.S. troops destroy an Iraqi bunker before pulling back to their positions inside Saudi Arabia (*see* **Wadi al-Bāṭin**).

*February 21:* The U.S. 2nd Marine Division begins screening actions to divert the Iraqis from the actual site of attack of the imminent ground war.

*February 22:* Bush delivers an ultimatum to Iraq: it must begin a large-scale withdrawal from Kuwait by noon the following day (EST) and complete the evacuation within one week, or face a ground war.

By this date Iraq has set fire to approximately 100 Kuwaiti oil wells, prompting Bush to declare that Iraq has "launched a scorched-earth policy destroying the entire oil production system of Kuwait." Within two days 450 wells are on fire.

When a final artillery brigade joins 7th Corps, all of the coalition armies are in position to initiate the ground campaign. In preparation for the assault the United States and Britain begin a massive artillery attack against Iraqi artillery positions, and U.S. aircraft drop napalm on oil-filled trenches to burn off the oil. Also, a team of CIA-trained Kuwaiti guerrillas lands on a beach south of Kuwait City.

*February 23:* After Iraq fails to meet the deadline for withdrawing from Kuwait, Bush authorizes General Schwarzkopf to initiate the ground campaign.

Allied units begin limited incursions into Iraqi-held territory for reconnaissance or gaining advantageous positioning for the main assault. Special Forces land reconnaissance units inside Iraq to report on Iraqi positions and movements, and six Apache helicopters from the 1st Armored Division fly a reconnaissance mission 60 miles to the north. In the desert to the west, the French 6th Light Armored Division and troops from the U.S. 82nd Airborne Division seize control of a position overlooking a major highway, and four Marine battalions advance into Kuwait to provide artillery fire direction and clear lanes through the minefields for the impending ground attack.

On the evening before the ground offensive begins, Navy SEALs simulate an attack at Mīnā Saʿūd, Kuwait, to convince Iraqi defenders that an amphibious attack against the Kuwaiti coastline has begun (*see* **Deceptions, Feints, and Ruses**).

*February 24:* At 4 A.M. local time, the allies launch the ground attack in full. During the day ground forces from the United States, Great Britain, France, Kuwait, Saudi Arabia, United Arab Emirates, Bahrain, Qatar, Oman, Syria, and Egypt participate in the assault.

The attack has two principle components. The first is an assault against dug-in Iraqi fortifications straight across the border into Kuwait and toward Kuwait City on the coast. The Iraqis are expecting this attack, which is conducted primarily by the U.S. 1st and 2nd Marine divisions, the U.S. Army's Tiger Brigade (1st Brigade of the 2nd Armored Division), and forces from the Joint Arab Forces Command (JFC), which has two segments (*see* **1st U.S. Marine Expeditionary Force, Joint Forces Command**). The heavily armored JFC–North flanks the Marines on their left. The highly mechanized and mobile JFC–East flanks them on the right and is responsible for coastal positions. Like the Marines, with whom they coordinate, their final objective is Kuwait City (*see* **Battle for Kuwait**).

At 4 A.M. the 1st Marine division breaches the first of two minefields filled with barbed wire and trenches filled with burning oil (*see* **Iraqi Fortifications**). By mid-afternoon they penetrate the second minefield and enter the Al Burqan oil field, taking large numbers of prisoners. Attacking 90 minutes later, the 2nd Marine Division destroys an Iraqi armored unit. The JFC commands begin their assaults later in the day, and the JFC–North completes its breaching operations on the following day.

The ground campaign's second component takes place in the desert to the west and surprises the Iraqis (*see* **Battle Against the Republican Guard**). On the first day of the ground offensive the heavily armored 7th Corps and the mobile 18th Airborne Corps pushes northward against lightly defended positions from Saudi Arabia into Iraq, before turning east to launch a surprise armored attack against the Republican western flank.

At the center of the 7th Corps, the 1st Infantry Division breaches Iraqi defenses and advances about nine miles into Iraq. To their left, the 2nd Armored Cavalry Regiment swings around the Iraqis and proceeds almost 50 miles before nightfall. It is followed by the 1st and 3rd Armored divisions.

West of 7th Corps, the 24th Mechanized Infantry Division begins its dash northward toward the Euphrates Valley, and in the desert farther to the west, helicopters ferry the 101st Airborne Division 93 miles inside Iraq, where they establish Forward Operating Base Cobra, a refueling and resupply point for helicopters and air-assault troops preparing to move far-

ther into the Euphrates Valley (*see* **Forward Operating Base Cobra**). To the west of them, the French 6th Light Armored Division, supported by the U.S. 82nd Airborne Division, defeats Iraqi resistance and takes many prisoners as it begins its advance against As-Salmān Airfield (*see* **As-Salmān Airfield**).

*February 25:* After determining that the Iraqis are not counterattacking, but are retreating from their defensive positions, General Schwarzkopf decides to quicken the pace of the attack in order to cut off and destroy the retreating Republican Guard. Consequently, that afternoon the 7th Corps begins to turn clockwise to the east to attack Republican Guard tanks and armored vehicles. This was the most decisive military maneuver in Desert Storm.

Farther to the west, the 24th Mechanized Infantry Division concludes its unprecedented drive northward into the Euphrates River Valley near An-Nāṣirīyah. Between the afternoons of February 24 and 25, the division covers almost 150 miles in 24 hours, faster than any mechanized ground force had ever traveled during warfare. It then turns eastward toward Basra to cut off Republican Guard forces that are retreating from 7th Corps. Meanwhile, the 1st Infantry Division completes breaching the Iraqi defenses, and the British 1st Armoured Division moves through lanes they opened and turns east to secure the allies' southern flank. They attack and destroy the Iraqi 52nd Armored Division. The British troops then engage in nearly continuous combat for the next two days as they continue moving east into Kuwait.

The 3rd Brigade of the 101st Airborne Division airlifts 150 miles to a point in the Euphrates River Valley and then marches an additional 20 miles to capture Highway 8, a key Iraqi supply route. This was the deepest airborne assault in military history. Within two days 7th Corp, the British 1st Armoured Division, and the 24th Mechanized Infantry Division had trapped the Republican Guard within a pocket outside of Basra, and the 101st Airborne Division had cut it off from reinforcements and supplies.

To the south in Kuwait, the 1st Marine Expeditionary Force wins decisive tank battles near the Burqan oil field against stiff Iraqi resistance and determined counterattacks. They then prepare to proceed to their final objective, Kuwait International Airport and the suburb of al-Jahrah. By the afternoon the JFC-East has overcome their opposition and proceed up the coastal highway toward Kuwait City, and the JFC–North has begun moving towards its objective, the 'Alī as-Salīm airfield. Late that night Marine aircraft detects Iraqi convoys fleeing from Kuwait City, and throughout the next two days they attack thousands of trucks, private cars, and other vehicles, damaging and destroying 3,000–4,000 of them along the "Highway to Hell." (*See* **Highway to Hell**.)

In Dhahran, Saudi Arabia, debris from an exploding Scud missile kills 28 U.S. Army Reserve personnel from the 14th Quartermaster Detachment and wounds 100.

*February 26:* Hussein announces on Baghdad Radio that Iraq is withdrawing its troops from Kuwait. In response, Bush calls the announcement "an outrage. He is not withdrawing. His defeated forces are retreating. The coalition forces will continue to prosecute the war with undiminished intensity."

By the end of the day, the allies destroy over 21 Iraqi divisions. The U.S. 24th Mechanized Infantry Division seals off the Euphrates River Valley by cutting off the strategic Highway 8. The 7th Corps and the British 1st Armoured Division begin their assaults against the Republican Guard's armored divisions in what becomes the largest tank battle since World War II. It begins when the 2nd Armored Cavalry Regiment encounters dug-in Iraqi tanks and soldiers along a ridge east of the map designation 73 Easting. The six hour Battle of 73 Easting produces some of the fiercest fighting of the war, as the Republican Guard sends waves of tanks and motorized infantry against the 2nd Armored Cavalry's 2nd Squadron. The unsuccessful Iraqi tank attack is one of the few Iraqi offensive operations of the war. At Wadi al-Bāṭin the British 1st Armoured Division cuts behind two dug-in Iraqi infantry divisions that have been opposing the U.S. 1st Cavalry Division. The British forces overrun the infantry's rear positions and attack Iraqi mechanized troops, who begin to surrender. However, nine British Royal Engineers are killed and 11 injured when mistakenly attacked by a U.S. warplane (*see* **Friendly Fire**).

In the desert to the west, the French 6th Light Armored Division completes its capture of the strategic As-Salmān airfield. It then joins up with the U.S. 101st Airborne Division in the Euphrates River Valley, with less than two Iraqi brigades intervening between the allied forces and the Iraqi capital.

In Kuwait, the 1st Marine Division encounters hordes of surrendering Iraqi soldiers as it proceeds toward Kuwait City. It reaches its ultimate objective, the Kuwaiti International Airport, and successfully captures it in the early morning of February 27. Meanwhile, the 2nd Marine Division captures the suburb of al-Jahrah after encountering heavy resistance. Following an afternoon tank battle, 12 Marines from the 2nd Force Reconnaissance unit become the first Americans to enter Kuwait City, where they retake the U.S. embassy at around 10 P.M.

The U.S. Army Tiger Brigade (1st Brigade of the 2nd Armored Division) destroys 33 armored vehicles and captures the police station at the main highway south of Kuwait City at Mutla Ridge, which commands all of the highways leading into and out of Kuwait City. It then directs its firepower against the Iraqi vehicles fleeing along the Highway to Hell.

Egyptian forces from the JFC–North approach and prepare to attack their objective, the 'Alī As-Salīm airbase near Kuwait City, and the JFC–East continues to progress up the coast.

U.S. Marine aircraft attack Iraqi troops at Faylakah and Būbiyān islands.

U.S. Air Force pilots discover and attack a Scud launching site containing approximately 25 missiles at Al Qā'im, near the Syrian border. According to a CIA operative in Baghdad, these missiles were in reserve for a possible desperation attack.

*February 27:* Following overwhelming allied victories on the battlefield, Bush declares that Kuwait has been liberated and Iraq defeated and that all coalition offensive combat operations will cease at midnight EST (8 A.M. on February 28, local time). In reply, Iraq announces its intention to comply with the terms of a U.N. cease-fire.

Prior to the cessation of hostilities, British and American forces trap approximately three divisions of Republican Guards in the Euphrates Valley and destroy approximately 200 tanks, 50 armored vehicles, and 20 artillery pieces in what General Schwarzkopf describes as a classic tank battle. To the south, the 1st Armored Division destroys 300 Republican Guard tanks and armored vehicles in the 40-minute Battle of Medina Ridge. To the north and west, the 101st Airborne Division cuts Highway 6, the Republican Guard's final avenue of escape.

In a press conference describing the military situation at the time the cease-fire was announced, Schwarzkopf declares that the Iraqi armored divisions are totally trapped within the Basra Pocket: "The gates are closed. There is no way out of here." In fact, however, the roads leading to Basra were not entirely cut off: a 30-mile gap existed between the 7th Corps and the 18th Airborne Corps. Nor were all the bridges leading across a key canal outside of Basra destroyed despite allied bombings. It was initially believed that only infantry carrying small arms were able to escape into Basra, though later the Defense Intelligence Agency estimated that as many as one-third of the Republican Guard's tanks made their way into the city, along with 70,000–80,000 soldiers. Approximately 800 tanks and 1,400 armored personnel carriers survived.

In Kuwait, the 1st Marine Division destroys more than 250 tanks and 70 armored vehicles while clearing the Kuwait International Airport in the early morning.

The JFC–North captures the 'Alī as-Salīm airfield and then passes through the Marine 2nd Division to enter the western part of Kuwait City. At the same time, the JFC–East liberates the city from the east.

Forty-two air strikes are flown against Baghdad's Muthena Airport, the Salmon Pak chemical-biological research facility, the Ba'ath Party Headquarters, the Al-Musayyib rocket-motor test facility, and the Al-Athir complex for missile research, development, and production.

*February 28:* At 8 A.M. local time (midnight, February 27, EST) the cease-fire takes effect. Due to some confusion within the U.S. 3rd Army as to whether the cease-fire would begin at 5 A.M. Zulu time or 5 A.M. local time, some units stopped offensive action at 5 A.M. local time. (Zulu is the military designation for Greenwich Mean Time, which is three hours behind local time in Kuwait. *See* **Cease-fire.**)

*March 1:* Iraq officially agrees to abide by Security Council Resolution 660. The Security Council passed the resolution calling for Iraqi troops to withdraw from Kuwait on August 2, 1990, immediately following the Iraqi invasion.

The U.S. British, French, and Canadian embassies open in Kuwait, and the international airport becomes operational.

An Iraqi brigade attacks the 3rd Armored Cavalry Regiment, which destroys the Iraqi unit in an hour-long battle near the Rumaila oil field.

*March 2:* The U.N. Security Council passes Resolution 686 setting down the conditions for a cease-fire: Iraq must cease all hostile military action, disclose the locations of mines, return all POWs and other detainees, rescind its annexation of Kuwait, return Kuwaiti property, and accept responsibility for damages it incurred. The vote is 11–1, with Cuba opposing and India, Yemen, and China abstaining.

The U.S. 24th Mechanized Infantry Division destroys two battalions of Republican Guards traveling west on Highway 8, after Iraqis attack them with small arms fire. One hundred seventy-seven Iraqi tanks and armored personnel carriers, eleven battlefield missile systems, and twenty-three trucks are destroyed in the fighting, which lasts for several hours. Several civilians are also killed, including a group of school children whose bus is struck during an air attack.

**March 3:** Iraqi generals meet with Schwarzkopf and other coalition military leaders in a tent at Safwān airfield in southern Iraq, where they accept the U.N.'s terms for a cease-fire, and work out the details for enforcing it. The Iraqis agree to show their good faith by immediately releasing some POWs.

Inspired by Bush's call for Iraqis to overthrow Hussein, Shī'ah Muslims in southern Iraq rebel against Hussein and claim to control several areas, including An-Nāṣirīyah. On March 5, Kurds in northern Iraq also revolt. On March 7, Hussein orders the Republican Guard to suppress both insurrections. The rebels, who were undergoing attacks from Iraqi tanks and helicopters that survived the war, request assistance from the coalition. Despite Bush's call for insurrection, the United States announces on March 10 that it will not actively support the rebellions, because those were "Iraqi internal affairs." The Shī'ite revolt is suppressed on March 28, when Iraqi troops recapture the city of Karbalā'. The Kurdish rebellion, which initially met with some military success, ends on April 13 after major Kurdish defeats and the creation of some 2 million Kurdish refugees leads to a cease-fire. The Kurds and Iraqi government then try unsuccessfully to negotiate an agreement providing limited autonomy for the Kurds (*see* **Kurdish Rebellion, Shī'ite Rebellion**).

## V. Aftermath

**March 4:** Iraq releases the first ten allied POWs.

**March 5:** Iraq releases an additional 35 additional POWs.

**March 8:** Operation Desert Farewell begins as the first 5,000 American troops leave for home from a port in Dhahran, Saudi Arabia.

The harbor of Kuwait City reopens, following the conclusion of two weeks of minesweeping.

Twenty-one American POWs arrive in Washington, D.C.

**March 14:** The emir of Kuwait, Sheik Jabir Āl Ṣabāḥ, returns to Kuwait City from his exile in Saudi Arabia.

**March 20:** As Iraqi forces suppress the Kurdish rebellion, a U.S. jet shoots down an Iraqi warplane flying in northern Iraq, near Tikrīt, in violation of the terms of the cease-fire.

**March 22:** Two more Iraqi jets are downed.

The French withdraw from the town of As-Salmān, which they captured during the war.

**March 27:** The first U.S. Navy air units return to the United States.

**March 28:** Three U.S. Marines in the al-Jubayl area of Saudi Arabia are wounded in a drive-by shooting.

**April 1:** By this date 165,000 troops have returned to the United States.

**April 3:** Security Council Resolution 687 establishes the terms for the formal cessation of hostilities.

**April 6:** Iraq accepts the U.N. terms for a formal cease-fire.

**April 7:** The United States inaugurates Operation Provide Comfort to send humanitarian aid and security assistance to Kurds in northern Iraq.

**April 9:** The U.N. Security Council passes Resolution 689, which establishes an observer mission to monitor the permanent cease-fire.

**April 11:** The U.N. Security Council announces that Operation Desert Storm has officially concluded.

**April 18:** Iraq reports that it still has 10,000 nerve-gas warheads, 1,000 tons of mustard and nerve gas, 1,500 chemical weapons, and 30 Scud missiles.

**May 7:** The U.S. completes its withdrawal of forces from southern Iraq.

**May 18:** The restored Kuwaiti government begins trials of 200 alleged collaborators, most of whom are convicted and sentenced to death. However, in response to objections by human rights organizations and world governments, the sentences are commuted on June 26 to life imprisonment. Following the Iraqi withdrawal from Kuwait, there are many reports of Kuwaitis torturing and committing other acts of vengeance against Iraqis, Kurds, and Palestinians.

# Bibliography

Allen, Thomas B., et al. *CNN: War in the Gulf: From the Invasion of Kuwait to the Day of Victory and Beyond.* Atlanta: Turner Publishing Company, 1991.

Alpher, Joseph, ed. *War in the Gulf: Implications for Israel.* Boulder, CO: Westview Press, 1992. [Report of a study group from the Jaffee Center for Strategic Studies, Tel Aviv University.]

Aspen, Les, and William Dickinson. *Defense for a New Era: Lessons of the Persian Gulf War.* Washington, D.C.: Brassey's, 1992.

Atkinson, Rick. *Crusade: The Untold Story of the Persian Gulf War.* Boston: Houghton Mifflin Co., 1993. [A comprehensive narrative history, this is one of the most useful books on the Persian Gulf War.]

BBC World Services. *Gulf Crisis Chronology: Day-to-Day Coverage of Events in the Gulf Conflict.* Essex, UK: Longman Group, 1991. [A particularly thorough chronology, this is especially useful for researching political developments.]

Bergot, Erwin, with Alain Gandy. *Operation Daguet.* Paris: Presses de la Cité, 1991.

Billiere, General Sir Peter de la. *Storm Command: A Personal Account of the Gulf War.* London: Harper-Collins, 1992. [The author commanded the British forces in the war.]

Blumberg, Herbert H., and Christopher C. French, eds. *The Persian Gulf War.* Lanham, MD: University Press of America, 1994.

Bresheeth, Haim, and Nira Yuval-Davis, eds. *The Gulf War and the New World Order.* London: Zed Books Ltd., 1991. [These essays provide avowedly socialist perspectives on the war, its causes, and its ramifications.]

Bulloch, John, and Harvey Morris. *Saddam's War.* London and Boston: Faber and Faber, 1991.

Chadwick, Frank. *Desert Shield Fact Book.* Bloomington, IL: GDW, 1991.

_____. *Gulf War Fact Book. Desert Shield Fact Book.* Bloomington, IL: GDW, 1992.

Clark, Ramsey, et al. *War Crimes: A Report on United States War Crimes Against Iraq.* Washington, D.C.: Maisonneuve Press, 1992.

Cohen, Roger, and Claudio Gatti. *In the Eye of the Storm: The Life of General Norman Schwarzkopf.* New York: Farrar, Straus and Giroux, 1991.

Cooke, James. *100 Miles from Baghdad: With the French in Desert Storm.* Westport, CT: Praeger, 1993.

Denton, Robert E., Jr., ed. *The Media and the Persian Gulf War.* Westport, CT: Praeger, 1993.

Dunnigan, James F., and Austin Bay. *From Shield to Storm.* New York: William Morrow, 1992.

Englehardt, Colonel Joseph P. *Desert Shield and Desert Storm: A Chronology and Troop List for the 1990-1991 Persian Gulf Crisis.* Carlisle Barracks, PA: U.S. Army War College, Strategic Studies Institute, 1991.

Fanning, David, exec. prod. *The Gulf War.* Boston: WGBH Educational Foundation, 1996. [A 4 hour special edition of *Frontline*, a television documentary series funded by the Corporation for Public Broadcasting. *The Gulf War* was co-produced by *Frontline* and the BBC. A very useful documentary, it features interviews with top U.S., British, and Iraqi leaders, historians, and other figures.]

Fialka, John J. *Hotel Warriors: Covering the Gulf War.* Washington, D.C.: The Woodrow Wilson Center Press, 1992.

Gordon, Michael, and Bernard Trainor. *The Generals' War: The Inside Story of the Conflict in the Gulf.* Boston: Little, Brown, 1995.

Grossman, Mark. *Encyclopedia of the Persian Gulf War*. Santa Barbara, CA: ABC-CLIO, 1995.

Hawley, T.M. *Against the Fires of Hell: The Environmental Disaster of the Gulf War*. New York: Harcourt Brace Jovanovich, 1992.

Hilsman, Roger. *George Bush vs. Saddam Hussein: Military Success! Political Failure?* Novato, CA: Lyford Books, 1992.

Holm, Major General Jeanne. *Women in the Military: An Unfinished Revolution*, rev. ed. Novato, CA: Presdio, 1992.

Hutchinson, Kevin Don. *Operation Desert Shield/Desert Storm: Chronology and Fact Book*. Westport, CT: Greenwood, 1995. [A thorough chronology, this is particularly useful for researching military developments.]

Kamiya, Jason K. *A History of the 24th Mechanized Infantry Division Combat Team During Operation Desert Storm: The Attack to Free Kuwait*. Fort Stewart, GA: Headquarters, 24th Mechanized Infantry Division, 1991.

Karsh, Efraim, and Inari Rautsi. *Saddam Hussein: A Political Biography*. New York: Free Press, 1991.

MacArthur, John. *Second Front: Censorship and Propaganda in the Gulf War*. New York: Hill & Wang, 1992.

Moore, Molly. *A Woman at War: Storming Kuwait with the U.S. Marines*. New York: Scribner's, 1993.

*Needless Deaths in the Gulf War: Civilian Casualties During the Air Campaign and Violations of the Laws of War*. New York: Middle East Watch/Human Rights Watch, 1991.

Nyang, Sulayman S. *A Line in the Sand: Saudi Arabia's Role in the Gulf War*. Washington, D.C.: P.T. Books, 1995.

Photographers of Sygma Photo News, Inc. *In the Eye of Desert Storm*. New York: H.N. Abramin Association with the Professional Photography Division of Eastman Kodak Co., 1991. [Images and text by photographers from Sygma Photo News, Inc.]

Powell, General Colin, with Joseph E. Persico. *My American Journey*. New York: Random House, 1995.

Pyle, Richard. *Schwarzkopf in His Own Words: The Man, The Mission, The Triumph*. New York: Signet, 1991.

Rashid, Nasser Ibrahim, and Esber Ibrahim Shaheen. *Saudi Arabia and the Gulf War*. Joplin, MO: International Institute of Technology, 1992.

Rubin, Barry, et al. *Gulfwatch Anthology: The Day-to-Day Analysis of the Gulf Crisis, August, 30, 1990 to March 28, 1991*. Washington, D.C.: Washington Institute for Near East Policy, 1991.

Sadiq, Muhammad, and John C. McCain, eds. *The Gulf War Aftermath: An Environmental Tragedy*. Boston: Kluwer Academic Publishers, 1993.

Sasson, Jean P. *The Rape of Kuwait: The True Story of Iraqi Atrocities Against a Civilian Population*. New York: Knightsbridge, 1991.

Schwarzkopf, H. Norman, with Peter Petre. *It Doesn't Take a Hero*. New York: Bantam, 1992.

Schwarzkopf, H. Norman. *How We Won the War: The Press Briefings of General H. Norman Schwarzkopf*. New York: Simon & Schuster Audioworks, 1991. [Sound recording.]

Simon, Bob. *Forty Days*. New York: Putnam, 1992.

Smallwood, William L. *Strike Eagle: Flying the F-15E in the Gulf War*. London: Brassey's, 1994.

Smith, Perry M. *How CNN Fought the War*. New York: Putnam, 1992.

Summers, Colonel Harry G., Jr. *On Strategy II: A Critical Analysis of the Gulf War*. New York: Dell, 1992.

_____. *Persian Gulf War Almanac*. New York: Facts on File, 1995.

Szabo, Grant. *The Gulf War Veterans Resource Pages*. <http://www.gulfweb.org/> [This is a useful website on the World Wide Web. It contains photos, personal narratives, and information about resources.]

U.S. Department of Defense. *Conduct of the Persian Gulf War: Final Report to Congress*. Washington, D.C.: U.S. Government Printing Office, 1992.

Warden, John A. III. *The Air Campaign: Planning for Combat*. Washington D.C.: National Defense University Press, 1988.

Weller, M., ed. *Iraq and Kuwait: The Hostilities and Their Aftermath*. Cambridge International Documents Series, vol 3. Cambridge, England: Grotius, 1993. [Contains copies of documents from the United Nations relating to the war, including resolutions and proceedings of the Security Council, the General Assembly, the Commission on Human Rights, and other agencies. It also contains pertinent documents and statements from Iraq, the United States, and other involved nations.]

Weiner, Robert. *Live from Baghdad: Gathering News from Ground Zero*. New York: Doubleday, 1992.

*Women in the Military: Deployment in the Persian Gulf War* (Report to the Secretary of Defense). Washington, D.C.: U.S. General Accounting Office, 1993.

Woodward, Bob. *The Commanders*. New York: Simon & Schuster, 1991.

Yant, Martin. *Desert Mirage: The True Story of the Gulf War*. Buffalo, NY: Prometheus, 1991.

# Index